Contents

At A Glance Colour Map showing zonal jurisdiction		inside front cover & flap
About the Atlas & Acknowledgements		2
Preface		3
Metro Maps (Delhi & Kolkata)		4
Rajdhani & Shatabdi Express Routes		5
Locator Map use this at a glance map to see which page on the atlas you need to refer to.		6
Main Maps		7-61
India Rail Network Map of 1893		62
Narrow Gauge in South Bengal (past & present routes)		63
Glossary		64
Station Index with Station Codes		65-84
Map Legend		inside back cover & flap
Metro Maps:	Delhi	15
	Kolkata	25
Sectional Maps:	Delhi region	15
	Patna region	25
	Ahmadabad region	28
	Kolkata region	37
	Mumbai region	38
	Coalfields region	45
	Secunderabad region	51
	Chennai region	59

About this Atlas

The Great Indian Railway Altas is an accurate graphical representation of the network and resources of the railways in India: spanning over 63,000 route kilometers on four different gauges. More than 13 million passengers travel on 14,000 trains and well over 1.4 million tonnes of freight are transported every day in 6,000 freight trains between the 8,000+ stations, aided by a fleet of over 7,300 locomotives, 45,000 coaching vehicles and 280,000 goods wagons

Within the massive Indian railway network there are always new projects and upgradations in progress, be it new lines, gauge conversions or electrification works. This Atlas charts out the entire network, showing every station big or small, and also gives up-to-date indication about ongoing projects.

The Great Indian Railway Atlas is intended to be a valuable source of information for train lovers, travelers, academicians & infrastructure developers and anyone interested in the Indian Railways.

I have long been interested in trains as well as maps and cartography. I feel that commonly available maps produced by the railway authorities as well as private organizations lack detail or are badly produced. An urge to change that made me start collecting information (such as existing maps, timetables, ongoing project details) and I produced my first railway map in early 2001. Based on the feedback from the small circle of fellow railfans who had a chance to look at the map through my website and on printed copies, I decided to go the whole way and create an atlas which covered the entire network, every little station, every nuance of track.

I like the Lonely Planet's India & Bangladesh Travel Atlas, which has inspired the design and layout of this atlas.

I hope this Atlas will be useful to you, whether you are a regular traveler on the Indian Railways, or a train lover.

This Atlas provides a wealth of information not available as a single publication. A project of this magnitude, undertaken without any official support, could well have some shortcomings, omissions or errors, because of the lack of readily available information from official sources.

I would appreciate any feedback, suggestions and corrections. You may use the postal address given on the inside front cover, or email me at atlas@indianrailstuff.com

For post publication updates and errata, visit http://indianrailstuff.com/atlas.

This page will be continuously updated to provide current status.

Acknowledgements

Being part of the IRFCA, the Indian Railways Mailing List (http://irfca.org) I have received tremendous help from many of its members, whose names I gratefully acknowledge: Alok Patel, Apurva Bahadur, Amlan Chakraborty, Aravind Sivaramakrishnan, Arnab Acharya, Ashish Mashelkar, Ashish Vashisht Ashwin Kurup, Avimanyu Pyne, Bharat Vohra, Bharath Moro, Binand Sethumadhavan, BM Shukla, Bratin Choudhury, Brian McKenzie, Buddhadeb Saha, CSR Murthy, David Churchill, Eljas Pölhö, Frank Hung, Giridhar Patnaik, Hari Menon, Harsh Vardhan, IS Anand, Jagadheep D Pandian, Jimmy Jose, John Lacey, Joy Brahma, Jaydeep Dutta, Kamesh, Karthik MV, Karthik Nagarajan, K Gopalakrishna, K Rajesh, K Bhanu Prakash, KN Manoj, KK Subramanian, Lakshman Thodla, Madhur Dubey, Milan Chatterjee, M Giridhar, MSM Saifullah, Mohan Bhuyan, Parag Dave, Pavan Kumar, Pitchumani Hariharasubramanian, PVS Praveen Kumar, Rabibrata Mukherjee, Rajan Roopesh Mathew, Rajeev Shrivastava, Rajendra Tunuguntla, Rajesh Kalmady, Rakesh Misra, Ramesh Krishnamurthy, Ramu Aravindan, Ranganath Eunny, Ratnendra Pandey, Ravi S Rajan, S Skandan, S Srinivas, S Shankar, Samar Hussain, Sandeep Mohan, Sandeep Sharma, Satish Gune, Shashanka Nanda, Shirish Paranjape, Shrinivas Joshi, Shyam AR, Saurab Basu, Sridhar Narayan, Steven Logan, Sudeep Hota, Sudhir Moghe, Sumanth Ganapavarapu, Sundar Coimbatore, Sundar Krishnamurthy, Tarini Ghosh, Terry Martin, Vaibhav Sarin, Vijay Balasubramanian, Vijay VJ, Vinay Wagh, Vrijilesh Rai, Zubin Dotivala... and especially to Ajai Banerjee who made this project possible, Dr SA Patekar and Satish Pai.

Others... Anil Ranjan Das Gupta, Ashoke Sengupta, Dipak Roychoudhury, Santayan Sengupta, Tanaaz Kothari, and especially John Yonge, who proposed the project; Rabi Mahapatra (SPRO, SER), Biswanath Mitra and the office of the STM (Coaching), SER; and Arun Ray and others of the Commissioner of Safety (NFR) Kolkata office, Mr Nandy of Metro Rly Kolkata, The CPRO & PRO of NER, Gorakhpur for sending me the entire NER Working TTs, Mr Ravi Kochak and Mr WK Pradhan. Thanks to Boris Chomenko, Thorsten Büker, Erika Yared Pérez Contreras, Ruth Saha and Malobika Chowdhury for translations, and to Mera, Dr Sunil Patekar and Niel Hirjee for their encouragement.

Special thanks to my father Samar & sister Sujata, and others, without whose support this wouldnt have seen the light of day.

References & Sources

Trains At a Glance, various Zonal Railway Timetables, various Divisional Working Timetables and Maps of the Indian Railways (Min. of Railways, Govt of India);

Websites of the various Zonal Railways and other Railway sites, Rajan Roopesh Mathew's KR Website

Indian Railways Map, Survey of India; Indian Railways Map, NATMO; Newman's Indian Bradshaw,W Newman & Co. Ltd

Indian Travel Atlas, Lonely Planet; India By Rail by Royston Ellis (Bradt Publications); Alphabetical List of Indian Railway Stations, Prince Publications;

Railway Map of India from 1893, unknown source.

Suburban Railway & other maps of Ahmedabad, Bangalore, Chennai, Delhi, Hyderabad, Kanpur, Kolkata, Lucknow, Mumbai,

Published with the assistance of **ABN Transcon Institute for Economic Research, Jaipur**

The Great
Indian Railway Atlas

A comprehensive atlas of the Indian railway network

Der Große **Indische Eisenbahnatlas**
Le grand **atlas des chemins de fer indiens**
First Edition, 2005

Samit Roychoudhury

Preface

There are many maps and atlases of India. Cartographic representations of this vast and complex country range from the simple to the sophisticated and cover a wide range of subjects. Curiously, though, there are hardly any accurate and detailed maps publicly available of the Indian Railways network, a vital and important part of India's economic infrastructure. What maps there are of the railways are not very detailed, and show signs of having the railway information added as an afterthought. Indian Railways itself publishes maps of its networks, of course, but these are not generally available to the public.

Samit Roychoudhury's new atlas fills this gap. A work whose raison d'être and sole focus is the documentation of the Indian Railways network, this atlas is refreshingly welcome to all who are interested in transportation and railways in India. It is a labour of love, and Samit's diligence and painstaking research, without the benefit of any institutional support, has resulted in a superlatively accurate and detailed picture of the railway network in India. Indian Railways has been undergoing rapid change in recent years, with the commissioning of new routes, gauge conversion, and more recently, administrative reorganizations. It is to be hoped that this atlas will help its readers to place these changes in context and understand their impact and significance.

A group that will especially appreciate this new atlas is the small but growing band of railfans interested in studying Indian Railways. These enthusiasts, spread across the world, have long bemoaned the lack of good maps of the Indian railway routes, a situation especially frustrating when seeing the availability of good maps for railway networks in some other countries. Samit is an avid railfan himself, and his earlier publication of a map of railway routes in India helped partially to address this long-felt need, but this new atlas should satisfy railfans much more thoroughly. The inclusion of data not available in any other railway maps produced so far, such as the locations of locomotive sheds, closed historical lines and proposed new lines, and the comprehensive display of all stations on the network, will especially appeal to them. As a railfan myself, I certainly am looking forward to spending many delightful hours with this atlas!

Satish Pai
The Indian Railways Mailing List

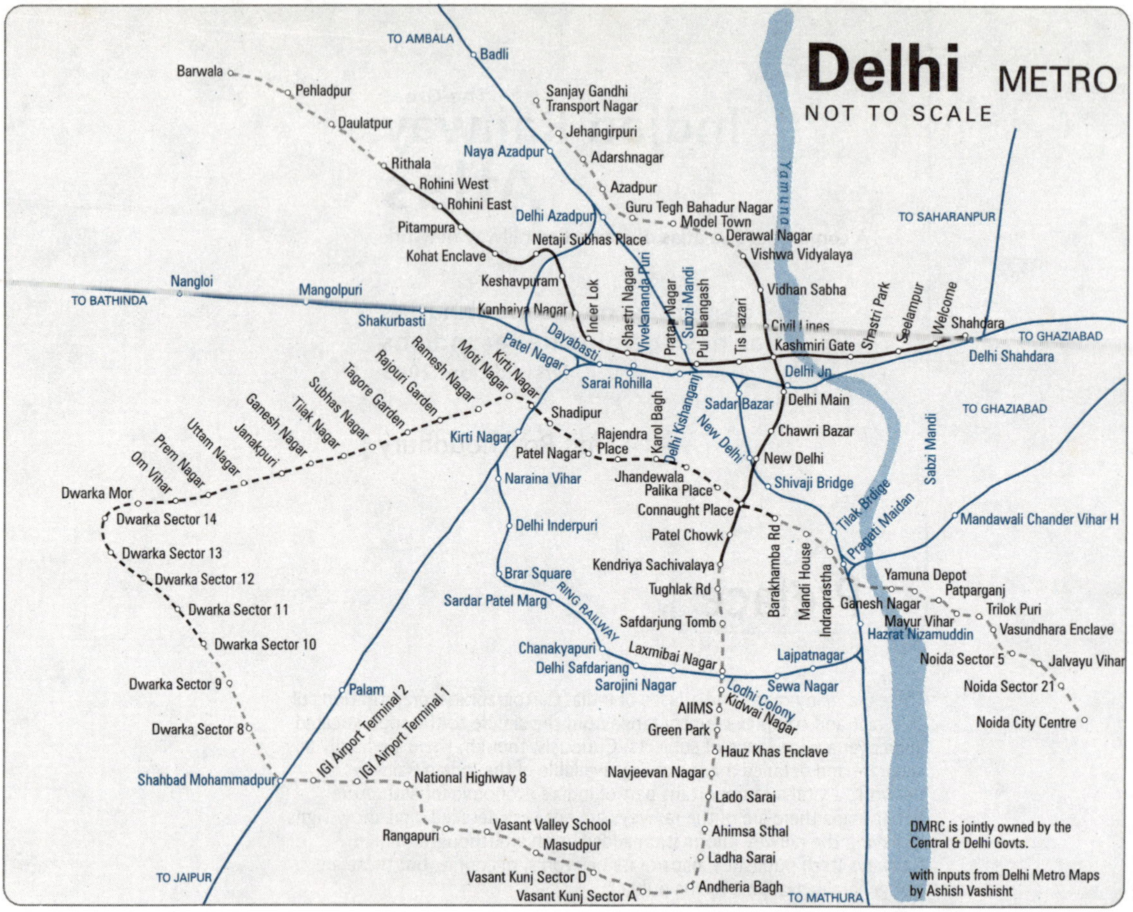

Legend

- ∘ Central — Metro Station
- ——— Commissioned Metro Line
- - - - Metro Line under construction
- - - - Proposed Metro Line
- ∘ Delhi Cantt — Regular Railway Station
- ——— Regular Railway Line
- - - - Railway Line under construction

The Delhi Metro route is still in its formative stages, and many deviations from plan may occur.

The regular railway stations (as opposed to Metro stations) shown are indexed, but not referred to this page.

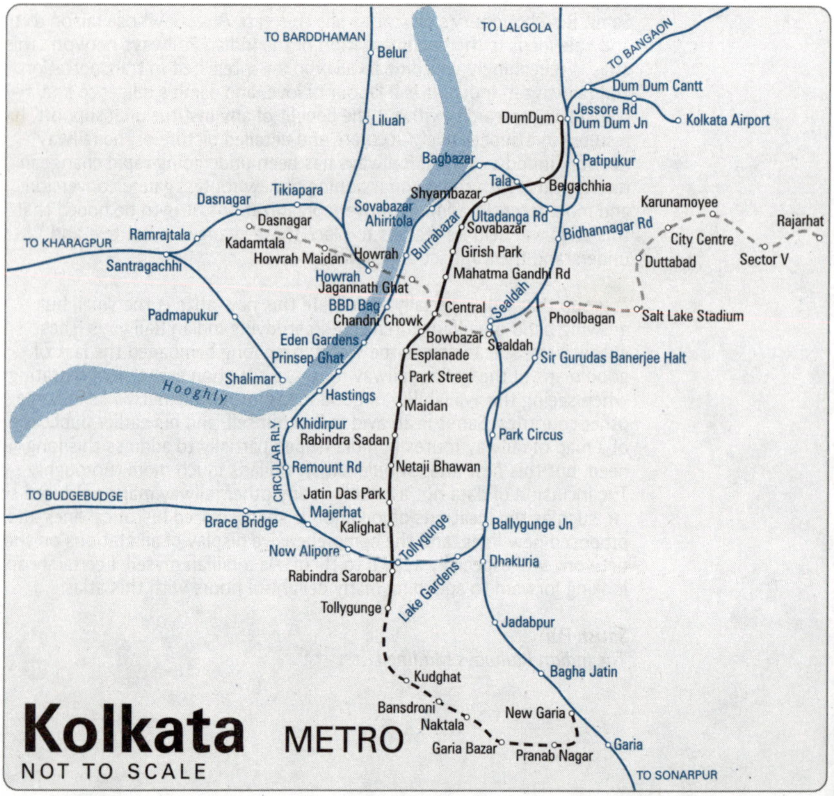

Special Trains

Rajdhani & Shatabdi Express Routes

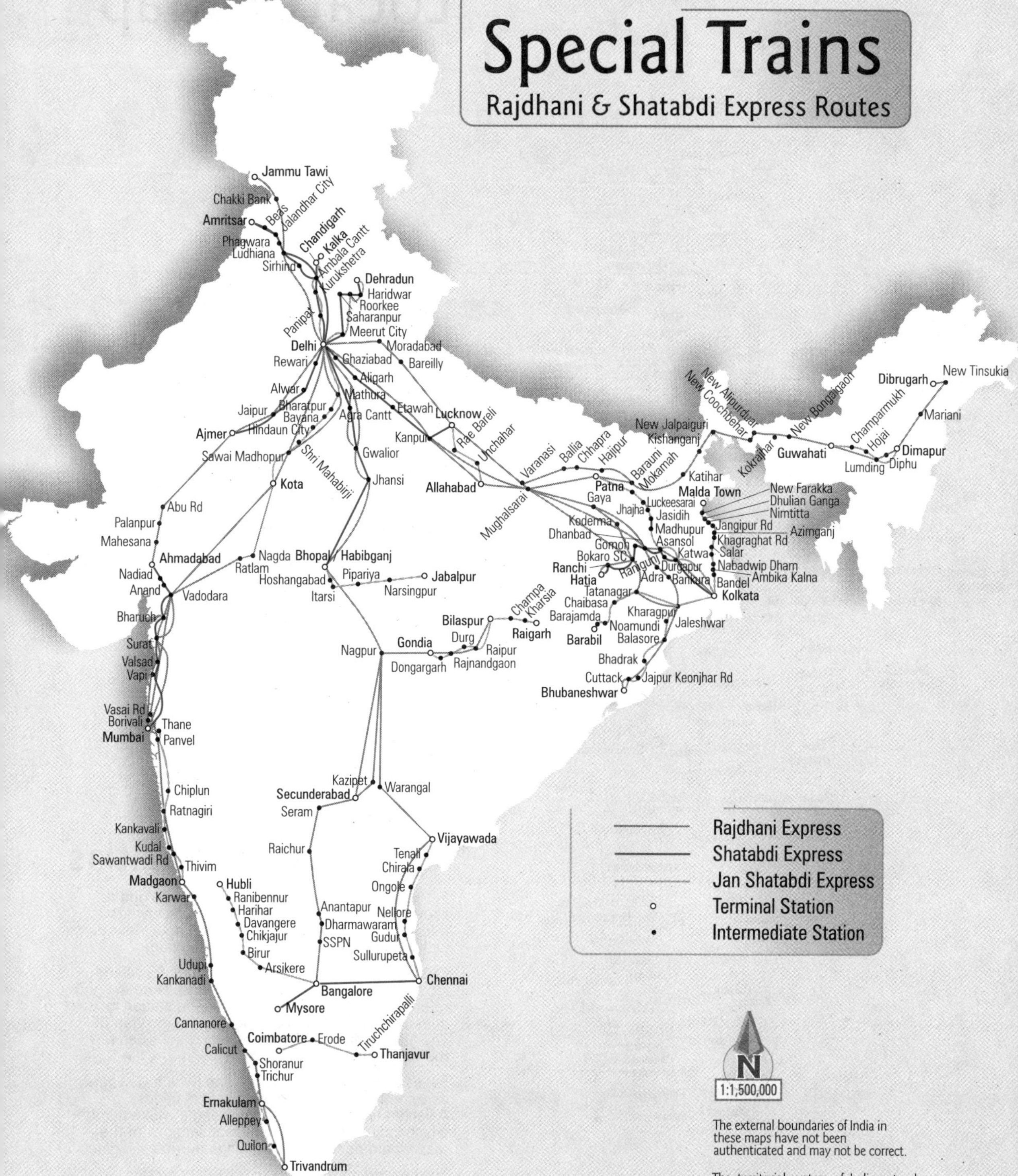

The external boundaries of India in these maps have not been authenticated and may not be correct.

The territorial waters of India extend into the sea to a distance of twelve nautical miles measured from the appropriate base line.

Locator Map

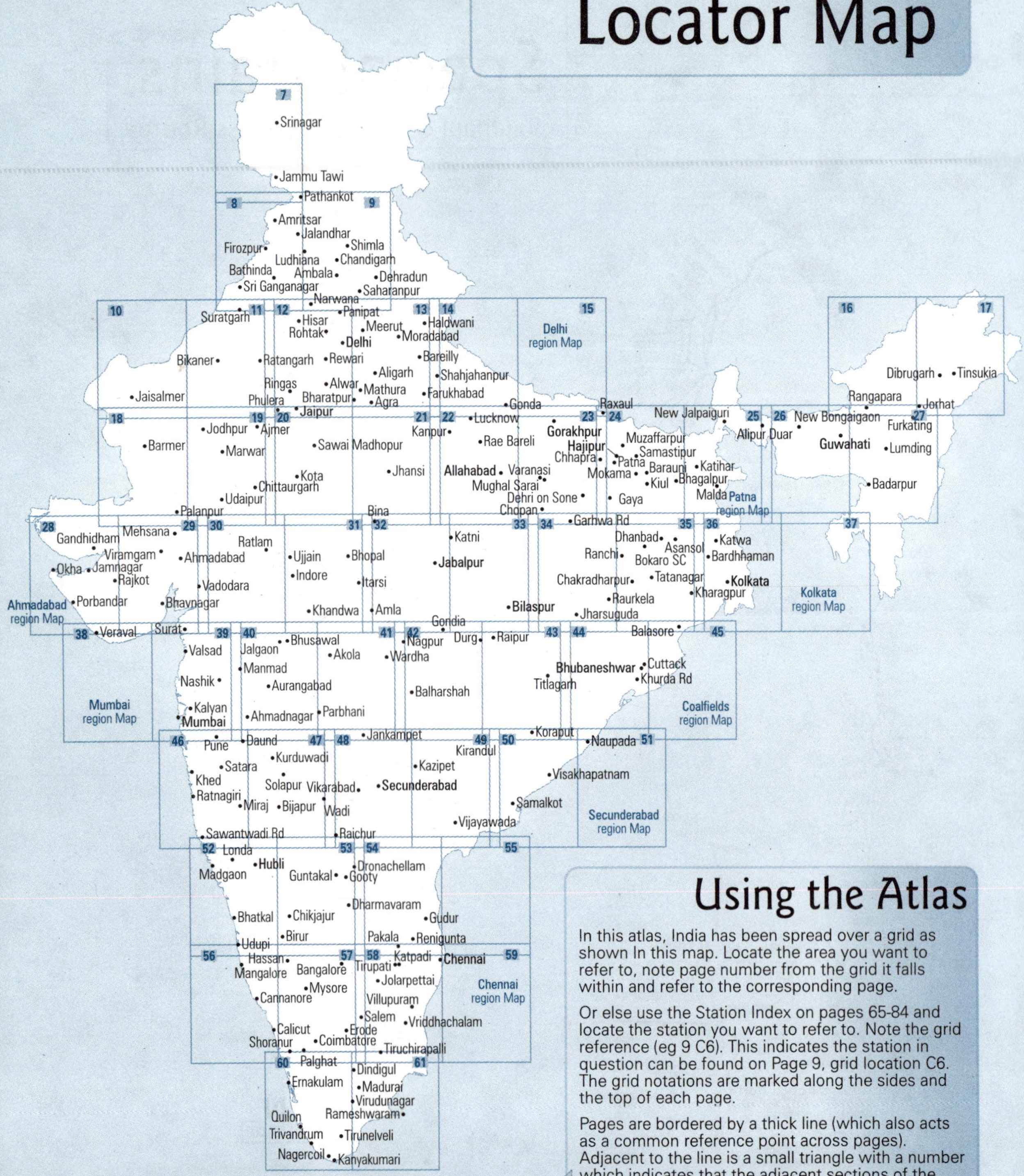

The territorial waters of India extend into the sea a distance of twelve nautical miles measured from the appropriate base line.

The external boundaries of India in these maps have not been authenticated and may not be correct.

Using the Atlas

In this atlas, India has been spread over a grid as shown In this map. Locate the area you want to refer to, note page number from the grid it falls within and refer to the corresponding page.

Or else use the Station Index on pages 65-84 and locate the station you want to refer to. Note the grid reference (eg 9 C6). This indicates the station in question can be found on Page 9, grid location C6. The grid notations are marked along the sides and the top of each page.

Pages are bordered by a thick line (which also acts as a common reference point across pages). Adjacent to the line is a small triangle with a number which indicates that the adjacent sections of the map would be found on the page number indicated.

27

The Legend on the Inside Back Cover & Flap describes all the conventions used in the atlas. You can keep the flap open and have the legend visible while browsing through the pages.

Jammu & Kashmir
PAKISTAN
Kupwara
Sopore
Hamre
Pattan
Jhelum
Baramula
Rajwiansher
Uri
Badgam
Srinagar
Kharaon
Pampore
Kakapora
Avantipora
PIR PANJAL
Panchgam
Bijbehera
Anantnag
Poonch
Sadura
Qazigund
Pir Panjal Tunnel (under construction)
Charil
Banihal
Rajouri
Arpinchla
Nachlana
Kohli
Laole
Sangaldan
PIR PANJAL
Barala
Chenab Br. (under construction) will be India's tallest bridge
Surukot
Salal B
Salal A
Doda
Riasi
The external boundaries of India in these maps have not been authenticated and may not be correct.
Katra
Chakarwaha
Udhampur
Ramnagar Rd
Sangar
Bajalata
Manwal
Lala Musa
Jammu Tawi
FZP
Bari Brahman
Jammu Cantt
Miran Sahib
Vijaypur Jammu
Ranbirsinghpura
Suchetgarh
Samba
Dalowali
Sialkot
Ghagwal
Chenab
Hiranagar
Budhi
Wazirabad
Chak Dayala
Chhan Arorian
Ravi
Kathua
Chak Amru
Madhopur Punjab
Pathankot Jn
Dalhousie Rd
Sujanpur
Bharoli Jn
Sarna
Chakki Bank Jn
FZP
FZP
FZP
8
E F G H
1 2 3 4 5 6

N
1:1,500,000
SCALE
0 5 10 15 20 25 Miles
0 5 10 15 20 25 30 35 40 45 50 Kms
A
B
C
D
1
2
3
4
5
6
6
11
12
PAKISTAN
The external boundaries of India in these maps have not been authenticated and may not be correct.
Punjab
Rajasthan
Ravi
Ravi
Chak Amru
Kathua
Madhopur Punjab
Sujanpur
Bharoli Jn
Sarna
Jakolari
Kandrori
Parma Nand
Ghiala Halt
Dinanagar
Gujranwala
Narowal
Jassar
Dera Baba Nanak
Gurdaspur
Chak Kalan
Rattar Chhattar Halt
Jhawar Halt
Bhangala
Harridas
Sohal
Musahibpur
Hardorawal
Dhariwal
Chhina
Mukerian
Ghaunspur
Fatehgarh Churian
Batala Sugar Mills Siding
Unchi Bassi
Batala Jn
Qadian
Sangla Hill
Kotla Gujran
Dasua
Sheikhpura
Vadala Granthan
Garna Sahib
Jaintipura
Majitha
Khudda Kurala
Kathunangal
Chak Jumra
Shahdara
Verka Jn
Tanda Urmar
Amritsar Jn
FZP
Mananwala
Cholang
Wagah
Jandiala
Sanaura
Atari
Khasa
Cheharta
Tangra
Baba Bakala Raiya Halt
Bhogpur Sirwal
Gurusar Sutlani
Bhagtanwala
Butari
Lahore
Sangrana Sahib H
Gohlwar Varpal
Beas Jn
Dhilwan
Kala Bakra
Dukhnawaran
Bhalujala
Kartarpur
Biaspind
Saidpur Jalalabad
Hamira
Alawalpur
Tarn Taran
Khadoor Sahib
Dera Baba Jaimal Singh
Sura Nussi
Rure Asal
DAV College Jalandhar H
Jandoke
Goindwal Sahib
Kapurthala
Khojewala
Kairon
RCF Halt
Patti
Husainpur
Lyalpur Khalsa
Pajian
College Jalandhar H
Raiwind
Gharyala
Boparai Halt
Dudwindi
Jamsher Khas
Chiher
Rattoke Gurdwara
Valtoha
FZP
Sultanpur Lodi
Thabalke
Phagw
Kasur Tabail
Lohian Khas Jn
Giddarpindi
Kasur
Khem Karan
Jogiwala
Shankar
Butewala
Makhu
Kang Khurd
Nakodar Jn
Talli Saida Sahu
Sindhar
Ganda Sindhwan
Mallanwala Khas
Mulewal Khaira
Malsian Shahkot
Gahndran Halt
Sidhwan
Nurmahal
Gumtali Halt
Bilga
Mahalam
Husainiwala
Firozpur City Jn
Firozpur Cantt Jn
Saidanwala
Maheshari Sandhuan
Partabpur
Khai Phameki
Dhindsa Halt
Model
Kasu Begu
Ghal Kalan
Parao Mahna
Dodh
Firozshah
Sulhani
Talwandi
Dagru
Moga
Ajitwal
Nanaksar
Jagraon
Chauki Man
Mulla
Jhok Tahal Singh
Golehwala
Kohar Singh Wala
Bhanohad Punjab
Guru Harsahai
Pipli Pakhi Kalan
Jiwa Arain
Faridkot
DAV College Jalalabad
Jalalabad
Giani Zail Singh Sandhwan
Bahminiwala
Budhai Balamgarh Halt
Charewan Halt
Bariwala
Kot Kapura Jn
Ladhuka
Romana Albel Singh
Theh Qalandar Halt
Wander Jatana
Ajit Gill Matta Halt
Fazilka Jn
FZP
Muktsar
Jhabelwale Halt
Gangsar Jaito
Chananwala
Chak Banawala
Chak Pakhewala
Roranwala
Lakhewali
Bhagsar
Amraka
Chand Bhan
Lehra Muhabbat
Rampura Phul
Jethuke
Tapa
Ghunas Halt
Hadaiya
Barnala
Sekha
Rajomaj
Goniana
Bhuchchu
Bathinda Cantt
Kotha Pakki
Bakayanwala
Panj-Kosi
Kikanwali Punjab
Qabarwala
Malout
Faqarsar
Giddarbaha
Daulakot Bhai Halt
Balluana
UMB
Bahman Diwana
UMB
Qasamwala
MacLeod Gunj Rd Jn
Abohar
Pakki
Karamgarh Sardargarh Halt
Bathinda Jn
Bathinda B Cabin
Hindumalkote
Bathinda A Cabin
DLI
Narauna Jodhpur Romana H
BKN
Kattar Singh Wala
Orki
Bahawal Bassi
Gurusar Sahnewala
BKN
Kot Fateh
Fatuhi
Garhi Bhagi H
Maisar Khana
Bharu
Bhawalnagar
Sangat
Kotli Kalan
Sadda Singh Wala
Kesri Singhpur
Prithvirajpur
Mohanpura Halt
Shergarh
Maur
BKN
UMB
Bagwali
Manwala Kot Bakhtu H
Mansa
Dalpat Singhpur Halt
Sri Ganganagar Jn
Pathrala Halt
Bangi Nihalsingh
Narinderpura
Fateh Singhwala Halt
Banwali
DKN
Sadulshahr
Mandi Dabwali
Govindgarh Kh
Raman
Sri Karanpur
Budh Singhwala Halt
Lehra
Longarh Abub Halt
Birang Khera
Budhlada
Buglanwali Halt
Dhaban
Ratangarh Kankawal
Datewas
Bareta
Zorawar Pura Halt
Dholipal
Kalanwali
Kahangarh
Sangaria
Hiranwali Halt
Gaj Singhpur
Sukh Chain Halt
Kudr
Jorkian Halt
Manaksar
Bara Gudha
Nawan Halt
Jamalpur Sh
Rai Singh Nagar
Hanumangah Jn
Hanumangarh Town
Dabhli Rathan
Sirsa
Tibi
Sherekan
Fatehabad
Mohan Nagar
Pilibanga
Bajekan Halt
Tilwara Jhil
Suchan Kotli
Amarpura Rathan Halt
Jodhka Halt
Masaniwal Halt
BKN
BKN
BKN
BKN

E
F
G
H
1
2
3
4
5
6
7
13
DHAULADHAR RANGE
Nurpur Rd
Talara
Balle Da Pir Larath Halt
Dharamshala
Bharmar
Jawanwala Shahr
Harsar Dehri
Megh Rajpura Halt
Nagrota Suriyan
Kangra
Kangra Mandir
Samloti
Nagrota
Chamunda Marg Halt
Paror Halt
Kopar Lahar
Jawalamukhi Rd
Guler
Lunsu Halt
Tripal Halt
Nandpur Bhatauli
Barial Himachal Halt
Sulah Himachal
Palampur Himachal
Patti Rajpura Halt
Panch Rukhi
Majheran Himachal
Baijnath Paprola
Baijnath Mandir Halt
Ahju
Chauntra Behetrah
Jogindernagar
Talwara
Kulu
Beas
Himachal Pradesh
Satluj
INDIA
Hoshiarpur
Nasrala
ChuraruTakrala
Panoh
Jaijon Doaba
Una Himachal
Mahngarwal Doaba
Saila Khurd
Satnaur Badesron Halt
Garhshankar
Khatkar Kalan Jhandalji
Alachor
Mandhali Halt
Kultham Abdullah Shah Halt
Bahram
Malupota
Banga
Kariha Halt
FZP
Nawashahr Doaba Jn
Rahon
UMB
Rai Mehatpur
Naya Nangal
Nangal Dam
Bhanupali
Baddi
Anandpur Sahib
Kiratpur Sahib
Bharatgarh
Ghanauli
Rup Nagar
Mianpur
Chatauli
Kurali
Morinda
Nogawan
Bassi Pathanan
Fatehgarh Sahib
PATIALA STATE MONORAIL
Beri
Bilaspur
Darlaghat
Summer Hill
Jutogh
Shimla
Taradevi
Shoghi
Kathleeghat
Kanoh
Kandaghat
Salogra
SHIVALIK HILLS
Solan
Solan Brewery
Barog
Barog Tunnel
Kumarhatti Dagshai
Sonwara
Gumman
Dharampur (Himachal)
Parwanoo
Koti
Jabli
Kalka
Taksal
Koti Tunnel
Surajpur
DW
Chandi Mandir
Chandigarh
Ghaggar
Dhappar
Lalru
Dhulkot
Ludhiana Jn
Block Hut 01
Dhandari Kalan
Sanehwal
Jassowal
Doraha
Kila Raipur
Jaspalon
Chawapail
Ghungrana Halt
Ahmedgarh
Khanna
Mandi Gobindgarh
Rohira Galllughara
Kup
Sirhind Jn
Sadhoo Garh
Sarai Banjara
Malerkotla
Himmatana
Rajpura Jn
Dhuri Jn
Kauliseri
Chhintanwala
Kakrala Halt
Nabha
Kaleh Majra Halt
Dhablan
Patiala Cantt
Kauli
Sambhu
Duankalan
Patiala
Ambala City
Bahadur Singhwala
Ambala Cantt Jn
PATIALA STATE MONORAIL
Bhawanigarh
Block Hut T
Dukheri
Mohri
Kesri
Tandwal
Barara
Shahabad Markand
Mustafabad
Dhola Mazra
Darazpur
Jagadhri Town
Abdullapur
Jagadhri Workshop
Jagadhri
Dhirpur
Dhoda Kheri
Kalanaur
Kurukshetra Jn
Thanesar City
Amin
Pindarsi
Pabnawa Jasmahinder Halt
Tik
Pehowa Road
Nilokheri
Geong Halt
Taraori
Kaithal
Qutabpur Halt
Sajuma
Bhaini Khurd
Kalayat
Karnal
Himmatpura
Tohana
Kalwan Halt
Dharodi
Gurthari Halt
Narwana Jn
Ghaso
Bajida Jattan
Gharunda
Haryana
DIVISIONS
BKN - Bikaner (NWR)
DLI - Delhi (NR)
FZp - Firozpur (NR)
MB - Moradabad ((NR)
UMB - Ambala (NR)
Bharkot
Uttaranchal
Yamuna
U.P.
GARHWAL HILLS
Dehradun
Harrawala
Doiwala
Rishikesh
Kansrao
Virbhadra
Maika Mandir
Bibiwala
Shyampura
Satnarain Temple
Raiwala Jn
Motichur
Bhimgoda Tank
Near Tunnel
Haridwar
Jwalapur
Ikkar
Pathri
Aithal
Laksar Jn
Raisi
Balawali
Chandok
Kotdwara
Saneh Rd
Najibabad Jn
Muazzampur Narain Jn
Fazalpur
Khanalampura West
Sarsawa
Pilkhani
Hindon Cabin
Baliakheri
Sunheti Kharkhari Halt
Chodiala
Iqbalpur
Roorkee
Dhandhera
Landhaura
Dausni
Saharanpur Jn
Khanalampura Goods Yard
Manani
Tapri Jn
Bhankla Halt
Nagal
Rampur Maniharan
Sona Arjunpur
Talheri Buzurg
Nanauta
Deoband
Thana Bhawan
Thana Bhawan Town
Rohana Kalan
DLI
MB

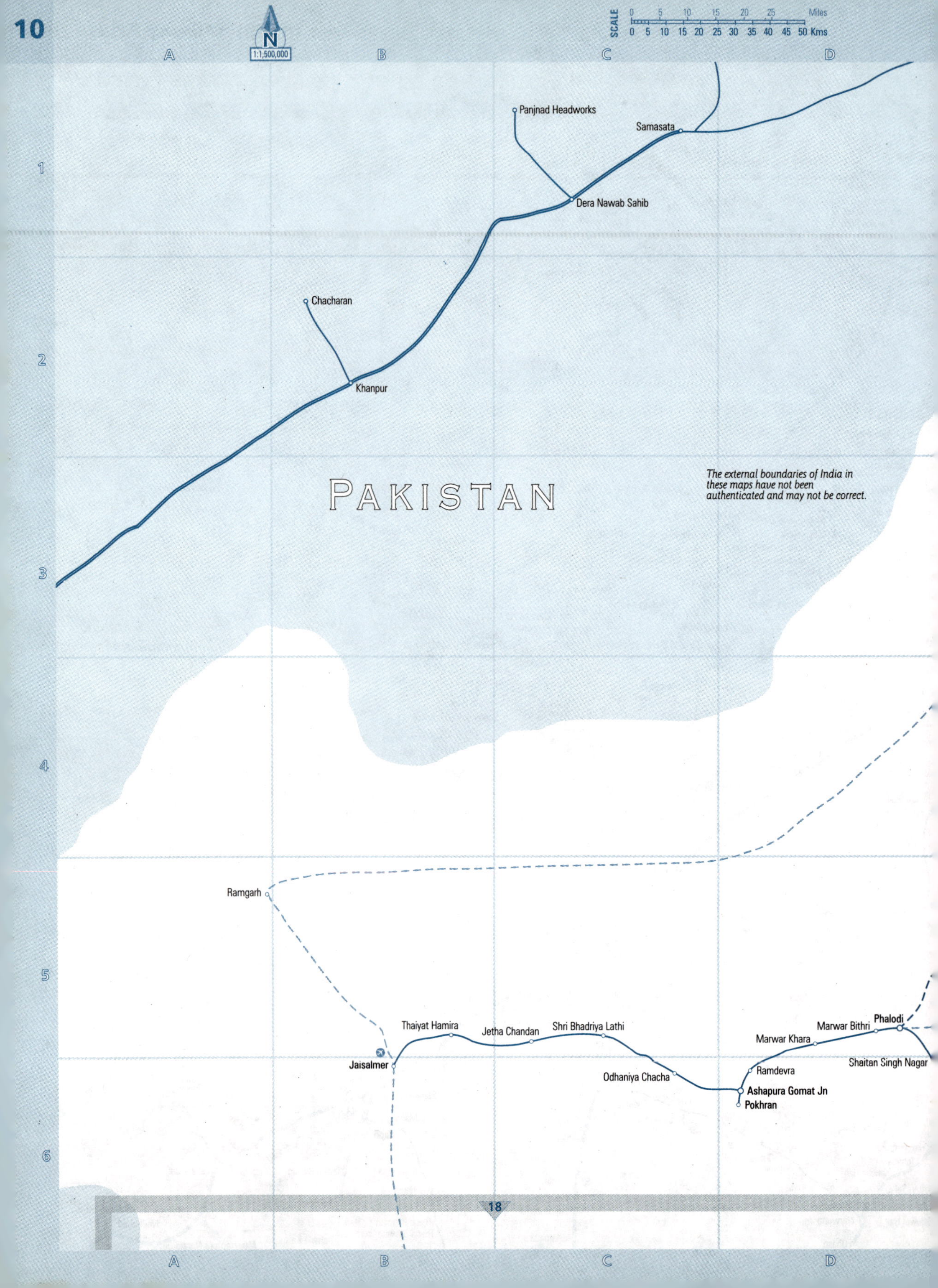
N
1:1,500,000
SCALE
0 5 10 15 20 25 Miles
0 5 10 15 20 25 30 35 40 45 50 Kms
A
B
C
D
1
2
3
4
5
6
Panjnad Headworks
Samasata
Dera Nawab Sahib
Chacharan
Khanpur
PAKISTAN
The external boundaries of India in these maps have not been authenticated and may not be correct.
Ramgarh
Thaiyat Hamira
Jetha Chandan
Shri Bhadriya Lathi
Jaisalmer
Odhaniya Chacha
Marwar Khara
Marwar Bithri
Phalodi
Ramdevra
Ashapura Gomat Jn
Pokhran
Shaitan Singh Nagar
18

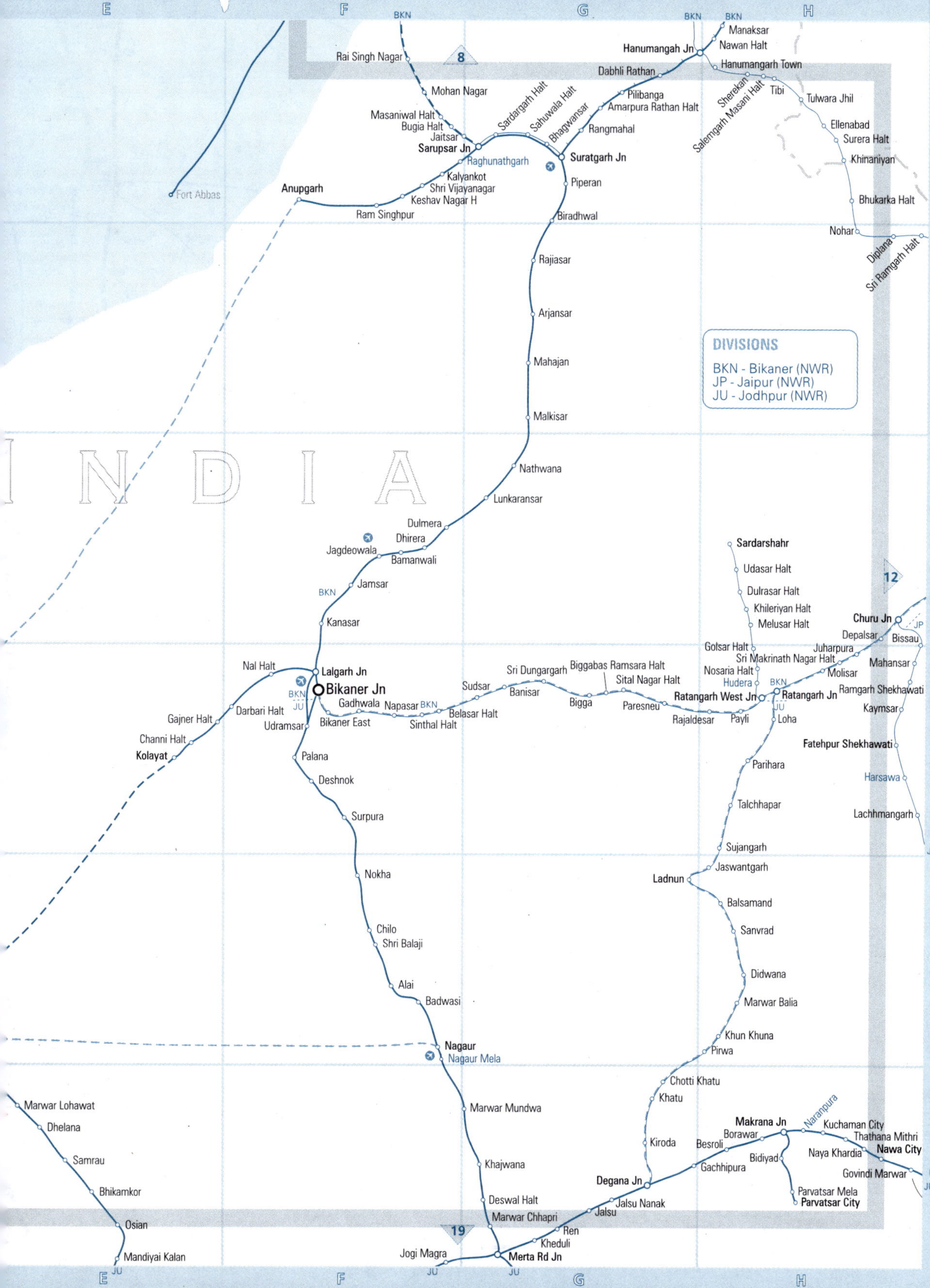
E
F
G
H
1
2
3
4
5
6
8
12
19
BKN
JU
JP
IZN
INDIA
Fort Abbas
Rai Singh Nagar
Mohan Nagar
Masaniwal Halt
Bugia Halt
Jaitsar
Sarupsar Jn
Raghunathgarh
Sardargarh Halt
Sahuwala Halt
Bhagwansar
Suratgarh Jn
Rangmahal
Amarpura Rathan Halt
Pilibanga
Dabhli Rathan
Hanumangah Jn
Manaksar
Nawan Halt
Hanumangarh Town
Sherekan
Salemgarh Masani Halt
Tibi
Tulwara Jhil
Ellenabad
Surera Halt
Khinaniyan
Bhukarka Halt
Nohar
Diplana
Sri Ramgarh Halt
Anupgarh
Kalyankot
Shri Vijayanagar
Keshav Nagar H
Ram Singhpur
Piperan
Biradhwal
Rajiasar
Arjansar
Mahajan
Malkisar
Nathwana
Lunkaransar
Dulmera
Dhirera
Jagdeowala
Bamanwali
Jamsar
Kanasar
DIVISIONS
BKN - Bikaner (NWR)
JP - Jaipur (NWR)
JU - Jodhpur (NWR)
Sardarshahr
Udasar Halt
Dulrasar Halt
Khileriyan Halt
Melusar Halt
Golsar Halt
Sri Makrinath Nagar Halt
Nosaria Halt
Hudera
Churu Jn
Depalsar
Bissau
Juharpura
Mahansar
Molisar
Ramgarh Shekhawati
Kaymsar
Fatehpur Shekhawati
Harsawa
Lachhmangarh
Nal Halt
Lalgarh Jn
Bikaner Jn
Gadhwala
Napasar
Belasar Halt
Sinthal Halt
Bikaner East
Udramsar
Darbari Halt
Gajner Halt
Channi Halt
Kolayat
Sudsar
Sri Dungargarh
Banisar
Biggabas Ramsara Halt
Sital Nagar Halt
Bigga
Paresneu
Rajaldesar
Ratangarh West Jn
Payli
Ratangarh Jn
Loha
Parihara
Talchhapar
Sujangarh
Jaswantgarh
Ladnun
Palana
Deshnok
Surpura
Nokha
Chilo
Shri Balaji
Alai
Badwasi
Nagaur
Nagaur Mela
Marwar Mundwa
Khajwana
Deswal Halt
Marwar Chhapri
Balsamand
Sanvrad
Didwana
Marwar Balia
Khun Khuna
Pirwa
Chotti Khatu
Khatu
Kiroda
Degana Jn
Jalsu Nanak
Jalsu
Ren
Kheduli
Merta Rd Jn
Jogi Magra
Besroli
Borawar
Gachhipura
Makrana Jn
Naranpura
Kuchaman City
Thathana Mithri
Nawa City
Naya Khardia
Bidiyad
Govindi Marwar
Parvatsar Mela
Parvatsar City
Marwar Lohawat
Dhelana
Samrau
Bhikamkor
Osian
Mandiyai Kalan

SCALE
0 5 10 15 20 25 Miles
0 5 10 15 20 25 30 35 40 45 50 Kms
N
1:1,500,000
A
B
C
D
1
2
3
4
5
6
8
9
11
20
BKN
UMB
DLI
JP
JU
AGC
KTT
Haryana
Rajasthan
Bara Gudha
Sirsa
Bajekan Halt
Suchan Kotli
Jodhka Halt
Ding
Mehuwala Halt
Bhattu
Khabra Kalan Halt
Mandi Adampur
Surera Halt
Khinaniyan
Bhukarka Halt
Nohar
Diplana
Sri Ramgarh Halt
Gogameri
Tehsil Bhadra
Kalana
Anupshahr
Sidhmukh
Hansiawas Halt
Narwasi
Paharsar Halt
Jamalpur Sheikhan
Pirthala Lalaunda
Fatehabad
Dhamtan Sahib
Gajuwal Halt
Uklana
Daulatpur Haryana
Barwala
Agroha
Jakhod Khera
Nyoli Kalan Halt
Hisar Jn
Dhansu
Raipur Haryana Jn
Satrod
Mayar Halt
Hansi
Charaud
Naloi Barwa
Siwani
Jhunpa
Laseri Halt
Suratpura Jn
Sadulpur Jn
Tohana
Kalwan Halt
Dharodi
Sajuma
Kalayat
Gurthari Halt
Narwana Jn
Ghaso
Uchana
Barsola
Jind Jn
Jind City
Pendu Pindara
Siwaha
Pilu Khera
Budha Khera
Sila Kheri Halt
Safidon
Karsindhu
Narah
Madlauda
Asan
Khukrana
Bhaini Khurd
Karnal
Bazida Jattan
Gharaunda
Kohand Halt
Babarpur
Panipat Jn
Gujran Balwa Halt
Binjhol Halt
Naulatha
Diwana
Israna
Dhurana Halt
Samalkha
Mudlana
Sarsadh H
Gohana
Bodhwal Majri
Qasimpur Khetri
Bishanpura Haryana
Kinana
Jai Jai Wanti
Julana
Kila Zafargarh
Karainthi
Bhainswan
Rukhi Halt
Jasia
Makrauli
Ganaur
Rajlu Garhi Halt
Sandal Kalan
Barka Halt
Alawalpur Idrispur
Sujra Halt
Sonipat
Baghpat Rd
Kandhla
Ailam H
Asara H
Bhudpur H
Aurangnagar Halt
Jita Kheri
Bawani Khera
Samar Gopalpur
Kalanaur Kalan
Dobh Bahali
Rohtak Jn
Asthal Bohar
Kharawar
Ismaila Haryana
Sampla
Sui Halt
Bamla
Kharak
Lahli
Bhiwani Jn
Bhiwani City
Dhana Ladanpur Halt
Manheru
Fatehgarh Haryana Halt
Charkhi Dadri
Patuwas Maharana Halt
Jharli
Sudrana
Kosli
Jhajjar
Harsana Kalan Halt
Rathdhana
Narela
Holambi Kalan
Khera Kalan
Ahera Halt
Sunhera Halt
Khekra
Fakharpur Halt
Gotra Halt
Nusratabad Khai
Rohand Nagar Halt
Asaudah
Bahadurgarh
Badli
Naya Azadpur
Ghevra
Mundka Halt
Nangloi
Shakurbasti
Sarai Rohilla
Delhi Jn
Behta Hazipur
Noli
Daya Basti
New Delhi
Delhi Cantt
Palam
Hazrat Nizamuddin
Delhi
Shahbad Mohammadpur
Bijwasan
Carterpuri
Gurgaon
Basai Dhankot
Okhla
Tuglakabad
Garhi Harsaru Jn
Junction Cabin
Faridabad
Faridabad New Town
Ballabhgarh
Asaoti
Palwal
Rundhi
Sholaka
Sultanpur Kaliwas Halt
Farukhnagar
Patli
Jataula Jauri Sampka
Pataudi Rd
Ichchapuri
Khalilpur
Kumbhawas Mundhalia Dabri Halt
Nangal Pathani Halt
Jatusana
Kishangarh Balawas H
Rewari Jn
Dokwa
Hadyal
Dudhwa Khara
Sirsala Halt
Aslu
Sri Makrinath Nagar Halt
Churu Jn
Depalsar
Bissau
Juharpura
Mahansar
Ramgarh Shekhawati
Kayamsar
Fatehpur Shekhawati
Harsawa
Lachhmangarh Sikar
Rashidpura Khori
Sikar Jn
Goriyan
Ranoli Shishu
Palsana
Baori Thikria
Sonthaliya
Ringas Jn
Kishan Manpura
Badhal
Pachar Malikpura
Renwal
Mindha
Bheslana
Sanodiya
Kandhran Halt
Harpalu
Bewar Bhojan Halt
Rampura Beri
Gugalwa Kirtan H
Parvezpur
Kushalpura Halt
Loharu Jn
Sohansara
Bhavdhari
Satnali
Narwan
Nangal Degrota Halt
Zerpur Pali
Bojawas Halt
Guha Kemla
Kanina Khas
Mahendergarh
Dahina Zainabad
Nangal Mundi
Surajgarh
Chirawa
Nari Khetri
Ratanshahar
Khajpur Naya
Jhunjhunu
Nua
Bhojasar
Dundlod Mukundgarh
Balwantpura
Nawalgarh
Kolida Beri
Jerthi Dadia
Singhana
Mirzapur Bachhod
Kathuwas
Ateli
Kund
Pali
Khori
Narnaul
Amarpur Jorasi
Nizampur
Dabla Jn
Jhilo
Maonda
Nim-ka-Thana
Bhagega
Kanwat
Kachera
Shri Madhopur
Chhota Gudha
Govindgarh Malikpur
Loharwara
Chomu-Samod
Bhaton-ki-Gali
Bharawas
Bawal
Manjri Nangal
Ajerka
Khanpur Ahir
Harsauli
Khairtal
Ghatala
Parisal
Alwar Byepass Cabin N
Alwar Branch Cabin
Alwar Jn
Ootwar
Ramgarh
Jadoli ka Bas
Mahwa
Malakhera
Dhigawara
Govindgarh
Brijnagar
Bedham
Deeg
Rajgarh
Surergoth
Baswa
Golana
Bandikui Jn
Arniya
Kolvagram
Bhankri
Khan Bhankri
Dausa
Talchera Baraoli Ran
Paprera
Ghosrana
Dantia
Kherli
Nadbai
Mandawar Mahwa Rd
Bhuda
Karanpura
Bhajera
Biwai
Shri Ghasi Nagar
Jaic
Pingora
Keladevi
Salabad
Bayana Jn
Dumariya
Thathana Mithri
Naya Khardia
Nawa City
Govindi Marwar
Gudha
Khandel
Pipli-Ka-Bas
Hirnoda
Dhindha
Sambhar Lake
Phulera Jn
Japog
Bhanwasa
Naraina
Dantra
Asalpur Jobner
Bobas
Sheosinghpura
Dhankya
Bindayaka
Baisgodam
Durgapura
Sanganer
Nindhar Benar
Kanakpura
Daharka Balaji
Jaipur Jn
Gandhinagar Jaipur
Getor Jagatpura
Khatipura
Kanauta
Jhir
Banskho
Bhandana

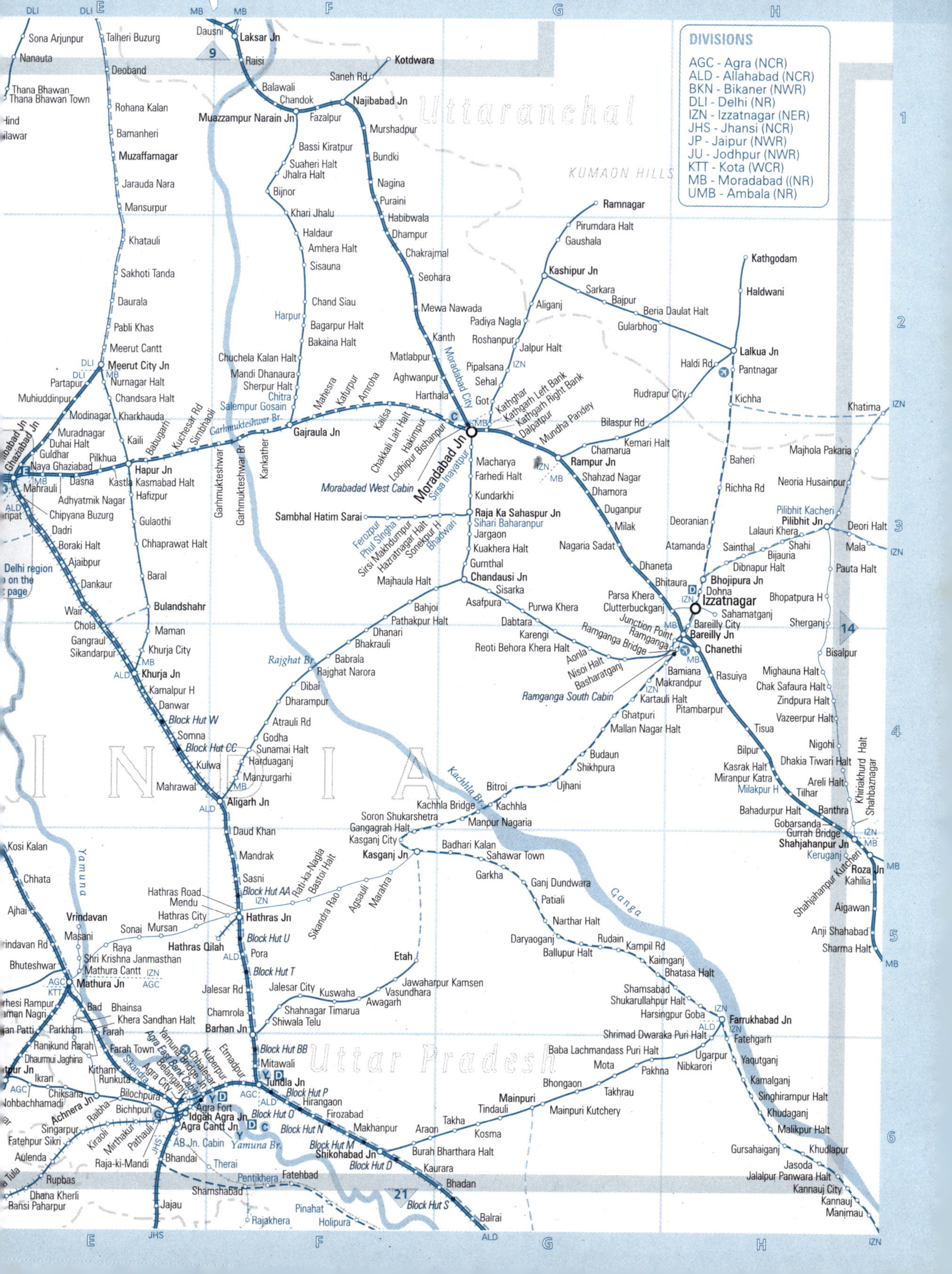
DIVISIONS
AGC - Agra (NCR)
ALD - Allahabad (NCR)
BKN - Bikaner (NWR)
DLI - Delhi (NR)
IZN - Izzatnagar (NER)
JHS - Jhansi (NCR)
JP - Jaipur (NWR)
JU - Jodhpur (NWR)
KTT - Kota (WCR)
MB - Moradabad ((NR)
UMB - Ambala (NR)
Uttaranchal
KUMAON HILLS
INDIA
Uttar Pradesh
Ganga
Yamuna
Delhi region on the page
Sona Arjunpur
Nanauta
Thana Bhawan
Thana Bhawan Town
Talheri Buzurg
Deoband
Rohana Kalan
Bamanheri
Muzaffarnagar
Jarauda Nara
Mansurpur
Khatauli
Sakhoti Tanda
Daurala
Pabli Khas
Meerut Cantt
Meerut City Jn
Nurnagar Halt
Chandsara Halt
Kharkhauda
Partapur
Muhiuddinpur
Modinagar
Muradnagar
Duhai Halt
Guldhar
Pilkhua
Naya Ghaziabad
Dasna
Mahrauli
Kaili
Hapur Jn
Kastla Kasmabad Halt
Hafizpur
Adhyatmik Nagar
Chipyana Buzurg
Dadri
Boraki Halt
Ajaibpur
Dankaur
Gulaothi
Chhaprawat Halt
Baral
Bulandshahr
Maman
Khurja City
Wair
Chola
Gangraul
Sikandarpur
Khurja Jn
Kamalpur H
Danwar
Block Hut W
Somna
Block Hut CC
Kulwa
Mahrawal
Aligarh Jn
Babugarh
Kuchesar Rd
Simbhaoli
Garhmukteshwar Br.
Garhmukteshwar
Kankather
Gajraula Jn
Salempur Gosain
Chitra
Chuchela Kalan Halt
Mandi Dhanaura
Sherpur Halt
Laksar Jn
Dausni
Raisi
Balawali
Chandok
Muazzampur Narain Jn
Fazalpur
Najibabad Jn
Saneh Rd
Kotdwara
Murshadpur
Bundki
Nagina
Puraini
Habibwala
Dhampur
Chakrajmal
Seohara
Mewa Nawada
Kanth
Matlabpur
Aghwanpur
Harthala
Bassi Kiratpur
Suaheri Halt
Jhalra Halt
Bijnor
Khari Jhalu
Haldaur
Amhera Halt
Sisauna
Chand Siau
Harpur
Bagarpur Halt
Bakaina Halt
Mahesra
Katurpur
Amroha
Kailsa
Chakkali Lait Halt
Hakimpur
Lodhipur Bishanpur
Moradabad Jn
Moradabad City
Morabadad West Cabin
Sirsa Inayatpur
Macharya
Farhedi Halt
Kundarkhi
Raja Ka Sahaspur Jn
Sihari Baharanpur
Jargaon
Kuakhera Halt
Gumthal
Chandausi Jn
Sambhal Hatim Sarai
Ferozpur
Phul Singha
Sirsi Makhdumpur
Hazratnagar Halt
Sonekpur H
Bhadwari
Majhaula Halt
Padiya Nagla
Roshanpur
Pipalsana
Sehal
Got
Kathghar
Kathgarh Left Bank
Kathgarh Right Bank
Dalpatpur
Mundha Pandey
Aliganj
Jalpur Halt
Ramnagar
Pirumdara Halt
Gaushala
Kashipur Jn
Sarkara
Bajpur
Beria Daulat Halt
Gularbhog
Kathgodam
Haldwani
Lalkua Jn
Haldi Rd
Pantnagar
Kichha
Rudrapur City
Bilaspur Rd
Kemari Halt
Chamarua
Rampur Jn
Shahzad Nagar
Dhamora
Duganpur
Milak
Nagaria Sadat
Dhaneta
Bhitaura
Bhojipura Jn
Dohna
Izzatnagar
Sahamatganj
Parsa Khera
Clutterbuckganj
Junction Point
Ramganga
Ramganga Bridge
Bareilly City
Bareilly Jn
Chanethi
Baheri
Richha Rd
Deoranian
Atamanda
Sainthal
Bijauria
Dibnapur Halt
Lalauri Khera
Shahi
Pilibhit Jn
Pilibhit Kacheri
Deori Halt
Mala
Pauta Halt
Bhopatpura H
Sherganj
Bisalpur
Khatima
Majhola Pakaria
Neoria Husainpur
Sisarka
Asafpura
Purwa Khera
Dabtara
Karengi
Reoti Behora Khera Halt
Aonla
Nisoi Halt
Basharatganj
Ramganga South Cabin
Bamiana
Makrandpur
Kartauli Halt
Rasuiya
Pitambarpur
Ghatpuri
Mallan Nagar Halt
Tisua
Budaun
Shikhpura
Ujhani
Bitroi
Kachhla
Kachhla Bridge
Kachhla Br.
Manpur Nagaria
Bilpur
Kasrak Halt
Miranpur Katra
Milakpur H
Tilhar
Dhakia Tiwari Halt
Areli Halt
Banthra
Khiriakhurd Halt
Shahbaznagar
Bahadurpur Halt
Gobarsanda
Gurrah Bridge
Shahjahanpur Jn
Keruganj
Shahjahanpur Kutcheri
Roza Jn
Kahilia
Aigawan
Anji Shahabad
Sharma Halt
Mighauna Halt
Chak Safaura Halt
Zindpura Halt
Vazeerpur Halt
Nigohi
Bahjoi
Pathakpur Halt
Dhanari
Bhakrauli
Babrala
Rajghat Br
Rajghat Narora
Dibai
Dharampur
Atrauli Rd
Godha
Sunamai Halt
Harduaganj
Manzurgarhi
Soron Shukarshetra
Gangagrah Halt
Kasganj City
Kasganj Jn
Badhari Kalan
Sahawar Town
Garkha
Ganj Dundwara
Patiali
Narthar Halt
Daryaoganj
Ballupur Halt
Rudain
Kampil Rd
Kaimganj
Bhatasa Halt
Shamsabad
Shukarullahpur Halt
Harsingpur Goba
Farrukhabad Jn
Fatehgarh
Shrimad Dwaraka Puri Halt
Baba Lachmandass Puri Halt
Ugarpur
Nibkarori
Yaqutganj
Kamalganj
Singhirampur Halt
Khudaganj
Malikpur Halt
Gursahaiganj
Khudlapur
Jasoda
Jalalpur Panwara Halt
Kannauj City
Kannauj
Manimau
Daud Khan
Mandrak
Sasni
Block Hut AA
Hathras Road
Mendu
Hathras City
Hathras Jn
Rati-ka-Nagla
Bastoi Halt
Sikandra Rao
Agsauli
Marahra
Block Hut U
Hathras Qilah
Pora
Block Hut T
Etah
Jawaharpur Kamsen
Vasundhara
Awagarh
Kuswaha
Jalesar City
Jalesar Rd
Shahnagar Timarua
Shiwala Telu
Chamrola
Barhan Jn
Block Hut BB
Mitawali
Etmadpur
Tundla Jn
Block Hut P
Hirangaon
Firozabad
Block Hut O
Block Hut N
Makhanpur
Block Hut M
Shikohabad Jn
Block Hut D
Araon
Takha
Kosma
Burah Bharthara Halt
Kaurara
Bhadan
Block Hut S
Balrai
Mainpuri
Tindauli
Mainpuri Kutchery
Bhongaon
Takhrau
Mota
Pakhna
Kosi Kalan
Chhata
Ajhai
Vrindavan
Masani
Sonai
Mursan
Raya
Shri Krishna Janmasthan
Mathura Cantt
Mathura Jn
Vrindavan Rd
Bhuteshwar
Bad
Bhainsa
Khera Sandhan Halt
Parkham
Farah
Ranikund Rarah
Dhaurmui Jaghina
Farah Town
Kitham
Runkuta
Ikran
Chiksana
Mohbachhamadi
Achnera Jn
Raibha
Bilochpura
Bichhpuri
Singarpur
Fatehpur Sikri
Kiraoli
Mirthakur
Pathauli
Aulenda
Raja-ki-Mandi
Rupbas
Dhana Kherli
Bansi Paharpur
Sikandra
Agra City
Agra East Bank Cabin
Yamuna Bridge
Chhalesar
Belanganj
Kuberpur
Agra Fort
Idgah Agra Jn
Agra Cantt Jn
AB Jn. Cabin
Yamuna Br.
Bhandai
Therai
Pentikhera
Fatehbad
Shamshabad
Jajau
Rajakhera
Pinahat
Holipura

N
1:1,500,000
SCALE
0 5 10 15 20 25 Miles
0 5 10 15 20 25 30 35 40 45 50 Kms
A
B
C
D
1
2
3
4
5
6
Pithoragarh
Uttaranchal
Tanakpur
Banbasa
Chakrapur Halt
Khatima
Majhola Pakaria
Neoria Husainpur
Pilibhit Kacheri
Pilibhit Jn
Deori Halt
IZT
Lalauri Khera
Mala
Sandei Halt
Shahgarh
Parsadpur
Puranpur
Pauta Halt
Udayapur Halt
Bhopatpura Halt
Dudhia Khurd
Kuraiya
Sherganj
Sehra Mau
13
Bisalpur
Akela Hanspur Halt
IZT
LJN
Mighauna Halt
Mailani Jn
Chak Safaura Halt
Zindpura Halt
Khotar
Vazeerpur Halt
Nigohi
Powayan
Dhakia Tiwari Halt
Areli Halt
Khiriakhurd Halt
Bahadurpur Halt
MB
Shahbaznagar
Shahjahanpur Jn
Mohammadi
Banthra
Gobarsanda
Gurrah Bridge
Shahjahanpur Kutcheri
Roza Jn
Keruganj
Unchaulia
Kahilia
Lakhnauria Halt
Jung Bahadurganj
Jahanikhera
Aigawan
Maigalganj
Anji Shahabad
Sharma Halt
Todarpur
Behtagokul
Kaurha
Hardoi
Karna
Masit
Baghauli
Ghausganj Halt
Atwa Kursath
Balamau Jn
Gauriphanta
Dingania
Paulaha
Phulwaria Phanta
Chandan Chauki
Dudwa Jn
Sonaripur
Paliakalan
Rehta
Bhirakheri
Raj Narainpur
Bhikhampur
Banke Ganj
Gola Gokarannath
Bahelia Buzurg Halt
Raja Ganj
Phardhan
Deokali
Lakhimpur
Khiri Town
Kadipur Sani Halt
Oel
Hargaon
Persehramal Halt
Jharekhapur
Bhujhia Bara Gaon Halt
Uttar Pradesh
Neri Halt
Maholi Halt
Urdauli Halt
Hempur Halt
Kateli Halt
Sitapur City Jn
Sitapur Kutcheri
Ramkot
MB
LJN
Sitapur Cantt Jn
Tappa Khajuria Halt
Persendi
Ramaipur Halt
Khairabad Awadh
Burmi Halt
Misrikh Tirath
Ghori Halt
Naimisharanya
Beniganj
Atwa Muthia Halt
Arseni
Gaju Halt
Barai Jalalpur
Kamlapur
Suraincha Halt
Sidhauli
Manwa Halt
Ataria
Itaunja
Belrayan
Tikunia
Kauriala Ghat
Katarnian Ghat
Khairatia Bandh Rd
Bichia
Manjhra Purab
Nishangara
Murtiha
Kakraha Rest House
Mahinpurwa
Raibojha
Nepalganj Rd
Babaganj H
Nanpara Jn
Matera
Risia
Bahraich
INDIA
The external boundaries of India in these maps have not been authenticated and may not be correc
Biswan
Shankerpur Halt
Sarayan
Babupur Halt
Mahmudabad (Awadh)
Munda Gopal Ashram
Paintipur
Tahsil Fatehpur
Bahramghat
Mahadewa
Sundhia Mau
Burhwal Jn
Bindaura
Rafinagar
Jahangirabad Raj
Chowka Ghat
Ghaghara Ghat
Jarwal Rd
Sarju
Colonelganj
Kasturi
Kathola
Gonda Kutcheri
Chilwaria
Yogendradham Halt
Payagpur
Bisheswarganj
Bangain
Gangadham
Maijapur
Lakshmanpur
Kauwapur
Gainjahwa
Jharkhandi Halt
Balrampur
Bhawanipurkalan
Intiathok
Subhagpur
Gonda Jn
Barua Chak
Motiganj
Jhilahi Flag H
Mankapur Jn
Tikri Ha
IZN
Khudlapur
Jasoda
Jalalpur Panwara Halt
Kannauj City
Kannauj
Manimau
Gauntra Halt
Madhoganj
Farhat Nagar Halt
Mallawan
Dalelnagar
Umar Tali
Sandila
Rahimabad
Dilawarnagar
Bakshi ka Talab
Kamlabad Barhauli
22
IZN
MB
MB
LJN
LKO
LJN

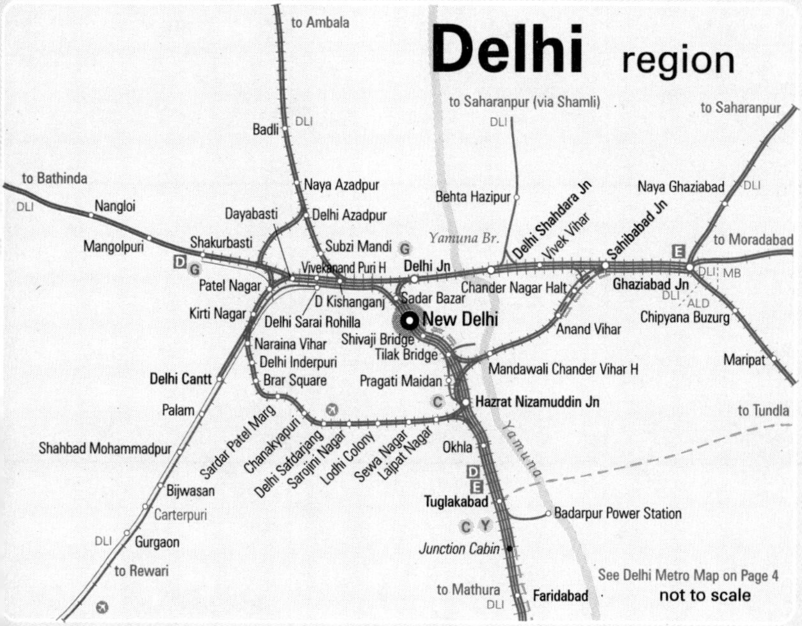

DIVISIONS

ALD - Allahabad (NCR)
BSB - Varanasi (NER)
DLI - Delhi (NR)
IZN - Izzatnagar (NER)
LJN - Lucknow (NER)
LKO - Lucknow (NR)
MB - Moradabad (NR)
SPJ - Samastipur (ECR)

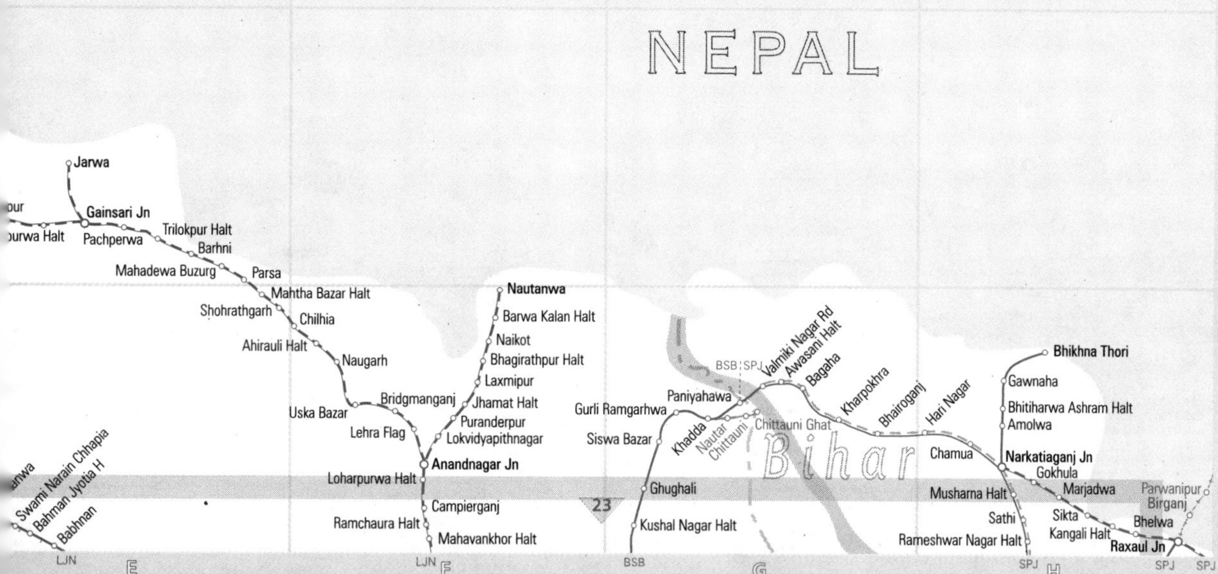

The external boundaries of India in these maps have not been authenticated and may not be correct.

E
F
G
H
1
2
3
4
5
6
Arunachal Pradesh
INDIA
Along
Passighat
Tezu
DIVISIONS
RNY - Rangiya (NFR)
TSK - Tinsukia (NFR)
Saikhoa Ghat
Dangari
TSK
Talap
Rupai
Sookerating
Hansara
Dumduma Town
Barhapjan
Makum Jn
Tinsukia Jn
Tingrai
Bogapani
Sripuriagaon
Chariali
Telpung
Digboi
Bordubi Rd
Duliajan
TRAMWAY
Bargolai
Ledo
Tirap Siding
Lekhapani
Tipongpani Wharf
Powai
TSK
Margherita
Namdong Wharf
COLLIERY LINES
New Tinsukia Jn
Naharkatia
Balimara
Namrup
Borhat
Barua Nagar
Sapekhati
Longpatia
Bhojo
Safrai
Lakwa
Mahutgaon
Simaluguri Jn
Santak
Naginimora
Bihubar
Nazira
Mezenga
Namtiali
Barahibari
Amguri Jn
Seleng Hat
Lahing
Nakchari
Tuli
Meleng
Nahorbari
Mariani Jn
TSK
Kharikatia
itabar
Dukhlangia
Koliapani
Cinnamara
Jorhat Town
Borigaon
Neamati Ghat
Kujibali
Sibsagar Town
Desang Siding
Kharahat
Mohkhuti
Sepon
Moran
Moranhat
TSK
Khowang
Dhamalgaon
New Dibrugarh Town
Dibrugarh Town
Dibrumukh
Chalkhoa
Lahoal
Dikom
Hatiali Ground Siding
Panitola
Chabua
TSK
Hijiguri
W
Murkong Selek
Jonekareng Halt
Laimekuri Halt
Telem
Dekapam Halt
Simenchapari Halt
RNY
Dipa Halt
Dimow Halt
Archipathar Halt
Silapathar
Sisibargaon
New Sisibargaon
Sripani Halt
Maridhal Halt
Dhemaji
RNY
Tangni
Jiadhal Halt
Nanadi Halt
Bordoloni Halt
Gogamukh
Subansiri
ginadi
Brahmaputra
Assam
MYANMAR
27

N
1:1,500,000
SCALE
0 5 10 15 20 25 Miles
0 5 10 15 20 25 30 35 40 45 50 Kms
A
B
C
D
1
2
3
4
5
6
10
28
29
The external boundaries of India in these maps have not been authenticated and may not be correct.
INDIA
PAKISTAN
Rajasthan
Gujarat
Luni
Munabao
Khokhaopar
Jaisingder
Lilma
JU
Tamlor
Gadra Rd
Ramsar
Gagariya
Bhachhbhar
Khadeen
Jasai
Ati Malani
Barmer
Gypsum Halt
Utarlai
Kavas
Baniya Sanda Dhora
Baytu
Bhimarlai
Gole
Tilwara
Tilwara Mela
Pachpadra Salt Depot
Pachpadra City
Khed Temple
Balotra Jn
Samdari
Janiyana
Parlu
Jethantri H
Bamsin
Rakhi Halt
Mokalsar
Balwara
Bishangarh
Jalor
Jagannathji Rd
Bakra Rd
Modran
Marwar Ba
Bheempura
Ledarmer
Marwar Bhinmal
Marwar Kori
Kagmala H
Malwara
Raniwara
Marwar Ratanpur
Dugdol
Jari
Dhanera
Ramsan
Jenal
Shri Amirgadh
Sarotra Rd
Iqbal Gadh
Jethi
Chitrasani
Karjoda
AII
Bhildi Jn
JU
ADI
Lorwada
Disa
Rasana
Chandisar
Chaddotar
Palanpur Jn
Umardashi
Jasali
Dhanakwada
Diyodar
Mitha
Bhabhar
Devgam
Piplee
Radhanpur
Kakoshi Metrana Rd
Dhanawada
Wagdod
Charup
Kosa Rd
Khalipur
Chhapi
Dharewada
Siddhapur
Taranga
Varetha
Kaderpur
ADI

E
F
G
H
JU
1
2
3
4
5
6
11
20
30
Bhikamkor
Osian
Mandiyai Kalan
Tiwari
Marwar Mathaniya
Manaklao
Daijar
Mandor
Mahamandir
Banar
Fedusar Quarry Siding
Fedusar
Marwar Musuria Siding
Rai Ka Bag Palace Jn
Jodhpur Jn
Bhagat-ki-Kothi
Basni
Salawas
Hanwant
Luni Jn
Satlana Halt
Dundara
Dudia
Miyon ka Bara
Khandi Halt
Rohat
Pir Dhule-Shah Halt
Kairla
Pali Marwar
Bomadra
Rajkiawas
Marwar Jn
Auwa
Banta Raghunathgarh
Bhinwaliya
Somesar
Jawali
Bhagwanpura
Rani
Khimei
Falna
Biroliya
Jawai Bandh
Mori Bera
Kothar
Nana
Keshavganj
Sirohi Rd
Banas
Swarupganj
Bhimana
Kivarli
Morthala
Abu Rd
Ambaji
Khed Brahma
Vadali
ADI
Asranada
Jajiwal
Kheri Salwa
Pipar Rd Jn
Sathin Rd
Umed
Kharia-Khangarh
Gotan
Jogi Magra
Merta Rd Jn
Merta City
Marwar Chhapri
Kheduli
Ren
Deswal Halt
Jalsu
Jalsu Nanak
Degana Jn
Pipar City
Silari H
Bhawi H
Bilara
Parvatsar Mela
Parvatsar City
Sakhun
JP
Sali
Gehlota
Tiloniya
Mandavariya
Kishangarh
Gegal Akhri
Ladpura
Pushkar
Madar
Ajmer Jn
Daurai
Adarshnagar
Hatundi
Lachipura
Rajoshi
Nasirabad
Saradhana
Makrera
Mangaliyawas
Lamana
Kharwa
Piplaj
Bangurgram
Amarpura
Beawar
Sendra
Bar
Haripur
Guriya
Chandawal
Bagri Sajjanpur
Bagrinagar
Sojat Rd
Bhesana
Dhareshwar
Marwar Ranawas
Goramghat
Phulad
ARAVALLI RANGE
Khambli Ghat
Devgarh Madariya
Delaji-ka-Khera
Kuwanthal
Khara Kameri
Charbhuja Rd
Lawa Sardargarh
Kaunriya
Soniyana Mewar
Kankroli
Bejnal
Nathdwara
Thamla Mogana
Mavli Jn
Bhimal
Khemli
Debari
Udaisagar
Udaipur City
Rana Pratap Nagar
Umra
Kharwa Chanda
Zawar
Padla
Jay Samand Rd
Surkhand-ka-Khera
Semari
Kundalgarh
Rikhab Dev Rd
Kotana
Vallabhnagar
Kheroda
Bhindar
Kanor
Bari Sadri
Bansi Bohera
Fatehnagar
Bhupalsagar
Kapasan
Pandoli
Netawal
Ghosunda
Chhaderiya
Berach Jn Cabin
Chittaurgarh Jn
RTM
KTT
Ordi
Shambhupura
Gambhiri Rd
Nimbahera
Jawad Rd
Bisalwas Kalan
Nimach
Jamuniya Kalan
Harkia Khal
Matyakheri
Malhargarh
Piplia
Sindpan
Mandsor
M.P.
Jharwasa
Bandanwara
Singwal
Mokhampura
Bijainagar
Gulabpura
Rupaheli
Bhojras
Sareri
Raila Rd
Lambiya
Dhuwala
Mandal
Bhilwara
Mandpiya
Hamirgarh
Soniana
Gangrar
Det
Mandalgarh
Genoli Rd
Singoli Shyam
Parsoli
Barundani
Jodhpuriya
Basi Berisal
Thambawati Nagari
DIVISIONS
ADI - Ahmadabad (WR)
AII - Ajmer (NWR)
JP - Jaipur (NWR)
JU - Jodhpur (NWR)
KTT - Kota (WCR)
RTM - Ratlam (WR)

N
1:1,500,000
SCALE
0 5 10 15 20 25 Miles
0 5 10 15 20 25 30 35 40 45 50 Kms
A
B
C
D
1
2
3
4
5
6
12
19
31
INDIA
Rajasthan
Madhy
Chambal
JU
JP
Gudha
Khandel
Pipalikabas
Hirnoda
Dhindha
Sambhar Lake
Phulera Jn
Japog
Bhanwasa
Naraina
Dantra
Sakhun
Sali
Gehlota
Tiloniya
Asalpur Jobner
Bobas
Sheosinghpura
Dhankya
Bindayaka
Kanakpura
Nindhar Benar
Daharka Balaji
Jaipur Jn
Gandhinagar Jaipur
Getor Jagatpura
Khatipura
Kanauta
Baisgodam
Durgapura
Sanganer
Goner Rd
Balawala
Chitora Renwal
Sheodaspura Padampura
Shitala Rd
Chaksu
Phagi
Nimera
Chosla
Channani
Diggi
Banasthali Niwai
Avikanagar
Malpura
Tordi Sagar
Kukar
Toda Rai Singh
Siras
Isarda
Sureli
Chauth ka Barwara
Devpura
Bassi
Jhir
Banskho
Bhandana
Jatwara
Dausa
Bhankri
Khan Bhankri
Kolvagram
Arniya
Keladevi
Salabad
Bayana Jn
AGC
Dumariya
Fateh Singhpura
Dhindhora Hukmikheda
Bandh Baretha
Hindaun City
Sikroda Mina
Shri Mahabirji
Khandip
Piloda
Chhoti Odai
Barauli
Sirmuttra
KTT
Gangapur City North Cabin
Gangapur City
Lalpur Umri
Narayanpur Tatwara
Nimoda
Malarna
Mokholi
Ranthambhor
Sawai Madhopur D Cabin
Sawai Madhopur Jn
Kushtala
Rawanjna Dungar
Amli
Indragarh Sumerganj Mandi
Lakheri
Laban
Ghat-ka-Varana
Kapren
Arnetha
Keshorai Patan
Pipalwali Chowki
Sabalgarh
Bijaipur Rd
Rampa
Birpur
Kaimarakalan
Sillipur
Ikdori
Tarrakalan
Seroni Rd
Khojeepura
Girdharpur
Durgapuri
JHS
Datarda Kalan
Sheopur Kalan
Bundi
Srinagar
Nimka Khera
Thalera
Dehit
Jalindri
Mandalgarh
Genoli Rd
Upramal
Shyampura
Singoli Shyam
Gurla North Cabin
Chambal Br.
Gurla Jn
Kota C Cabin
Kota Jn
Chandresal
Shri Kalyanpura
Bhonra
Digod
Kota Jn South Cabin
Kota City
Sogaria Cabin
Dakaniya Talav
Antah
Bijora
Sundlak
Baran
Dadhdevi
Alniya
Dhani-Kasar
Ravtha Rd
Chhajawa
Pipalda Rd
Atru
Dara
Kanwalpura
Morak
Ramganj Mandi
Salpura
Kesholi
Chhabra Gugor
Bhulon
Motipura Chauki
Raiserjagir
Miyana
Bhadora Jagir
Tarawata
Guna Jn
Pagara
Dharnoda
Mahugarha
Chaurakheri
BPL
Ruthiyai Jn
Vijaipur
Raghogarh
Kumbhraj
Ramri
Jhalawar Rd
Jhalawar
Dhuankheri
Bhawani Mandi
Pachpahar
Kurlasi
Garot
Shamgarh
Hanspura
Suwasra
RTM
Sindpan
Mandsor
G
D
W

DIVISIONS
AGC - Agra (NCR)
ALD - Allahabad (NCR)
BPL - Bhopal (WCR)
IZN - Izzatnagar (NER)
JBP - Jabalpur (WCR)
JP - Jaipur (NWR)
JHS - Jhansi (NCR)
JU - Jodhpur (NWR)
KTT - Kota (WCR)
RTM - Ratlam (WR)
E
F
G
H
1
2
3
4
5
6
13
22
32
Uttar Pradesh
Pradesh
Yamuna
Betwa
Chambal Br.
Pentikhera
Fatehpur Sikri
Aulenda
Rupbas
Dhana Kherli
Bansi Paharpur
Bhandai
Therai
Shamshabad
Rajakhera
Fatehbad
Pinahat
Holipura
Bah
Shikohabad Jn
Makhanpur
Araon
Burah Bharthara Halt
Block Hut M
Block Hut D
Kaurara
Bhadan
Block Hut S
Balrai
Jaswantnagar
Sarai Bhopat
Etawah
Ekdil
Block Hut X
Bharthana
Block Hut G
Samhon
Ghasara Halt
Achalda
Pata
Phaphund
Block Hut HH
Kanchausi
Parajani Halt
Jhinjhak
Block Hut L
Ambiapur
Block Hut I
Rura
Block Hut Y
Roshan Mau Halt
Maitha
Gursahaiganj
Khudlapur
Jasoda
Jalalpur Panwara Halt
Kannauj City
Kannauj
Manimau
Jajau
Tantpur
Bagthar
Baseri
Mania
Mohari Jn
Nurpura
Dhaulpur Jn
Gher
Bari
Garhi Sandra
Soorothee
Talshahi
Hetampur
Sikroda Kwari
Morena
Sank
Nurabad
Banmor
Malanpur
Rethora Kalan
Nonera
Rayatpura
Gohad Rd
Sondha Rd
Soni
Asokhar
Itehar
Bhind
Udi
Sanichara
Bhadroli
Rayaru
Golaka Mandir
Birla Nagar
Gwalior Jn
Scindia-ka-Chhaoni
Ambikeshwar
Kailaras
Bhatpura
Jora Alapur
Thara
Sumaoli
Sikroda
Bamouragaon
Milavali
Motijheel
Ghosipura
Jiwajigunj
Nangaon
Sithouli
Sandalpur
Antri
Anant Paith
Simariatal
Dabra
Kotra
Sonagir
Datia
Karari
IBP
Garhmau
Paricha
Paricha Thermal Siding Cabin
Chirgaon
Nandkhas
Moth
Erich Rd
Parauna
Ait Jn
Konch
Bhua
Orai
Ata
Usargaon
Kalpi
Chaunrah
Pokhrayan
Malasa
Lalpur
Tilaunchi
Panihar
Naunanda
Ghatigaon
Renhat
Mohana
Indargarh
Bhangarh
Parakheda
Chorepura
Khajuri
Satanwara
Mansapooran
Shivpuri
Raishree
Khonkar
Kolaras
Lukwasa
Jhansi Jn
Bijauli
Khajraha
Babina
Burhpura
Basai
Orchha
Barwasagar
Niwari
Magarpur
Teharka
Ranipur Rd
Mau-Ranipur
Rora
Harpalpur
Ghutai
Bela-Tal
Kulpahar
Charkhari Rd
Mahoba
Baripura
Rath
Matalila
Talbahat
Daulta
Bijrotha
Jakhaura
Dailwara
Lalitpur
Tikamgarh
Khajuraho
Jiron
Jakhlaun
Dhaura
Mohasa
Karonda
Agasod
Malkhedi
Bina Jn
Karod
Mahadeokhedi
Semarkheri
Kanjia
Mungaoli
Guneru Bamori
Pipraigaon
Rehatwas
Orr
Ashoknagar
Shadoragon

N
1:1,500,000
SCALE
Miles
Kms
Uttar Pradesh
Madhya Pradesh
KAIMUR RANGE
Ganges
Yamuna
Betwa
14
21
33
Lucknow
Lucknow Jn (Charbagh)
Lucknow West
Manaknagar Jn
Amausi
Alamnagar
Kakori
Aishbagh Jn
Lucknow City
Daliganj Jn
Badshahnagar
Gomti Nagar Halt
Mohibullahpur
Bakshi ka Talab
Itaunja
Utraitia Jn
Mohanlalganj
Kankaha
Nigohan
Shri Rajnagar
Bachhrawan
Kundanganj
Harchandpur
Gangaganj
Rae Bareli Jn
Daryapur Jn
Ubarni
Surajkund
Bela Bhela Halt
Radhabalampur H
Dalmau Jn
Lachhmanpur
Ramchandrapur
Jalalpur Dhai
Manjhlepur Halt
Unchahar Jn
Arkha
Pariawan Kalankakar Rd
Garhi Manikpur
Kunda Harnamganj
Bhadri
Lalgopalganj
Ramchaura Rd
Sarai Gopal Halt
Phaphamau Jn
Curzon Br.
Prayag
Allahabad City
Prayag Ghat
Daraganj
Allahabad Jn
Jhusi
Izat Br.
Naini Jn
Jamuna Br.
Link Jn Cabin
Chheoki
Block Hut A
Block Hut B
Block Hut C
Meja Rd
Iradatganj
Jasra
Madaraha
Lohgara
Shankargarh
Bargarh
Kataiya Dandi
Majhiari
Dabhaura
Panhai
Manikpur Jn
Barahmuafi
Bansapahar
Ohan
Bahilpurwa
Khoh
Chitrakootdham Karwi
Shivrampur
Bharat Kup
Badausa
Atarra
Khurhand
Dingwahi
Banda
Khairar Jn
Mataundh
Kabrai
Baripura
Mahoba
Ichauli
Akona
Ragaul
Ingohta
Bharwa Sumerpur
Yamuna South Bank
Dapsaura
Hamirpur Rd
Dohru
Ghatampur
Patara
Shambhua
Kathara Rd
Paman
Lalpur
Malasa
Pokhrayan
Tilaunchi
Rasulpur Gogamau
Binaur
Bhimsen Jn
Block Hut Z
Panki
Govindpuri
Juhi Cabin
Sirhitara
Kanpur Central Jn
Chandari Jn
Chakeri
Rooma
Sirsaul
Prempur
Karbigwan
Aung
Bindki Rd
Kanspur Gugauli
Malwan
Kurasti Kalan
Fatehpur
Ramva
Faizullahpur
Rasulabad
Sath Naraini
Khaga
Katoghan
Kunwar
Athsarai
Sirathu
Block Hut KK
Shujatpur
Bidanpur
Bharwari
Manoharganj
Saiyed Sarawan
Manauri
Bamhrauli
Subedarganj
Kanpur Br.
Kanpur Bridge Left Bank
Magarwara
Unnao Jn
Sonik
Ajgain
Kusumbhi
Jaitipur
Harauni
Pipar Sand
Patiyara
Makhi
Methi Tikur Halt
Baradev Halt
Safipur
Ugu Halt
Fatehpur Chaurasi Halt
Bangarmau
Ganj Muradabad
Mallanwan
Farhat Nagar Halt
Madhoganj
Ghausganj Halt
Atwa Kursath
Gauntra Halt
Gursahaiganj
Khudlapur
Jasoda
Jalalpur Panwara Halt
Kannauj City
Kannauj
Manimau
Gangwapur Halt
Araul Makanpur
Bakothi Khas
Bilhaur
Dhaursalar Halt
Utripura
Barrajpur
Chaubepur
Brahmavart
Mandhana Jn
Kalianpur
Rawatpur
Collectorganj
Kanpur Anwarganj
Bhaupur
Block Hut FF
Maitha
Roshan Mau Halt
Block Hut Y
Rura
Block Hut I
Ambiapur
Dalelnagar
Umar Tali
Sandila
Rahimabad
Dilawarnagar
Mahilabad
Kamlabad Barhauli
Alamnagar Cabin
Transport Nagar
Dilkusha Cabin
Block Hut A
Harauni
Korari
Achalganj
Band Hamirpur Halt
Tikauli Rawatpur
Kulha Halt
Bighapur
Indamau Halt
Takia
Baiswara
Raghuraj Singh
Nihastha Halt
Lalganj
Bahi
Bani
Jais
Fursatganj
Rupamau
Kasimpur Halt
Gauriganj
Talakhajuri
Amethi
Misrauli
Sahajipur Halt
Antu
Jagesharganj
Ramganj
Musafirkhana
Shivnagar
Bandhua Kalan
Sultanpur Jn
Dwarkaganj
Adhinpur
Nihalgarh
Sindurwa
Akbarganj
Chaubisi
Haidergarh
Tribediganj
Chhandrauli
Harmatnagar
Anupganj
Bani
Tahsil Fatehpur
Bahramghat
Mahadewa
Sundhia Mau
Burhwal Jn
Bindaura
Barabanki Jn
Rafinagar
Jahangirabad Raj
Safedabad
Jugaur
Malhaur
Rasauli
Safdarganj
Saidkhanpur
Daryabad
Patranga
Rauzagaon
Rudauli
Gauriamau
Baragaon
Devrakot
Sohawal
Salarpur
Faizabad Jn
Acharya Narendra Dev Nagar
Ayodhya Ghat
Katra
Ramghat
Nawabganj
Tikri Halt
Lakhpat Nagar
Mankapur Jn
Motiganj
Barua Chak
Jhilahi Flag
Gonda Jn
Gonda Kutcheri
Kathola
Maijapur
Kasturi
Colonelganj
Sarju
Jarwal Rd
Ghaghara Ghat
Chowka Ghat
Masodha
Darshannagar
Bharat Kund
Bilhar Ghat
Malethu Kanak
Khajurhat
Chaure Bazar
Kurebhar
Pakhrauli
Bhadaiya
Piparpur
Maharani Paschim
Chanda Halt
Kohndaur
Koiripur
Chilbila Jn
Pratapgarh Jn
Pirthiganj
Dandupur
Gaura
Suwansa
Badshahpur
Nibhapur
Barya Ram
Ugrasenpur
Phulpur
Sarai Chandi
Dayalpur
Siwaith
Tharwai
Atrampur
Mau Aimma
Dhirganj
Bishnathganj
Bhupiamau
Kuwandih H
Ramnathpur
Manhgupur
Saidabad
Handia Khas
Bhiti
Ataura Halt
Jangiganj
Sarai Jagdish
Karchana
Bheerpur
Unchadih
Mandah Rd
Block Hut JJ
Markundi
Tikaria
Itwandundail
Mahjgawan
Chitahara
Khutaha
Jaitwar
Hati
Sagma
Kaima
Satna Jn
Baghai Rd
Hinauta Ramban
Turki
Rewa
Lagargawan
Unchehara
Maihar
Khajuraho
Panna
Sidhi
IZN
MB
LJN
ALD
LKO
JHS
JBP
A
B
C
D
1
2
3
4
5
6

DIVISIONS
ALD - Allahabad (NCR)
BSB - Varanasi (NER)
DHN - Dhanbad (ECR)
DNR - Danapur (ECR)
IZN - Izzatnagar (NER)
JBP - Jabalpur (WCR)
JHS - Jhansi (NCR)
LJN - Lucknow (NER)
LKO - Lucknow (NR)
MB - Moradabad ((NR)
MGS - Mughal Sarai (ECR)
SEE - Sonpur (ECR)
SPJ - Samastipur (ECR)
INDIA
Bihar
Jharkhand
Ghaghara
Gandak
Ganga
Son
15
24
34
E
F
G
H
1
2
3
4
5
6
Lehra Flag
Lokvidyapithnagar
Anandnagar Jn
Loharpurwa Halt
Campierganj
Ramchaura Halt
Mahavankhor Halt
Rawatganj
Pipiganj
Kauria Jungle
Gorakhpur City
Nakaha Jungle
Maniram
Gorakhpur Jn
Gorakhpur Cantt Jn
Kushmi
Sardar Nagar
Chauri Chaura
Gauri Bazar
Baitalpur
Deoria Sadar
Ahilyapur Halt
Nunkhar
Bhatni Jn
Peokol
Barahajbazar
Siswa Bazar
Ghughali
Kushal Nagar Halt
Mathiabar Ghat
Laxmiganj
Barharaganj Halt
Kaptanganj Jn
Bodarwar
Ram Kola
Padrauna
Kathkuiyan
Chaf Halt
Dudahi
Gauri Sriram Halt
Tamkuhi Rd
Mahuawa Khurd Halt
Pipraich
Unaula
Basti
Orwara
Munderwa
Chureb
Khalilabad
Maghar
Sahjanwa
Sihapar Halt
Jagatbela
Domingarh
Swami Narain Chhapia
Bahman Jyotia H
Babhnan
Gaur
Tinich
Govindnagar
Bhairoganj
Hari Nagar
Chamua
Amolwa
Narkatiaganj Jn
Musharwa Halt
Gokhula
Marjadwa
Sikta
Kangali Halt
Bhelwa
Birganj
Sirsiya
Sathi
Rameshwar Nagar Halt
Chanpatia
Kumarbagh
Prajapati
Bettiah
Raxaul Jn
Masanadih
Ram Garhwa
Majhwalia
Nakardei
Dharminia H
Parsa Nagar Halt
Sagauli Jn
Semra
Motihari
Motihari Court Halt
Jiwdhara
Taraya Sujan
Tinpheriya Halt
Jalalpur
Sipaya Halt
Sasa Musa
Katea
Narkatia Bazar
Phulwaria
Salarkhurd
Lain Bazar
Gopalganj
Thawe Jn
Hathuwa
Manjhagarh
Ratansarai
Sher Halt
Sidhwalia
Brajkishore H
Trivikramdeonagar H
Dighwa Dubauli
Katalpur Halt
Rajapatti
Nonapar Halt
Bhatpar Rani
Amlori Sarsar
Bankata
Mairwa
Jiradei
Karchhui
Siwan Kacheri
Siwan Jn
Chakra H
Pachrukhi
Duraundha Jn
Maharajganj
Mushrakh
Sham Kauria
Chainwa
Mahendra Nath Halt
Ekma
Marhaura
Tejpurwa Halt
Paterhi
Daudpur
Bani Mohammanpatti Halt
Kopa Samhota
Khairah
Tekanwas
Revelganj Ghat
Chhapra Jn
Chhapra Kacheri Jn
Gautam Asthan
Goldinganj
Dumari Juwara H
Revelganj
Ramanand Tiwari H
Tanda
Goshainganj
Surapur
Akbarpur Jn
Jafarganj
Malipur
Tulsinagar Halt
Bilwai
Shahganj Jn
Kheta Sarai
Mani Kala Halt
Mehrawan
Mehgawan
Jaunpur Jn
Yadvendranagar
Jaunpur City
Jaunpur Kuchery
Zafarabad Jn
Kajgoan Terhwan
Salkhapur
Shudnipur
Bhanaur
Mariahu
Warigaon Newada
Barsathi
Harpalganj
Sri Krishan Nagar
Sarai Harkhu
Bakhsha
Khanja Halt
Deedarganj Rd
Khorasan Rd
Sarai Mir
Sanjharpur Halt
Sarai Rani
Fariha
Azamgarh
Sidhari Halt
Sathiaon
Muhammadabad
Khurhat
Pali Garh Halt
Paniara Halt
Pipridih
Nayakdih Halt
Dullahpur
Jakhanian
Hurmujpur Halt
Sadat
Mahpur
Dohrighat
Muradpur Halt
Amila
Ghoshi
Banyapur
Kopaganj
Chakra Rd Halt
Indara Jn
Mau Jn
Haldharpur
Ratanpura
Rajmalpur Rd
Rasra
Sanwara Halt
Chil Kahar
Jegani Khas Halt
Sagarpali
Bansdih Rd
Chhata Aschaura H
Sahatwar
Reoti
Ballia
Phephna Jn
Sisai Gulab Rai Halt
Satraon
Deorawababa Rd
Salempur Jn
Lar Rd
Turtipar
Belthara Rd
Govindpur Dugauli Halt
Kinharapur
Karimuddinpur
Dhondhadih
Yusufpur
Shahbazkuli
Ghazipur Ghat
Ghazipur City
Ankushpur
Chitbaragaon
Tajpur Dehama
Baruna
Dumraon
Twiniganj
Raghunathpur
Sikaria
Banahi
Bihiya
Kauriya
Karisath
Jagjivan
Jamira Halt
Kulharia
Koelwar
Son Br.
Ara
Veer Kuwar Singh Dharauli H
Amar Shaheed Jagdeo Prasad H
Sarvodaya H
Udwantnagar
Kasap
Garhani
Semraon
Charpokhri
Dhanauti
Piru
Nonar
Hasanbazar
Kastar Mahadev
Bikramganj
Ghusia Kalan
Sujhauli
Garh Nokha
Kharadih
Dalchhapra Halt
Suraimanpur
Bakulha
Manjhi
Block Hut C
Binta
Patel
Sadisopur
Gandhi Halt
Sarkoni
Kerakat
Dobhi
Muftiganj
Gungauli Halt
Kusarna H
Faridaha Halt
Dudhaunda Halt
Jalalganj
Trilochan Mahadev
Bahjai
Aunrihar Jn
Rajwari
Kadipur
Baba Bhagwan Ram H
Sarnath
Taraon
Saiyedpur Bhitari
Basuchack Halt
Nand Ganj
Saheri Halt
Tarighat
Nagsar Halt
Sarahula Halt
Dildarnagar Jn
Buxar
Chausa
Pawani Kamarpur
Barakalan
Gahmar
Karahia
Bhadaura
Usia Khas
Darauli BH
Zamania
Bahora Chandil
Kuchman
Sakaldiha
Tulsi Ashram
Dheena
Khalispur
Pindra Rd Halt
Babatpur
Birapatti
Umarha
Varanasi Jn
Shivpur
Sewapuri
Bankat
Lohta
Kapsethi
Chaukhandi
Bhadohi
Parsipur
Suriawan
Mondh
Gyanpur Rd
Ahimanpur
Almau Halt
Katka
Nigatpur
Hardattpur
Bulanpur Halt
Varanasi City
Malaviya Br.
Kashi
Vyasnagar
Mughal Sarai Jn
Ganjkhwaja
Block Hut K
Jeonathpur
Ahraura Rd
West Outer BH B
Manduadih
Rajatalab
Baherwan Halt
Block Hut DD
Kailahat
Chunar Jn
Block Hut R
Madho Singh Jn
Kachhwa Rd
Mirzapur Ghat
Chilh
Vindyachal
Mirzapur
Block Hut EE
Jhingura
Pahara
Dagmagpur
Vishwanath Puri
Saktesgarh
Lusa
Khairahi
Robertsganj
Churk
Agori Khas
Chopan
Billi Jn
Obra Dam
Salai Banwa BH
Paraspani
Paprakund
Gurmura
Magardah
Sukhra
Mirchandhori
Jogidih
Karaila Rd Jn
Chandauli Majhwar
Saidraja
Karamnasa
Dhanaicha
Durgauti
Bhabua Rd
Muthani
Pusauli
Kudra
Kurmabad Rd BH
Kumahu
Shiu Sagar Rd
Sasaram
Karwandiya
Pahleza
Dehri On Sone
Upper Son Br.
Sonnagar Jn
Chiralla Pauthu BH
Anugrah Narayan Rd
Phesar
Baghoikusa
Jakhim
Deo Rd BH
Rafiganj
Ismailpur
Guraru
Paraiya
Kastha
Dehri City
Bidiha Shankarpuri
Indrapuri
Tilothu Bazar
Tilothu
Ramdhira-on-Sone
Tumba
Bagha Bisnupur
Ankorah
Barki Salaiya
Nabinagar Rd
Banjari
Rohtas
Rohtas Fort
Beolia Rd
Mahadeopuri Bhadara
Tiura Pipardih
Nimhat
Kajrat Nawadih
Japla
Kosiara
Haidar Nagar
Mohammadganj
Satbahini
Untari Rd
Karkatta
Sigsigi
Garhwa Rd Jn
Imamganj
Chatra

N
1:1,500,000

SCALE
0 5 10 15 20 25 Miles
0 5 10 15 20 25 30 35 40 45 50 Kms

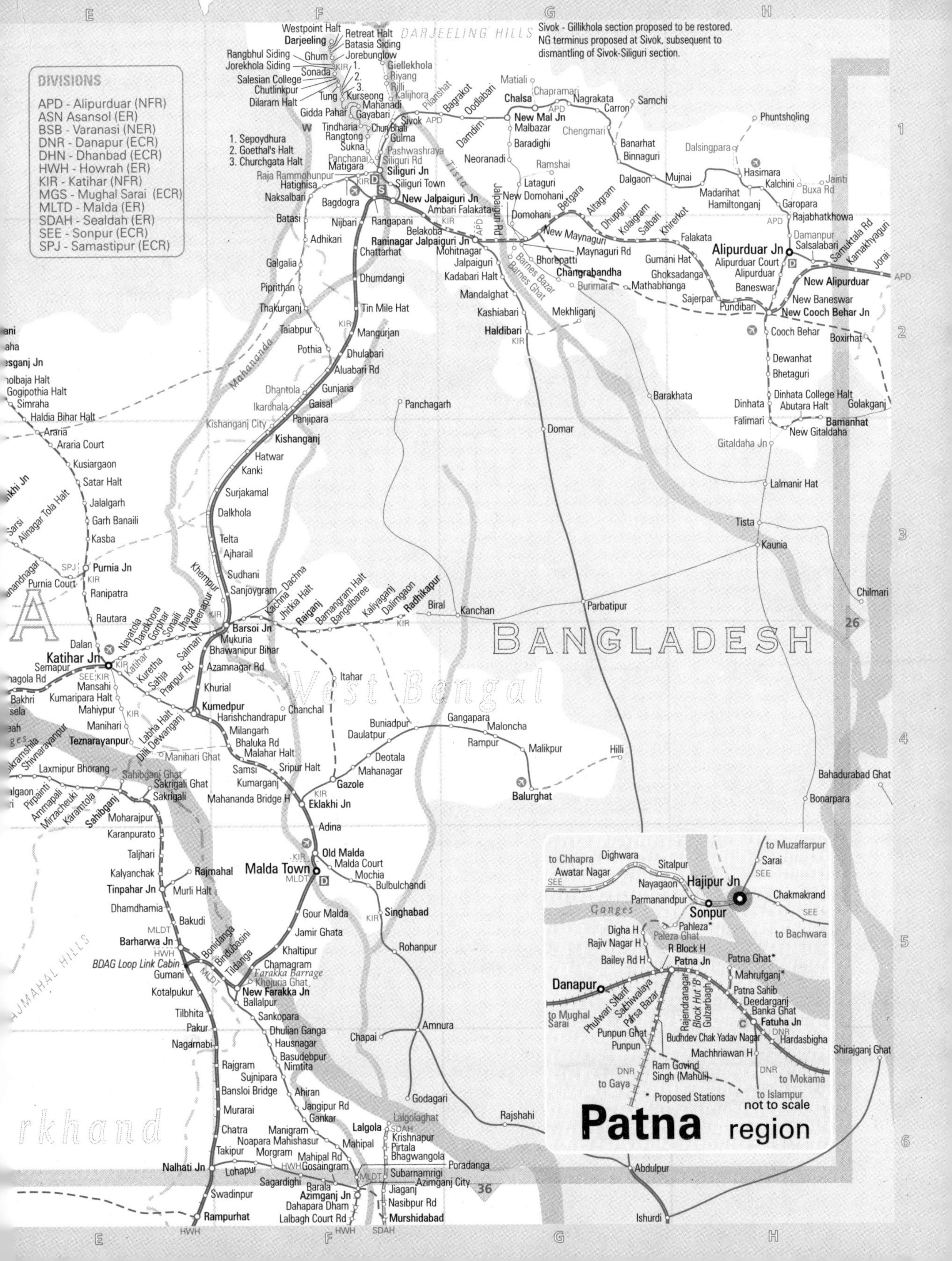
DIVISIONS
APD - Alipurduar (NFR)
ASN Asansol (ER)
BSB - Varanasi (NER)
DNR - Danapur (ECR)
DHN - Dhanbad (ECR)
HWH - Howrah (ER)
KIR - Katihar (NFR)
MGS - Mughal Sarai (ECR)
MLTD - Malda (ER)
SDAH - Sealdah (ER)
SEE - Sonpur (ECR)
SPJ - Samastipur (ECR)
Sivok - Gillikhola section proposed to be restored. NG terminus proposed at Sivok, subsequent to dismantling of Sivok-Siliguri section.
1. Sepoydhura
2. Goethal's Halt
3. Churchgata Halt
DARJEELING HILLS
Westpoint Halt
Darjeeling
Retreat Halt
Batasia Siding
Ghum
Jorebunglow
Rangbhul Siding
Jorekhola Siding
Sonada
Salesian College
Chutlinkpur
Dilaram Halt
Tung
Kurseong
Gidda Pahar
Mahanadi
Gayabari
Giellekhola
Riyang
Rilli
Kalijhora
Tindharia
Chunbhati
Rangtong
Gulma
Sukna
Sivok
Pashwashraya
Panchanai
Siliguri Rd
Matigara
Siliguri Jn
Siliguri Town
Raja Rammohunpur
Hatighisa
Naksalbari
Bagdogra
New Jalpaiguri Jn
Ambari Falakata
Batasi
Nijbari
Rangapani
Adhikari
Belakoba
Raninagar Jalpaiguri Jn
Chattarhat
Mohitnagar
Jalpaiguri
Kadabari Halt
Mandalghat
Kashiabari
Haldibari
Mekhliganj
Galgalia
Piprithan
Thakurganj
Dhumdangi
Tin Mile Hat
Taiabpur
Mangurjan
Pothia
Dhulabari
Aluabari Rd
Mahananda
Dhantola
Gunjaria
Ikarchala
Gaisal
Kishanganj City
Panjipara
Kishanganj
Hatwar
Kanki
Surjakamal
Dalkhola
Telta
Ajharail
Sudhani
Sanjoygram
Khempur
Barsoi Jn
Mukuria
Bhawanipur Bihar
Azamnagar Rd
Khurial
Kumedpur
Harishchandrapur
Milangarh
Bhaluka Rd
Malahar Halt
Samsi
Kumarganj
Sripur Halt
Mahananda Bridge H
Eklakhi Jn
Gazole
Adina
Old Malda
Malda Court
Malda Town
Mochia
Bulbulchandi
Singhabad
Gour Malda
Jamir Ghata
Khaltipur
Chamagram
Farakka Barrage
Khejuria Ghat
New Farakka Jn
Ballalpur
Sankopara
Dhulian Ganga
Hausnagar
Basudebpur
Nimtita
Ahiran
Jangipur Rd
Gankar
Manigram
Noapara Mahishasur
Morgram
Mahipal Rd
Gosaingram
Sagardighi
Barala
Azimganj Jn
Dahapara Dham
Lalbagh Court Rd
Lalgola
Lalgolaghat
Krishnapur
Pirtala
Bhagwangola
Mahipal
Subarnamrigi
Azimganj City
Jiaganj
Nasibpur Rd
Murshidabad
Poradanga
Kachna
Dachna
Jhitkia Halt
Raiganj
Bamangram Halt
Bangalbaree
Kaliyaganj
Dalimgaon
Radhikapur
Biral
Kanchan
Parbatipur
Itahar
Chanchal
Buniadpur
Daulatpur
Gangapara
Maloncha
Rampur
Malikpur
Hilli
Deotala
Mahanagar
Balurghat
Panchagarh
Domar
Chapai
Amnura
Godagari
Rajshahi
Abdulpur
Ishurdi
BANGLADESH
West Bengal
Matiali
Chapramari
Chalsa
Nagrakata
Carron
Samchi
New Mal Jn
Malbazar
Chengmari
Baradighi
Damdim
Oodlabari
Bagrakot
Pilanshat
Neoranadi
Ramshai
Lataguri
New Domohani
Domohani
Jalpaiguri Rd
Tista
Betgara
Altagram
Dhupguri
Kolaigram
Salbari
Khirerkot
New Maynaguri
Maynaguri Rd
Bhorepatti
Barnes Bazar
Barnes Ghat
Changrabandha
Burimara
Mathabhanga
Falakata
Gumani Hat
Ghoksadanga
Sajerpar
Banarhat
Binnaguri
Dalsingpara
Dalgaon
Mujnai
Phuntsholing
Hasimara
Madarihat
Hamiltonganj
Kalchini
Jainti
Buxa Rd
Garopara
Rajabhatkhowa
Damanpur
Alipurduar Jn
Salsalabari
Samuktala Rd
Kamakhyaguri
Jorai
Alipurduar Court
Alipurduar
Baneswar
New Alipurduar
Pundibari
New Baneswar
New Cooch Behar Jn
Cooch Behar
Boxirhat
Dewanhat
Bhetaguri
Barakhata
Dinhata
Dinhata College Halt
Abutara Halt
Golakganj
Falimari
Bamanhat
New Gitaldaha
Gitaldaha Jn
Lalmanir Hat
Tista
Kaunia
Chilmari
Bahadurabad Ghat
Bonarpara
Shirajganj Ghat
Katihar Jn
Semapur
Dalan
Rautara
Ranipatra
Purnia Jn
Purnia Court
Kasba
Garh Banaili
Jalalgarh
Satar Halt
Kusiargaon
Araria Court
Araria
Haldia Bihar Halt
Simraha
Gogipothia Halt
Mansahi
Kumaripara Halt
Mahiypur
Manihari
Teznarayanpur
Labha Halt
Dilli Dewanganj
Manihari Ghat
Navatola
Dandkhora
Gorphar
Sonaili
Jhaua
Meenapur
Katihar
Kuretha
Sahja
Pranpur Rd
Salmari
Laxmipur Bhorang
Sahibganj Ghat
Sakrigali Ghat
Sakrigali
Sahibganj
Karamtola
Mirzacheuki
Ammapali
Pirpainti
Moharajpur
Karanpurato
Taljhari
Kalyanchak
Rajmahal
Tinpahar Jn
Murli Halt
Dhamdhamia
Bakudi
Barharwa Jn
Bonidanga
Bindubasini
Tildanga
BDAG Loop Link Cabin
Gumani
Kotalpukur
Tilbhita
Pakur
Nagarnabi
Rajgram
Sujnipara
Bansloi Bridge
Murarai
Chatra
Takipur
Nalhati Jn
Lohapur
Swadinpur
Rampurhat
RAJMAHAL HILLS
rkhand
Patna region
not to scale
* Proposed Stations
to Chhapra
Dighwara
Awatar Nagar
Sitalpur
Nayagaon
Hajipur Jn
to Muzaffarpur
Sarai
Chakmakrand
Parmanandpur
Sonpur
Ganges
Pahleza*
Paleza Ghat
to Bachwara
Digha H
Rajiv Nagar H
R Block H
Bailey Rd H
Patna Jn
Patna Ghat*
Mahrufganj*
Danapur
Patna Sahib
Deedarganj
Banka Ghat
Fatuha Jn
Hardasbigha
to Mughal Sarai
Phulwari Sharif
Sachiwalaya
Parsa Bazar
Rajendranagar
Block Hut 'B'
Gulzarbagh
Punpun Ghat
Punpun
Budhdev Chak Yadav Nagar
Machhriawan H
Ram Govind Singh (Mahuli)
to Gaya
to Mokama
to Islampur

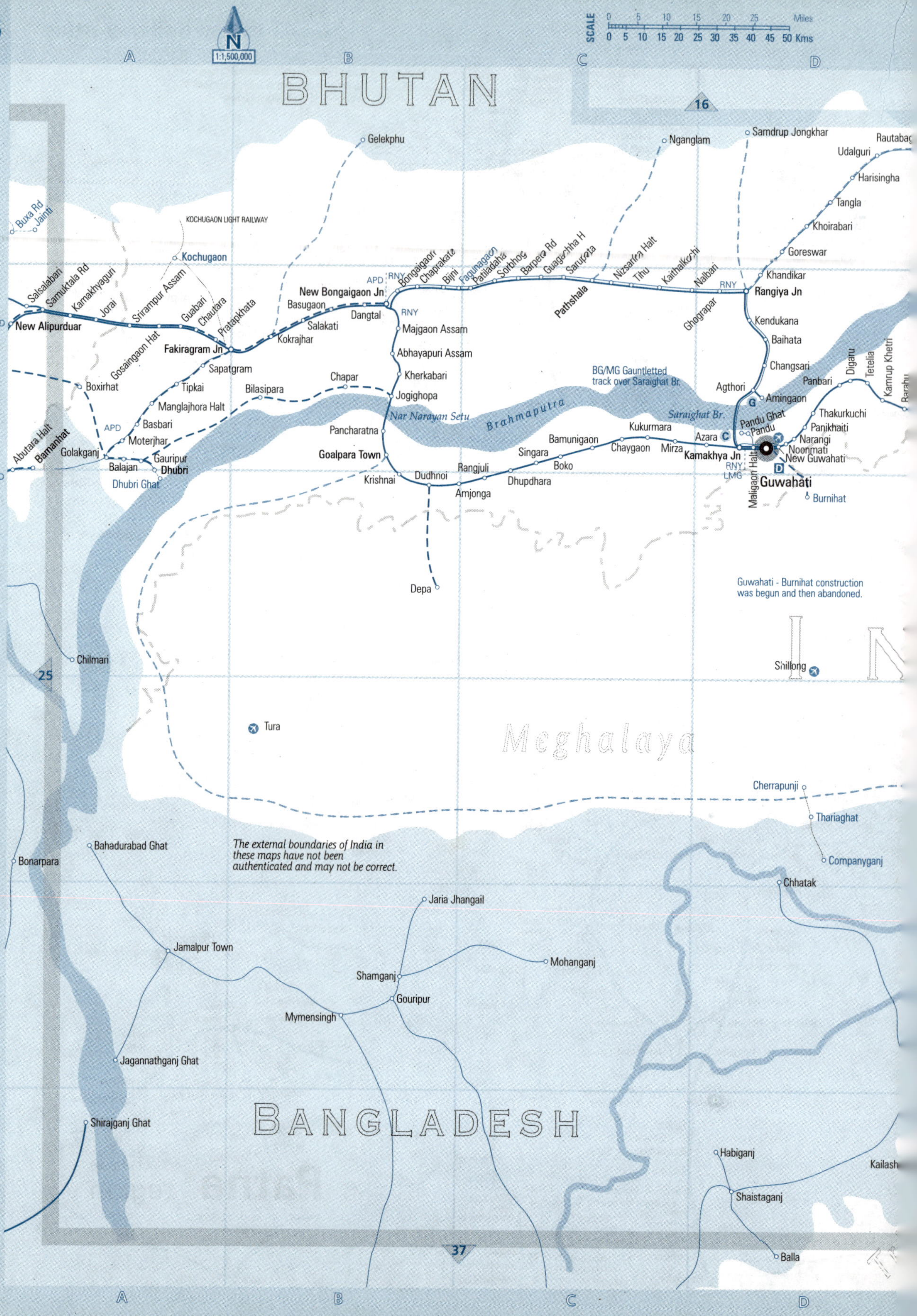

N
1:1,500,000
SCALE
0 5 10 15 20 25 Miles
0 5 10 15 20 25 30 35 40 45 50 Kms
A
B
C
D
1
2
3
4
5
6
BHUTAN
16
25
37
BANGLADESH
Meghalaya
Brahmaputra
KOCHUGAON LIGHT RAILWAY
Gelekphu
Nganglam
Samdrup Jongkhar
Rautabag
Udalguri
Harisingha
Tangla
Khoirabari
Goreswar
Khandikar
Rangiya Jn
RNY
Kendukana
Baihata
Changsari
Amingaon
Agthori
G
Buxa Rd
Jainti
Kochugaon
Salsalabari
Samuktala Rd
Kamakhyaguri
Jorai
Srirampur Assam
Guabari
Chautara
Pratapkhata
APD
New Alipurduar
Fakiragram Jn
Gosaingaon Hat
Basugaon
Salakati
Kokrajhar
New Bongaigaon Jn
Dangtal
Bongaigaon
Chaprakata
Bijni
Fagunagaon
Patiladaha
Sorbhog
Barpeta Rd
Guagachha H
Sarupeta
Pathshala
Nizsarita Halt
Tihu
Kaithalkuchi
Nalbari
Ghograpar
Majgaon Assam
Abhayapuri Assam
Kherkabari
Jogighopa
Chapar
Bilasipara
Sapatgram
Tipkai
Boxirhat
Manglajhora Halt
Basbari
Moterjhar
Abutara Halt
Bamanhat
Golakganj
Balajan
Gauripur
Dhubri
Dhubri Ghat
BG/MG Gauntletted track over Saraighat Br.
Saraighat Br.
Nar Narayan Setu
Pancharatna
Goalpara Town
Krishnai
Dudhnoi
Rangjuli
Amjonga
Dhupdhara
Singara
Boko
Bamunigaon
Chaygaon
Kukurmara
Mirza
Azara
C
Kamakhya Jn
Pandu Ghat
Pandu
Maligaon Halt
LMG
D
Guwahati
Noonmati
New Guwahati
Narangi
Panikhaiti
Thakurkuchi
Panbari
Digaru
Tetelia
Kamrup Khetri
Barahu
Burnihat
Depa
Guwahati - Burnihat construction was begun and then abandoned.
Shillong
Chilmari
Tura
Cherrapunji
Thariaghat
Companyganj
Chhatak
Bahadurabad Ghat
Bonarpara
The external boundaries of India in these maps have not been authenticated and may not be correct.
Jaria Jhangail
Jamalpur Town
Shamganj
Mohanganj
Gouripur
Mymensingh
Jagannathganj Ghat
Shirajganj Ghat
Habiganj
Shaistaganj
Kailash
Balla

E
F
G
H
RNY
TSK TSK
17
1
2
3
4
5
6
Charduar
Dhalaibil
Balipara Jn
Jiabharali
Nagshankar H
Nizchetia
Vishwanath Charali
Nahorani Siding
Rangapara North Jn
Dhekiajuli Rd
Belsiri
Misamari
Thakurbari
chnoi
Hugrajuli
Rangapara
Sessa
New Misamari
Bindukuri
Monmohinipur Rd Siding
Dekargaon
Dhekiajuli
Dhadhera Halt
Dhekiajuli TE Siding
Tezpur
Sirajuli Siding
Singri Ghat
Hugrajuli Siding
Sapoi Siding
Dibru Darrang Siding
Dherai Siding
Silghat Town
Jakalabandha
Salona
Batadrawa
Baikotia
Dagaon
Juriagaon
Tarabari
Rupahigaon
Mairabari
Dhing
Dhing Bazar
Samaguri
Haibargaon
Puranigudam
Senchoa
Nowgong Assam
Bebejia
Phulaguri
Haibargaon - Mairabari & Senchoa - Silghat identified for restoration
Raha
Chaparmukh Jn
Thekeraguri
Dharamtul
Laopani
Kampur
Aujuri
Jamunamukh
Jugijan
Hojai
Dhalpukhuri
Lanka
Habaipur
Lamsakhang
Lumding South
Patharkhola
Langcholiet
Lumding Jn
Barlangfer
Diphu
Daldali
Dhansiri
Nailalung
Mandardisa
Hatikhali
Dijaobra
Langting
Dihakho
Mupa
Kalachand
Maibong
Wadrengdisa
Daotuhaja
Phiding
Mahur
Migrendisa
Lower Haflong
Jatinga
Doyang Viaduct
Bagetar
Haflong Hill
Longrangajao
Mailongdisa
Harangajao
Ditokcherra
Bandarkhal
Damchara
Chandranathpur
Bihara
BARAIL RANGE
Assam
RENGMA HILLS
NAGA HILLS
Nagaland
Manipur
Mizoram
D I A
Kohima
Karong
Borigaon
Jorhat
Jorhat Town
Rowriah
Bhalukmara
Khelmati
Cinnamara
Koliapani
Dukhlangia
Lahing
Nakchari
Meleng
Nahorbari
Tuli
Barua Bamungaon
Rangaliting
Mariani Jn
Badulipar
Dhekiajuli
Sycotta
Rangajan
Kharikatia
Khumtai
Moabund
Titabar
Numaligarh
Chakiting
Hautly
Adharsatra
Kamarbandha Ali
Golaghat
Furkating Jn
Oating
Jamguri
Bhilgaon
Barpathar
Sarupathar
Naojan
Chongajan
Bokajan
Khotkhoti
Dimapur
Rangapahar Crossing
Rangapahar
Sukritipur
Hilara
Badarpur Jn
Badarpur Ghat
Karimganj Jn
Rupasibari
Langai
Maishashan
Chargola Bhanga
Salchapra
Katakhal Jn
Silchar
Mainarbandh
Sukona Halt
Arunachal Jn
New Silchar Halt
Ranigaon
Sribar
Kamranga
Jirighat
Jiribam
Imphal Rd
Imphal
Latu
Suprakandi H
Nilambazar
Kayasthagram
Panchgram
Algapur
Hailakandi
Baraigram Jn
Eraligul
Phakoagram
Kanai Bazar
Patharkhandi
Bazarghat Halt
Kalkalighat
Ratabari
Anipur
Chandkhirabagan
laura
Dullabcherra
Monacherra
Amala Halt
Lalabazar
Lalaghat
Mohammadpur
Katlicherra
Manipurbagan
Tilbhum
Kathaltali
Churaibari
Nadiapur
Dharmanagar
Jamira
Ramnathpur
Bhairabi
Panisagar
Pencharthal
Kumarghat
Nalkata H
Manu
Aizawl
DIVISIONS
APD - Alipurduar (NFR)
LMG - Lumding (NFR)
RNY - Rangiya (NFR)
TSK - Tinsukia (NFR)

N
1:1,500,000
SCALE
0 5 10 15 20 25 Miles
0 5 10 15 20 25 30 35 40 45 50 Kms
A
B
C
D
1
2
3
4
5
6
Koteshwar
Baranda
Naliya
Naliya Cantt
Kothara
ADI
Mothala
Dhanvala Wada
Sanosara
Mothala Halt
Sukhpur Roha
Deshalpur
Sukhpur
Bhuj
Madhapur Rd
Kukma
Ratnal
Sapada
Warsamedi
Ajapur Rd
Bhimasar
Bhachau
Vondh
ADI
Samkhiali Jn
Chirai
Anjar
Antarjal
Galpadar
Gopalpuri
Adipur Jn
D
Gandhidham C Cabin
Gandhidham Jn
Shirva
Khari Rohar Rd
Devalia Rd
ADI
Kandla
Kandla Port
Tuna Port
C
Bhadresar Rd
Mundra
Mundra Port
Adipur - Mundra Port is a private line
Kidiyanagar
Chitrod
Shivlakha
Lakadiya
Katariya
Surbari
Indira Nagar
Maliya Miyana
Maliya Miyana
Nani Baral
RJT A
Bhavpura
Vavaniya
Navlakhi
Lawanpur
Dahinsara Jn
Piplia Rd
Barwala Rd
Khakhrala Rd
Shakti Para
Rajpar
Sanala
Amram Rd
Khanpur
Chanchapar
Virpar
Tanka
Jodiya Bandar
Jodiya
Bhadra
Gunatitnagar
Dhrol
Jaiwa
Gulf of Kuchchh
Rozi
Bedi Port
Rozi Block Hut
Windmill
Hapa
Jamnagar
Aliya Vada
Lakhabawal
Chanol
RJT
Kanako
Padadhari
Khorana
Bileshwar
Khanderi
Rajkot City
Rajkot Jn
Rajkot Town
Bhaktinagar
RJT
BVP
Kothariya
Ribad
Semla
Gonda
Okha
Aramda
Mithapur
Bhimrana
RJT
Varvala
Dwarka
Baradiya
Gorinja
Okha Madhi
Arabian Sea
Sikka
Moti Khavdi
RJT
Pipli
Kanalus East BH
BVP
Kanalus South BH
Kanalus Jn
Salaya
Sinhan
Modpur
Dabasang
Khambhaliya Jn
Jam Wanthali
Jaliya Devani
Hadmatiya
Viramdad
Bhatel
Meghpur Titodi
Bhopalka
Bhatiya
Kuranga
Lalpur (Jamnagar)
Gop (Jamnagar)
Bhanvad
Balwa
Jam Jodhpur
Paneli Moti
Jashapar
Katkola
Wansjaliya Jn
BVP
Bhayavadar
Khakhi Jalia
Tarsai
Sakhpur
Rana Bordi
Ranavav
Porbandar Dock
Porbandar
Upleta
Dumiyani
Supedi
Dhoraji
Fareni
Navagadh
Jetpur
Jetalsar Jn
Choki Sorath
Gomta
Virpur
Vavdi
Vadiya D
Khakhariya
Vadal
Saradiya
Bantwa
Manavadar
Galvav
Meghpur
Vanthali
W
BVP
Junagadh Jn
Shahpur
Bandhnath
Dungarpur Quarry
Iorniya
Bilkha
Bagasr
Lushala
Badodar
Junichavand
Jetalvad
Keshod
Visavadar Jn
Bhad
Satadhar
Kansiya Nes
GIRNAR HILL
Maliya Hatina
Sasan Gir
Chitravad
Chorwad Rd
Talala Jn
Jambur
BVP
BVP
BVP
The external boundaries of India in these maps have not been authenticated and may not be correct.
38
to Mahesana
not to scale
to Gandhinagar
Saij Sertha Rd
ADI
ADI
Sabarmati
Khodiyar Jn
Chandkheda Rd
to Himatnagar
Sabarmati D Cabin
Chandlodiya Jn
ADI
Kali Rd
C
Naroda
Ambli Rd
ADI
Sabarmati Jn
D
BVP
Sardargram
Sahijpur
to Viramgam
Sabarmati A Cabin
ADI
Shahibag B Cabin
Asarva
Gandhigram
Ahmadabad Jn
Vastrapur
Kankariya Cabin
Maninagar
Sarkhej
C
to Botad
ADI
Vatva
D
Y
Vatva Yard
to Vadodara
Ahmadabad region

DIVISIONS
ADI - Ahmadabad (WR)
AII - Ajmer (NWR)
BVP - Bhavnagar (WR)
MCT - Mumbai (WR)
RJT - Rajkot (WR)
BRC - Vadodara (WR)
Gujarat
INDIA
Gulf of Khambhat
Narmada
Tapi
see Ahmadabad region Map on the opposite page
The external boundaries of India in these maps have not been authenticated and may not be correct.
18
30
38
39
Ahmadabad Jn
Vadodara Jn
Bhavnagar Terminus
Surendranagar Jn
Viramgam Jn
Mahesana Jn
Gandhinagar Capital
Kalol Jn
Sabarmati Jn
Anand Jn
Nadiad Jn
Bharuch Jn
Ankleshwar Jn
Surat
Udhna Jn
Botad Jn
Dhola Jn
Sihor Jn
Palitana
Rajula Rd Jn
Khijadiya Jn
Dhasa Jn
Wankaner Jn
Dhrangadhra Jn
Halvad
Kharaghoda
Jhund Jn
Patan
Ranuj Jn
Chanasma Jn
Katosan Rd Jn
Ambliyasan Jn
Himatnagar Jn
Khed Brahma
Taranga Hill
Modasa
Kapadvanj
Nandol Dahegam
Dakor
Vasad Jn
Samlaya Jn
Pratapnagar
Vishvamitri Jn
Dabhoi
Miyagam Karjan Jn
Jambusar Jn
Samni Jn
Dahej
Khambhat
Dhandhuka
Limbdi
Ningala
Jasdan
Chotila
Than
Joravarnagar
Radhanpur
Santalpur
Kosamba
Hazira Port
Jhagadiya Jn
Netrang
Moti Koral
Talaja
Bhavnagar Port
Chhapi
Dharewada
Devgam
Kakoshi Metrana Rd
Lotana
Timba Rd Jn

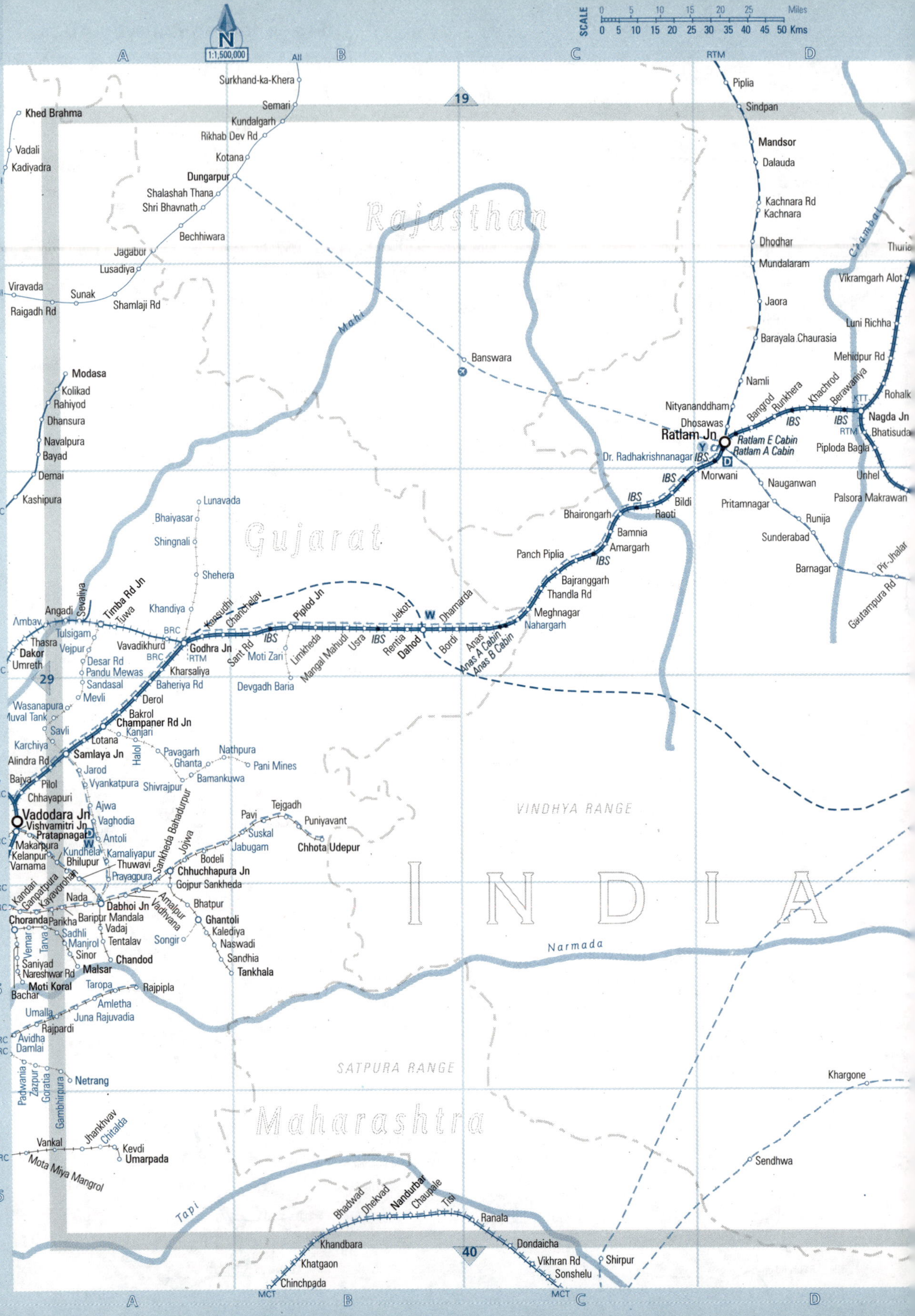
N
1:1,500,000
SCALE
0 5 10 15 20 25 Miles
0 5 10 15 20 25 30 35 40 45 50 Kms
A
B
C
D
1
2
3
4
5
6
19
29
40
Rajasthan
Gujarat
Maharashtra
INDIA
VINDHYA RANGE
SATPURA RANGE
Mahi
Narmada
Tapi
Chambal
Surkhand-ka-Khera
Semari
Kundalgarh
Rikhab Dev Rd
Kotana
Dungarpur
Shalashah Thana
Shri Bhavnath
Bechhiwara
Jagabor
Lusadiya
Shamlaji Rd
Sunak
Viravada
Raigadh Rd
Khed Brahma
Vadali
Kadiyadra
Modasa
Kolikad
Rahiyod
Dhansura
Navalpura
Bayad
Demai
Kashipura
Banswara
Lunavada
Bhaiyasar
Shingnali
Shehera
Khandiya
Timba Rd Jn
Tuwa
Sevaliya
Angadi
Ambav
Thasra
Tulsigam
Dakor
Umreth
Vejpur
Desar Rd
Pandu Mewas
Sandasal
Mevli
Vavadikhurd
Godhra Jn
Kharsaliya
Baheriya Rd
Derol
Bakrol
Champaner Rd Jn
Kanjari
Lotana
Wasanapura
Muval Tank
Savli
Karchiya
Alindra Rd
Samlaya Jn
Halol
Pavagarh
Ghanta
Nathpura
Pani Mines
Bamankuwa
Jarod
Vyankatpura
Shivrajpur
Bajva
Pilol
Chhayapuri
Vadodara Jn
Vishvamitri Jn
Pratapnagar
Makarpura
Kelanpur
Varnama
Ajwa
Vaghodia
Antoli
Kundhela
Kamaliyapur
Bhilupur
Thuwavi
Prayagpura
Sankheda Bahadurpur
Jojwa
Bodeli
Pavi
Tejgadh
Suskal
Jabugam
Puniyavant
Chhota Udepur
Chhuchhapura Jn
Gojpur Sankheda
Bhatpur
Ghantoli
Kalediya
Naswadi
Sandhia
Tankhala
Songir
Amalpur
Vadhvana
Kandari
Ganpatpura
Kayavorohan
Nada
Dabhoi Jn
Choranda
Parikha
Baripur Mandala
Vadaj
Sadhli
Manjrol
Tentalav
Sinor
Chandod
Vemar
Tarva
Saniyad
Nareshwar Rd
Malsar
Moti Koral
Bachar
Taropa
Rajpipla
Amletha
Juna Rajuvadia
Umalla
Rajpardi
Avidha
Damlai
Padwania
Zazpur
Goratia
Gambhirpura
Netrang
Vankal
Jhankhvav
Chitalda
Kevdi
Umarpada
Mota Miya Mangrol
Kansudhi
Chanchelav
Piplod Jn
Sant Rd
Moti Zari
Limkheda
Mangal Mahudi
Usra
Rentia
Dahod
Jekot
Devgadh Baria
Dhamarda
Bordi
Anas
Anas A Cabin
Anas B Cabin
Nahargarh
Meghnagar
Thandla Rd
Bajranggarh
Panch Piplia
Amargarh
Bamnia
Bhairongarh
Raoti
Bildi
Morwani
Dr. Radhakrishnanagar
Ratlam Jn
Dhosawas
Nityananddham
Ratlam E Cabin
Ratlam A Cabin
Bangrod
Runkhera
Khachrod
Berawaniya
Nagda Jn
Bhatisuda
Piploda Bagla
Unhel
Palsora Makrawan
Rohalk
Naugawan
Pritamnagar
Runija
Sunderabad
Barnagar
Pir-Jhalar
Gautampura Rd
Piplia
Sindpan
Mandsor
Dalauda
Kachnara Rd
Kachnara
Dhodhar
Mundalaram
Jaora
Barayala Chaurasia
Namli
Vikramgarh Alot
Thuria
Luni Richha
Mehidpur Rd
Khargone
Sendhwa
Shirpur
Bhadwad
Dhekvad
Nandurbar
Chaupale
Tisi
Ranala
Khandbara
Khatgaon
Chinchpada
Dondaicha
Vikhran Rd
Sonshelu
IBS
W
D
Y
ADI
All
BRC
RTM
KTT
MCT

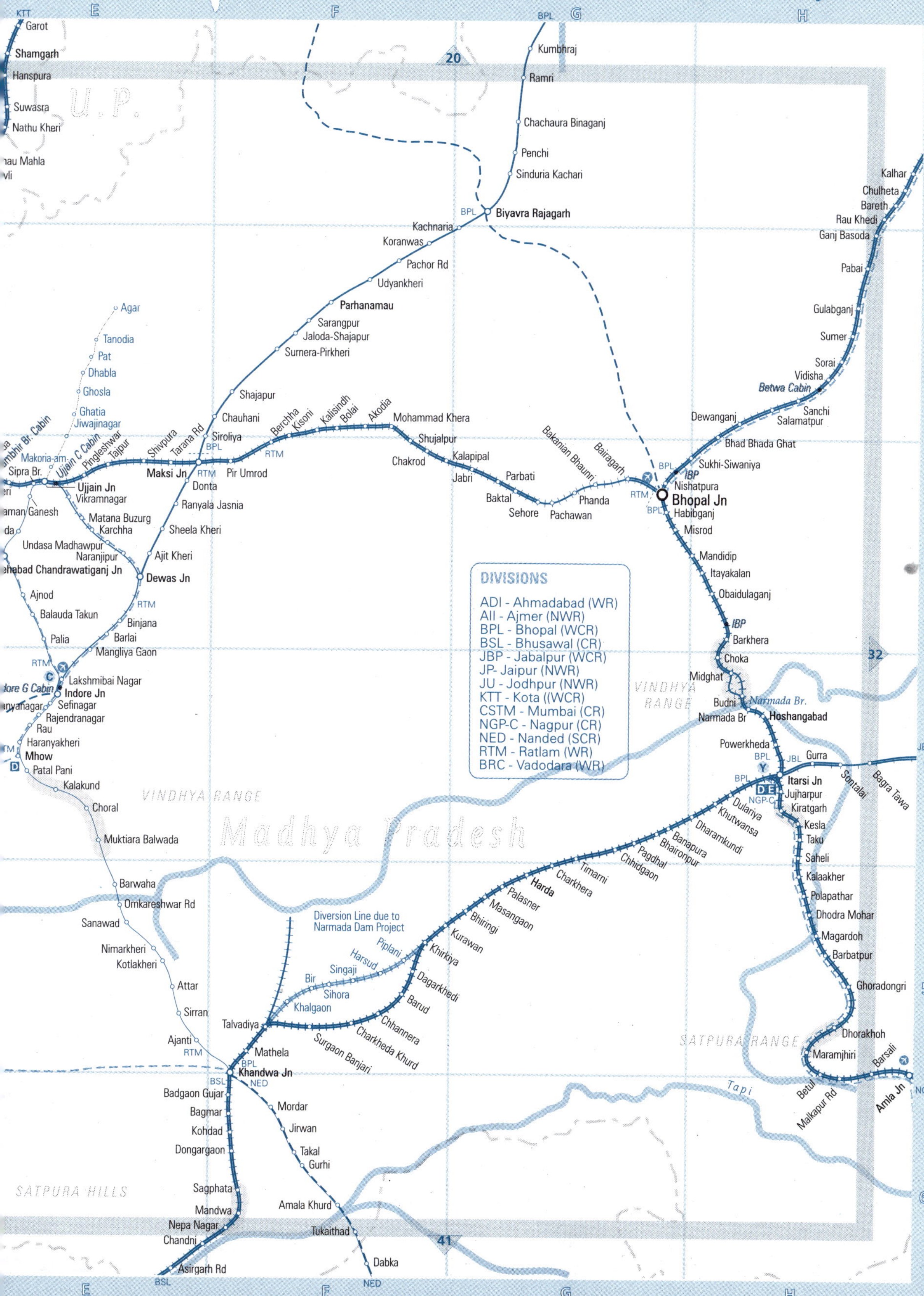

DIVISIONS
ADI - Ahmadabad (WR)
AII - Ajmer (NWR)
BPL - Bhopal (WCR)
BSL - Bhusawal (CR)
JBP - Jabalpur (WCR)
JP- Jaipur (NWR)
JU - Jodhpur (NWR)
KTT - Kota ((WCR)
CSTM - Mumbai (CR)
NGP-C - Nagpur (CR)
NED - Nanded (SCR)
RTM - Ratlam (WR)
BRC - Vadodara (WR)
E
F
G
H
1
2
3
4
5
6
20
32
41
U.P.
Madhya Pradesh
VINDHYA RANGE
SATPURA RANGE
SATPURA HILLS
Narmada Br.
Tapi
Diversion Line due to Narmada Dam Project
KTT
Garot
Shamgarh
Hanspura
Suwasra
Nathu Kheri
BPL
Kumbhraj
Ramri
Chachaura Binaganj
Penchi
Sinduria Kachari
Biyavra Rajagarh
Kachnaria
Koranwas
Pachor Rd
Udyankheri
Parhanamau
Sarangpur
Jaloda-Shajapur
Surnera-Pirkheri
Shajapur
Chauhani
Siroliya
Agar
Tanodia
Pat
Dhabla
Ghosla
Ghatia
Jiwajinagar
Makoria-am
Sipra Br.
Ujjain C Cabin
Pingleshwar
Tajpur
Shivpura
Tarana Rd
Maksi Jn
Pir Umrod
Donta
Ranyala Jasnia
Sheela Kheri
Ajit Kheri
Dewas Jn
Berchha
Kisoni
Kalisindh
Bolai
Akodia
Mohammad Khera
Shujalpur
Kalapipal
Chakrod
Jabri
Parbati
Baktal
Sehore
Pachawan
Phanda
Bakanian Bhaunri
Bairagarh
Bhopal Jn
Nishatpura
Habibganj
Misrod
Mandidip
Itayakalan
Obaidulaganj
IBP
Barkhera
Choka
Midghat
Budni
Narmada Br
Hoshangabad
Powerkheda
Itarsi Jn
Gurra
Sontalai
Bagra Tawa
JBP
JBL
Jujharpur
Kiratgarh
Kesla
Taku
Saheli
Kalaakher
Polapathar
Dhodra Mohar
Magardoh
Barbatpur
Ghoradongri
Dhorakhoh
Maramjhiri
Barsali
Betul
Malkapur Rd
Amla Jn
NGP-C
Kalhar
Chulheta
Bareth
Rau Khedi
Ganj Basoda
Pabai
Gulabganj
Sumer
Sorai
Vidisha
Betwa Cabin
Sanchi
Salamatpur
Dewanganj
Bhad Bhada Ghat
Sukhi-Siwaniya
Ujjain Jn
Vikramnagar
Ganesh
Matana Buzurg
Karchha
Undasa Madhawpur
Naranjipur
Chandrawatiganj Jn
Ajnod
Balauda Takun
Palia
Binjana
Barlai
Mangliya Gaon
Lakshmibai Nagar
Indore Jn
Indore G Cabin
Sefinagar
Rajendranagar
Rau
Haranyakheri
Mhow
Patal Pani
Kalakund
Choral
Muktiara Balwada
Barwaha
Omkareshwar Rd
Sanawad
Nimarkheri
Kotlakheri
Attar
Sirran
Ajanti
Khandwa Jn
Talvadiya
Mathela
Badgaon Gujar
Bagmar
Kohdad
Dongargaon
Sagphata
Mandwa
Nepa Nagar
Chandni
Asirgarh Rd
BSL
Mordar
Jirwan
Takal
Gurhi
Amala Khurd
Tukaithad
Dabka
NED
Bir
Singaji
Harsud
Piplani
Sihora
Khalgaon
Khirkiya
Dagarkhedi
Barud
Chhannera
Charkheda Khurd
Surgaon Banjari
Kurawan
Bhiringi
Masangaon
Palasner
Harda
Charkhera
Timarni
Chhidgaon
Pagdhal
Bhaironpur
Banapura
Dharamkundi
Khutwansa
Dulariya

N
1:1,500,000
SCALE
0 5 10 15 20 25 Miles
0 5 10 15 20 25 30 35 40 45 50 Kms
A B C D
1 2 3 4 5 6
21
31
42
U.P.
VINDHYA RANGE
BHANNER RANGE
Madhya Pradesh
MAHADEO HILLS
MAHADEO HILLS
Narmada
Pench
Wainganga
BPL
JHS
Mohasa
Kanjia
Karonda
Semarkheri
Mahadeokhedi
Agasod
Karod
JHS
Bina Jn
Malkhedi
Kurwai Kethora
JBL
BPL
Baghora
Mandi Bamora
Khurai
Kalhar
Sumreri
Chulheta
Jeruwa Khera
Bareth
Isharwara
Rau Khedi
Nariaoli
Ganj Basoda
Pabai
Gulabganj
Sumer
Sorai
BPL
Vidisha
Makronia
Lidhora Khurd
Ratona
Sagar
Girwar
Dangidhar
Ganeshganj
Patharia
Aslana
Karhiya Bhadoli
Bandakpur
Damoh
Ghatera
Golapatti
Sagoni
Ratangaon
Salaia
Bakhleta
Rithi
Patohan
Mahjgawan Phata
Katni
Madhav Naga
Niw
Sansarpur
Sleemanabad Rd
Dundi
Sihora Rd
Gosalpur
Deori
JBP
Adhartal
JBP
Kachhpura
Bheraghat
Jabalpur Jn
Bhitoni
Madanmahal
D
Howbagh
Guwarighat
Bikrampur
Shridham
Jamtara Paraswara
NGPS
Belkhera
Ghat Pindrai
Karakbel
Bargi
Charghatpipariya
Karapgaon
Kareli
Narsingpur
Gadarwara
Bohani
Salichauka Rd
Sukrimangela
Bankhedi
Pipariya
Junehta
Shikara
Sohagpur
Sobhapur
Mehpani
JBP
Bagra Tawa
Guramkhedi
Sontalai
Binaiki
Ghunsor
Nidhani
NGP-S
Mandla Fo
NGP-S
Tulyapani
Pindrai
Limarua
Jeonara
Bamhani Bajha
Nainpur Jn
D
Gangatola
Keolari
Khairee
Palari
Dhatura
Alipur
Jamgaon
Rampuri
Chiraidongri
Padriganj
Gudru
Nagarwada
Jurtara
Kanhiwara
Bhoma
NGP-S
Lamta
Charegaon
Titwa
Samnapur
Dhapewara
Balaghat
Kanhadga
Hatta Rd
Khara
Birsola
Gatra
Pratapbag
Gondia Jn
NGP-C
Barbatpur
Ghoradongri
Dhorakhoh
NGP-C
NGP-C
Betul
Malkapur Rd
Barsali
Amla Jn
Lalwadi
Jambara
Barchi Rd
Bordhai
Barelipar
Nawegaon
Markadhana
Hirdagarh
Junnor Deo
Barkuhi
Chandameta
Digha Wani
Palachuri
Iklehra
Parasia
Khirsadoh
Bardhana Halt
Gangiwara Town
Gangiwara Halt
NGP-C
Chhindwara Jn
NGP-S
NGP-S
Umaria Isra
Jhilimili
Markandi Udadon
Chaurai
Karaboh
Kapurdah
Somaswara
Pipardahi
Seoni
Shikarpur
Linga
Bisapur Kalan
Umranala
Kukrakhapa
Bhimalgondi
Ghadela
Devi
Kachchhidhana
Ramakona
Sausar
Bardi
Lodhikhera
Paradsinga
Saonga
Kelod
Jaulkhera
Multai
Hatnapur
Chichonda
Ghudankhapa
Teegaon
Pandhurna
Darimeta
Narkhed
Pusla*
Benoda*
Warud*
Mowad*
Niwarkhed*
NGP-C
NGP-S
Ramramatola
Saongi
Waraseoni
Garra
Katangi
Lakhanwara
Kochewahi
Kaydi
Tirodi
Sukli
Makhaper Rd
Dongri Buzurg
Goberwahi
NGP-S
NGP-S
NGP-S
NGP-S

DIVISIONS
BPL - Bhopal (WCR)
BSP - Bilaspur (SECR)
BSL - Bhusawal (CR)
DHN - Dhanbad (ECR)
JBP - Jabalpur (WCR)
JHS - Jhansi (NCR)
NGPC - Nagpur (CR)
NGPS - Nagpur (SECR)
R - Raipur (SECR)
E
F
G
H
1
2
3
4
5
6
22
34
43
JBP
Unchehara
Maihar
Bhadanpur
Amdara
Pakaria Rd
Jukehi
Patwara
New Katni Jn
Katangi Khurd
Lachakheri
Salhana
Pipariya Kalan
Mahroi
Khanna Banjari
Damoy
Vijaysota
Bara
Chhateni
Beohari
Dubri Kalan
Kanchanpur Rd
Joba
Marwasgram
Shankarpur Bhadoura
Niwas Rd
Bharsendi
Surasaraighat Jhara
Saraigram
Gajara Bahra
Deoragram
Majholi
Bargawan
Mahadiya
Gondwali
Singrauli
Shaktinagar
Krishna Shila
Anpara
Karaila Rd Jn
Mirchandhori
Sukhra
Magardah
DHN
JBP
DHN
JBP
BSP
Jhalwara
Rupaund
Vilayatkalan Rd
Chandia Rd
Lorha
Umaria
Karkeli
Nowrozabad
Birsinghpur
Mudaria
Ghunghuti
Badhwabara
Shahdol
Singhpur
Chhada
Burhar
Amlai
BSP
Anuppur Jn
Chhulha
Mauhari
Jaithari
Dhurwasin
Harrad
Kotma
Bhaitola
Bijuri
Boridand Jn
BSP
Manendragarh
Paradol
Chirimiri
Udalkachhar
Darritola Jn
Nagar
Baikunthpur Rd
Katora
BSP
Tiger Hill
Sheo Prasad Nagar
DEOGARH HILLS
Son
Narmada
Nigaura
Venkatnagar
Harri
Pendra Rd
Sarbahara
Khodri
Bhanwartonk
Khongsara
Tengenmanda
Belghana
Salka Rd
Kargi Rd
Kalmitar
BSP
Ghutku
Uslapur
Bilaspur Jn
Gatora
Jairamnagar
Kotmisonar
Akaltara
Kapan
Naila
Champa Jn
Saragaon Rd
Baraduar
Jetha
BSP
Balpur
Kothari Rd
Madwarani
Saragbundia
Urga
Korba
BSP
Gevra Rd
Latia
BSP
R
Dadhapara
Chakrabhata
Belha
Dagori
Nipania
Bhatapara
Hathbandh
Tilda
Baikunth
Silyari
R
INDIA
MAIKAL RANGE
MAIKAL RANGE
Chhattisgarh

N
1:1,500,000
SCALE
0 5 10 15 20 25 Miles
0 5 10 15 20 25 30 35 40 45 50 Kms
A
B
C
D
1
2
3
4
5
6
DHN
Obra Dam
Salai Banwa BH
Paprakund
Paraspani
Magardah
Gurmura
Sukhra
Jogidih
Mirchandhori
Karaila Rd Jn
Renukut
Muirpur Rd
Jharokhas
Dudhinagar
Mahuariya
Wyndhamganj
Nagar Untari
Ramna
Meralgram
Garhwa
Anpara
Krishna Shila
Shaktinagar
U.P.
Satbahini
Untari Rd
Karkatta
23
Sigsigi
Garhwa Rd Jn
Tolra
Lalgarh Bihar
Rajhura
Kajri
Daltonganj
Chianki
Kechki
Mangra
Barwadih
Chipadohar
Hehegara
Kumendi
Bendi
Latehar
Demu
Richughuta
Chetar
Tori
Mahua Milan
Nindra BH
Mccluskieganj
Khalari
Ray
Kole BH
Chatra
Shibpur
HAZARIBAGH RAN
M.P.
DEOGARH HILLS
Katora
Sheo Pasad Nagar
Surajpur Rd
Karonji Jn
Kumsa
BSP
Bishrampur
Ambikapur
INDIA
Lohardaga
Irgaon
Akashi
Nagjua
Narkopi
Tangerbansli
Itki
RNC
Ranchi - Lohard
old 2'6" line
Jharkhand
HAZARIBAGH RANGE
33
Jariagar
Bakaspur
Mahabuang
Bano
Tati
Parbatonia
MAIKAL RANGE
Birmitrapur
Purnapani
Orga
CKP
Kuarmunda
Bispur
Quarry Siding
Bangurkela
Kalunga
Kansbahal
Rajgangpur
Sogra
Sonakhan
Garposh
Tangarmunda
Bamra
Panposh
Rourkela Jn
Bondamunda
Bisra
Dumetra
Lathika
Champajharan
Chandiposi
Patasahi
Bimlagarh Jn
Gognaposh
Brahmani
Gevra Rd
Korba
Urga
Saragbundia
Madwarani
Kothari Rd
Balpur
Saragaon Rd
Baradwar
Jetha
Sakti
Jaradih
Kharsia
Robertson
Bhupdeopur
Kirodimalnagar
Raigarh
Champa Jn
Chhattisgarh
Ghuriadhor Mines
GANGPUR LIGHT RAILWAY
Dharuadih
Bagdehi
Panpali
Dhutra
Kotarlia
Jamga
Daghora
Himgir
Belpahar
Ib
Jharsuguda Jn
SBP
Brundamal
Lajkura Cabin
Brajrajnagar
Lapanga
Rengali
Sason
Sambalpur Jn
Sambalpur Rd
Sarla Jn
Sambalpur City
Hirakud
44

DIVISIONS
ADA - Adra (SER)
ASN - Asansol (ER)
BSP - Bilaspur (SECR)
CKP - Chakradharpur (SER)
DHN - Dhanbad (ECR)
HWH - Howrah (ER)
KGP - Kharagpur (SER)
RNC - Ranchi (SER)
SBP - Sambalpur (ECR)
see Coalfields region Map on Page 45
West Bengal
Orissa
existing NG line closed for conversion
Damodar
24
36
45
E
F
G
H
1
2
3
4
5
6
Koderma
Larabad BH
Hirodih
Sarmatanr
Jajudih
Parsabad
Dasarah BH
Chaube
Keshwari BH
Hazaribagh Rd
Garea Bihar BH
Chichaki
Karmabad BH
Chaudhuribandh
Chegro BH
Parasnath
Nimiaghat
Hazaribagh
Mathurapur
Nawa Patra BH
TP 6/3
Madhupur Jn
TP 7/11
Jagadishpur
Krishnaballabh Sahay Halt
Giridih
Maheshmunda
Joramow
Madankata
Vidyasagar
Kaseetar
Jamtara
Bodma BH
Kulti Link Cabin
Chittaranjan
Rupnarayanpur
Salanpur
Kulti
Sitarampur Link Cabin
Sitarampur Jn
Dumka
Mallarpur
Gadadharpur
Sainthia Jn
Bataspur
Ahmadpur Jn
Kopai
Prantik
Bolpur
Bhedia
Dhanbad Jn
Gomoh Jn
Bholidih BH
IBP No. 3
Matari
Nichitpur Jn
Tetulmari
Bhuli
Katrasgarh Jn
Telo
Chandrapura Jn
Bhandaridah
Phusro
Bermo
Amlo BH
Jarangdih
Bokaro Thermal
Gomia
Dumri Bihar
Danea
Jageswar Bihar
Chainpur
Rajabera BH
Tupkadih
Dugda
Jamunatanr
Khanoodih
Mohuda Jn
Bhaga
Jharia
Dokra
Pradhankhunta Jn
Chhota Ambona
Kalubathan
Thapamagar
Mugma
Kumardubi
Barakar
Rakhitpur
Sindri BH
Sindri Marshalling Yard
Sindri Town
Chaurashi
Pathardih Jn
Talgoria Jn
Sudamdih
Bhojudih Jn
Bhojudih Washery
Santaldih
Radhagaon
Pundag
Bokaro Steel City Jn
Radhanagar
Burnpur
Barachak
Asansol Jn
Kalipahari
Mohishila
Asansol Court
Damodar Jn
Madhukunda
Muradih
Ramkanali
Bero
Nimcha BH
Raniganj
Bakhtarnagar BH
Andal Jn
Pinjrapole BH
Waria
DCOP
Durgapur
Rajbandh
Panagarh
Mankar
Paraj
Galsi
Barabani
Jamuria
Churulia
Sreepur
Ikra Jn
Tapasi Jn
Sonachara
Siduli
Ukhra
Kajoragram
Chinchuria
Gaurangdi
Palasthali
Lachhmanpur Rd
Barhagram
Raswan
Hazaratpur
Chinpai
Kachujor
Jibdharpur
Siuri
Mahishadahari
Kunuri
Kherua
Dubrajpur
Panchra
Bhimgara Jn
Pandabeswar
Tokisud
Patratu
Bhurkunda
Barkakana Jn
Ramgarh Town
Arigada
Ranchi Rd
Karmahat
Mael
Barkipona
Gola Rd
Harubera
Sondimra
Barlanga
Muri Jn
Tulin
Silli
Burwadag
Kherwakocha
Jonha
Gangaghat
Tatsilwai
Namkom
Ranchi Jn
Hatia
Balsiring
Lodhma
Karra
Hesabera
Gautamdhara
Kita
Ilioo
Torang
Suisa
Jhalda
Tiruldih
Latemda
Heslang
Jhimri
Gonda Bihar
Kotshila Jn
Barbenda
Garjapur
Chas Rd
Gourinathdham
Damrughutu
Purulia Jn
Tamna
Kantadih
Urma
Barabhum
Biramdih
Nimdih
Chandil Jn
Manikui
Kumki
Kandra Jn
Birajpur
Gamharia Jn
Sini Jn
Birbans
Mahali Marup
Raj Kharsawan Jn
Barabamboo
Chakradharpur
Adityapur
Tatanagar Jn
Salgajhari
Asanboni
Rakha Mines
Galudih
Ghatsila
Dalbhumgarh
Kokpara
Chakulia
Kanimahuli
Gidhni
Khatkura
Jhargram
Banstala
Sardiha
Khemasuli
Kalaikunda
Nimpura Jn
Haludpukur
Bahalda Rd
Aunlajori Jn
Gurumahisani
Rairangpur
Kuldiha
Chhanua
Badampahar
Talbandh
Rajaluka
Bangriposi
Buramara
Kuchai
Bhanjpur
Baghra Rd
Baripada
Jamsole
Krishnachandrapur
Betnoti
Jogal
Jugpura
Thakurtala
Rupsa Jn
Haldipada
Tikirapal
Balasore
Nilgiri
Nilgiri Rd
Garhdhrubeshwar
Rukni
Sanka
Joychandipahar
Adra Jn
Anara
Bagalia
Kustaur
Chharrah
Metyal Sahar
Indrabil
Sirjam
Jhantipahari
Chhatna
Anchuri
Belboni
Beliator
Chandar
Brindabanpur
Sirampur
Hamirhati
Sonamukhi
Dhansimla
Dhangaria
Patrasayer
Betur
Kumrul
Indus
Shankrul
Sahaspur Rd
Bowaichandi
Nobanda
Bikna
Bankura Jn
Bheduasole
Ondagram
Ramsagar
Bishnupur
Mukutmanipur
Piardoba
Bogri Rd
Garbeta
Chandrakona Rd
Salboni
Godapaisal
Midnapur
Cossye Halt
Gokulpur
Giri Maidan
Kharida
Kharagpur Jn
Jakpur
Madpur
Shyamchak
Balichak
Radhamohanpur
Khirai
Haur
Hijli Jn
Benapur
Narayangarh
Bakhrabad
Contai Rd
Nekurseni
Dantan
Angua
Lakhannath Rd
Jaleswar
Rajghat
Amarda Rd
Basta
Nuagaon Mayurbhanj Rd
Ramnagar
Tirkha
Digha
Lotapahar
Sonua
Tunia
Goilkera
Derowan
Posoita
Pendrasali
Chaibasa
Singhpokharia
Jhinkpani
Talaburu
Kendposi
Gua
Bara Jamda Jn
Noamundi
Padapahar Jn
Maluka
Dangoaposi
Kiriburu
Karampada
Barabil
Bolanikhadan
Deojhar
Murga Mahadev Rd
Banspani
Jaruli
Kendujhargarh
DHN
ASN
ADA
RNC
CKP
KGP
HWH

The territorial waters of India extend into the sea a distance of twelve nautical miles measured from the appropriate base line.

The external boundaries of India in these maps have not been authenticated and may not be correct.

E
F
G
H
1
2
3
4
5
6
26
LMG
Shaistaganj
Pencharthal
Kumarghat
Nalkata H
Manu
Balla
Bhairab Bazar
Tungi
Akhaura
Agartala
INDIA
Tripura
DIVISIONS
ADA - Adra (SER)
ASN - Asansol (ER)
HWH - Howrah (ER)
KGP - Kharagpur (SER)
LMG - Lumding (NFR)
MLDT - Malda (ER)
SDAH - Moradabad (ER)
Dhaka
Narayanganj
Comilla
BANGLADESH
The external boundaries of India in these maps have not been authenticated and may not be correct.
Sabrum
Phatikchhari
Sholashahar
Chittagong
Chittagong Port
Dohajari
not to scale
See Kolkata Metro Map on Page 4
to Barddhaman (main line)
to Katwa
to Barddhaman (chord line)
to Krishnanagar
Magra
Tribeni
Kalyani Simanta
Kalyani Ghoshpara
Kalyani Silpanchal
Madanpur
Banshberia
Adisaptagram
Kalyani Jn
Kanchrapara
Kanchrapara Workshop
to Tarakeshwar
Chandanpur
Bandel Jn
Halisahar
Hooghly
Jubilee Br.
Naihati Jn
Chuchura
Kankinara
Madhusudanpur
Chandannagar
Jagaddal
Kamarkundu
Nalikul
Hooghly Ghat
Garifa
to Bongaon
Balarambati
Singur
Mankundu
Shyamnagar
Mirzapur Bankipur
Nasibpur
Bhadreshwar
to Champadanga
Ichhapur
Sheakhala
Baruipara
Diara
Baidyabati
Palta
Seoraphuli Jn
Barrackpore
Barasat Jn
Bamangachi
Begampur
Shrirampur
Titagarh
to Hasnabad
Janai Rd
Janai
Khardaha
Hridaypur
Gobra
Rishra
Madhyamgram
Chanditala Jn
Konnagar
Sodpur
New Barrackpore
Karea Kadambagachhi
Dankuni Jn
Uttarpara
Agarpara
Bisharpara Kodalia
Hindmotor
Vivekananda Br.
Baranagar Rd
Birati
Belanagar
Dakshineshwar
Belgharia
Durganagar
Bally Halt
Rajchandrapur
Dum Dum Cantt
Bargachia
Dakshinbari
Pantihal
Munsirhat
Domjur
Maju
Mahendralalnagar
Domjur Rd
Dakshin Maju
Jalalsi
Panpur
Harish Dadpur
to Amta
Makardaha
Jhaluarber
Dansi
Bhattanagar
Kona
Belur
Belur Math
Bally
Bally Ghat
Jessore Rd
Kolkata Airport
Dum Dum Jn
Bagbazar
Tala
Patipukur
Ultadanga Rd
Liluah
Baltikuri
Howrah
Bidhannagar Rd
Kankurgachi Rd Jn
Bankranayabaz
Tikiapara
Burrabazar
Sealdah
Sovabazar Ahiritola
Howrah Jn Cabin
Dasnagar
BBD Bag
Eden Gardens
Princep Ghat
Hastings
Sir Gurudas Banerjee Halt
Park Circus
Sankrail
Andul
Abada
Nalpur
Mourigram
Padmapukur
Ramrajatala
Shalimar
Khidirpur
Remount Rd
Ballygunge Jn
Dhakuria
Chitpur new terminal station coming up near Tala
Bauria
Chengail
Phuleswar
Uluberia
to Kharagpur
Santragachi Jn
Hooghly
Majerhat
Jadabpur
Pujali
Budge Budge
Nangi
Akra
Santoshpur
Brace Bridge
Kalighat
New Alipore
Tollygunge
Mile 5B Cabin
Lake Gardens
Bagha Jatin
Garia
Narendrapur
Sonarpur Jn
Bidyadharpur
Kalikapur
to Canning
Subhasgram
Mallikpur
to Falta
Baruipur Jn
Kalyanpur
Shashan Rd
to Diamond Harbour
to Kakdwip
Kolkata region
see Narrow Gauge Map Page 63

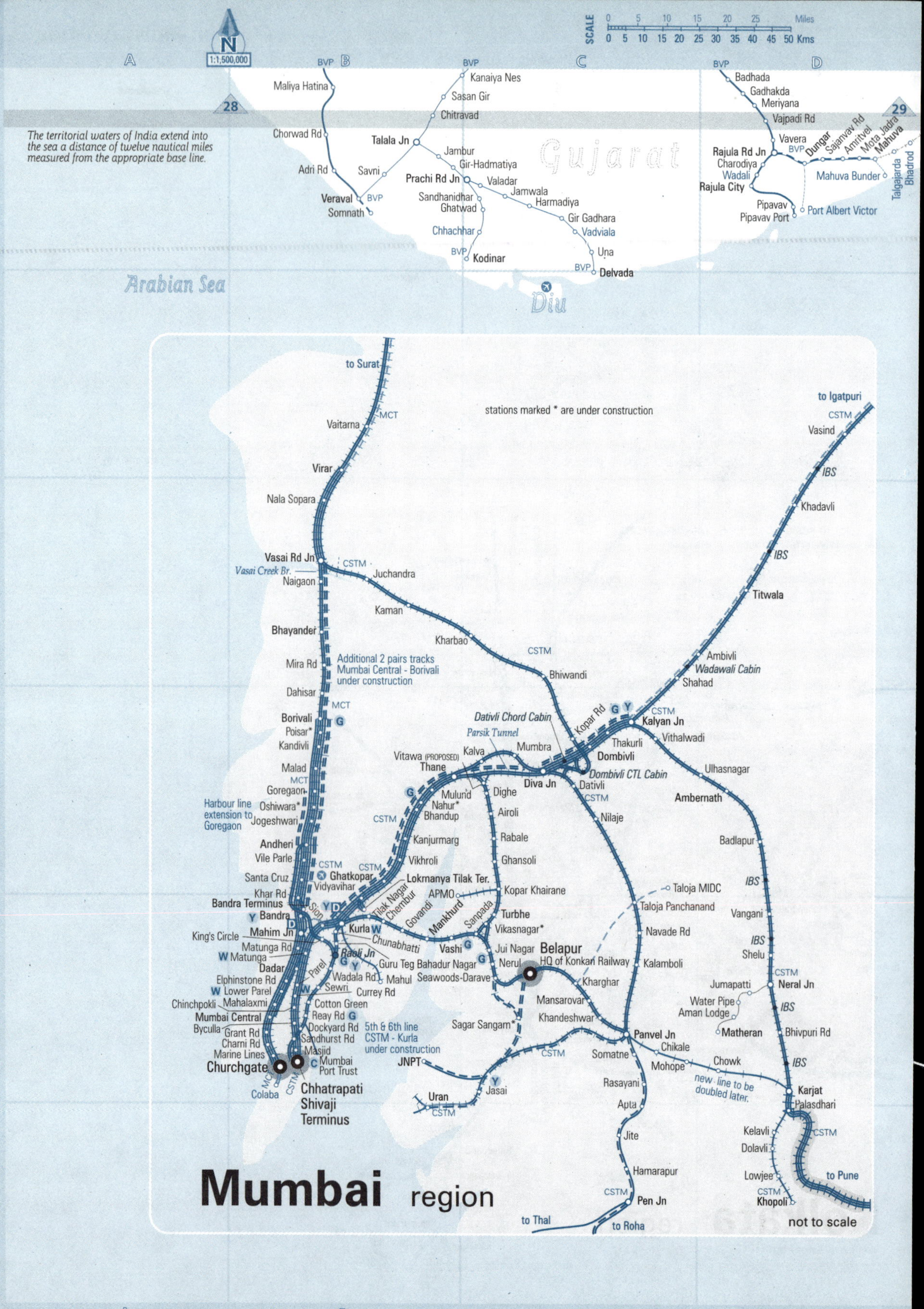
N
1:1,500,000
SCALE
Miles 0 5 10 15 20 25
0 5 10 15 20 25 30 35 40 45 50 Kms
A
B
C
D
1
2
3
4
5
6
28
29
The territorial waters of India extend into the sea a distance of twelve nautical miles measured from the appropriate base line.
Gujarat
Arabian Sea
Diu
BVP
Maliya Hatina
Chorwad Rd
Adri Rd
Veraval
Somnath
Kanaiya Nes
Sasan Gir
Chitravad
Talala Jn
Savni
Jambur
Gir-Hadmatiya
Prachi Rd Jn
Valadar
Jamwala
Harmadiya
Sandhanidhar
Ghatwad
Chhachhar
Kodinar
Gir Gadhara
Vadviala
Una
Delvada
Badhada
Gadhakda
Meriyana
Vajpadi Rd
Vavera
Rajula Rd Jn
Charodiya
Wadali
Rajula City
Pipavav
Pipavav Port
Port Albert Victor
Dungar
Sajanvav Rd
Amritvel
Mota Jadra
Mahuva
Mahuva Bunder
Talgajarda
Bhadrod
Mumbai region
not to scale
stations marked * are under construction
to Surat
MCT
Vaitarna
Virar
Nala Sopara
Vasai Rd Jn
Vasai Creek Br.
Naigaon
CSTM
Juchandra
Kaman
Kharbao
Bhiwandi
Bhayander
Mira Rd
Dahisar
Additional 2 pairs tracks Mumbai Central - Borivali under construction
Borivali
Poisar*
Kandivli
Malad
Goregaon
Harbour line extension to Goregaon
Oshiwara*
Jogeshwari
Andheri
Vile Parle
Santa Cruz
Khar Rd
Bandra Terminus
Bandra
Mahim Jn
King's Circle
Matunga Rd
Matunga
Dadar
Elphinstone Rd
Lower Parel
Mahalaxmi
Chinchpokli
Mumbai Central
Byculla
Grant Rd
Charni Rd
Marine Lines
Churchgate
Colaba
Chhatrapati Shivaji Terminus
Masjid
Mumbai Port Trust
Sandhurst Rd
Dockyard Rd
Reay Rd
Cotton Green
Sewri
Wadala Rd
Parel
Curry Rd
Mahul
Raoli Jn
Guru Teg Bahadur Nagar
Sion
Kurla
Chunabhatti
Tilak Nagar
Chembur
Govandi
Mankhurd
Vashi
Sanpada
Lokmanya Tilak Ter.
Ghatkopar
Vidyavihar
Vikhroli
Kanjurmarg
Bhandup
Nahur*
Mulund
Thane
Vitawa (PROPOSED)
Kalva
Parsik Tunnel
Mumbra
Dativli Chord Cabin
Diva Jn
Dativli
Dombivli CTL Cabin
Dombivli
Thakurli
Kopar Rd
Kalyan Jn
Vithalwadi
Ulhasnagar
Ambernath
Badlapur
Vangani
Shelu
Neral Jn
Bhivpuri Rd
Karjat
Palasdhari
Kelavli
Dolavli
Lowjee
Khopoli
to Pune
Shahad
Ambivli
Wadawali Cabin
Titwala
Khadavli
IBS
Vasind
to Igatpuri
Dighe
Airoli
Rabale
Ghansoli
Kopar Khairane
APMC
Turbhe
Vikasnagar*
Jui Nagar
Nerul
Seawoods-Darave
Belapur
HQ of Konkan Railway
Kharghar
Mansarovar
Khandeshwar
Sagar Sangam*
Panvel Jn
Nilaje
Taloja Panchanand
Taloja MIDC
Navade Rd
Kalamboli
Chikale
Mohope
Chowk
new line to be doubled later.
Jumapatti
Water Pipe
Aman Lodge
Matheran
Somatne
Rasayani
Apta
Jite
Hamarapur
Pen Jn
to Roha
to Thal
JNPT
Jasai
Uran
5th & 6th line CSTM - Kurla under construction

E
F
G
H
BRC
Phulsar
Gopnath Rd
Mangela
Lilwan
Datha Rd
KBCS Siding
KWAE Siding
Kawas Jn Cabin
Tapti Br.
Surat
Udhna Jn
Sayan
Gothangam
Kosad
Utran
Niyol
Chalthan
Bagumra
Gangadhra
Bardoli
Mangrolia
Madhi
Kaher
Lotarva
Vyara
Timbarva
Kikakui Rd
Ukai Songadh
Dosvada
Lakkadkot
Bhadbunja
Navapur
Kolde
Chinchpada
Khatgaon
Khandbara
Bhadwad
Dhekvad
Nandurbar
MCT
30
Tapi
Bhestan
Sachin
Maroli
Gujarat
Navsari
Gandhi Smriti
Hansapore
Vedchha
Ancheli
Amalsad
Unai & Vansada Rd
Kevdi Rd
Dungarda
Waghai
Kala Amba
Anaval
Dholikuva
Rankuva
Chikhli Rd
Gandevi
Bilimora Bunder
Bilimora Jn
Jora Vasan
Dungri
IBS
Valsad
Atul
Pardi
Udvada
Bagwada
Vapi
Karambeli
Bhilad
Daman
Sanjan
Umbargaon
Bordi Rd
Gholvad
Dahanu Rd
Dadra & Nagar Haveli
INDIA
Manmad Jn
Summit
BSL
NED
Lasalgaon
Niphad
Ugaon
Kherwadi
Kasbe Sukene
Odha
Nashik
Nashik Rd
Devlali
40
Godavari
Lahavit
Asvali
Padli
Ghoti
WESTERN GHATS
TGR Cabin 3
TGR Cabin 2
TGR Cabin 1
Kasara
Igatpuri
CSTM
Ehegaon Viaduct
Umbermalli
Khardi
Thal Ghats
Tansit
Atgaon
Tambadmal IBS
Asangaon
Vasind
Khadavli
Titwala
Ambivli
Shahad
Vithalwadi
Ulhasnagar
Ambarnath
Badlapur
Vangani
Shelu
Neral Jn
Bhivpuri Rd
Karjat
Palasdhari
Jambrung
Nagnath Cabin
Thakurwadi
Bhor Ghats
Shirawata Dam
Monkey Hill Cabin
Khandala Tunnel
Lonavla
Khandala
Khopoli
Lowjee
Dolavli
Kelavli
Vangaon
Boisar
Umroli
Palghar
Kelve Rd
Saphale
Vaitarna
Virar
Vasai Rd Jn
Juchandra
Kaman
Kharbao
Kalyan Jn
Bhiwandi
Bhayandar
Borivali
Dombivli
Thane
Diva Jn
Nilaje
Lokmanya Tilak Terminus
Andheri
Ghatkopar
Kurla Jn
Bandra Terminus
Bandra
Dadar
Mumbai Central
Churchgate
Mumbai
Belapur
Navade Rd
Matheran
Kalamboli
JNPT
Uran
Jasai
Panvel Jn
Rasayani
Apta
Jite
Hamarapur
Pen Jn
Thal
Kasu
Nagothane
see Mumbai region Map
Panvel - Roha, Panvel - JNPT & Uran, Pen - Thal
proposed to be handed over to KRCL
46
Malavli
Kamshet
Kanhe
Talegaon
Vadgaon
Ghorawadi
Begdewadi
Dehu Rd
Akurdi
Chinchwad
Kasarwadi
Dapodi
Khadki
Pimpri
Shelarwadi Cabin
Shivaji Nagar
Pune Jn
Hadapsar
Manjari Budruk
Loni
PA
Bhima
Maharashtra
DIVISIONS
BRC - Vadodara (WR)
BSL - Bhusawal (CR)
BVP - Bhavnagar (WR)
CSTM - Mumbai (CR)
MCT - Mumbai (WR)
NED - Nanded (SCR)
PA - Pune (CR)
SUR - Solapur (CR)
1
2
3
4
5
6

N
1:1,500,000
SCALE
0 5 10 15 20 25 Miles
0 5 10 15 20 25 30 35 40 45 50 Kms
A
B
C
D
1
2
3
4
5
6
30
39
47
SATPURA HILLS
M.P.
AJANTA RANGE
BALAGHAT RANGE
INDIA
Maharashtra
Tapi
Godavari
MCT
BSL
SUR
NED
SC
Dhekvad
Nandurbar
Chaupale
Tisi
Ranala
Dondaicha
Vikhran Rd
Shirpur
Sonshelu
Sindkheda
Hol
Nardana
Betawad
Padse
Bhortex
Amalner
Takarkheda
Bhone
Dharangaon
Chaval Kheda
Paldhi
Jalgaon Jn
Bhadli
Shirsoli
Bhusawal Jn
Varangaon
Duskheda
Savda
Nimbhora
Raver
Waghoda
Burhanpur
Asirgarh Rd
Chandni
Nepa Nagar
Mandwa
Sagphata
Achegaon
Bodwad
Kolhadi
Khamkhed
Malkapur
Wadodara
Biswa Bridge
Khamgaon Burti
Nandura
Jalamb Jn
Khamgaon
Dhule
Mohade Pargane Laling
Borvihir
Shirud
Mordad Tanda
Rajmane
Jamdha
Bhoras Budrukh
Chalisgaon Jn
Mhasawad
Maheji
Pardhade
Pachora Jn
Jamner
Bhagdara
Pahur
Shendurni
Pimpalgaon
Varkhedi
Galan
Nagardevla
Kajgaon
Vaghali
Hirapur
Rohini
Nayadongri
Pimparkhed
Nandgaon
Panjhan
Hisvahal
Panewadi
Malegaon
Manmad Jn
Summit
Lasalgaon
Ankai-Killa
Ankai
Nagarsol
Yeola
Tarur
Anchalgaon
Rotegaon
Kopargaon
Parsoda
Lasur
Potul
Daulatabad
Aurangabad
Mukundawadi
Chikalthan
Karmad
Gevrai
Badnapur
Dinagaon
Jalna
Sarwari
Kodi
Ranjani
Paradgaon
Partur
Usmanpur
Satuna
Selu
Dhengli Pimpalgaon
Manvat Rd
Devalgaon Avchar
Pergaon
Sanvatsar
Kanhegaon
Shirdi
Puntamba
Chitali
Belapur
Nipani Vadgaon
Padhegaon
Taklimiya
Rahuri
Vambori
Dehare
Vilad
Nimbalak
Ahmednagar
Akolner
Sarola
Ranjangaon Rd
Visapur
Belvandi
Pargaon Sudrik
Shrigonda Rd
Beed
Vadgaon
Ukhali Halt
Parli Vaijnath
Ghatnandur
Murti
Pangaon

E
F
G
H
M. P.
GAWILGARH HILLS
RMAL RANGE
SATMALA RANGE
NIRMAL RANGE
Andhra Pradesh
Penganga
31
42
48
1
2
3
4
5
6
Amala Khurd
Tukaithad
Dabka
Dhulghat
Wan Rd
Hiwarkhed
Adgaon Buzurg
Akot
Patsul
Karatwadi
Ugwe
Shegaon
Shri Khetra Nagjhari
Paras
Gaigaon
Akola Jn
Yavalkhed
Borgaon
Katepurna
Murtazapur Jn
Mana
Mandura
Kuram
Takli
Badnera Jn
Timtala
Malkhed
Chandur
Dipore
Dhamangaon
Talni
Pulgaon Jn
Kaotha
Dahegaon
Wardha Jn
Varud
Seloo Rd
Tuljapur
Sindi
Barkhedi
Buti Bori Jn
Gumgaon
Khapri
Aini
Nagpur Jn
Godhani
Bharatwada
Motibagh
Koradih
Kalmeshwar
Sonkhamb
Metpanjra
Katol
Kalambha
Tinkheda
Narkhed
Darimeta
Pandhurna
Teegaon
Sausar
Bardi
Lodhikhera
Paradsinga
Saonga
Kelod
Saoner
Khapa
Malegaon
Takli Bhansali
Patan Saongi
Patan Saongi Town
Kohli
Pipla
Khaparkheda
Benoda*
Pusla*
Warud*
Mowad*
Niwarkhed*
Palasin*
Morshi*
Ashtegaon*
Kolwihir*
Chandur Bazar*
Shirala*
Walgaon*
Amravati Rd
Amravati
Achalpur
Nowbagh
Chamak
Pathrot
Khusta Buzurg
Anjangaon
Kapustalni
Kokalda
Lehgaon
Banosa
Bhujvad
Lakhanpuri
Murtazapur Town
Kinkhed
Vilegaon
Bhadsivni
Pohe
Karanja
Karanja Town
Dadgaon
Somthan
Sangwi
Ramgaon Rameshwar
Warud Khed
Bhandegaon
Darwa Motibagh
Tapuna
Ladkhed
Ling
Lasina
Yavatmal
Pusad
Arvi
Khubagaon
Pachegaon
Pargothan
Dhanori
Rohna Town
Virul
Sorta
Sewagram
Chitoda
Bhugaon
Sonegaon
Wagholi
Hinganghat
Yenor
Nagri
Chikni Rd
Warora
Majri Khadan
Majri Jn
Rajur
Wani Jn
Dhandak
Ghughus
Mukutban
Pimpalkuti
Chanakh
Adilabad
Ambari (Deccan)
Talamadugu
Kosai
Kinwat
Madanapur
Bodhani Bujrug
Dhanora (Deccan)
Mahimba
Sahasrakund
Jirona
Himayatnagar (Deccan)
Khadki Bazar
Julagaon (Deccan)
Hadgaon Rd
Parwakhurd
Terban
Devthana
Bhokar
Bimbari
Jambhali
Mudkhed Jn
Mugat
Pathrad
Nanded
Limbgaon
Chudawa
Wanegaon
Purna Jn
Marsul
Pimplachauri
Basmet
Chondi
Junona
Sirlli
Pangara Shinde
Bolda
Nandapur
Dhamni
Kanjara
Hingoli Deccan
Navalgaon
Kanhargaon Naka
Penganga
Kekatumar
Washim
Kata Rd
Jaulka
Amanwadi
Lohagad
Barsi Takli
Sivni Shivpuri
Parbhani Jn
Pingli
Mirkhal
gannapur
nani Narasimha
ondi
angakher
Sivungaon
Shelgaon
Umri
Bolsa
Karkheli
Samrala
Dharmabad
Basar
Fakhrabad
Navipet
Jankampet Rd
Ali Sagar
Jankampet Jn
Nizamabad
Yadapalli
Shakar Nagar
Jagtial
BSL
NED
NGPC
NGPS
HYB
W
G
E
C
DIVISIONS
BSL - Bhusawal (CR)
CSTM - Mumbai (CR)
HYB - Hyderabad SCR)
MCT - Mumbai (WR)
NED - Nanded (SCR)
NGPC - Nagpur (CR)
NGPS - Nagpur (SECR)
SC - Secunderabad (SCR)
SUR - Solapur (CR)

N
1:1,500,000
SCALE
0 5 10 15 20 25 Miles
0 5 10 15 20 25 30 35 40 45 50 Kms
A
B
C
D
1
2
3
4
5
6
32
41
49
NGPS
NGPC
SC
Lodhikhera
Paradsinga
Saonga
Kelod
Khapa
Saoner
Malegaon
Takli Bhansali
Kumeshwar
Patan Saongi
Patan Saongi Town
Pipla
Khaparkheda
Koradih
Kalumna
Motibagh
Bharatwada
Godhani
Nagpur Jn
Ajni
Itwari Jn
Kamptee
Bhandewadi
Dighori Buzurg
Kempalsad
Titur
Mahuli
Kuhi
Mohadara
Bamhani
Umred
Khapri
Gumgaon
Buti Bori Jn
Barkhedi
Sindi
Ramtek
Amdi
Dumri Khurd
Kanhan Jn
Salwa
Chachel
Tharsa
Rewral
Khat
Koka
Bhandara Rd
Sukli
Makhepar Rd
Dongri Buzurg
Goberwahi
Chicholi
Mitewani
Tumsar Town
Tumsar Rd Jn
Mundikota
Tirora
Gangajhari
Kachewani
Gankhera
Hirdamali
Pindkepar
Gondia Jn
Khara
Birsola
Gotra
Pratapbagh
Gudma
Amgaon
Dhanoli
Salekasa
Darekasa
Bortalao
Paniajob
Dongargarh
Musra
Jatkanhar
Bakal
Parmalkasa
Murhipar
Rajnandgaon
Rasmara
Durg Jn
Durg Link Cabin
Maraud
Pauwa
Risama
Gunderdehi
Sikosa
Latabor
Balod
Kusumkasa
Dallirajhara
R
Gonglee
Khodseoni
Sondad
Gondumri
Dewalgaon
Barabati
Arjuni
Wadegaon
Arunnagar
Wadsa
Chicholi Buzurg
Brahmapuri
Kirtimenda
Naghbir Jn
Kargaon
Bhiwapur
Pauni Rd
Bhuyar
Tempa
Mangli
Kotgaon
Meodala
Talodi Rd
Alewahi
Sindewahi
Rajoli
Mulmarora
Tolewahi
Kelzar
Chichpalli
Wainganga
Gad Chiroli
Maharashtra
Nagri
Chikni Rd
Warora
Rajur
Majri Jn
Majri Khadan
Bhandak
Wani Jn
Tadali Jn
Choti Padoli
Vivekanandnagar
Chandrapur
Ghughus
Chanda Fort
Babupeth
Chanda Fort
Visapur
Balharshah Jn
Old Chanda Fort stn on NG line was west of the main line
Manikgarh Jn
Wihirgaon
Pandur Pawani
Gadchandur
Wirur
Makudi
Sirpur Town
Vempalli
Sirpur Kaghaznagar
Ralapet
Asifabad Rd
Repalliwada
Rechni Rd
Andhra Pradesh
Bellampalli
IBS
Mandamari
Ravindrakhani
IBS
Manchiryal
Peddampet
Ramagundam
IBS
INDIA
BASTAR HILLS
Indravati
Dantewa
Kamalur
Bhansi
Bache

E
F
G
H
1
2
3
4
5
6
33
44
50
Bhatapara
Hathbandh
Tilda
Baikunth
Silyari
Mandhar
Bhilai Power House
Bhilai
Devbalodacharoda
Urkura
WRS Colony
Raipur BH
Mandirhasaud
Kumhari
Sarona
Saraswatinagar
Raipur Jn
Raipur City
SBP
Mana
Lakholi
Arangmahanadi
Belsonda
Mahasamund
Arand
Bhimkhoj
Bagbahara
Komakhan
Khariar Rd
Nawapara Rd
SBP
Lakhna
Harishankar Rd
Turekela Rd
Kantabanji
Muribahal
Rahenbata
Titlagarh Jn
Bhatgaon
Kendri
Abhanpur Jn
Manik Chouree
Rajim
Chataud
Sirri
Kurud
Charmuria
Sarsanpuri
Sankra
Dhamtari
Mahanadi
Chhattisgarh
RAIPUR FOREST TRAMWAY
Likhma
Godbhaga
SBP
Attabira
Bargarh Rd
Barapali
Dungripali
Khaliapali
Loisingha
Padampur
Bolangir Rd
Bolangir
SBP
Deogaon Rd
Saintala
Badmal
Sikir
Kesinga
Kandel Rd
Rupra Rd
Norla Rd
Orissa
Utkela
Junagarh
Lanjigarh Rd
Ambodala
Doikallu
Muniguda
Bissam Cuttack
Kondagaon
DIVISIONS
NGPC - Nagpur (CR)
NGPS - Nagpur (SECR)
R - Raipur (SECR)
SBP - Sambalpur (ECoR)
SC - Secunderabad (SCR)
VSKP - Waltair (ECoR)
Keutuguda
Therubali
Bhalumaska
VSKP
SBP
VSKP
Singhapuram Rd Jn
Lelligumma
Rauli
Rayagada
Tikiri
Ladda
Singaram
Lakshmipur Rd
Jimidipeta
Gunupur
VSKP
Palasingi
Bansidhara
VSKP
Kuneru
Kakrigumma
Gumada
A.P.
KONDHAN HILLS
MADAGULA KOUDAS RANGE
Nawarangpur
Dilmili
Bodearapur
Tokopal
Jagdalpur
Kaklur
VSKP
Silakjhori
Kumharsodra
Kumarmaranga
Kawargaon
Dabpal
Naktisemra
Amagura
Ambagaon
Kotpar Rd
Charamula Kusumi
Khadapa
Dhanapur
Jeypore Rd
Maligura
Chattriput
Jarati
Manabar
A Cabin BH
VSKP
Koraput Jn
B Cabin BH
Damanjodi
Dumuriput
VSKP
Parvatipuram Town
Parvatipuram
Narshipuram
VSKP
E
F
G
H

N
1:1,500,000
SCALE
0 5 10 15 20 25 Miles
0 5 10 15 20 25 30 35 40 45 50 Kms
A
B
C
D
1
2
3
4
5
6
34
43
51
SBP
Rengali
Sambalpur Rd
Sason
Sambalpur Jn
Sarla Jn
Hirakud
Sambalpur City
Godbhaga
Maneswar
Attabira
Hatibari
Bargarh Rd
Rairakhol
Jujomura
Charmal
Bamur
Sarayipalli
Handapa
Boinda
Jarapada
Kerejanga
Angul
KUR
D
Talcher
NTPC BH
Talcher Thermal
Talcher Junction Cabin
Budhapank Junction Cabin
Talcher Rd
Budhapank
Mermandoli
Nayabhagirathipur
Hindol Rd
Sadashibpur
Dandimal
Dhenkanal
Shyamacharanpur
Joranda Rd
Machapur Jn BH
Gurudijhatia
Badapadagaon
Charbatia
Salagaon
Sri Jhadeswar
Kapilas Rd Jn
Byree
Barithengarh
Kendujhargarh
Daitari
Tumka
Sukinda
Brahmani
Mahanadi
Orissa
Rajatgarh Jn
Radhakishorepur
Ghantikal Nidipur
Birpura BH
Kendrapara Rd
Sarpeswar
Naraj Marthapur
Gopalpur-Balikuda
Manguli
Chawdwar
Kathajori
Cuttack
Barang Jn
Kalajhari BH
Mattagazpur
Kandarpur
Patia
Mancheswar
Vani Vihar
W
Bhubaneshwar
Sarkantra BH
Lingaraj Temple
Retang
Argul
Khurda Rd Jn
Haripur Gram
Kaipadar Rd
Motari
Dhaulimuhan
Tapang
Kanas Rd
Delang
Jenapur Rd
Golabai
Birpurusottampur
Nirakarpur
Sakhigopal
Bhusandpur
Janakidei
Mukteswarpuri
Kaluparaghat
Malatipatpur
Kuhuri
Puri
Solari
Gangadharpur
Balugaon
Chilka
Kalijai
Khallikot
Rambha
Humma
Ganjam
Phulbani
INDIA
Chatrapur
Chatrapur Court
Jagannathpur
Narasimhapura
Brahmapur
Berhampore Court
Gopalpur-on-Sea
Golanthara
Surla Rd
Ichchapuram
Jhadupudi
Sompeta
Baruva
Mandasa Rd
Summadevi
Palasa
VSKP
Gunupur
Palasingi
Bansidhara
existing NG line
Lihuri
Kashinagar
Sitapuram
Hadobanghi
Parlakimidi
Patapatnam
A.P.
Bay of Bengal
The territorial waters of India extend into the sea a distance of twelve nautical miles measured from the appropriate base line.

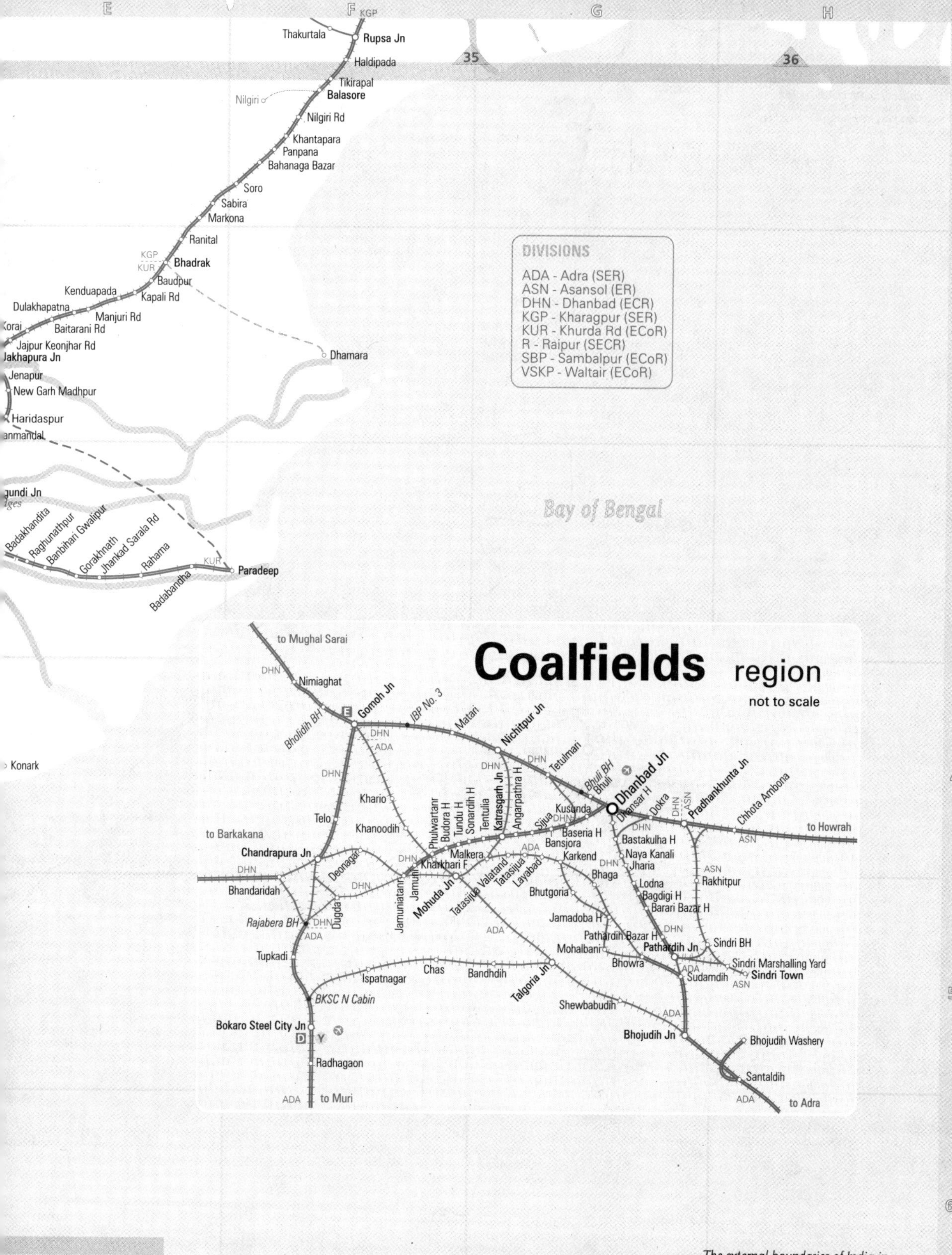

The external boundaries of India in these maps have not been authenticated and may not be correct.

N
1:1,500,000
SCALE
0 5 10 15 20 25 Miles
0 5 10 15 20 25 30 35 40 45 50 Kms
A
B
C
D
1
2
3
4
5
6
39
52
Thal
Panvel - Roha, Panvel - JNPT & Uran, Pen - Thal
proposed to be handed over to KRCL
The territorial waters of India extend into the sea a distance of twelve nautical miles measured from the appropriate base line.
CSTM
Kasu
Nagothane
Nidi
Roha
CSTM
RN
Kolad
Indapur
Mangaon
Goregaon Rd
Veer
Sape Wamne
Karanjadi
Nathuwadi Tunnel
Diwan Khauti
Khed
Nilik Tunnel
Ashti Tunnel
Anjani
Chiplun Tunnel
Chiplun
Kamathe
Guhagar
Arabian Sea
Savarde Tunnel
Savarde
Khershet Tunnel
Aravali Rd
Aravali Tunnel
Shinde Ambri Tunnel
Sangameshwar
Ambed Tunnel
Bhirkond Tunnel
longest tunnel in India (6506m)
Karbude Tunnel
Parchuri Tunnel
Bhoke
Ukshi
Ratnagiri
Math Tunnel
Banewadi Tunnel
Panval Nadi Viaduct
tallest viaduct in India
Tike Tunnel
Nivasar
Adavali
Berdewadi Tunnel
Lanja
Vilvade
Shiravali Tunnel
Tiware Tunnel
Raipatan Rd
Rajapur Rd
Gopalwadi Tunnel
Vaibhavwadi Rd
Nandgaon Rd
Kankavli
Sindhudurg
Kudal
Sawantwadi Rd
RN
Mulshi
WESTERN GHATS (SAHYADRIS)
MAHADEO RANGE
Maharashtra
Krishna
PA
Bagdewadi
Dehu Rd
Akurdi
Chinchwad
Pimpri
Kasarwadi
Dapodi
Khadki
Shivaji Nagar
Pune Jn
Hadapsar
Manjari Budruk
Loni
Ghorpuri
Sasvad Rd
Phursungi
Alandi
Guroli
Uruli
Yevat
Khutbhav
Kedgaon
Kadhethan
Patas
Shindawane
Ambale
Rajewadi
Jejuri
Daundaj
Valha
Nira
Lonand
Salpa
Phaltan
Adarki
Wathar
Palsi
Jarandeswar
Satara
Koregaon
Rahimatpur
Targaon
Masur
Shiravade
Karad
Shenoli
Bhavananinagar
Takari
Kirloskarwadi
Amnapur
Bhilavdi
Nandre
Madhavnagar
Budhgaon
Sangli
Vishrambag
Wanlesswadi H
Miraj North Cabin
Miraj Jn
Bolwad
Jayasingpur
Nimshirgaon Tamdalge
Hatkanagale
Rukadi
Valivade
Gur Market
Chhattrapati Shahu Majaraj Terminus (Kolhapur)
SUR
UBL
Belvandi
Pargaon Sudrik
Shrigonda Rd
Kashti
Daund Jn
Bori
Malad-Gaon
Rawangaon
Malthan
Shirsai
Shirsupha
Katphal
Barama
Vijaynag
Ugarkhurd
Kuda
Chinch
Raybag
Chikodi Rd
Bage
Ghatp
Gokak
Parakanaha
Pachchapur
Suldhal
Sulebhavi
Sambre
Belgaum

E
F
G
H
1
2
3
4
5
6
40
48
53
SC
Ghatnandur
Murti
Pangaon
Karepur
Janwal
Manjra
Wadwal Nagnath
Latur Rd
Chakur
Nageshwadi
Ambika Rohina
Gharani
Bhatangali
Her
Kumthakurd
Udgir
Belshakarga
Kamalnagar
Kalgupur
Bhalki
Jinti Rd
Parewadi
Washimbe
Katraj
Pomalwadi
Bhima
Pophalaj
Jeur
Bhalvani
Kem
Dhavalas
SUR
Kurduvadi Jn
D
Chink Hill
Mahisgaon
Wadsinge
Madha
Shendri
Uplai
Barsi Town
Kuslamb
Pangri
Ramling
Yedshi
Kalamb Rd
Dhoki
Thair
Palsap
Murud
Neoli
Ausa Rd
Harangul
Latur
Osmanabad
Tuljapur
DIVISIONS
GTL - Guntakal (SCR)
CSTM - Mumbai (CR)
KAWR - Karwar (KR)
PA - Pune (CR)
RN - Ratnagiri (KR)
SC - Secunderabad (SCR)
SUR - Solapur (CR)
UBL - Hubli (SWR)
Laul
Padsali
Vakav
Angar
Modlimb
Malikpeth
Ashti
Mohol
Babulgaon
Mundhewadi
Wellingdon Br.
Pandharpur
Pakni
Solapur Jn
Bale
UBL
Tikekarwadi
Hotgi Jn
Tilati
Akkalkot Rd
Nagansur
Boroti
Dudhani
Kulali
Gaudgaon
Gangapur Rd
Hunsi-Hadgil
Savalgi
Bablad
Gulbarga
Bohali
Bamani
Sangola
Wasud
Javale
Jath Rd
Gulvanchi
Dhalgaon
Langerpeth
Kavathe Mahankal
Agran Dhulgaon
Sulgare
Belanki
Aherwadi
Sulerjavalge
Tadwal
Padnur
Lachyan
Mavinahalli
Indi Rd
Chorgi
Nimbal
INDIA
Kyatanakeri Rd
Minchnal
Aliyabad
Bijapur
Ibrahimpur
Jumnal
Honaganahalli
Mulvad
Karlgurki
Kudgi
Basavana Bagewadi Rd
Angadageri
Wandal
Benal
Almatti
Kudala Sangama Rd
Sitimani
Kadlimatti
Mugalolli
Bagalkot
Guledagudda Rd
Badami
Yeragoppa
Lakhmapur
Karnataka
Krishna
Hirenanduru
Martur
Shahabad
Y
Wadi Jn
GTL
Malkhaid Rd
Chittapur
Sulehalli
Hallakatta
Hallakatta H
Nalwar
Shampur Halli
Thangundi
Yadgir
Lingiri
Narayanpet Rd

N
1:1,500,000
SCALE
0 5 10 15 20 25 Miles
0 5 10 15 20 25 30 35 40 45 50 Kms
A
B
C
D
1
2
3
4
5
6
41
47
54
Maharashtra
Karnataka
Andhra Pradesh
INDIA
Manjra
Krishna
HYB
Basar
Fakhrabad
Navipet
Jagtial
Jankampet Rd
Ali Sagar
Jankampet Jn
Nizamabad
Yadapalli
Bodhan
Shakar Nagar
Dichpalli
Indalvai
Sirnapalli
Raghavapuram
IBS
Sultanabad
Kothapalli
SC
Karimnagar
Kumthakurd
Udgir
Belshakarga
Uppalavi
Kamareddi
Kamalnagar
Talmadla
Kalgupur
Bhiknur
Akanapet
Bhalki
Mirzapalli
Sidheswar
Halbarga
Wadiaram
Khanapur
Bidar
Srinivasanagar
Masaipet
Brahmanapalli
Chitta
Matalkunta
Zahirabad
Manoharabad
Kuchavaram H
Dabilpur
Medchal
Gowdavalli
Kohir (Deccan)
Marpalli
BHEL Halt
Patancheru
Ramchandrapuram
Sanatnagar Jn
Hafizpeta
Bolarum
Ammuguda
Maula Ali
Charlapalli
Ghatkesar
Bibinagar
Begumpet
Telapur
Sadashivpeth Rd
Ravalapalli Kalan
Gulaguda
Chitgidda
Shankarpalli
Nagalapalli
Lingampally
Hussainsagar Jn
Secunderabad Jn
Kacheguda
(HQ of HYB Div.)
Khairatabad
Hyderabad
Falaknuma
Budvel
see Secunderabad region Map on the next page
Umdanagar
Pagidipalli Jn
GNT
Nagireddipalli
Mamdapur
Valigonda
Bhongir
Raigir
Wangapalli
Aler
Pembarti
Jangaon
Raghunathpalli
Yeshwantapuram
Ippaguda
Ghanpur
Nashk
Ramannapet
Chityala
Srirampuram
Nalgonda
Thipparthi
Vikarabad Jn
Godamgura
Dharur
Rukmapur
Tandur
Mantatti
Nawandgi
Kurgunta
Seram
Mailaram
Malkhaid Rd
Chittapur
Sulehalli
Timmapur
Kottur
Shadnagar
Burgula
Balanagar
Rangareddi Guda
Rajapur
Gollapalli
Jadcherla
GTL
Shampur Halli
Thangundi
Yadgir
Lingiri
Yenugonda
Mahbubnagar
Mahbubnagar Town
Divitipalli
Kotakadra
Manyamkonda
Devarkadra
Narayanpet Rd
Chegunta
Kaukuntla
Kurumurti
Krishna
Konnur
Yadalapur
Chiksugur
Wanaparti Rd
Ajjakollu
Sriramnagar
Yermaras
Arepalli
Raichur
Gadwal
Poodoor
Peddadinne
Itikyala
Marichethal
Matmari
Hanumapura
Manopad
Mantralayam Rd
Macherla

E
F
G
H
1
2
3
4
5
6
42
50
55
Manchiryal
Peddampet
Ramagundam
dapalli Jn
Kolanur
Odela
Potkapalli
IBS
Bisugirshariff
Jamikunta
Uppal
Hasanparti Rd
KZJ E Cabin
KZJ F Cabin
Warangal
Kazipet Jn
Vanchangiri
Chintalapalli
Yelgur
Nekonda
Intekanne
Kesamudram
Tadalapusapalli
Mahbubabad
Singareni Collieries
Gandhipuram Halt
Chimalpahad
Gundratimadugu
Karepalle Jn
Garla
Dornakal Jn
Pocharam
Tadikalapudi
Bethampudi
Bhadrachalam Rd
Gajulagudem
Bhadrachalam
Pandurangapuram
Aswapuram
Manguru
Godavari
Chhattisgarh
BAILADILA HILLS
Kamalur
Bhansi
Bacheli
Kirandul
VSKP
SC
Papatapalli
Mallemadugu
Khammam
Pandillapalli
Chintakani
Nagalwancha
Bonakalu
Motumari Jn
Madhira
Dendukur
Tondalagopavaram
Errupalem
Gangineni
Cheruvu Madhavaram
Kondapalli
Jaggayyapet Town
Miryalaguda
Vishnupuram
Pondugula
Nadikudi Jn
Gurujala
GNT
Tummalacheruvu
Piduguralla
Bellamkonda
Reddigudem
Krishna
DIVISIONS
BZA - Vijayawada (SCR)
HYB - Hyderabad (SCR)
GNT - Guntur (SCR)
GTL - Guntakal (SCR)
SC - Secunderabad (SCR)
VSKP - Waltair (ECoR)
Rajahmundry
Godavari Br.
Godavari
Kovvur
Pasivedala
Chagallu
Brahmanagudem
Nidadavolu Jn
Kaldhari
Satyavada
Tanuku
Velpuru
Relangi
Attili
Manchili
Aravalli
Pennada Agraharam
Chintaparru
Sitampet
Dendukuru
Bhimadolu
Pulla
Kaikoram
Chebrol
Unguturu
Badampudi
Tadepalligudem
Prattipadu
Navabpalem
Marampalli
Eluru
Powerpet
Vatlur
Nuzvid
Viravalli
Telaprolu
Pedda Avutapalli
Gannavaram
Mustabada
Gunadala
Vijayawada NE
Rayanapadu WS
Rayanapadu
Krishna Br.
Vijayawada New West Block Cabin
Vijayawada Jn
Ramavarappadu Gate
Krishna Canal Jn
Satyanarayanapuram
New Station
Ramavarappadu
Nidamanuru
Tenneru
Tarigoppula
Moturu
Mokhasakalavapudi
Mandavalli
Kaikaluru
Pallevada
Lakshminarayanapuram
Vendra
Akividu
Cherukuvada
Undi
Bhimavaram Town
Bhimavaram Jn
Sringavruksham
Viravasaram
Sivadevunichikkala
Lankalakoderu
Narasapur
Gorintada
Palakollu
Putlacheruvu
Pasalapudi
Guntakoduru
Gudivada Jn
Nujella
Gudlavalleru
Kavutaram
Vadlamannadu
Pedana
Chilakalapudi
Machilipatnam
Bay of Bengal
Kolanukonda
Uppalluru
Peddavadlapudi
Indupalli
Ventrapragada
Dosapadu
Chiluvur
Morampudi
Duggirala
Kolakalur
Tenali Jn
Chinnaravuru
Zampani
Valliveru
Vemuru
Tsunduru
Modukuru
Penumarru
Bhattiprolu
Pallikona
Repalle
Machavaram
Nidubrolu
Angalakuduru
Sangamjagarlamudi
Vejendla
Manipuram Block Cabin
Guntur Jn
New Guntur
Pedakakani
Namburu
Mangalagiri
Limgamguntla
Sripuram
Mandapadu
Pedakurapadu
Gudipudi
Sattenapalli
Bandarupalli
Nallapadu
Phirangipuram
Nudurupadu
Satulur
Perecherla
Munumaka
Narasaraopet
Santmagulur
Vellalacheruvu
Savalyapuram
Vinukonda
Gundlakamma
achintala
ondrapol
The territorial waters of India extend into the sea a distance of twelve nautical miles measured from the appropriate base line.

N
1:1,500,000
SCALE
0 5 10 15 20 25 Miles
0 5 10 15 20 25 30 35 40 45 50 Kms
A
B
C
D
1
2
3
4
5
6
VSKP
43
49
55
Chattisgarh
KONDHAN HILLS
Orissa
MADAGULA KOUDAS HILLS
INDIA
Andhra Pradesh
Bay of Bengal
Godavari
Godavari Br.
Malkangiri
Charamula Kusumi
Khadapa
Dhanapur
Maligura
Jarati
Jeypore Rd
Chattriput
Manabar
A Cabin BH
Koraput Jn
B Cabin BH
Damonjodi
Dumuriput
Suku
Paliba
Machhakund Rd
Bheja
Padua
Darliput
Gorapur
Arakku
Arakku Valley H
Shimliguda
Borraguhalu
Karakavalasa
Gajapathinagaram
Chimidipalli
Tyada
Shivalingapuram
Bodavara
Srungavarapukota
Mallividu
Gumada
Lihuri
Kashinagar
Parvatipuram Town
Parvatipuram
Narshipuram
Sitanagaram
Narayanappavalasa
Rompalli
Gollaveta
Parannavalasa
Bobbili Jn
Salur
Donkinvalsa
Komatipalli
Urlam
Srikakulam Rd
Sigadam
Ponduru
Dusi
Batuva
Chipurupalli
Garividi
Gujjangivalasa
Garudabilli
Gotlam
Nellimarla
Vizianagaram Jn
Korukonda
Alamanda
Kantakapalli
Kottavalasa Jn
Pendurti
BZA
Simhachalam North Jn
Simhachalam
Gopalapatnam BH
Kottapalam BH (ex Gopalapatnam Cabin)
Maripalem
Duvvada
Visakhapatnam Jn
Visakhapatnam Town
Visakhapatnam Port
Visakhapatnam Steel Plant
E
D
Y
Thadi
Anakapalle
Kasimkota
Bayyavaram
Narasingapalli
Elamanchili
Regupalem
Narsipatnam Rd
Gullipadu
Tuni
Hamsavaram
Timmapuram
Annavaram
Ravikampadu
Durgada Gate
Mallavaram
Gollaprolu
Pithapuram
Chandrapalem
Samalkot Jn
Gudaparti
Medapadu
Peddabrahmadevam
Bikkavolu
Balabhadrapuram
Anaparti
Dwarapudi
Kesavaram
Kakinada Town
Kakinada Port
Kovvada
Aratlakatla
Karapa
Vakada
Velangi
Narasapurapupeta
Ramachandrapuram
Draksharama
Kunduru
Gangavaram
Kotapalle
Kovvur
Godavari
Pasivedala
Chagallu
Rajahmundry
Brahmanagudem
Kadiyam
Nidadavolu Jn
Kaldhari
Satyavada
Tanuku
Velpuru
Relangi
Attili
Manchili
Aravalli
Navabpalem
Marampalli
Vendra
Lakshminarayanapuram
Pennada Agraharam
Lankalakoderu
Chintaparru
Palakollu
Gorintada
Narsapur
Sringavruksham
Viravasaram
Sivadevunichikkala
C
The territorial waters of India extend into the sea a distance of twelve nautical miles measured from the appropriate base line.

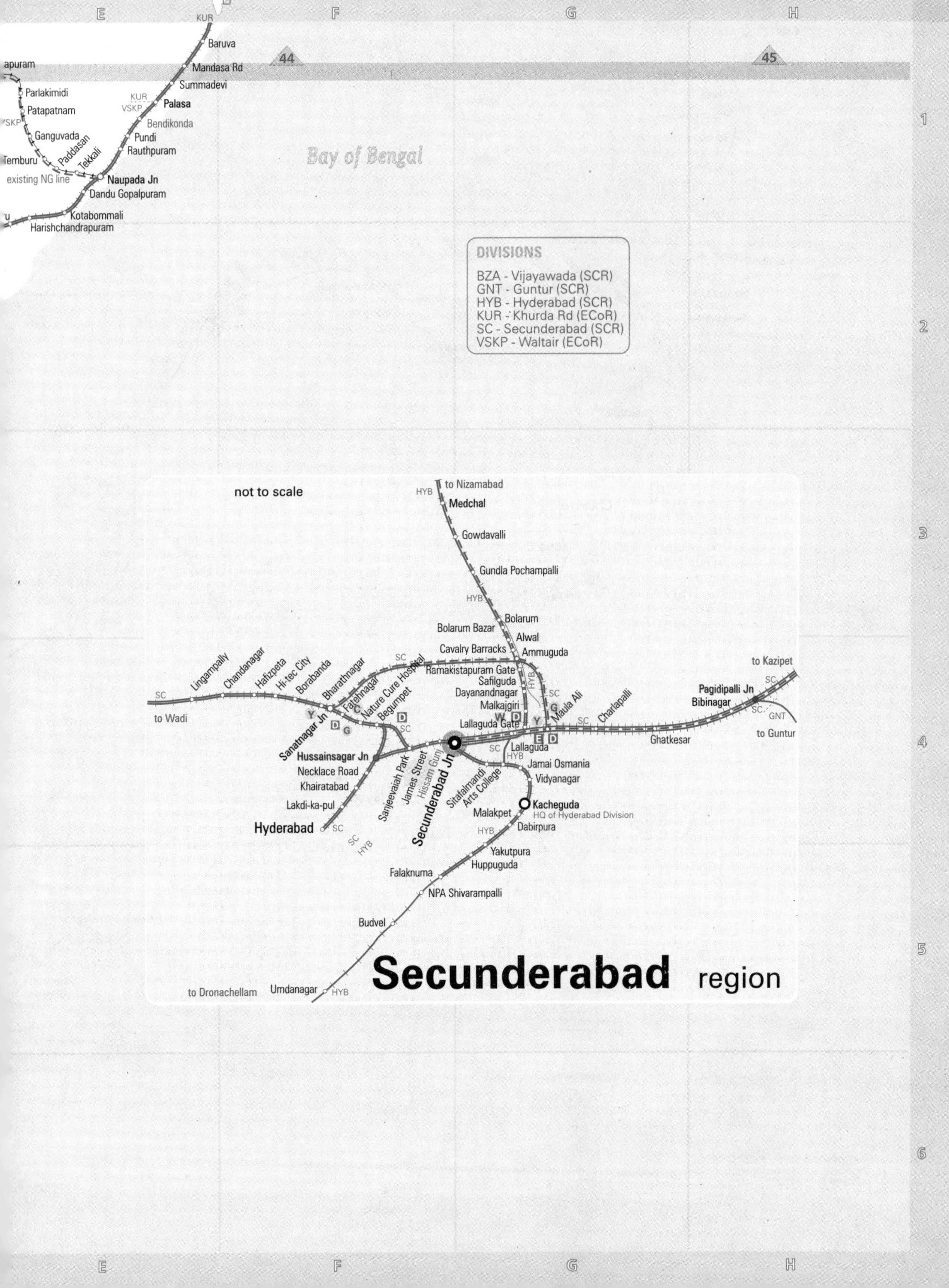
E
F
G
H
1
2
3
4
5
6
44
45
KUR
Baruva
apuram
Mandasa Rd
Summadevi
Parlakimidi
KUR
VSKP
Palasa
Patapatnam
VSKP
Bendikonda
Ganguvada
Paddasan
Pundi
Rauthpuram
Temburu
Tekkali
Naupada Jn
existing NG line
Dandu Gopalpuram
Kotabommali
Harishchandrapuram
Bay of Bengal
DIVISIONS
BZA - Vijayawada (SCR)
GNT - Guntur (SCR)
HYB - Hyderabad (SCR)
KUR - Khurda Rd (ECoR)
SC - Secunderabad (SCR)
VSKP - Waltair (ECoR)
not to scale
HYB
to Nizamabad
Medchal
Gowdavalli
Gundla Pochampalli
HYB
Bolarum
Bolarum Bazar
Alwal
Cavalry Barracks
Ammuguda
SC
Ramakistapuram Gate
Safilguda
Dayanandnagar
Malkajgiri
Lallaguda Gate
Maula Ali
Charlapalli
to Kazipet
Pagidipalli Jn
Bibinagar
SC
GNT
to Guntur
Ghatkesar
SC
to Wadi
Lingampally
Chandanagar
Hafizpeta
Hi-tec City
Borabanda
Bharathnagar
Fatehnagar
Nature Cure Hospital
Begumpet
Sanatnagar Jn
Hussainsagar Jn
Necklace Road
Khairatabad
Lakdi-ka-pul
Hyderabad
SC
Sanjeevaiah Park
James Street
Hissam Gunj
Secunderabad Jn
Sitafalmandi
Arts College
Lallaguda
HYB
Jamai Osmania
Vidyanagar
Kacheguda
HQ of Hyderabad Division
Malakpet
Dabirpura
HYB
Yakutpura
Huppuguda
Falaknuma
NPA Shivarampalli
Budvel
to Dronachellam
Umdanagar
HYB
Secunderabad region
E
F
G
H

N
1:1,500,000
SCALE
Miles 0 5 10 15 20 25
0 5 10 15 20 25 30 35 40 45 50 Kms
A B C D
1 2 3 4 5 6
46
56
RN
UBL
KAWR
MYS
Kudal
Sawantwadi Rd
Madure
Satorda (proposed)
Pernem Tunnel
Pernem
Thivim
Karmali
Maharashtra
Goa
Mormugao Harbour
Vasco-da-Gama
Dabolim
Sankaval
Neura O Grande* (proposed)
Verna
Cansaulim
Majorda Jn
Suravali
Madgaon Jn
San Juje da Areyal
Chandargao
Kudchade (Sanvordem)
Kalem
Dudhsagar Falls
Kulem
Castle Rock
Caranzol
Dudhsagar
Sonaulim
Braganza Ghat
Ghotgewadi
Tinaighat
Londa Jn
Devarayi
Nagargali
Tavargatti
Kambaraganvi
Naglavi
Mugad
Kyarkop
Dharwad
Navalur
Amargol
Unkal
Alnavar Jn
Shingatgeri
Shirgur
Ambewadi
Dandeli
Hubli Jn
Hubli East Cabin
Kusagal
Hebsur
Sisvinahalli
Navalgund Rd
Annigeri
Hulkoti
Gadag Jn
Sulebhavi
Suldhal
Sambre
Belgaum
Desur
Idalhond
Khanapur
Gunji
Guledagudda R
Badami
Yeragoppa
Lakhmapur
Jakanur
Hole-Alur
Somankatti
Mallapur
Balganur
Hombal
Kundgol
Saunshi
Gudgeri
Kalas Halt
Yalvigi
Savanur
Kalsur
Karajgi
Haveri
Byadgi
Davargudda
Ranibennur
Chalg
Wardha
Balli
Padi Tunnel
Barcem Tunnel
Canacona
WESTERN GHATS
Asanoti
Kalinadi Br.
Karwar
Karwar Tunnel
Harwada
Ankola
Gokarna Rd
Kumta
Honnavar
Honnavar Tunnel
Sharavati Br.
INDIA
Kanale Halt
Baradavalli
Talguppa
Sagar Jambagaru
Balgundi
Adderi Halt
Anandapuram
Manki
Murdeshwar
Chitrapur H
Bhatkal
Arabian Sea
Kechanalu Halt
Arasalu
Kumsi
Harnahalli
Konagavalli Halt
Kotegangur
Shimoga Town
Shimoga
Shimoga Bidare Halt
Bhadra
Shiroor
Byndoor Tunnel
Byndoor
Bijur
Mandagadde
Masarahalli
Bolenahalli
Tarikere
Senapura
Tungabhadra
Lakkavali
Hoshahalli
Duggala
Narasimharajapuram
Tadasa
Rangenhalli
Agasanhadlu
Hebbe
Kemmanugund
Kundapura
Barkur
Udupi
Innanje
Padubidri
Chikmagalur
The territorial waters of India extend into the sea a distance of twelve nautical miles measured from the appropriate base line.

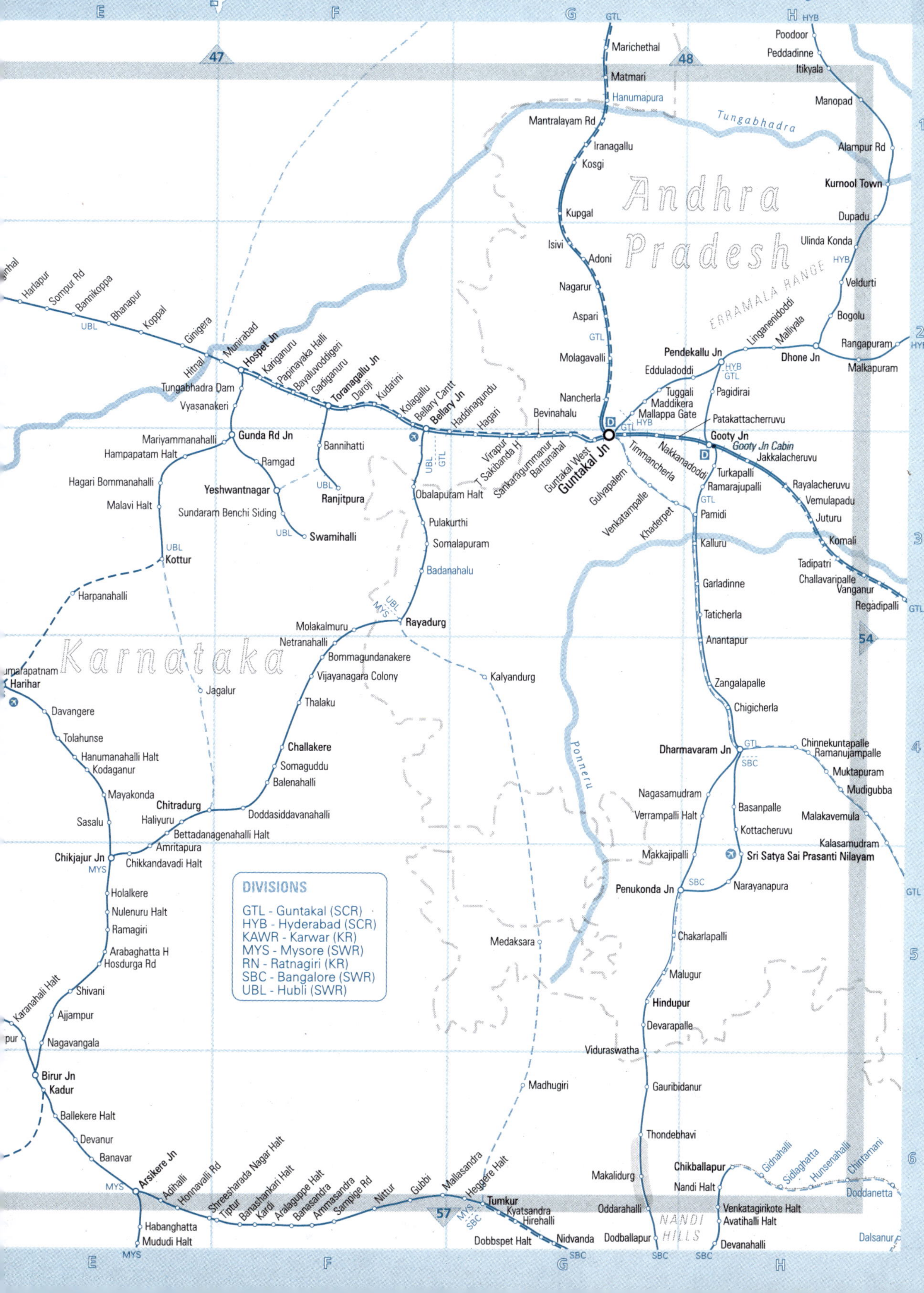
E
F
G
H
GTL
HYB
47
48
54
57
1
2
3
4
5
6
Andhra Pradesh
Karnataka
Tungabhadra
ERRAMALA RANGE
Ponneru
NANDI HILLS
Poodoor
Peddadinne
Itikyala
Manopad
Alampur Rd
Kurnool Town
Dupadu
Ulinda Konda
Veldurti
Bogolu
Rangapuram
Malkapuram
Dhone Jn
Marichethal
Matmari
Hanumapura
Mantralayam Rd
Iranagallu
Kosgi
Kupgal
Isivi
Adoni
Nagarur
Aspari
Molagavalli
Nancherla
Bevinahalu
Pendekallu Jn
Linganenidoddi
Malliyala
Edduladoddi
Tuggali
Maddikera
Mallappa Gate
Pagidirai
Patakattacherruvu
Gooty Jn
Gooty Jn Cabin
Jakkalacheruvu
Guntakal Jn
Guntakal West
Timmancherla
Nakkanadoddi
Gulyapalem
Venkatampalle
Khaderpet
Turkapalli
Ramarajupalli
Pamidi
Kalluru
Rayalacheruvu
Vemulapadu
Juturu
Komali
Tadipatri
Challavaripalle
Vanganur
Regadipalli
Garladinne
Taticherla
Anantapur
Zangalapalle
Chigicherla
Dharmavaram Jn
Chinnekuntapalle
Ramanujampalle
Muktapuram
Mudigubba
Malakavemula
Kalasamudram
Sri Satya Sai Prasanti Nilayam
Nagasamudram
Verrampalli Halt
Basanpalle
Kottacheruvu
Makkajipalli
Penukonda Jn
Narayanapura
Chakarlapalli
Malugur
Hindupur
Devarapalle
Viduraswatha
Gauribidanur
Thondebhavi
Makalidurg
Chikballapur
Nandi Halt
Oddarahalli
Venkatagirikote Halt
Avatihalli Halt
Dodballapur
Devanahalli
Dalsanur
Gidnahalli
Sidlaghatta
Hunsenahalli
Chintamani
Doddanetta
Nidvanda
Dobbspet Halt
Tumkur
Kyatsandra
Hirehalli
Heggere Halt
Mallasandra
Gubbi
Nittur
Sampige Rd
Ammasandra
Banasandra
Aralaguppe Halt
Kardi
Banashankari Halt
Tiptur
Shreesharada Nagar Halt
Honnavalli Rd
Adihalli
Arsikere Jn
Habanghatta
Mududi Halt
Banavar
Devanur
Ballekere Halt
Kadur
Birur Jn
Nagavangala
Ajjampur
Karanahali Halt
Shivani
Hosdurga Rd
Arabaghatta H
Ramagiri
Nulenuru Halt
Holalkere
Chikjajur Jn
Chikkandavadi Halt
Amritapura
Bettadanagenahalli Halt
Haliyuru
Chitradurg
Doddasiddavanahalli
Balenahalli
Somaguddu
Challakere
Thalaku
Vijayanagara Colony
Bommagundanakere
Netranahalli
Molakalmuru
Rayadurg
Kalyandurg
Medaksara
Madhugiri
Jagalur
Sasalu
Mayakonda
Kodaganur
Hanumanahalli Halt
Tolahunse
Davangere
Harihar
Kumarapatnam
Harpanahalli
Kottur
Malavi Halt
Hagari Bommanahalli
Hampapatam Halt
Mariyammanahalli
Gunda Rd Jn
Ramgad
Yeshwantnagar
Sundaram Benchi Siding
Swamihalli
Ranjitpura
Bannihatti
Vyasanakeri
Tungabhadra Dam
Hitnal
Munirabad
Hospet Jn
Kariganuru
Papinayaka Halli
Bayaluvoddigeri
Gadiganuru
Toranagallu Jn
Daroji
Kudatini
Kolagallu
Bellary Cantt
Bellary Jn
Haddinagundu
Hagari
Virapur
T Sakibanda H
Sankaragummanur
Bantanahal
Obalapuram Halt
Pulakurthi
Somalapuram
Badanahalu
Ginigera
Koppal
Bhanapur
Bannikoppa
Sompur Rd
Harlapur
UBL
MYS
SBC
DIVISIONS
GTL - Guntakal (SCR)
HYB - Hyderabad (SCR)
KAWR - Karwar (KR)
MYS - Mysore (SWR)
RN - Ratnagiri (KR)
SBC - Bangalore (SWR)
UBL - Hubli (SWR)

SCALE 0 5 10 15 20 25 Miles
0 5 10 15 20 25 30 35 40 45 50 Kms
N
1:1,500,000
INDIA
Andhra Pradesh
Karnataka
Krishna
Ponneru
ERRAMALA RANGE
NALLAMALAY RANGE
VELLIKONDA RANGE
SHESHACHALAM HILLS
PALKONDA RANGE
TIRUMALA HILLS
Nakdikanama Pass
Chelama Tunnel
Bogada Tunnel
48
53
58
Peddadinne
Itikyala
Manopad
Alampur Rd
Kurnool Town
Dupadu
Ulinda Konda
Veldurti
Bugganipalli Cement Nagar
Krishnammakona
Panyam
Bogolu
Betamcherla
Dhone Jn
Rangapuram
Malkapuram
Nandyal
Gazulapalli
Basavapuram
Chelana
Bogada
Diguvametta
Gudimetta
Giddalur
Kistam Settipalli
Somidevipalli
Jaggambhotla Krishnapuram
Cumbum
Tarlupadu
Markapur Rd
Gajjelakonda
Donakonda
Potlapadu
Kurichedu
Gundlakamma
Vinukonda
Savalyapuram
Vellalacheruvu
Santmagulur
Munumaka
Kadavakuduru
Chinnaganjam
Uppugundur
Raparla
Ammanabrolu
Karavadi
Ongole
Pelluru
Surareddipale
Tanguturu
Singarayakonda
Ulavapadu
Chakicherla
Tettu
Kavali
Musunur
Sri Venkateswarapalem
Bitragunta
Alluru Rd
Talamanchi
Kodavaluru
Padugupadu
Nellore
Nellore South
Vedayapalem
Venkatachalam
Krishnapatnam
Manubolu
Gudur Jn
Odur
Kondagunta
Vendodu
Nidigallu
Pedapariya
Venkatagiri
Yataluru
Yellakaru
Akkurti
Srikalahasti
Rachagunneri
Yerpedu
Srivasava Udasipuram H
Renigunta Jn
Nayudupetta
Nelaballi
Doravarichattram
Polireddipalem
Sullurupeta
Akkampet
Tada
Arambakkam
Elavur
Gummidipundi
Kavaraipettai
Anuppampattu
Por
Juturu
Komali
Tadipatri
Challavaripalle
Vanganur
Regadipalli
Kondapuram
Mangapatnam
Muddanuru
Kalamalla
Yerraguntla
Yerragudipadu
Kamalapuram
Gangayapalle
Krishnapuram
Cuddapah
Kanamalopalle
Bhakrapeta
Ontimitta
Mantapampalle
Nandalur
Hastavaramu
Razampeta
Pullampeta
Reddipalli
Obulavaripalle
Anantarajupet
Koduru
Settigunta
Balapalle
Mamanduru
Tiruchanur
Tirupati
Tirupati West
Mangapuram
Chandragiri
Kotala
Pudi
Taduku
Puttur
Vepagunta
Ekambarakuppam
Nagari
Pallipattu
Panapakam
Muktapuram
Mudigubba
Malakavemula
Kalasamudram
Kadiri
Nallacheruvu
Nallcheruvu East
Tanakallu
Mulakala Cheruvu
Battulapuram
Burakayalakota
Tummanamgutta
Kurabalakota
Madanapalle Rd
Vayalpad
Chintapatri
Itlamvaripalle
Kalikiri
Piler
Pulicherla
Mangalampeta
Vallivedu
Damalcheruvu
Pakala Jn
Kottakota
Putalapattu
Chintamani
Doddanetta
Hunsenahalli
Srinivaspur
Dalsanur
HYB
GNT
GTL
BZA
MAS
IBS
D
W
A B C D
1 2 3 4 5 6

E
F
G
H
1
2
3
4
5
6
BZA
IBS
Zampani
Vemuru
Tsunduru
Modukuru
Penumarru
Bhattiprolu
Nidubrolu
Pallikona
Repalle
Machavaram
Appikatla
Bapatla
Stuartpuram
Ipurupalem
Chirala
Vadarevu
Vetapalem
Jandrapeta
Chilakalapudi
Machilipatnam
Krishna
49
50
59
C
DIVISIONS
BZA - Vijayawada (SCR)
GNT - Guntur (SCR)
GTL - Guntakal (SCR)
HYB - Hyderabad (SCR)
MAS - Chennai (SR)
Bay of Bengal
The territorial waters of India extend into the sea a distance of twelve nautical miles measured from the appropriate base line.

N
1:1,500,000
SCALE
0 5 10 15 20 25 Miles
0 5 10 15 20 25 30 35 40 45 50 Kms
A
B
C
D
1
2
3
4
5
6
52
60
KAWR
Innanje
Padubidri
Chikmagalur
Mulki
Thokur - Panumbur & Thokur - Kankanadi proposed to be handed over to KRCL
Suratkal
Thokur
Suratpete Halt
Kankanadi Jn
Farangepetta Halt
Bantawala
Kallataka
Neralakatte Halt
Kabakaputtur
Narimogaru
Kaniuru Halt
Yedamangala Halt
Panambur
PGT
MYS
Mangalore
Mangalore Harbour
Netravathi H
Tokuttu Halt
Ullal
Shribagilu
Subramanya Rd
Kadimbala Halt
Bajakere Halt
Manjeshwar
Uppala
Kumbla
Kasaragod
Kalanad Halt
Kotikulam
Pallikere
Kanhangad
KODAGU HILLS
Madikere
WESTERN GHATS
Nileshwar
Charvattur
Chandera Halt
Trikarpur
Payyanur
Elimala
Payangadi
Kannapuram
Pappinisseri
Valapattinam
Chirakkal Halt
Cannanore
Cannanore South
Etakkot
Dharmadam Halt
Tellicherry
Jagannath Temple Gate
Mahe
Mukkali Halt
Nadapuram Rd Halt
Badagara
Iringal Halt
Payyoli
Tikkoti
Vellarakkad Halt
Quilandi
Elattur
Vellayil Halt
Kallayi
Kadalundi
Vallikunnu
Parpanangadi
Tanur
Arabian Sea
The territorial waters of India extend into the sea a distance of twelve nautical miles measured from the appropriate base line.

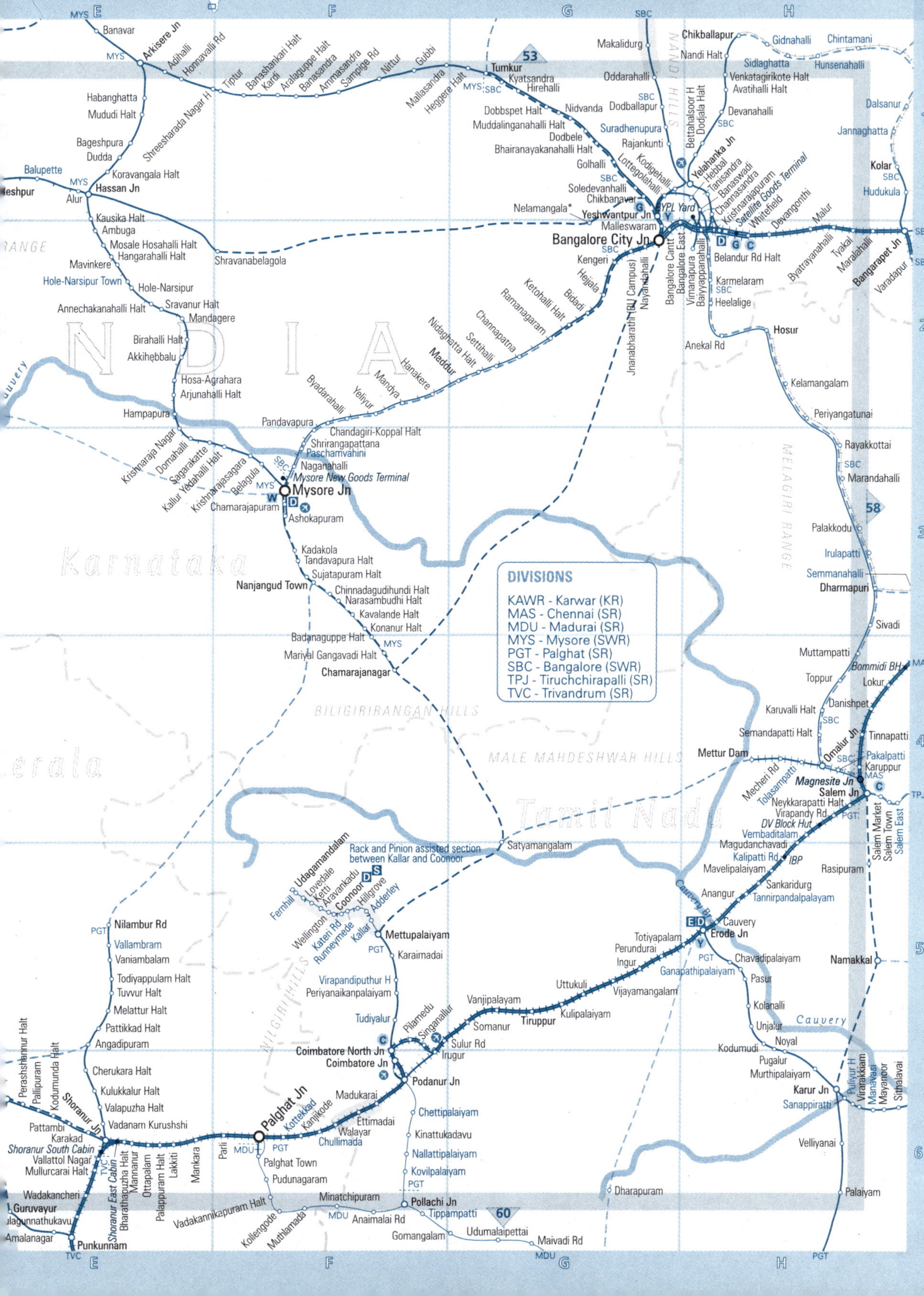
E
F
G
H
1
2
3
4
5
6
53
58
60
DIVISIONS
KAWR - Karwar (KR)
MAS - Chennai (SR)
MDU - Madurai (SR)
MYS - Mysore (SWR)
PGT - Palghat (SR)
SBC - Bangalore (SWR)
TPJ - Tiruchchirapalli (SR)
TVC - Trivandrum (SR)
INDIA
Karnataka
Kerala
Tamil Nadu
NANDI HILLS
MELAGIRI RANGE
BILIGIRIRANGAN HILLS
MALE MAHDESHWAR HILLS
NILGIRI HILLS
Cauvery
Rack and Pinion assisted section between Kallar and Coonoor
Banavar
Arkisere Jn
Adihalli
Honnavalli Rd
Tiptur
Banashankari Halt
Kardi
Aralaguppe Halt
Banasandra
Ammasandra
Sampige Rd
Nittur
Gubbi
Mallasandra
Heggere Halt
Tumkur
Kyatsandra
Hirehalli
Habanghatta
Mududi Halt
Shreesharada Nagar H
Bageshpura
Dudda
Koravangala Halt
Balupette
Hassan Jn
Alur
Kausika Halt
Ambuga
Mosale Hosahalli Halt
Hangarahalli Halt
Mavinkere
Shravanabelagola
Hole-Narsipur Town
Hole-Narsipur
Annechakanahalli Halt
Sravanur Halt
Mandagere
Birahalli Halt
Akkihebbalu
Hosa-Agrahara
Arjunahalli Halt
Hampapura
Krishnaraja Nagar
Dornahalli
Sagarakatte
Kallur Yedahalli Halt
Krishnarajasagara
Belagula
Mysore Jn
Chamarajapuram
Ashokapuram
Naganahalli
Mysore New Goods Terminal
Paschamvahini
Shrirangapattana
Chandagiri-Koppal Halt
Pandavapura
Byadarahalli
Yeliyur
Mandya
Hanakere
Maddur
Nidaghatta Halt
Settihalli
Channapatna
Ramanagaram
Ketohalli Halt
Bidadi
Hejjala
Kengeri
Jnanabharathi (BU Campus)
Nayandahalli
Bangalore City Jn
Malleswaram
Yeshwantpur Jn
Nelamangala*
Chikbanavar
Soledevanhalli
Golhalli
Lottegollahalli
Kodigehalli
Bhairanayakanahalli Halt
Dodbele
Muddalinganahalli Halt
Dobbspet Halt
Nidvanda
Dodballapur
Surdhenupura
Rajankunti
Oddarahalli
Makalidurg
Nandi Halt
Chikballapur
Bettahalsoor H
Dodjala Halt
Yelahanka Jn
Hebbal
Tanisandra
Banaswadi
Channasandra
Krishnarajapuram
Satellite Goods Terminal
Whitefield
Devangonthi
Malur
BYPL Yard
Bangalore Cantt
Bangalore East
Vimanapura
Baiyyappanahalli
Belandur Rd Halt
Karmelaram
Heelalige
Anekal Rd
Hosur
Byatrayanahalli
Tyakal
Maralahalli
Bangarapet Jn
Varadapur
Gidnahalli
Chintamani
Sidlaghatta
Hunsenahalli
Venkatagirikote Halt
Avatihalli Halt
Devanahalli
Dalsanur
Jannaghatta
Kolar
Hudukula
Kelamangalam
Periyangatunai
Rayakkottai
Marandahalli
Palakkodu
Irulapatti
Semmanahalli
Dharmapuri
Sivadi
Muttampatti
Bommidi BH
Lokur
Toppur
Danishpet
Karuvalli Halt
Semandapatti Halt
Tinnapatti
Pakalpatti
Karuppur
Mettur Dam
Omalur Jn
Magnesite Jn
Salem Jn
Mecheri Rd
Tolasampatti
Neykkarapatti Halt
Virapandy Rd
DV Block Hut
Vembaditalam
Magudanchavadi
Kalipatti Rd
IBP
Mavelipalaiyam
Sankaridurg
Tannirpandalpalayam
Anangur
Salem Market
Salem Town
Salem East
Rasipuram
Namakkal
Cauvery
Erode Jn
Totiyapalam
Perundurai
Ingur
Ganapathipalaiyam
Chavadipalaiyam
Pasur
Kolanalli
Unjalur
Noyal
Kodumudi
Pugalur
Murthipalaiyam
Karur Jn
Sanappiratti
Pulliyur H
Virarakkiam
Manavasi
Mayanoor
Sithalavai
Velliyanai
Palaiyam
Dharapuram
Uttukuli
Vijayamangalam
Kulipalaiyam
Tiruppur
Vanjipalaiyam
Somanur
Sulur Rd
Irugur
Singanallur
Pilamedu
Coimbatore North Jn
Coimbatore Jn
Podanur Jn
Madukarai
Ettimadai
Walayar
Chullimada
Kanjikode
Kottekkad
Palghat Jn
Palghat Town
Pudunagaram
Vadakannikapuram Halt
Kollengode
Muthlamada
Minatchipuram
Anaimalai Rd
Pollachi Jn
Tippampatti
Gomangalam
Udumalaipettai
Maivadi Rd
Kovilpalaiyam
Nallattipalaiyam
Kinattukadavu
Chettipalaiyam
Satyamangalam
Chamarajanagar
Mariyal Gangavadi Halt
Badanaguppe Halt
Konanur Halt
Kavalande Halt
Narasambudhi Halt
Chinnadagudihundi Halt
Nanjangud Town
Sujatapuram Halt
Tandavapura Halt
Kadakola
Udagamandalam
Lovedale
Ketti
Aravankadu
Coonoor
Hillgrove
Adderley
Fernhill
Wellington
Kateri Rd
Runneymede
Kallar
Mettupalaiyam
Karaimadai
Virapandiputhur H
Periyanaikanpalaiyam
Tudiyalur
Nilambur Rd
Vallambram
Vaniambalam
Todiyappulam Halt
Tuvvur Halt
Melattur Halt
Pattikkad Halt
Angadipuram
Cherukara Halt
Kulukkalur Halt
Valapuzha Halt
Vadanam Kurushshi
Perashshannur Halt
Pallipuram
Kodumunda Halt
Shoranur Jn
Pattambi
Karakad
Shoranur South Cabin
Vallattol Nagar
Mullurcarai Halt
Shoranur East Cabin
Bharathapuzha Halt
Mannanur
Ottapalam
Palappuram Halt
Lakkiti
Mankara
Parli
Wadakancheri
Guruvayur
Punkunnam
Amalanagar

N
1:1,500,000
SCALE
0 5 10 15 20 25 Miles
0 5 10 15 20 25 30 35 40 45 50 Kms
A
B
C
D
1
2
3
4
5
6
54
57
61
Andhra Pradesh
INDIA
Tamil Nadu
Pondicherry
JAVADI HILLS
SHEVAROY HILLS
Cauvery
see Chennai region Map
Doddanetta
Srinivaspur
Dalsanur
Jannaghatta
Kolar
SBC
Hudukula
Byatrayanahalli
Tyakal
Malur
BEML Nagar
Coromandel
Oorgaum
Champion
Marikuppam
Maralahalli
Bangarapet Jn
Varadapur
Kamasamudram
Bisanattam
Gudupulli
Kuppam
Mulanur
Jolarpettai A Cabin
Patchur
Somanayakkanpatti
Jolarpettai Jn
Jolarpettai B Cabin
Tirupattur
Periyangatunai
Krishnagiri
Kandikuppam
Bargur
Peria Kandili
Periagaram
Rayakkottai
Marandahalli
Palakkodu
Irulapatti
Semmanahalli
Ranimukkanur
Dharmapuri
Sivadi
Muttampatti
Karuvalli Halt
Toppur
Semandapatti Halt
Omalur Jn
Danishpet
Lokur
Bommidi
Bommidi BH
Buddireddipatti
Buddireddipatti BH
Thonganur Halt
Morappur
Doddampatti
Dasampatti
Samalpatti
Kunnattur Halt
Kagankarai
Molakarampatti
Tinnapatti
MAS
Karuppur
Magnesite Jn
Salem Jn
Pakalpatti
PGT
DV Block Hut
Virapandy Rd
Neykkarapatti Halt
Salem Market
Salem Town
Salem East
Rasipuram
Ayodhyapattinam Halt
Minnampalli
Seshanchavadi
Valappadi Gate Halt
Ettapur Rd
Peddanayakkanpalayam
Kalpaganur
Attur
Kattukottai
Sarvay
Talaivasal
Melnariyappanur Halt
Chinna Salem
Siruvattur Halt
Pukkiravari
Asakalattur
Kuttakudi
Damalcheruvu
GTL
Pakala Jn
Kottakota
Putalapattu
Chittoor
Siddampalli
Peyanapalli
Hamapuram
Bommasamudram
Thalangai
Latteri
Virinchipuram
Kavanur
Gudiyattam
Melathur
Valathoor
Katpadi Jn
Vellore Town Halt
Vellore Cantt
TPJ
Pennathur
Melpatti
Pachchakuppam
Ambur
Ambur IBH
Vinnamangalam
Vinnamangalam IBH
Vaniyambadi
Vaniyambadi IBH
Kettandapatti
Kaniyambadi
Kannamangalam
Onnupuram
Sedarampattu Halt
Arni Rd
Madimangalam
Polur
Kalasapakkam
Agaram Sibbandi Halt
Turinjapuram Halt
Tiruvannamalai
Velanandal
Tandarai
Andampallam
Adichchanur
Tirukkovilur
Mugaiyur Halt
Ayandur
Mambalapattu
Teli Halt
Venkatesapuram
Villupuram Jn
Kandambakkam
Tiruvennainallur Rd
Parikkal
Padur H
Ulundurpet
Meppuliyur
Puvanur
Mukhasa Parur
Vriddhachalam Town
Vriddhachalam Jn
Talanallur
Pennadam
Ichchangadu
Mathur
Ichchangadu Halt
Sendurai
Vellur Halt
Ottakovil
Ariyalur
Sillakkudi
Kallagam
Kallakkudi Palanganatham
Perambdur
Thuraiyur
Namakkal
Tiruvalam
Sevur
Mukundarayapuram
Walajah Rd Jn
Ranippettai
Arcot
Arani
Cheyyar
Vandavasi
MAS
Taduku
Puttur
Vepagunta
Ekambarakuppam
Nagari
Pallipattu
Venkatanarasimharajuvaripetta
Ponpadi
Tiruttani
Ichchiputtur
Arakkonam North Cabin
Melpakkam
Marudalam
Sholingur
Mahendravadi
Anvardikanpettai
Chitteri
Arakkonam West Cabin
Arakkonam Jn
Mosur
Tiruvalangadu
Manavur
Senjipanambakkam
Kadambattur
Egattur
Puliyamangalam
Takkolam
Tirumalpur
Kanchipuram
Nathapettai
Walajabad
Palayasivaram
Palur
Villiambakkam
Reddipalayam
Kanchipuram East
Sriperumbudur
Urapakkam
Potheri
Chengalpattu Jn
Tirumani
Ottivakkam
Padalam
Karunguzhi
Mahabalipuram
Madurantakam
Pakkam
Melmaruvathur
Acharapakkam
Tozhupedu
Karasangal
Olakur
Panchalam
Tindivanam
Mailam
Nedimoliyanur
Perani
Vikravandi
Mundiyambakkam
Kolianur
Valavanur
Pallinellianur
Chinnababu Samudram
Villianur
Pondicherry
Pondicherry Port
Semdanur
Thiruthuraiyur Halt
Nellikuppam
Karamanikkuppam H
Varakalpattu
Tiruppadirippuliyur
Cuddalore Port Jn
Panruti
Melpattambakkam
Kullanchavadi
Annavalli
Kurinjipadi
Vadalur
Neyveli
Uttangal Mangalam
Capper Quarry
Alapakkam
Puduchattiram
Parangipettai
Kille
Chidambaram
Vallampadugai Halt
Kollidam
Tirumayiladi
Arasur
Sirkazhi
Vaithisvarankoil
Anandatandavapuram
Nidur
Mayiladuturai Jn
Malliyam
Kutralam
Narasinganpet
Aduturai
Tiruvidaimarudur
Mayavaram Town
Mannampandal
Sembanarkoil
Akkur
Tirukkadaiyur
Tillaiyadi
Tarangambadi
Elantangudi
Manganallur H
Kollumangudi
Peralam Jn
Poraiyar
Ambagarattur
Tirunageswaram
Kumbakonam
Punthottam
Nannilam
Visalur
Patecoudy
Tirunalar
Karai-Kovilpathu
Karaikal
Nagore
Velippalaiyam
Nagapattinam Beach
Nagapattinam
Andanapettai Halt
Vailankanni
Virkudi
Kodikkalpalayam Halt
Thiruvarur Jn
Kadaramkondan H
Adiyakkamangalam
Haridranadhi
Mannargudi
Mavur Rd
Tirunellikaval
Kuthur Halt
Kizhvelur H
Sikkal
Elavur
Gummidipundi
Kavaraipettai
Ponneri
Anuppampattu
Minjur
Nandiyambakkam
Attipattu
Ennore
Wimco Nagar
Tiruvottiyur
Tiruvallur
Pattabiram
Avadi
Villivakkam
Mambalam
Guindy
Tambaram
Perungalattur
Vandalur
Guduvancheri
Kattangulathur
Maraimalai Kamarajar Nagar
Singaperumal Kovil
Paranur
Murthipalaiyam
Karur Jn
Sanappiratti
Virarakkam
Manavasi
Mayanoor
Sithalavai
Mahadanapuram
Lalapet
Timmachipuram Halt
Kulittalai
Marudur Halt
Pettaivaytalai
Perugamani
Tirupparaithurai H
Elamanur
Jiyapuram Halt
Mukkudi Halt
Muttarasanallur
Tiruchchirappalli Fort
Tiruchchirappalli Goods
Tiruchchirappalli Town
Tiruchchi Palakkarai
Srirangam
Uttamarkovil Halt
Pichchandarkovil
Valadi
Mandurai Halt
Puliyur H
Velliyanai
Palaiyam
Sirugamani H
Cauvery Br.
Tiruchchirappalli Jn
Ariyamangalam H
Sircarpalayam
Ponmalai (Golden Rock)
Thanjavur Jn
DW
Pudur H
Punggudi
Kolatur
Samudram
Manaparai
MDU
Udaiyanpatti
Kumaramangalam
Manjattidal
Tiruverumbur
Tondamanpatti
Solagampatti
Aiyanapuram
Budalur
Alakkudi
Pulliarpatti
Mariamman Kovil H
Saliyamangalam
Kudikadu
Ammapet
Koyilvenni H
Nidamangalam Jn
Koradacheri
Tirumathikkunam
Kulikarai
Lalgudi
Kattur
Pullambadi
Sundaraperumal Koil
Papanasam
Pandaravadai
Ayyampet
Pasupathikoil
Titte
Vadavar
Rajappayyan Chavadi
Swamimalai
Darasuram
Tondaman Nallur
E
W
C
D
G
Y

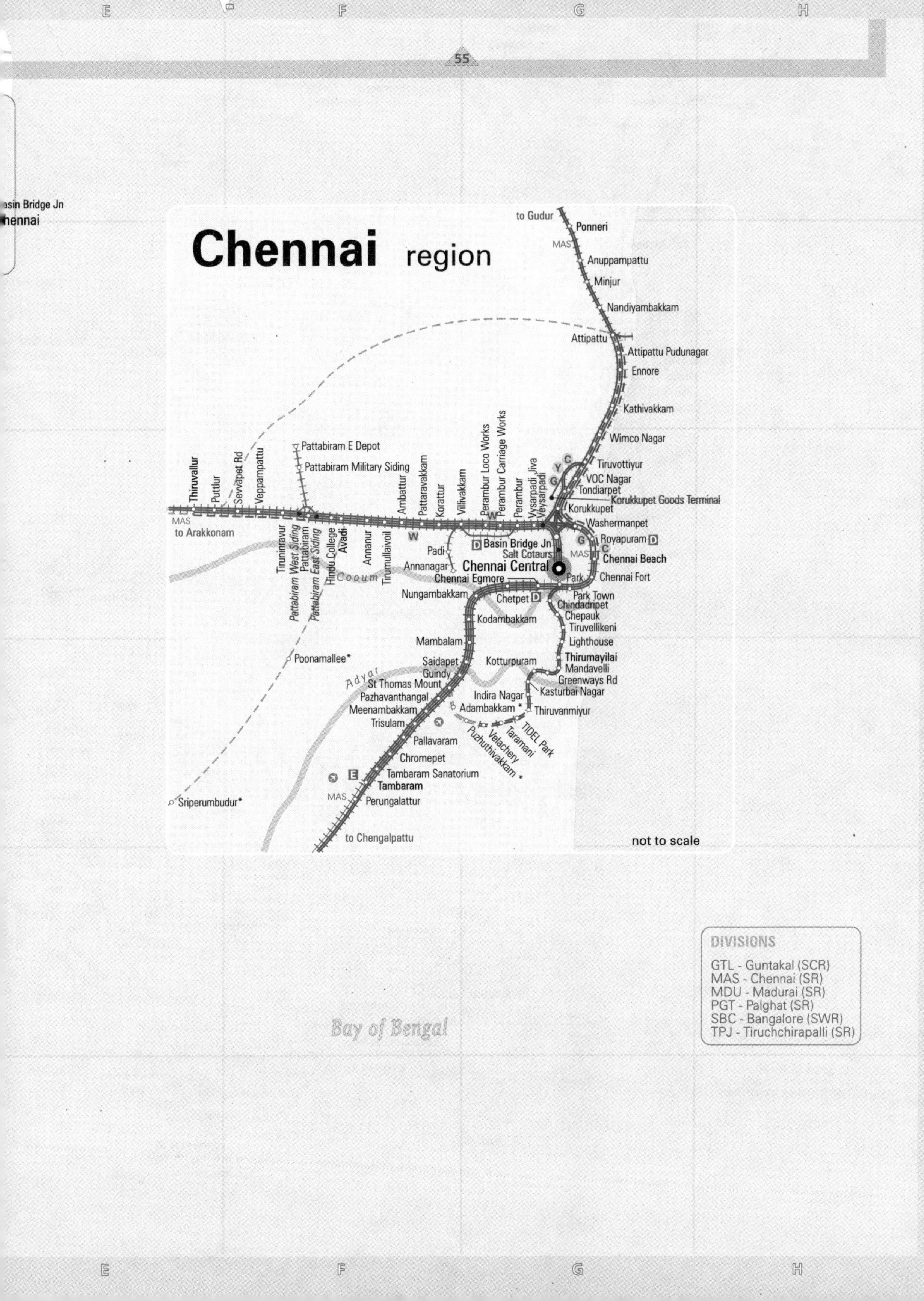

DIVISIONS

GTL - Guntakal (SCR)
MAS - Chennai (SR)
MDU - Madurai (SR)
PGT - Palghat (SR)
SBC - Bangalore (SWR)
TPJ - Tiruchchirapalli (SR)

N
1:1,500,000
SCALE
0 5 10 15 20 25 Miles
0 5 10 15 20 25 30 35 40 45 50 Kms
A
B
C
D
1
2
3
4
5
6
PGT
TVC
PGT MDU
PGT
MDU
57
Vallattol Nagar
Mullurcarai Halt
Wadakancheri
Mulagunnathukavu
Guruvayur
Amalanagar
Punkunnam
Trichur
Kanimangalam H
Ollur
Pudukkad
Nellayi
Irinjalakuda
Chalakudi
Divine Nagar Halt
Koratti Angadi Halt
Karukutty
Angamali
Chovvara
Alwaye
Kalamasseri
Idapalli
Ernakulam Goods
Ernakulam Town
Vallarpadam
Ernakulam Jn
ERS C Cabin
ERS D Cabin
Cochin Pier
Cochin Harbour Terminus
Mattancheri Halt
Tripunittura
Kurikad Halt
Mulanturutti
Kanjiramittam
Piravam Rd
Kumbalam
Arur Halt
Ezhuppunna
Tirunettur
Perumanur H
Thuravur
Vayalar
Vaikam Rd
Vaikam
Kaduturutti Halt
Kuruppantara
Shertalai
Tiruvizha
Ettumanur
Mararikulam
Kalavur Halt
Kumaranallur Halt
Kottayam
Tumboli Halt
Chingavanam
Ittittanam
Erumeli
Alleppey
Changanacheri
Punnapra
Nalukody
Ambalapuzha
Tiruvalla
Odara
Chengannur
Takazhi
Karuvatta Halt
Cheriyanad
Haripad
Mavelikara
Cheppad
Sabarimalai
Kayankulam Jn
Ochira
Karunagapalli
Sasthankotta
Munrothuruttu Halt
Ezhukone
Kottarakara
Kuri Halt
Avaneeswarem
Punalur
Edamann
Ottakkal
Tenmalai
Kalthuruthy Halt
Bhagavathipuram
Sengottai
Perinad
Kilikollur
Kundara East Halt
Kundara
Chandanattop Halt
Quilon Jn
Ashramam Maidan
Iravipuram Halt
Mayyanad
Paravur
Edapalayam Halt
Aryankavu
Kappil
Edavai
Varkala
Kadakavur
Akathumuri Halt
Chirayinkil
Perunguzhi Halt
Murukkampuzha
Kaniyapuram
Kazhakuttam
Veli Halt
Kochuveli
Trivandrum Pettah
Trivandrum Central
Nemam Halt
Balaramapuram
Neyyattinkara
Amaravilla Halt
Dhanuvachapuram Halt
Parassala
Kulitturai West Halt
Kulitturai
Palliyadi Halt
Eraniel
Virani Alur
Nagercoil Town Halt
Nagercoil Jn
Suchindram H
Tamrakulam H
Agastiswaram H
Kanniyakumari
Palghat Town
Pudunagaram
Minatchipuram
Vadakannikapuram Halt
Kollengode
Muthalamada
Anaimalai Rd
Nallattipalaiyam
Kovilpalaiyam
Pollachi Jn
Tippampatti
Gomangalam
Udumalaipettai
Pulankinar
Maivadi Rd
Madathukulam H
Pushpattur
Dharapuram
Palani
Kanakkanpatti
Chatrappati
Oddanchatram
Palakkanuth
Reddiarchatram
Akkaraipatti
PALANI HILLS
ANAIMALAI HILLS
Anapantham
Parambikulam
KUNDALA VALLEY RAILWAY
Buchanan
Kundala
Top Station
Munnar
Mattupetti
Kodaikanal Rd
I N D
Vaigai
Bodinayakkanur
Teni
Collectorate
Vallanadi Rd
Andipatti
Doddappanayakkanur
Nagamalai West Ha
Vadapalanji Ha
Karumathur Ha
Usilampatti
Sikkampatti
ENAMALAI HILLS
Periyar
Kerala
Arabian Sea
Ramakrishnapuram
Srivilliputtur
Sankarilingapuram
Tirutthangal
Sivakasi
Vaithilingapuram
Rajapalayam
Tulukapat
Veppilaipatti Chattiram
Cholapuram
Satur
Karivalam Vandanallur
Nalli
Sankarankovil
Kovilpatti
Pambakovil Shandy
Nalattinputtur
Kadayanallur
Kumarapuram
Nainaragaram
Kurumalai
Tenkasi Jn
Kizhapuliyur
Kadambur
Pavurchutram
Ilavelangal
ENAIMALAI HILLS
Mettur
Vanchi Maniyachchi Jn
Naraikkinar
Kilakkadaiyam
Ravanasamudram
Azhwarkurichi
Kizha Ambur Halt
Ambasamudram
Kallidaikurichi
Viravanallur
Karaikurichchi Halt
Cheranmahadevi
Melakallur
Pettai
Tirunelveli Town
Gangaikondan
Talaiyuthu
Tirunelveli Jn
Palayankottai
Srivaikuntam
Melappalayam Halt
Kurichchi
Sengulam
Seydunganallur
Thathankulam
ASHAMBU HILLS
Nanguneri
Dalapathisamudram
Valliyur
N Panakudi Halt
Kavalkinaru H
Aralvaymoli
Tovalai
Tisaiyanvilai
Indian Ocean
The territorial waters of India extend into the sea a distance of twelve nautical miles measured from the appropriate base line.

DIVISIONS
MDU - Madurai (SR)
PGT - Palghat (SR)
TPJ - Tiruchchirapalli (SR)
TVC - Trivandrum (SR)
E
F
G
H
1
2
3
4
5
6
MDU
TPJ
58
Tiruchchirapalli Jn
Ponmalai (Golden Rock)
Pudur H
Punggudi
Kolatur
Samudram
Udaiyanpatti
Kumaramangalam
Manjattidal
Tiruverumbur
Tondamanpatti
Solagampatti
Aiyanapuram
Budalur
Alakkudi
Vadavar
Titte
Pulliarpatti
Thanjavur Jn
Nidamangalam Jn
Tirumathikkunam
Koradacheri
Kulikarai
Virkudi
Kodikkalpalayam H
Kadaramkondan H
Nagore
Velippalaiyam
Nagapattinam Beach
Nagapattinam
Vailankanni
Rajappayyan Chavadi
Mangudi
Mavur Rd
Tirunellikaval
Ammanur
Alattambadi
Manali Halt
Adiyakkamangalam
Kuthur Halt
Kizhvelur Halt
Sikkal
Andanapettai Halt
Mariamman Kovil Halt
Kudikadu
Saliyamangalam
Ammapet
Koyilvenni Halt
Haridranadhi
Mannargudi
Palaiyam
Manaparai
Elangakurichi
Chettiyapatti
Eriodu
Kalpattichatram
Vaiyampatti
Ayyalur
Thangamapatti
Vadamadura
Tamaraipadi
Dindigul Jn
Vellodu
mbaturai
Tamil Nadu
Tondaman Nallur
Keeranur
Narthamalai
Vellannur
Pudukkottai
Namanasamudram
Tirumayam
Nemaththanpatti H
Chettinad
Kottaiyur
Kadanur Puduvayal
Devakottai Rd
Karaikkudi Jn
Anattidal H
Aranmanai Siruvayal H
Kallal
Panangudi
Nattarasankottai
Sivaganga
Nedungulam
Melakkonnakulam
Manamadurai East
Manamadurai Jn
Idaiyar
Arantangi
Valaramanikkam Halt
Periyakottai Rd
Ayingudi
Merppanaikkadu
Peravurani
Tiruchchittrambalam
Ottankadu
Pattukottai
Rajamatam Rd
Adirampattinam
Mutupet
Tillaivilagam
Pandi Halt
Nedumbalam
Tirutturaipundi Jn
Adirangam
Sundaram
Thambikkottai
Maravakkadu
Melamarudhur
Tennampalam
Neyvilakku
Kariyapattinam
Kuravapulam
Yadhavapuram
Topputhurai
Vedaranyam
Agasthiampalli
Kodikkarai
ipatti
Karupatti
Sholavandan
Samayanallur
Kudal Nagar
Madurai Bridge
Madurai Jn
Parsumalai
Madurai East
ppalur
Silaiman
Tiruparankundram
Tiruppuvanam
Thirumangalam
Tiruppachetti
Sivarakottaii
Muttanendal
Rajagambiran Halt
Kalligudi
Kokkalanjeri
Virudunagar Jn
Kadambankulam Halt
Mallankinar H
Narikkudi
lakarai
Aruppukottai
Tiruchchuli
Sudiyur
Vaigai
Kamudakkudi
Paramakkudi
Pandikanmoi Halt
Sattirakkudi
Uttarakosamangai
Ramanathapuram
Valantaraval
Uchippuli
Pirappanvalasai
Mandapam Camp Halt
Mandapam
Thangachimadam
Pamban Br.
Pamban
Rameshwaram Port
Rameshwaram
Rameshwaram Rd
Kothandaramankoil
Dhanushkodi Halt
Dhanushkodi Pier
Bay of Bengal
asapuram
Tattaparai
Milavittan
Tuti-Melur
Tuticorin
Kurumbur
Arumuganeri
Kayalpattinam
Nallur Rd
Adaikalapuram
Virapandiyanpattanam H
Tiruchendur
lasekharapatnam

India

Rail Network Map of 1893

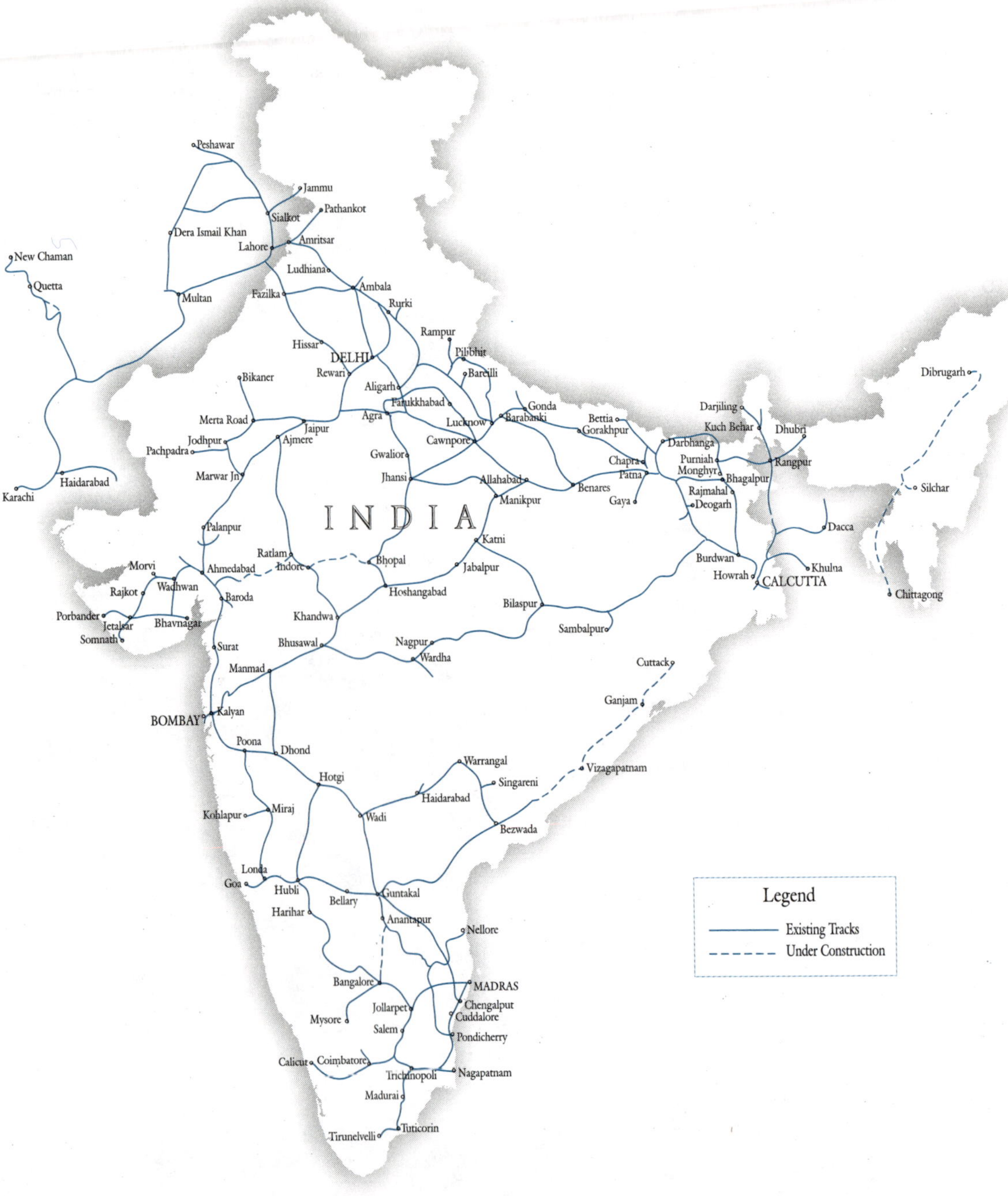

* *based on a map of unknown origin*

Narrow Gauge in South Bengal
Old & Present Routes

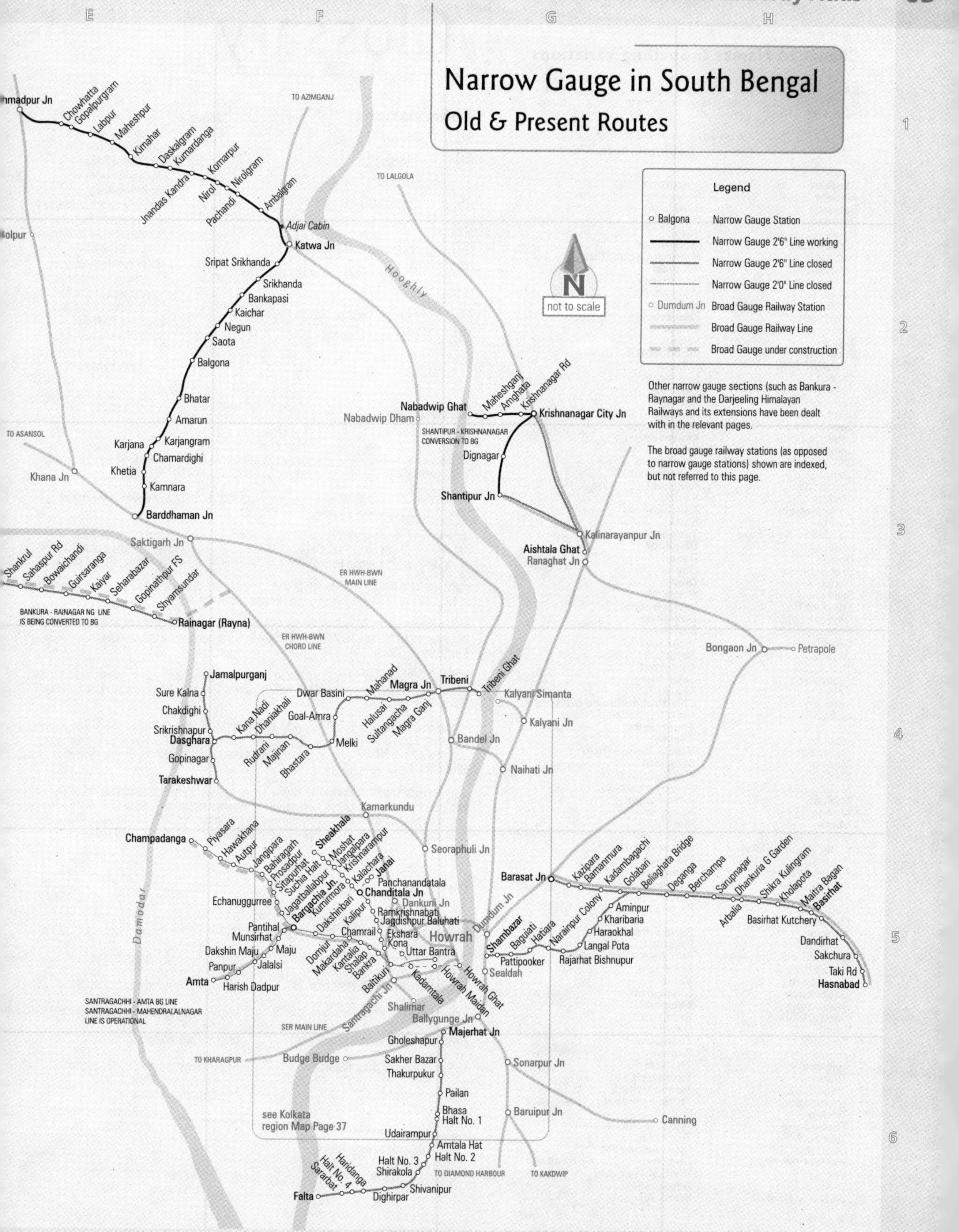
E
F
G
H
1
2
3
4
5
6
Legend
Balgona Narrow Gauge Station
Narrow Gauge 2'6" Line working
Narrow Gauge 2'6" Line closed
Narrow Gauge 2'0" Line closed
Dumdum Jn Broad Gauge Railway Station
Broad Gauge Railway Line
Broad Gauge under construction
Other narrow gauge sections (such as Bankura - Raynagar and the Darjeeling Himalayan Railways and its extensions have been dealt with in the relevant pages.
The broad gauge railway stations (as opposed to narrow gauge stations) shown are indexed, but not referred to this page.
N
not to scale
TO AZIMGANJ
TO LALGOLA
Hooghly
Damodar
TO ASANSOL
ER HWH-BWN MAIN LINE
ER HWH-BWN CHORD LINE
SHANTIPUR - KRISHNANAGAR CONVERSION TO BG
BANKURA - RAINAGAR NG LINE IS BEING CONVERTED TO BG
SANTRAGACHHI - AMTA BG LINE
SANTRAGACHHI - MAHENDRALALNAGAR LINE IS OPERATIONAL
SER MAIN LINE
TO KHARAGPUR
TO DIAMOND HARBOUR
TO KAKDWIP
see Kolkata region Map Page 37
nmadpur Jn
Chowhatta
Gopalpurgram
Labpur
Maheshpur
Kirnahar
Daskalgram
Kumardanga
Jnandas Kandra
Niroi
Komarpur
Nirolgram
Pachandi
Ambalgram
Adjai Cabin
Bolpur
Katwa Jn
Sripat Srikhanda
Srikhanda
Bankapasi
Kaichar
Negun
Saota
Balgona
Bhatar
Amarun
Karjana
Karjangram
Chamardighi
Khetia
Kamnara
Khana Jn
Barddhaman Jn
Saktigarh Jn
Shankrul
Sahaspur Rd
Bowaichandi
Guirsaranga
Kaiyar
Seharabazar
Gopinathpur FS
Shyamsundar
Rainagar (Rayna)
Nabadwip Ghat
Nabadwip Dham
Maheshganj
Amghata
Krishnanagar Rd
Krishnanagar City Jn
Dignagar
Shantipur Jn
Kalinarayanpur Jn
Aishtala Ghat
Ranaghat Jn
Bongaon Jn
Petrapole
Jamalpurganj
Sure Kalna
Chakdighi
Srikrishnapur
Dasghara
Gopinagar
Tarakeshwar
Kana Nadi
Dhaniakhali
Rudrani
Majinan
Bhastara
Dwar Basini
Goal-Amra
Melki
Halusai
Sultangacha
Magra Ganj
Mahanad
Magra Jn
Tribeni
Tribeni Ghat
Kalyani Simanta
Kalyani Jn
Bandel Jn
Naihati Jn
Kamarkundu
Champadanga
Piyasara
Hawakhana
Autpur
Jangipara
Bahiragarh
Prosadpur
Sitapurhat
Suchia Halt
Sheakhala
Moshat
Vangaipara
Krishnarampur
Kalachara
Janai
Seoraphuli Jn
Jagatballavpur
Bargachia Jn.
Kumirmora
Panchanandatala
Chanditala Jn
Dankuni Jn
Echanuggurree
Dakshinbari
Kalipur
Ramkrishnabati
Jagdishpur Baluhati
Pantihal
Munsirhat
Dakshin Maju
Maju
Panpur
Jalalsi
Amta
Harish Dadpur
Domjur
Makardaha
Kantalia
Shalap
Bankra
Chamrail
Ekshara
Kona
Uttar Bantra
Howrah
Baltikuri
Kadamtala
Howrah Maidan
Howrah Ghat
Santragachi Jn
Shalimar
Dumdum Jn
Shambazar
Baguiati
Hatiara
Narainpur Colony
Pattipooker
Rajarhat Bishnupur
Langal Pota
Haraokhal
Kharibaria
Aminpur
Sealdah
Barasat Jn
Kazipara
Bamanmura
Kadambagachi
Golabari
Beliaghata Bridge
Deganga
Berchampa
Sarupnagar
Arbalia
Dhankuria G Garden
Shikra Kulingram
Kholapota
Maitra Bagan
Basirhat
Basirhat Kutchery
Dandirhat
Sakchura
Taki Rd
Hasnabad
Ballygunge Jn
Majerhat Jn
Gholeshapur
Budge Budge
Sakher Bazar
Thakurpukur
Pailan
Bhasa
Halt No. 1
Udairampur
Amtala Hat
Halt No. 2
Halt No. 3
Shirakola
Shivanipur
Dighirpar
Haridanga
Halt No. 4
Sararbat
Falta
Sonarpur Jn
Baruipur Jn
Canning

Glossary

Change of Names & Spelling Variations

Spellings of names have evolved over the years. Some of the ones reflected below are ancient. The Railways do not necessarily use the newest spellings. The list includes both changes in spellings of towns and railway stations.

The column on the left has the old name/spelling while on the right, the newer name/spelling. The versions currently used by the Railways are in bold.

Alleppey	Alappuzha
Alwaye	Aluva
Balasore	Baleshwar
Baroda	**Vadodara**
Bassein	**Vasai**
Begumabad	**Modinagar**
Bellasis Road	**Mumbai Central (local)**
Benares	**Varanasi**
Berhampur	**Brahmapur**
Bezwada	**Vijayawada**
Bombay	**Mumbai**
Bowringpet	**Bangarapet**
Broach	**Bharuch**
Bulsar	**Valsad**
Burdwan	**Barddhaman**
Calcutta	**Kolkata**
Calicut	Kozhikode
Callian	**Kalyan**
Cambay	**Khambat**
Campoolie	**Khopoli**
Cannanore	Kannur
Cape Comorin	**Kanyakumari**
Cawnpore	**Kanpur**
Chicacole	**Srikakulam**
Chingleput	**Chengalpattu**
Cocanoda	**Kakinada**
Cochin	Kochi
Conjeewaram	**Kanchipuram**
Coorla	**Kurla**
Cuddalore New Town	**Tiruppadirippuliyur**
Dholpur	**Dhaulpur**
Dhond	**Daund**
Dronachellam	**Dhone**
Dhulia	**Dhule**
Ellichpur	**Achalpur**
Erinpura Rd	**Jawai Bandh**
Gauhati	**Guwahati**
Gotegaon	**Shridham**
Goya Gate	**Vishvamitri**
Jagatpur	**Nergundi**
Jhalukbari	**Kamakhya**
Jullunder	**Jalandhar**
Kirkee	**Khadki**
Kohlapur	**Chhattrapati Shahu Maharaj T.**
Koliwada	**Guru Teg Bahadur Nagar**
Luz	**Thirumayilai**
Madras	**Chennai**
Maniyachi	**Vanchi Maniyachchi**
Margao	**Madgaon**
Mayuram	**Mayiladuturai**
McDonalds Choultry	**Magudanchavadi**
Mihijam	**Chittaranjan**
Munger	**Monghyr**
Muttra	**Mathura**
Olavakkot	**Palghat Jn**
Ootacamund (Ooty)	**Udagamandalam**
Palghat	Palakkad
Point Calimere	**Kodikkarai**
Pokhran Road	**Ashapura Gomat**
Poona	**Pune**
Porto Novo	**Parangipettai**
Quilon	Kollam
Ramnad	**Ramnathapuram**
Ropar	**Rupnagar**
Sanvordem Curchorem	**Kudchade (Sanvordem)**
Serampore	**Srirampur**
Sewagram	**Varud**
Shencottah	**Shengottai**
Shrirampur	**Belapur**
Sone East Bank	**Sonnagar**
Tabiji	**Daurai**
Tanjore	**Thanjavur**
Tannah	**Thane**
Tellicherry	**Thalasseri**
Tinnevely	**Tirunelveli**
Tranquebar	**Tarangambadi**
Trichinopoly	**Thiruchchirapalli**
Trichur	Trissur
Trivandrum	Thiruvananthapuram
Trivellore	**Tiruvallur**
Ultadanga Rd	**Bidhannagar Rd**
Victoria Terminus	**Chhatrapati Shivaji Terminus**
Waltair	**Vishakhapatnam**
Wardha East	**Sevagram**
Welseley Ganj	**Waris Aleganj**

Abbreviations

BG	Broad Gauge
BH	Block Hut
Br.	Bridge
Cantt	Cantonment
H	Halt
IBP	Intermediate Block Post
IBS	Intermediate Block Section
Jn	Junction
MG	Metre Gauge
NG	Narrow Gauge

Zones:

CR	Central Railway
ECR	East Central Railway
ECoR	East Coast Railway
ER	Eastern Railway
KR	Konkan Railway
NCR	North Central Railway
NER	North Eastern Railway
NFR	Northeast Frontier Railway
NR	Northern Railway
NWR	North Western Railway
SCR	South Central Railway
SECR	Southeast Central Railway
SER	South Eastern Railway
SR	Southern Railway
SWR	South Western Railway
WCR	West Central Railway
WR	Western Railway

Resources

Timetables:

Newman's Indian Bradshaw, published quarterly; available at many railway stations - W Newman & Co., 3 Old Court House Street, Calcutta 700 069 India.

Trains at a Glance, published every year; available at railway stations. Ministry of Railways, Government of India.

India by Rail, by Royston Ellis, a comprehensive guide to railway travel in India. 1st ed. 1989, 3rd ed. 1997, ISBN 1-898323-49-6, Bradt Travel Guides, Bradt Publications (UK), or The Globe Pequot Press (USA, 1997), or Hunter (USA, 1987 1st ed.)

Railways of India, by J N Westwood, A concise and comprehensive history of railways in India. ISBN 0-7153-6295-X David & Charles : Newton Abbot, 1975

Indian Railways, by M A Rao, General overview of IR, some pictures and interesting material on IR history. ISBN 81-237-2589-2, National Book Trust of India, New Delhi, 1975 (3rd edition, 1999)

History of Indian Railways: Constructed and in progress, periodical (annual), till c.1960, not available now. Government of India, Railway Department (Railway Board) Simla, Government of India Press

Alphabetical List of Indian Railway Stations, by M. K. Jain Subtitled: All-Indian Railway Distance Table and Code Book. Contains an extensive list of stations with their codes, distances from New Delhi, and route information. 1997 (?) Prince Publication, G. T. Road, Shahdara, New Delhi, INDIA

Alphabetical List of Railway Stations in India, Contains a comprehensive list of passenger and goods stations, sidings, cabins, etc. Published irregularly every few years. The last one was published in 1995.(?) Published by the Indian Railway Conference Association. Available from offices of the Chief Commercial Managers of the zonal railways.

Online Resources:

The Indian Railways Fan Club Mailing List. http://irfca.org
Here you will find an incredible range of information on the Indian Railways.

Indian Railways FAQ: Bibliography	http://irfca.org/faq/faq-books.html
Indian Railways FAQ: History of IR	http://irfca.org/faq/faq-hist.html
Indian Railways FAQ: Research into IR	http://irfca.org/faq/faq-research.html
Links to various Railways websites	http://shankaronline.com
Indian Railways Official Site	http://www.indianrailways.gov.in
Railway Board	http://rb.railnet.gov.in

Chief Public Relations Officer
Indian Railways
Rail Bhavan

Index

Separate Index on Page 84 for Metro Stations and Bridges & Tunnels.

Where Two Codes are given against a station, usually the first one is for the Broad Gauge section, and the second one for the Metre Gauge section.

* indicates proposed station
Closed stations are shown in Light Blue
Non-Commercial operational locations (such as block huts) are shown in **Dark Blue**.

A
A Cabin BH 50 B1 -
Abada 37 inset ABB
Abdullapur 9 G5 -
Abhaipur 24 C4 AHA
Abhanpur Jn 43 E2 AVP
Abhayapuri Assam 26 B2 AYU
Abohar 8 B5 ABS
Abu Rd 19 E5 ABR
Abutara Halt 25 H3 ABW
AB Jn Cabin 13 E6 -
Achalda 21 G1 ULD
Achalganj 22 B2 ACH
Achalpur 41 F1 ELP
Acharapakkam 58 D3 ACK
Acharya Narendra Dev Nagar 22 D1 ACND
Achegaon 40 C2 ACG
Achnera Jn 13 E AH
Achaura 24 B4 ACU
Adaikalapuram 61 E5 AQM
Adambakkam 59 inset *
Adapur 24 A1 ADX
Adarki 46 C2 AKI
Adarshnagar 19 H2 AHO
Adas Rd 29 H4 ADD
Adavali 46 B4 ADVI
Adderi Halt 52 C4 AEX
Adderley 57 F5 ADY
Adesar 29 E1 AAR
Adgaon Buzurg 41 E1 ABZ
Adharsatra 27 G1 AYS
Adhartal 32 D3 ADTL
Adhewada 29 F5 ADV
Adhikari 25 F2 ADQ
Adhinpur 22 D2 AHZ
Adhyatmik Nagar 13 E3 AKNR
Adichchanur 58 C3 ACN
Adihalli 53 E6 ADHL
Adilabad 41 G4 ADB
Adina 25 F5 ADF
Adipur Jn 28 C2 AI
Adirampattinam 61 G1 AMM
Adirangam 61 H1 ADC
Adisaptagram 36 B3, 37 inset ADST
Adityapur 35 F4 ADTP
Adiyakkamangalam 58 C6 AYM
Adjai Cabin 36 B2, 63 F2 -
Adoni 53 G2 AD
Adra Jn 35 G2 ADRA
Adraj Moti 29 G2 AJM
Adri Rd 38 B1 ADE
Aduturai 58 C6 ADT
Agar 31 E2 AGAR
Agaram Sibbandi Halt 58 B3 AGM
Agarpara 37 inset AGP
Agartala 37 G2 ATLA
Agas 29 H4 AGAS
Agasanhadlu 52 D5
Agasod 32 A1 AGD
Agasthiampalli 61 H2 AGX
Agastiswaram H 60 D6 AXM
Aghwanpur 13 G2 AWP
Agori Khas 23 F6 AGY
Agra Cantt Jn 13 E6 AGC
Agra City 13 E6 AGA
Agra East Bank Cabin 23 F6 AEB
Agra Fort 13 E6 AF
Agradwip 36 B2 AGAE
Agran Dhulgaon 47 E4 AGDL
Agroha 12 B1 *
Agsauli 13 F5 AUL
Agthori 26 D2 AGT
Ahera Halt 12 D2 AHQ
Aherwadi 47 F3 AHD
Ahilyapur Halt 23 G2 AHLR
Ahimanpur 23 E4 AHM
Ahiran 25 F6 AHN
Ahirauli Halt 15 F6 AHU
Ahju 9 F2 AHJU
Ahmadabad Jn 29 G3, 28 inset ADI
Ahmadpur Jn 36 A2, 63 E1 AMP, ADP
Ahmedgarh 9 E4 AHH
Ahmednagar 40 A5 ANG
Ahraura Rd 23 F5 ARW
Aigawan 14 A5 AIG
Ailam Halt 12 D2 AILM
Airoli 38 inset AIRL
Aishbagh Jn 22 B1 ASH
Aishtala Ghat 63 G3 -
Ait Jn 21 G3 AIT
Aithal 9 H6 ATMO
Aizawl 27 F6 *
Ajaibpur 13 E3 AJR
Ajanti 31 E5 ANI
Ajapur Rd 28 C2 AJPR
Ajerka 12 C4 AIA
Ajgain 22 B2 AJ
Ajhai 13 E5 AJH
Ajharail 25 F3 AHL
Ajit 19 E3 AJIT
Ajit Gill Matta Halt 8 C4 AJTM
Ajit Kheri 31 E3 AJKI
Ajitwal 8 D4 AJL
Ajjakollu 48 B6 AJK
Ajjampur 53 E5 AJP
Ajmer Jn 19 H2 AII
Ajni 42 A2 AJNI
Ajnod 31 E3 AJN
Ajwa 30 A4 AJW
Akaipur 36 C3 AKIP
Akalkot Rd 47 G3 AKOR
Akaltara 33 H5 AKT
Akanapet 48 C2 AKE
Akashi 34 D3 AKZ
Akathumuri Halt 60 B5 AMY
Akbarganj 22 C2 AKJ
Akbarnagar 24 D4 AKN
Akbarpur Jn 23 E2 ABP
Akela Hanspur Halt 14 A4 ALNP
Akividu 49 H5 AKVD
Akkampet 54 D6 AKAT
Akkaraipatti 60 D1 API
Akkihebbalu 57 E2 AKK
Akkur 58 D6 AKQ
Akkurti 54 C5 AKY
Akodia 31 F2 AKD
Akola Jn 41 E2 AK
Akolner 40 A6 AKR
Akona 22 A4 AKW
Akot 41 E2 AKOT
Akra 37 inset AOR
Akurdi 39 G6 AKRD
Alachor 9 E3 AEE
Alai 11 F5 ALAI
Alal 8 D5 ALAL
Alakkudi 58 B6 ALK
Alamanda 50 C2 ALM
Alambagh Cabin 22 B1 AMV
Alamnagar 22 B1 AMG
Alampur 29 F5 ALMR
Alampur Rd 54 A1 ALPR
Alandi 46 C1 ALN
Alapakkam 58 C4 ALP
Alattambadi 61 H1 ATB
Alau 29 F4 ALAU
Alawalpur 8 D3 AWL
Alawalpur Idrispur 12 D2 AIH
Aler 48 D3 ALER
Alewahi 42 B3 AWH
Algapur 27 E5 ALGP
Ali Sagar 48 B1 ALSR
Aliganj 13 G2 ALJ
Aligarh Jn 13 F4 ALJN
Alinagar Tola Halt 25 E3 ATX
Alindra Rd 29 H4 AIR
Alipurduar 25 H2 APD
Alipurduar Court 25 H2 APDC
Alipurduar Jn 25 H2 APDJ
Aliya Vada 28 C3 ALB
Aliyabad 47 F4 AYB
Allahabad City 22 D4 ALY
Allahabad Jn 22 D4 ALD
Alleppey 60 B3 ALLP
Alluru Rd 54 D4 AXR
Almatti 47 F5 LMT
Almau Halt 23 E4 ALMU
Alnavar Jn 52 C2 LWR
Alniya 20 B5 ALNI
Altagram 25 G1 ATM
Aluabari Rd 25 F2 AUB
Alur 57 E1 ALUR
Alwal 51 inset ALW
Alwar Branch Cabin 12 C5 -
Alwar Byepass Cabin N 12 C5 -
Alwar Jn 12 C5 AWR
Alwarthirunagari 60 D5 AWT
Alwaye 60 B2 AWY
Alyanapuram 58 B6 AYN
Amagura 43 F6 AGZ
Amala Halt 27 E5 ALO
Amala Khurd 31 F6 AMX
Amalanagar 60 A1 AMLR
Amalner 40 B1 AN
Amalpur 30 A4 AMLP
Amalsad 39 F2 AML
Aman Lodge 38 inset -
Amanwadi 41 E3 AMW
Amaravilla Halt 60 C5 AMVA
Amarda Rd 35 H6 ARD
Amargarh 30 C3 AGR
Amargol 52 C2 AGL
Amarpur Jorasi 12 B4 APJ
Amarpura 19 G2 APA
Amarpura Rathan Halt 11 G1 AMPR
Amarsar 29 E3 AXA
Amar Shaheed Jagdeo Prasad H 23 H4
Amarun 36 A3, 63 E2 ARNB
Amausi 22 B1 AMS
Ambagaon 43 F6 AGB
Ambagarattur 58 C6 ABT
Ambaji 19 E1 *
Ambala Cantt Jn 9 F5 UMB
Ambala City 9 F5 UBC
Ambalapuzha 60 B3 AMPA
Ambale 46 C1 ABLE
Ambalgram 36 A2, 63 F1 ABGM
Ambari (Deccan) 41 G4 ABX
Ambari Falakata 25 F1 ABFC
Ambarnath 39 F5 ABH
Ambasamudram 60 D5 ASD
Ambattur 59 inset ABU
Ambaturai 61 E2 ABI
Ambav 29 H3 AAV
Ambernath 38 inset ABH
Ambewadi 52 C2 AVA
Ambiapur 21 H2 AAP
Ambika Kalna 36 B3 ABKA
Ambika Rohina 47 H1 AMBR
Ambikapur 34 A3 *
Ambikeshwar 21 E2 ABE
Ambivli 39 F5, 38 inset ABY
Ambli Rd 29 G3, 28 inset ABD
Ambliyasan Jn 29 G2 UMN
Ambodala 43 H4 AMB
Ambuga 57 E2 ABV
Ambur 58 B2 AB
Ambur IBH 58 B2 AVBH
Amdara 33 E1 UDR
Amdi 42 A1 AMDI
Amethi 22 D3 AME
Amgaon 42 C1 AGN
Amghata 36 B3, 63 G2 AHT
Amguri Jn 17 E6 AGI
Amha-Pendapur H 24 B4
Amhera Halt 13 F2 ARH
Ami Rd 58 C2 ARV
Amila 23 F3 AMD
Amin 9 F6 AMIN
Amingaon 26 D2 AM
Aminpur 63 G5 -
Amjonga 26 B3 AMGA
Amla Jn 32 A5 AMLA
Amlai 33 F3 AAL
Amletha 30 A5 ALE
Amli 20 C3 AMLI
Amlo BH 35 F2 AMLO
Amlori Sarsar 23 H2 ALS
Ammanabrolu 54 D2 ANB
Ammanur 61 H1 AMNR
Ammapali 25 E4 AMPL
Ammapet 58 C6 AMT
Ammasandra 57 F1 AMSA
Ammuguda 48 C3, 51 inset AMQ
Amnapur 46 D4 ANQ
Amod 29 H5 AMOD
Amolwa 15 H6 AMO
Amram Rd 28 D3 ARO
Amravati 41 F2 AMI
Amravati Rd 41 F2 *
Amreli 29 E5 AE
Amreli Para 29 E5 AEP
Amritapura 53 E5 AMC
Amritsar Jn 8 C2 ASR
Amritvel 38 D1 AVL
Amroha 13 F2 AMRO
Amta 36 A4, 63 F5 AMTA
Amtala Hat 63 F6 -
Anaimalai Rd 60 C1 ANM
Anakapalle 50 C3 AKP
Anakhi 29 H5 ANKI
Anakhol 29 G2 AKL
Anand Jn 29 H4 ANND
Anand Vihar 15 inset ANVR
Anandapuram 52 C4 ANF
Anandatandavapuram 58 C5 ANP
Anandnagar Jn 15 F6 ANDN
Anandpur Sahib 9 F3 ANSB
Anangur 57 H5 ANU
Anant Paith 21 F3 AEH
Anantapur 53 H4 ATP
Anantarajupet 54 C5 ANE
Anantnag 7 G3 ANTG
Anapantham 60 B1 -
Anaparti 50 A5 APT
Anara 35 G2 ANR
Anas 30 C3 ANAS
Anas A Cabin 30 C3 ANAS'A'
Anas B Cabin 30 C3 ANAS'B'
Anattidal H 61 F2 ANZ
Anaval 39 G2 ANW
Anchalgaon 40 A4 ANCG
Ancheli 39 F2 ACL
Anchuri 35 G3 ANCR
Andal Jn 35 H2 UDL
Andapallam 58 C3 AND
Andanapettai Halt 58 D6 APE
Andheri 39 F5, 39 inset ADH
Andipatti 60 D2 ADPT
Andul 36 B4, 37 inset ADL
Anekal Rd 57 H2 AEK
Angadageri 47 F5 ANGR
Angadi 30 A3 AGCI
Angadipuram 57 E5 AAM
Angai 21 E1 AGE
Angalakuduru 49 F6 AKU
Angamali 60 B2 AFK
Angar 47 F2 AAG
Angar Ghat 24 B3 ARG
Angarpathra H 45 inset ANJE
Angua 35 H6 AGV
Angul 44 C2 ANGL
Anipur 27 E5 APU
Aniyali 29 E2 AYL
Anjangaon 41 F1 ANJ
Anjani 46 B3 ANO
Anjar 28 C2 AJE
Anji Shahabad 14 A5 AJI
Ankai 40 A3 ANK
Ankai-Killa 40 A3 AAK
Ankalav 29 H4 ALV
Ankleshwar Jn 29 H5 AKV
Ankola 52 B3 ANKL
Ankorah 23 G5 ANH
Ankushpur 23 F4 AKS
Annanagar 59 inset
Annanur 59 inset ANNR
Annavalli 58 C4 ANVL
Annavaram 50 B4 ANV
Annechakanahalli Halt 57 E2 ANC
Annigeri 52 D2 NGR
Anpara 33 H1 ANPR
Antah 20 C4 ATH
Antarjal 28 C2 -
Antoli 30 A4 ANL
Antri 21 F3 ARI
Antu 22 D3 ANTU
Anugrah Narayan Rd 23 H5 AUBR
Anupganj 22 C1 APG
Anupgarh 11 F1 APH
Anuppampattu 58 D1, 59 inset APB
Anuppur Jn 33 G3 APR
Anupshahr 12 A2 AUS
Anvardikanpettai 58 C1 AVN
Aonla 13 G4 AO
Appikatla 55 E1 APL
APMO 38 inset *
Apta 39 F6, 38 inset APTA
Ara 23 H4 ARA
Arabaghatta H 53 E5 ABGT
Arag 46 D4 ARAG
Arakkonam Jn 58 C1 AJJ
Arakkonam North Cabin 58 C1
Arakkonam West Cabin 58 C1 AJJW/C
Arakku 50 C2 ARK
Arakku Valley H 50 C2 -
Aralaguppe Halt 57 F1 ARGP
Aralvaymoli 60 D6 AAY
Arambakkam 54 D6 AKM
Aramda 28 B3 ARM
Arand 43 F2 ARN
Aranghata 36 B3 AG
Arangmahanadi 43 F2 ANMD
Aranmanai Siruvayal H 61 F2 ASVL
Arani 58 C2 *
Arantangi 61 F2 ATQ
Araon 13 F6 AON
Araria 25 E3 ARR
Araria Court 25 E3 ARQ
Arasalu 52 D5 ARU
Arasur 58 C5 ARS
Araul Makanpur 22 A1 ARL
Aravali Rd 46 B3 AVRD
Aravalli 49 H5 AVLI
Aravankadu 57 F5 AVK
Arbalia 63 H5 -
Archipathar Halt 17 E4 AVK
Arcot 58 C2 *
Areli Halt 14 A4 ARX
Arepalli 48 B6 ARPL
Argora 35 E3 AOR
Argul 44 D3 ARGL
Arigada 35 E2 AGVD
Ariyalur 58 B5 ALU
Ariyamangalam 58 B6 ARMG
Arjansar 11 G2 AS
Arjunahalli Halt 57 E2 ARNH
Arjuni 42 B2 AJU
Arkha 22 C3 ARKHA
Arnej 29 G4 AEJ
Arnetha 20 B4 ARE
Arni Rd 58 C2 ARV
Arniya 12 C6 ARNA
Arpinchla 7 G4 *
Arseni 14 B6 ASI
Arsikere Jn 53 E6 ASK
Arts College 51 inset ATC
Arumuganeri 61 E5 ANY
Arunachal Jn 27 F5 ARCL
Arunnagar 42 B2 ARNG
Aruppukottai 61 E3 APK
Arur Halt 60 B2 ROR
Arvi 41 G2 ARVI
Aryankavu 60 C4 AYV
Asafpura 13 G3 AFR
Asakalattur 58 B4 ACT
Asalpur Jobner 12 A6 JOB
Asan 12 D1 ASAN
Asanboni 35 F4 ASB
Asangaon 39 G4, 38 inset ASO
Asanoti 52 B3 AT
Asansol Jn 35 G2 ASN
Asansol Court 35 G2 -
Asaoti 12 D4 AST
Asara H 12 D2
Asarganj 24 D5 *
Asarma 29 H6 ASM
Asarva 29 G3, 28 inset ASV
Asaudah 12 D3 ASE
Ashapura Gomat Jn 10 D6 AQG
Ashokapuram 57 F3 AP
Ashoknagar 21 E6 ASKN
Ashoknagar Rd 36 B4 ASKR
Ashramam Maidan 60 B4 -
Ashtegaon 41 G1 *
Ashti 47 F2 AHI
Asifabad Rd 42 A5 ASAF
Asirgarh Rd 40 D1 AGQ
Aslana 32 C2 ANA
Aslaoda 31 E3 ASL
Aslu 12 A3 ASLU
Asnera 29 H5 AER
Asokhar 21 F2 AXX
Aspari 53 G2 ASP
Asranada 19 F2 AAS
Asthal Bohar 12 C2 ABO
Asvali 39 G4 AV
Aswapuram 49 G3 AWM
Ata 21 H3 ATA
Atamanda 13 H3 AMA
Atari 8 C2 ATT
Ataria 14 B6 AA
Atarra 22 B4 ATE
Ateli 12 C4 AEL
Atgaon 39 G4, 38 inset ATG
Athmal Gola 24 B4 ATL
Athsarai 22 C3 ASCE
Ati Malani 18 B3 ATNI
Atladara 29 H4 ATDA
Atrampur 22 D4 ARP
Atrauli Rd 13 F4 AUR
Atraura Halt 22 D4 ATRR
Atru 20 C5 ATRU
Attabira 44 A1 ATS
Attar 31 E5 ATR
Attili 49 H5 AL
Attipattu 58 D1, 59 inset AIP
Attipattu Pudunagar 59 inset AIPP
Attur 58 B4 ATU
Atul 39 F2 ATUL
Atwa Kursath 14 A6 ATKS
Atwa Muthia Halt 14 B6 ATWC
Aujuri 27 E2 AJRE
Aulenda 13 E6 AED
Aung 22 B2 AUNG
Aungaridham H 24 A5 -
Aunlajori Jn 35 F5 OND
Aunrihar Jn 23 F4 ARJ
Aunta 24 B4 ANAH
Aurahi 24 D3 AUI
Aurangabad 40 B4 AWB
Aurangnagar Halt 12 B2 AUN
Ausa Rd 47 G1 OSA
Autpur 36 A4, 63 F5 AUT
Auvaneeswarem 60 C4 AVS
Auwa 19 F3 AUWA

Avadi 58 D1, 59 inset AVD
Avantipora 7 G3 *
Avatihalli Halt 57 H1 AVT
Avidha 29 H5 AVH
Avikanagar 20 A2 AVR
Awagarh 13 F5 AWG
Awapur Halt 24 B2 APR
Awasani Halt 15 G6 AWS
Awatar Nagar 24 A3, 25 inset ATNR
Ayandur 58 C4 AYD
Ayingudi 61 G2 AYI
Ayodhya 22 D1 AY
Ayodhya Ghat 22 D1 AJG
Ayodhyapattinam Halt 58 A4 APN
Ayyalur 61 E1 AYR
Ayyampet 58 C6 AZP
Azamgarh 23 F3 AMH
Azamnagar Rd 25 E4 AZR
Azara 26 D2 AZA
Azhwarkurichi 60 C5 AZK
Azimganj City 36 B1 ACLE
Azimganj Jn 36 B1 AZ

B

B Cabin BH 50 B1 -
Baba Bakala Raiya Halt 8 D2 BRKR
Baba Bhagwan Ram H 23 F4 BBRM
Baba Lachmandass Puri Halt 13 G6 BBLK
Babaganj H 14 C4 BBJ
Babarpur 12 D1 BBDE
Baba Sodhai Nagar 8 D3 BBSL
Babatpur 23 E4 BTP
Babhnan 23 E1 BV
Babina 21 F4 BAB
Bablad 47 H4 BBD
Babra 29 E5 *
Babrala 13 F4 BBA
Babugarh 13 E3 BBO
Babulgaon 47 F3 BBV
Babupeth 42 A4 BUPH
Babupur Halt 14 C6 BBPR
Bachar 29 H5 BCHR
Bacheli 49 H1 BCHL
Bachhrawan 22 C2 BCN
Bachwara Jn 24 B4 BCA
Bad 13 E5 BAD
Badabandha 45 E3 BDBA
Badagara 56 D4 BDJ
Badakhandita 45 E3 BNKT
Badalpur 36 A6
Badami 47 F6 BDM
Badampahar 35 F5 BMPR
Badampudi 49 H5 BPY
Badanaguppe Halt 57 F4 BDGP
Badanahalu 53 H3 BDV
Badapadagaon 44 D3 -
Badarpur Ghat 27 E5 BPG
Badarpur Jn 27 E5 BPB
Badausa 22 B4 BUS
Baddi 9 E3 *
Baddowal 8 D4 BWZ
Badgam 7 G3 *
Badgaon Gujar 31 F6 BRGJ
Badhada 29 E6 BDHA
Badhal 12 A6 BDHL
Badhari Kalan 13 G5 BHK
Badhwabara 33 F3 BDWA
Badkulla 36 B3 BDZ
Badla Ghat 24 D4 BHB
Badlapur 39 F5, 38 inset BUD
Badli 12 D3, 15 inset BHD
Badmal 43 H3 BUDM
Badnapur 40 C4 BDU
Badnera Jn 41 F2 BD
Badodar 28 C6 BDDR
Badshahnagar 22 B1 BNZ
Badshahpur 22 D4 BSE
Badulipar 27 G1 BLPR
Badwasi 11 F5 BWS
Bagaha 15 G6 BUG
Bagalia 35 G3 BGA
Bagalkot 47 F6 BGK
Bagarpur Halt 13 F2 BGRP
Bagasra 28 D6 BAG
Bagbahara 43 F2 BGBR
Bagbazar 37 inset BBR
Bagdehi 34 C6 BEH
Bagdewadi 39 G6 BGWD
Bagdigi H 45 inset BEH
Bagdogra 25 F1 BORA
Bageshpura 57 E1 BGPA
Bagetar 27 F4 BF
Bagewadi 46 D5 BGWD
Bagha Bisnupur 23 G5 BCJ
Bagha Jatin 37 inset BGJT
Baghai Rd 22 C6 BGHI
Baghauli 14 A6 BGH
Baghi Bardiha 24 B5 BBF
Baghi Ghauspur 24 B5 BFX
Baghoikusa 23 H5 BHKH
Baghora 32 A1 BJQ
Baghpat Rd 12 D2 BPM
Baghra Rd 35 G5 BHRD
Bagila 36 B3 BGF
Baginadi 17 E5 BGND
Bagmar 31 F6 BMA
Bagnan 36 A4 BZN
Bagnapara 36 B3 BGRA
Bagra Tawa 31 H4 BGTA
Bagrakot 25 G1 BRQ
Bagri Sajjanpur 19 F3 BGX
Bagrinagar 19 F3 BQN
Bagthar 21 E1 BFG
Baguiati 63 G5 -
Bagula 36 B3 BGL
Bagumra 39 F1 BGMR
Bagwada 39 F3 BAGD
Bagwali 8 C5 BWR
Bah 21 F1 *
Bahadur Singhwala 9 E5 BSS
Bahadurgarh 12 D3 BGZ
Bahadurpur 36 B2 BPD
Bahadurpur Halt 13 H4
Bahalda Rd 35 F5 BDO
Bahanaga Bazar 45 F1 BNBR
Baharu 36 B5 BARU
Bahawal Bassi 8 B5 BFE
Bahelia Buzurg Halt 14 B4 BFV
Bahera 24 C3 *
Baheri 13 H3 BHI
Baheriya Rd 30 A4 BOA
Baherwan Halt 23 E4 BRWH
Bahi 22 B3 -
Bahilpurwa 22 B5 BIP
Bahira Kalibari 36 B4 BHKA
Bahiragarh 63 F5 BAGR
Bahirgachhi 36 B3 BHGH
Bahirkhanda 36 A4 BAHW
Bahirpuya 36 B5 BHPA
Bahjai 23 E4
Bahjoi 13 F3 BJ
Bahman Diwana 8 C5 BWX
Bahman Jyotia H 23 E1
Bahminiwala 8 B4 BVW
Bahmrauli 22 C4 BMU
Bahora Chandil 23 F4 BHCL
Bahraich 14 C5 BRK
Bahram 9 E3 BHM
Bahramghat 14 C6 BYG
Baidyabati 37 inset BBAE
Baidyanathdham 24 D6 BDME
Baihata 26 D2 BIZ
Baijnath Mandir Halt 9 F1 BJMR
Baijnath Paprola 9 F1 BJPL
Baijnathpur 24 D3 BYP
Baijnathpur Andoli 24 D2 VDNP
Baikunth 43 E1 BKTH
Baikunthpur Rd 33 H3 BRH
Bailey Rd H 25 inset
Bainchi 36 B3 BOI
Bainchigram 36 B3 BCGM
Bairagarh 31 G3 BIH
Bairagnia 24 A1 BGU
Baisgodam 20 B1 BSGD
Baiswara 22 B2 BSWA
Baitalpur 23 G2 BALR
Baitarani Rd 45 E2 BTV
Baiyyappanahalli 57 H2 BYPL
Bajakere Halt 56 D2 BAJE
Bajalata 7 G5 BLA
Bajana 29 F2 BAJN
Bajekan Halt 12 A1 BJKN
Bajpatti 24 B2 BJT
Bajpur 13 G2 BPZ
Bajranggarh 30 C3 BJG
Bajrangpura 29 F3 BRGP
Bajud 29 F5 BJUD
Bajwa 29 H4 BJW
Bakaina Halt 13 F2 BKNA
Bakal 42 D1 BAKL
Bakanian Bhaunri 31 G3 BJJ
Bakaspur 34 D3 BKPR
Bakayanwala 8 B5 BKWA
Bakhleta 32 D2 BOQ
Bakhrabad 35 H5 VKD
Bakhri 25 E4 BKHR
Bakhsha 23 E3 BKSA
Bakhtarnagar BH 35 H2 BQT
Bakhtiyarpur Jn 24 B4 BKP
Bakkas 22 C1 BKKS
Bakothi Khas 22 A1 KHSP
Bakra Rd 18 D4 BK
Bakrol 30 A4 BKRL
Bakshi ka Talab 22 B1 BKT
Baktal 31 G3 BKTL
Bakudi 25 E5 BKLE
Bakulha 23 H3 BKLA
Bala Rd 29 F3 BLRD
Balabhadrapuram 50 A5 BBPM
Balagarh 36 B3 BGAE
Balaghat Jn 32 D6 BTC
Balahpur H 24 C5
Balajan 26 A2 BLF
Balamau Jn 14 A6 BLM
Balanagar 48 C4 BABR
Balapalle 54 C5 BLPE
Balaramapuram 60 C5 BRAM
Balarambati 37 inset BLAE
Balasore 45 F1 BLS
Balauda Takun 31 E3 BLDK
Balawala 20 B1 BLWL
Balawali 13 F1 BLW
Baldana Rd 29 F3 BLDR
Bale 47 F3 BALE
Balenahalli 53 F4 BAHI
Balganur 52 D2 BLR
Balgona 36 A2, 63 E2 BGNA
Balgundi 52 C4 BGV
Balharshah Jn 42 A4 BPQ
Baliakheri 9 G6 BAE
Balichak 35 H5 BCK
Balikotia 27 C2 BKS
Balimara 17 F5 BTZ
Balipara Jn 16 B6 BVU
Ballabhgarh 12 D4 BVH
Ballalpur 25 F5 BQZ
Balle Da Pir Larath Halt 9 E1 BLDL
Ballekere Halt 53 E6 BLKR
Balli 52 B2 BLLI
Ballia 23 G3 BUI
Balluana 8 C5 BHX
Ballupur Halt 13 G5 BAPR
Bally 36 B4, 37 inset BLY
Bally Ghat 37 inset BLYG
Bally Halt 37 inset BLYH
Ballygunge Jn 36 B4, 37 inset BLN
Balod 42 D1 BXA
Balotra Jn 18 D2 BLT
Balpur 33 H5 BPRH
Balrai 21 G1 BBL
Balrampur 14 D6 BLP
Balsamand 11 H5 BLSD
Balsiring 35 E3 BLRG
Baltikuri 37 inset, 63 F5 BLTR
Balugaon 44 C4 BALU
Balupette 57 E1 BLLT
Balurghat 25 G4 BGTO
Balwa 28 C5 WAB
Balwantpura 12 A4 BWPA
Balwara 18 D3 BAWA
Bamangachi 36 B4, 37 inset BMG
Bamangram Halt 25 F4 BMGR
Bamanhat 25 H3 BXT
Bamanheri 13 E1 BMHR
Bamani 47 E3 BMNI
Bamankuwa 30 A4 BMX
Bamanmura 63 G5 -
Bamanwali 11 F3 BMNL
Bamhani 42 A2 BMW
Bamhani Bajhar 32 D4 BIV
Bamiana 13 G4 BMY
Bamla 12 C2 BMLL
Bamnia 30 C3 BMI
Bamouragaon 21 E2 BMZ
Bamra 34 C5 BMB
Bamsin 18 D3 BMSN
Bamunigaon 26 C2 BMGN
Bamur 44 B1 BAMR
Banahi 23 H4 BYN
Banapura 31 G4 BPF
Banar 19 E2 BNO
Banarhat 25 G1 BNQ
Banas 19 E5 BNS
Banasandra 57 F1 BSN
Banashankari Halt 57 F1 BNK
Banasthali Niwai 20 B2 BNLW
Banaswadi 57 H1 BAND
Banavar 53 E6 BVR
Banbasa 14 A2 BNSA
Banbihari Gwalipur 45 E3 BNHR
Banchari 12 D4 BNCR
Band Hamirpur Halt 22 B2 BAHP
Banda 22 A4 BNDA
Bandakpur 32 C2 BNU
Bandanwara 19 H2 BDW
Bandarkhal 27 F4 BXK
Bandarupalli 49 F6 BDPL
Bandel Jn 36 B3, 37 inset BDC
Bandh Bareta 20 D1 BR
Bandhdih 45 inset BDIH
Bandhnath 28 D6 BNTH
Bandhua 24 A5 BNF
Bandhua Kalan 22 D2 BDKN
Bandikui Jn 12 C6 BKI
Bandra 39 F5, 38 inset BA
Bandra Terminus 39 F5, 38 inset BDTS
Baneswar 25 H2 BSW
Banga 9 E3 BXB
Bangain 14 D6 BGAN
Bangalbaree 25 F4 BJY
Bangalore Cantt 57 G2 BNC
Bangalore City Jn 57 G2 SBC
Bangalore East 57 G2 BNCE
Bangarapet Jn 58 A2 BWT
Bangari Halt 24 A2 BGAR
Bangarmau 22 A1 BGMU
Bangi Nihalsingh 8 C5 BNLS
Bangriposi 35 G5 BGY
Bangrod 30 D2 BOD
Bangurgram 19 G2 BNGM
Bangurkela 34 D5 BGKA
Bani 22 C2 BANI
Banihal 7 G4 *
Bani Mohammanpatti Halt 23 H3 BMPT
Banisar 11 G4 BS
Baniya Sanda Dhora 18 C2 BSDA
Banjari 23 G6 BVE
Banka 24 D5 BNK
Banka Ghat 24 A4, 25 inset BKG
Bankapasi 36 A2, 63 F2 BCF
Bankat 23 E4 BNKT
Bankata 23 G2 BTK
Banke Ganj 14 B4 BNKJ
Bankhedi 32 B4 BKH
Bankimnagar 36 B3 BNKA
Bankra 63 F5 BKM
Bankranayabaz 37 inset BKNM
Bankura Jn 35 H3 BQA
Banmankhi Jn 24 D3 BNKI
Banmol 7 G4 *
Banmor 21 E2 BAO
Bannihatti 53 F3 BNHT
Bannikoppa 53 E2 BNA
Bano 34 D4 BANO
Banosa 41 F2 BASA
Banpas 36 A3 BPS
Banpur 36 C2 BPN
Bansapahar 22 B5 BANSA
Bansdih Rd 23 G3 BCD
Banshberia 36 B3, 37 inset BSAE
Bansi Bohera 19 G6 BYE
Bansi Paharpur 21 E1 BIQ
Bansidhara 44 A6 BSDR
Bansinala 24 A6 BNSL
Bansipur 24 C5 BSQP
Bansjora 45 inset BZS
Banskho 20 C1 BSKO
Bansloi Bridge 25 F6 BSBR
Banspani 35 E6 BSPX
Banstala 35 H5 BNST
Banswara 30 C2 *
Banta Raghunathgarh 19 F3 BGG
Bantanahal 53 G3 BLL
Bantawala 56 C1 BNTL
Banthra 13 H4 BTRA
Bantwa 28 C5 BATA
Banwali 8 B5 BWC
Banyapur 23 F3 BNAP
Baoli H 12 D2 BAOL
Baori Thikria 12 B5 BOTI
Bapatla 55 E1 BPP
Bar 19 G2 BAR
Bar Bigha 24 B4 *
Bara 33 F1 BARA
Bara Gopal 24 A3 BAGL
Bara Gudha 8 C6 BGD
Bara Jamda Jn 35 E5 BJMD
Barabamboo 35 E4 BRM
Barabani 35 G2 BBI
Barabanki Jn 22 C1 BBK
Barabati 42 B2 BFF
Barabhum 35 F3 BBM
Barabil 35 E5 BBN
Barachak 35 G2 BCQ
Baradavalli 52 C4 -
Baradev Halt 22 B1 BRDV
Baradighi 25 G1 BDS
Baradiya 28 B4 BRDA
Baraduar 34 A5 BUA
Baragaon 22 D1 BNM
Baraghop 16 D6 -
Barahajbazar 23 G2 BHJ
Barahat 24 D5 BHLB
Barahibari 17 E6 BRBY
Barahu 26 D2 BRHU
Barai Jalalpur 14 B5 BJLP
Baraigram Jn 27 E5 BRGM
Barakalan 23 G4 BQW
Barakar 35 G2 BRR
Baral 13 E3 BARL
Barala 36 B1 BAA
Barala 7 G4 *
Baramati 46 D2 BRMT
Barahmuafi 22 B5 BQF
Baramula 7 F2 BMRL
Barapali 43 H2 BRPL
Baran 20 C4 BAZ
Baranagar Rd 37 inset BARN
Baranda 28 A1 *
Barang Jn 44 D3 BRAG
Barara 9 F5 RAA
Barari 24 D4 BARR
Barari Bazar H 45 inset BRZR
Barari Ghat 24 D4 BARG
Barasat Jn 36 B4, 37 inset, 63 G5 BT
Barauli 20 D2 BRLI
Barauni Flag 24 C4 BUJ
Barauni Jn 24 C4 BJU
Baraut 12 D2 BTU
Barayala Chaurasia 30 D2 BRLA
Barbatpur 31 H5 BBTR
Barbenda 35 F3 BBDA
Barbera 34 D4 BRBR
Barchi Rd 32 A5 BCRD
Barda 36 A5 BRDL
Barddhaman Jn 36 A3, 63 E3 BWN
Bardhana Halt 32 B5 BRDH
Bardi 32 B6 BDHT
Bardoli 39 F1 BIY
Bareilly City 13 H3 BC
Bareilly Jn 13 H4 BE, BRY
Barejadi Nandej 29 G3 BJD
Barelipar 32 A5 BQM
Barepura Halt 24 C3 BAPN
Bareta 8 D6 BRZ
Bareth 32 A1 BET
Bargachia 36 B4, 37 inset, 63 F5 BAO
Bargarh 22 C5 BRG
Bargarh Rd 43 H1 BRGA
Bargawan 33 H1 BRGW
Bargi 32 D4 BUQ
Bargolai 17 G5 BGLI
Bargur 58 A2 -
Barh 24 B4 BARH
Barh Court 24 B4
Barhan Jn 13 F6 BRN
Barhat 24 C5 *
Barhapjan 17 F4 BPJ
Barhapur 24 B4 BHAP
Barhara Halt 24 C2 BHHT
Barhara Kothi 24 D3 BAKT
Barharaganj Halt 23 G1 BAGJ
Barharwa Jn 25 E5 BHW
Barhiya 24 C4 BRYA
Barhni 15 E5 BNY
Barhragram 35 H2 BRHM
Bari 21 E1 BARI
Bari Brahman 7 G5 BBMN
Bari Sadri 19 G6 BI
Barial Himachal Halt 9 E1 BRHL
Bariarpur 24 C4 BUP
Baripada 35 G5 BPO
Baripur Mandala 30 A5 BRPM
Baripura 22 A4 BPRA
Barithengarh 44 D2 BRTG
Bariwala 8 C4 BRW
Barka Halt 12 D2 BADK
Barkakana Jn 35 E2 BRKA
Barkhedi 42 A2 BOK
Barkhera 31 H3 BKA
Barki Salaiya 23 G5 BSYA
Barkipona 35 E2 BRKP
Barkuhi 32 B5 BCS
Barkur 52 C6 BKJ
Barlai 31 E3 BLAX
Barlanga 35 F2 BLNG
Barlangfer 27 F3 BRLF
Barmer 18 C3 BME
Barnagar 30 D3 BNG
Barnala 8 D5 BNN
Barnes Bazar 25 G2 BSG
Barnes Ghat 25 G2 BSG
Barog 9 F4 BOF
Barpathar 27 G2 BXP
Barpeta Rd 26 C2 BPRD
Barrackpore 36 B4, 37 inset BP
Barrajpur 22 A2 BJR
Barsali 32 A5 BYS
Barsathi 23 E4 BSY
Barsi Takli 41 E3 BSQ
Barsi Town 47 F2 BTW
Barsoi Jn 25 F4 BOE
Barsola 12 C1 BZO
Barsuan 34 D6 BXF
Barua Bamungaon 27 G1 BBGN
Barua Chak 14 D6 BRNR
Barua Nagar 17 F5 BRNR
Barud 31 F5 BRUD
Baruipara 37 inset BRPA
Baruipur Jn 36 B4, 37 inset BRP
Baruna 23 G4 BUE
Barundani 19 H4 BNDI
Baruva 44 B6 BAV
Barwa Kalan Halt 15 F6 BRCA
Barwadih 34 C2 BRWD
Barwaha 31 E5 BWW
Barwala 12 B1 BXC
Barwala Rd 28 D3 BRL
Barwasagar 21 F4 BWR
Barya Ram 22 D4 BYHA
Basai 21 F4 BZY
Basai Dhankot 12 D3 BDKT
Basanpalle 53 H4 BSPL
Basar 41 F6 BSX
Basavana Bagewadi Rd 47 F5 BSRX
Basavapuram 54 B2 BSV
Basbari 26 A2 BSI
Baseri 21 E1 BED
Baseria H 45 inset BZE
Basharatganj 13 G4 BTG
Basi Berisal 19 H4 BSSL
Basin Bridge Jn 58 D1, 59 inset BBQ
Basirhat 36 C4, 63 H5 BSHT
Basirhat Kutchery 63 H5 -
Baskatwa BH 24 B6 BSCP
Basmet 41 E5 BMF
Basni 19 E2 BANE
Bassi 20 B1 BAI
Bassi Kiratpur 13 F1 BSKR

Bassi Pathanan 9 E4 BSPN
Basta 35 H6 BTS
Bastakulha H 45 inset BYK
Basti 23 E1 BST
Bastoi Halt 13 F5 BTRO
Basuchack Halt 23 F4 BSCK
Basuchak H 24 C5
Basudebpur 25 F6 BDBP
Basudeopur Chandel Halt 24 B4 BDUA
Basugaon 26 B2 BSGN
Basuldanga 36 B5 BSD
Basulyasutahata 36 B5 BYSA
Baswa 12 C6 BU
Batadrawa 27 E2 BTDR
Batala Jn 8 D2 BAT
Batala Sugar Mills Siding 8 D2 BATM
Batasi 25 F2 BTSI
Batasia Siding 25 F1 -
Bataspur 36 A2 BSLE
Bathinda A Cabin 8 C5 BTI'A'
Bathinda B Cabin 8 C5 BTI'B'
Bathinda Cantt 8 C5 BTIC
Bathinda Jn 8 C5 BTI
Bathna Krittibas 36 B3 BTKB
Bathnaha 24 D2 BTF
Battulapuram 54 A5 BTM
Batuva Rd 50 D2 BTVA
Baudpur 45 E2 BUDR
Bauria 36 B4, 37 inset BVA
Bavla 29 G3 VLA
Bawal 12 C4 BWL
Bawani Khera 12 C2 BWK
Bayad 29 H2 BAYD
Bayaluvoddigeri 53 F2 BYO
Bayana Jn 20 D1 BXN
Baytu 18 C2 BUT
Bayyavaram 50 C3 BVM
Bazarghat Halt 27 E5 BZGT
Bazarsau 36 B1 BZLE
Bazida Jattan 12 D1 BZJT
BBD Bag 37 inset BBDB
BDAG Loop Link Cabin 25 E5 BDAGLC
Beas Jn 8 D2 BEAS
Beawar 19 G2 BER
Bebejia 27 E2 BEE
Bechhiwara 30 A1 BHWA
Bechraji 29 G2 BHRJ
Bedeti 16 C6 BVV
Bedham 12 D5 BEDM
Bedi Port 28 C3 BEDI
Beed 40 C6 *
Begampur 37 inset BPAE
Begumpet 48 C3, 51 inset BMT
Begusarai 24 C4 BGS
Behta Hazipur 12 D3, 15 inset BHHZ
Behtagokul 14 A5 BEG
Behula 36 B3 BHLA
Bejnal 19 F5 BJN
Bela 24 A5 BLA
Bela Bhela Halt 22 C3 BBHL
Belagula 57 F3 BLGA
Belakoba 25 G2 BLK
Belanagar 37 inset BZL
Belandur Rd Halt 57 H2 BLRR
Belanganj 13 E6 BLJN
Belanki 47 E4 BLNK
Belapur 38 inset BEPR
Belapur 40 A4 BAP
Belasar Halt 11 F4 BLSR
Bela-Tal 21 H4 BTX
Belboni 35 H3 BWX
Beldanga 36 B1 BEB
Belerhat 36 B2 BOY
Belgaum 52 B1 BGM
Belghana 33 G5 BIG
Belgharia 37 inset BLH
Belha 33 G6 BYL
Belhar 24 D5 *
Beliaghata Bridge 63 G5 -
Beliaghata Rd 36 B4 BGRD
Belitor 35 H3 BZC
Belkhera 32 C3 BELD
Bellamkonda 49 E5 BMKD
Bellampalli 42 A6 BPA
Bellary Cantt 53 F2 BYC
Bellary Jn 53 F2 BAY
Belmuri 36 B3 BMAE
Belpahar 34 B6 BPH
Belrayan 14 B4 BXM
Belshakarga 48 A2 BLKA
Belsiri 16 B6 BLRE
Belsonda 43 F2 BLSN
Belthara Rd 23 G3 BLTR
Belur 37 inset BEQ
Belur Math 37 inset BMCB
Belvandi 40 A6 BWD
BEML Nagar 58 A2 BEML
Benal 47 F5 BENL
Benapur 35 H5 BPE
Bendi 34 C2 BFQ
Bendikonda 51 E1 BKY
Beniganj 14 B6 BEJ
Benipatti Pirapur H 24 B3 BNPT
Benoda 41 G1 *

Beohari 33 F1 BEHR
Beolia Rd 23 G6 -
Berach Jn Cabin 19 H5 BEC
Berawaniya 30 D2 BRNA
Berchampa 63 H5 -
Berchha 31 F3 BCH
Berhampore Court 36 B1 BPC
Berhampore Court 44 C5 -
Beri 9 F3 *
Beria Daulat Halt 13 G2 BRDT
Bermo 35 F2 BRMO
Bero 35 G2 BERO
Besroli 11 H6 BSRL
Betamcherla 54 A2 BMH
Betawad 40 B1 BEW
Betberia Ghola 36 B4 BTBG
Betgara 25 G1 BYXA
Bethampudi 49 F3 BTPD
Bethuadahari 36 B2 BTY
Betnoti 35 G6 BTQ
Bettadanagenahalli Halt 53 E4 BTGH
Bettahalsoor H 57 H1 TLS
Bettiah 23 H1 BTH
Betul 31 H5 BZU
Betur 35 H3 BTRB
Betwa Cabin 31 H2 BETWA CABIN
Bevinahalu 53 G3 BNL
Bewar Bhojan Halt 12 B3 BWBN
Bhabhar 18 C6 BAH
Bhabta 36 B1 BFT
Bhabua Rd 23 F5 BBU
Bhachau 28 D2 BCOB, BCO
Bhachhbhar 18 B3 BBC
Bhad Bhada Ghat 31 H2 BVB
Bhadaiyan 22 D3 BDIN
Bhadan 21 G1 BDN
Bhadanpur 33 E1 BUU
Bhadaura 23 G4 BWH
Bhadbunja 39 G1 BBAI
Bhader 28 D6 BADR
Bhadi 29 F5 BDI
Bhadi Bhandariya 29 F5 BDBN
Bhadli 40 C2 BDI
Bhadohi 23 E4 BOY
Bhadora Jagir 20 D5 BDJR
Bhadra 28 D3 BHAD
Bhadrachalam 49 G3 *
Bhadrachalam Rd 49 G3 BDCR
Bhadrak 45 E2 BHC
Bhadran 29 H4 BDRN
Bhadravadi 29 F4 BDRD
Bhadravati 52 D5 BDVT
Bhadreshwar 37 inset BHR
Bhadresar Rd 28 C3 BDSR
Bhadri 22 C3 BHDR
Bhadrod 38 D1 BAHR
Bhadroli 21 F2 BBY
Bhadsivni 41 F3 BDKE
Bhadwad 30 B6 BAWD
Bhadwari 13 G3 -
Bhaga 35 F2, 45 inset VAA
Bhagalpur Jn 24 D4 BGP
Bhagalpur Kacheri 24 D4 BGRK
Bhagat-ki-Kothi 19 E2 BGKT
Bhagavathipuram 60 C4 BJM
Bhagdara 40 C2 BGR
Bhagega 12 B5 BAGA
Bhagirathpur Halt 15 F6 BHGP
Bhagsar 8 B4 BSGR
Bhagtanwala 8 C2 BGTN
Bhagwangola 25 F6 BQG
Bhagwanpur 24 A3 BNR
Bhagwanpur Desua 24 B3 BGDS
Bhagwanpura 19 F4 BGPR
Bhagwansar 11 G1 BNSR
Bhaili 29 H4 BAL
Bhainswan 12 D2 BASN
Bhaini Khurd 9 F6 BZK
Bhainsa 13 E5 BSA
Bhairabi 27 F6 BHRB
Bhairanayakanahalli Halt 57 G1 BNKH
Bhairoganj 15 G6 BRU
Bhairongarh 30 C3 BOG
Bhaironpur 31 G4 BIF
Bhairopatti Halt 24 D3 BHTH
Bhaitola 33 G3 BATL
Bhaiyasar 30 A3 BSAR
Bhajera 12 D6 BJRA
Bhakrapeta 54 B4 BKPT
Bhakrauli 13 F4 BHKL
Bhaktinagar 28 D4 BKNG
Bhalej 29 H4 BAJ
Bhalki 48 A2 BHLK
Bhalui 24 C5 BFM
Bhalujala 8 D2
Bhaluka Rd 25 F4 BKRD
Bhalukmara 27 G1 BLMR
Bhalukpong 16 B6 BHNG
Bhalulata 34 D5 BUL
Bhalumaska 43 H5 BLMK
Bhalvani 47 E2 BLNI
Bhanapur 53 E2 BNP
Bhanaur 23 E4 VNN
Bhandai 13 E6 BHA

Bhandak 42 A4 BUX
Bhandana 20 C1 BNDN
Bhandara Rd 42 B1 BRD
Bhandaridah 35 F2, 45 inset BHME
Bhandartikuri 36 B2 BFZ
Bhandegaon 41 F3 BDGN
Bhandewahi 42 A2 BNWD
Bhandu Motidau 29 G1 BHU
Bhandup 38 inset BND
Bhaner Minawada Rd 29 H3 BMVR
Bhanga 27 E5 BXG
Bhangala 8 D1 BNGL
Bhangarh 21 E3 BNGH
Bhanjpur 35 G5 VZR
Bhankla Halt 9 G6 BNQL
Bhankoda 29 G2 BKD
Bhankri 12 C6 BAK
Bhanohad Punjab 8 D4 BHQ
Bhansi 49 H1 BHNS
Bhanupali 9 F3 BNLY
Bhanvad 28 C4 BNVD
Bhanwartonk 33 G4 BHTK
Bhanwasa 20 A1 BNWS
Bhaptiahi 24 D2
Bharatgarh 9 F3 BARJ
Bharat Khand Halt 24 D4 BRKB
Bharat Kund 22 D2 BTKD
Bharat Kup 22 B4 BTKP
Bharathapuzha Halt 57 E6 BPZA
Bharathnagar 51 inset BTNR
Bharatpur Jn 13 E6 BTE
Bharatwada 41 H1 BWRA
Bharawas 12 C4 BFS
Bharmar 9 E1 BRMR
Bharoli Jn 8 D1 BHPL
Bharsendi 33 G1 BSDL
Bharthali 29 H5 BRTL
Bharthana 21 G1 BNT
Bharuch Jn 29 H5 BH
Bharur Halt 8 D5 BZ
Bharwa Sumerpur 22 A3 BSZ
Bharwari 22 C4 BRE
Bhasa 63 F6 -
Bhasila 36 C4 BSLA
Bhaskarpara 29 F3 BMM
Bhatangali 47 G1
Bhatapara 33 G6 BYT
Bhatar 36 A2, 63 E2 BTRH
Bhatariya 29 G2 BTYA
Bhatasa Halt 13 G5 BHTS
Bhatel 28 B4 BHTL
Bhatgaon 43 E2 BOV
Bhatiel 29 H4 BHAL
Bhatisuda 30 D2 BTSD
Bhatiya 28 B4 BHTA
Bhatkal 52 C5 BTKL
Bhatni Jn 23 G2 BTT
Bhaton-ki-Gali 12 B6 BHG
Bhatpar Rani 23 G2 BHTR
Bhatpur 30 A5 BTPR
Bhatpura 21 E2 BHAT
Bhatsar 29 G1 BATS
Bhattain 9 E3 BTTN
Bhattanagar 37 inset BTNG
Bhattiprolu 55 E1 BQU
Bhattu 12 A1 BHT
Bhaupur 22 A2 BPU
Bhavaninagar 46 D4 BVNR
Bhavdhari 12 B3 BOTR
Bhavnagar Para 29 F5 BVP
Bhavnagar Port 29 G5 BVRV
Bhavnagar Terminus 29 F5 BVC
Bhavpura 28 D2 BHVP
Bhawanigarh 9 E6 -
Bhawani Mandi 20 B6 BWM
Bhawanipur 24 D3 *
Bhawanipur Bihar 25 E4 BWPB
Bhawanipurkalan 14 D6 BWP
Bhawi H 19 F2 BCW
Bhayandar 39 F5, 38 inset BYR
Bhayavadar 28 C5 BHY
Bhayna 36 B3 BHNA
Bhedia 36 A2 BDH
Bheduasole 35 H3 BXL
Bheempura 18 D4 BIPR
Bheerpur 22 D4 BEP
Bheja 50 B2 BHJA
BHEL Halt 48 C3 BHEL
Bhela 29 E3 -
Bhelwa 23 H1 BLV
Bhenswadi 29 E6 BSWD
Bheraghat 32 D3 BRGT
Bhesana 19 F3 BFY
Bhesana Mankanaj 29 G2 BSKN
Bheslana 12 A6 BILA
Bhestan 39 F1 BHET
Bhetaguri 25 H2 VTG
Bhetasi 29 H4 BETI
Bhigwan 47 E1 BGVN
Bhikamkor 11 E6E BKC
Bhikhampur 14 B4 BKHP
Bhikhna Thori 15 H6 BKF
Bhiknur 48 C2 BKU
Bhilad 39 F3 BLD

Bhilai 43 E2 BIA
Bhilai Nagar 43 E2 BQR
Bhilai Power House 43 E2 BPHB
Bhilavdi 46 D4 BVQ
Bhildi Jn 18 C6 BLDI
Bhilgaon 27 G2 BHGN
Bhilupur 30 A4 BIL
Bhilwara 19 H4 BHL
Bhimadolu 49 H5 BMD
Bhimal 19 F5 BIML
Bhimgoda Tank 9 H6 -
Bhimalgondi 32 B6 BMC
Bhimana 19 E5 BMN
Bhimarlai 18 C2 BMQ
Bhimasar 28 C2 BMSR
Bhimavaram Jn 49 H5 BVRM
Bhimavaram Town 49 H5 BVRT
Bhimgara Jn 35 H2 BMGA
Bhimkhoj 43 F2 BMKJ
Bhimnath 29 F4 BNH
Bhimrana 28 A4 BMRN
Bhimsen Jn 22 A2 BZM
Bhind 21 G2 BIX
Bhindar 19 G5 BNNR
Bhinwaliya 19 F3 BWA
Bhirakheri 14 B4 BIK
Bhiringi 31 G5 BRI
Bhisa H 24 B2 BHSA
Bhitaura 13 G3 BTO
Bhiti 22 D4 BYH
Bhitiharwa Ashram Halt 15 H6 BHWR
Bhitoni 32 C3 BHTN
Bhivpuri Rd 39 G5, 38 inset BVS
Bhiwandi Rd 39 F5, 38 inset BIRD
Bhiwani City 12 C2 BNWC
Bhiwani Jn 12 C2 BNW
Bhiwapur 42 B2 BWV
Bhogpur 36 A5 BOP
Bhogpur Sirwal 8 D2 BPRS
Bhoj Padra 29 H4 BHOJ
Bhojasar 12 4A BOX
Bhojipura Jn BPR
Bhojo 17 F5 BOJ
Bhojras 19 H3 BHAS
Bhojudih Jn 35 F2, 45 inset BJE
Bhojudih Washery 35 G2, 45 inset BWSB
Bhokar 41 F5 BOKP
Bhoke 46 B4 BOKE
Bholidih BH 35 F2 BLME
Bhoma 32 C5 BHV
Bhone 40 B2 BHNE
Bhongaon 13 G6 BGQ
Bhongir 48 D3 BG
Bhonra 20 B4 BON
Bhopal Jn 31 G3 BPL
Bhopalka 28 B4 BPKA
Bhopatpura Halt 13 H3 BPPA
Bhoras Budrukh 40 B2 BFJ
Bhorepatti 25 G2 BPV
Bhortex 40 B1 BRTK
Bhowra 45 inset BCB
Bhoyani 29 G2 BHAN
Bhua 21 G3 BHUA
Bhubaneshwar 44 D3 BBS
Bhuchchu 8 C5 BCU
Bhuda 12 D6 BUDA
Bhudpur H 12 D2 BDHP
Bhugaon 41 H3 BPK
Bhuj 28 C2 BHUJ
Bhujhia Bara Gaon Halt 14 B5 BUGN
Bhujvad 41 F2 BHWD
Bhukarka Halt 11 H1 BKKA
Bhuli 35 F2, 45 inset BHN
Bhuli BH 45 inset BHHB
Bhulon 20 D5 BLO
Bhupalsagar 19 G5 BSJ
Bhupdeopur 34 A5 BEF
Bhupiamau 22 D3 VPO
Bhurkunda 35 E2 BHKD
Bhusandpur 44 D4 BSDP
Bhusawal Jn 40 C2 BSL
Bhutakiya Bhimasar 29 E1 BUBR
Bhuteshwar 13 E5 BTSR
Bhutgoria 45 inset BTGA
Bhuyar 42 B2 BHRH
Bhyabla 36 C4 BBLA
Biaspind 8 D2 BSP
Bibhuti Bhusan 36 C3 BNAA
Bibinagar 48 C3, 51 inset BN
Bibiwala 9 H5 BBVL
Bichhpuri 13 E6 BCP
Bichia 14 C4 BIC
Bidadi 57 G2 BID
Bidanpur 22 C4 BDNP
Bidar 48 A2 BIDR
Bidhannagar Rd 37 inset BNXR
Bidiha Shankarpuri 23 G5 -
Bidiyad 11 H6 BIDD
Bidupur 24 B4 BIU
Bidyadharpur 36 B4, 37 inset BDYP
Bigga 11 G4 BIGA
Biggabas Ramsara Halt 11 G4 BGRM
Bighapur 22 B2 BQP
Bihar Kutchery 24 B5 BKY

Bihar Sharif 24 B5 BEHS
Bihara 27 E4 BHZ
Bihariganj 24 D3 BHGJ
Bihat H 24 C4
Bihiya 23 H4 BEA
Bihta 24 A4 BTA
Bihubar 17 E6 BFB
Bijainagar 19 H3 BJNR
Bijaipur Rd 20 D2 BJPR
Bijapur 47 F5 BJP
Bijauli 21 F4 BJI
Bijauria 13 H3 BJV
Bijbehera 7 G3 *
Bijni 26 B2 BJF
Bijnor 13 F1 BJO
Bijora 20 C4 BJK
Bijrotha 21 F5 BJA
Bijur 52 C5 BIJR
Bijuri 33 G3 BJRI
Bijwasan 12 D3, 15 inset BWSN
Bikaner East 11 F4 BKN EAST
Bikaner Jn 11 F4 BKN
Bikkavolu 50 A4 BVL
Bikna 35 H3 BKNO
Bikramganj 23 G5 BKJ
Bikrampur 32 C3 BMR
Bikramshila 25 E4 BKSL
Bilara 19 F2 BARA
Bilasipara 26 B2 *
Bilaspur 9 F3 BLSP
Bilaspur Jn 33 G5 BSP
Bilaspur Rd 13 G3 BLQR
Bildi 30 C3 BILD
Bileshwar 28 D4 BLWR
Bilga 8 D3 BZG
Bilhar Ghat 22 D2 BLG
Bilhaur 22 A1 BLU
Bilimora Bunder 39 F2 BIMB
Bilimora Jn 39 F2 BIM
Bilkha 28 D6 BILK
Billi Jn 23 F6 BXLL
Bilochpura 13 E6 BFP
Bilpur 13 H4 BLPU
Bilwai 23 E3 BWI
Bimbari 41 F5 BMBE
Bimlagarh Jn 34 D6 BUI
Bina Jn 32 A1 BINA
Binaiki 32 D4 VNK
Binaur 22 A2 BNAR
Bindaura 22 C1 BUR
Bindayaka 12 B6 BDYK
Bindki Rd 22 B3 BKO
Bindubasini 25 F5 BDBS
Bindukuri 27 E1 BKTB
Binjana 31 E3 BNJN
Binjhol Halt 12 D1 BNJL
Binnaguri 25 G1 BNV
Bir 31 F5 BIR
Bira 36 B4 BIRA
Biradhwal 11 G1 BDWL
Birahalli Halt 57 E2 BRBL
Birambad 20 D1 BAMA
Biramdih 35 F3 BRMD
Birang Khera 8 C6 BMK
Birapatti 23 E4 BRPT
Birarajpur 35 F4 BIRP
Birati 37 inset BBT
Birbans 35 F4 BRBS
Birla Nagar 21 F2 BLNR
Birmitrapur 34 D5 BRMP
Birnagar 36 B3 BIJ
Birohe 23 E5 BEO
Biroliya 19 E4 BRLY
Birpur 20 D2 BIB
Birpur 24 D2 -
Birpura BH 44 D3
Birpurusottampur 44 D4 BRST
Birshibpur 36 A4 BSBP
Birsinghpur 33 E3 BRS
Birsola 32 D6 BRA
Birur Jn 53 E6 RRB
Bisalpur 13 H4 BSUR
Bisalwas Kalan 19 H5 BIWK
Bisanattam 58 A2 BSM
Bisapur Kalan 32 B6 BRKH
Bishangarh 18 D3 BISH
Bishanpura Haryana 12 C2 BSPH
Bisharpara Kodalia 37 inset BRPK
Bisheswarganj 14 D6 BEU
Bishnathganj 22 D3 BTJ
Bishnupriya 36 B2 VSPR
Bishnupur 35 H3 VSU
Bishrampur 34 A3 BSPR
Bispur 34 D5 BSPK
Bisra 34 D5 BZR
Bissam Cuttack 43 H5 BMCK
Bissau 12 A3 BUB
Bisugirshariff 49 E2 BGSF
Biswa Bridge 40 D2 BIS
Biswan 14 B5 BVN
Bithauli 24 B3 BTHL
Bithia Rd 24 D5 *
Bitragunta 54 D3 BTTR
Bitroi 13 G4 BTRI

Biwai 12 D6 BW
Biyavra Rajagarh 31 G1 BRRG
BKSC N Cabin 45 inset 'N' CABIN BKSC
Block Hut 01 9 E4 BH01
Block Hut A 22 D4 BH'A'
Block Hut A 22 B1 BH'A'
Block Hut AA 13 F5 BHAA
Block Hut 'B' 25 inset BH'B'
Block Hut B 22 D4 BH'B'
Block Hut BB 13 F6 BHBB
Block Hut C 22 D4 BH'C'
Block Hut CC 13 E4 -
Block Hut D 13 F6 BH'D'
Block Hut DD 23 E5 BHDD
Block Hut EE 23 E5 BHEE
Block Hut FF 22 A2 BHFF
Block Hut G 21 G1 BH'G'
Block Hut HH 21 H2 BHHH
Block Hut I 21 H2 BH'I'
Block Hut JJ 22 D5 BHJJ
Block Hut K 23 F4 BH'K'
Block Hut KK 22 C4 BHKK
Block Hut L 21 H2 BH'L'
Block Hut M 13 F6 BH'M'
Block Hut N 13 F6 BH'N'
Block Hut O 13 F6 BH'O'
Block Hut P 13 F6 BH'P'
Block Hut R 23 E5 BH'R'
Block Hut S 21 G1 BH'S'
Block Hut 'T' 9 F5 -
Block Hut T 13 F5 BH'T'
Block Hut U 13 F5 BH'U'
Block Hut W 13 E4 -
Block Hut X 21 G1 BH'X'
Block Hut Y 22 A2 BH'Y'
Block Hut Z 22 A2 BH'Z'
Bobas 12 B6 BOBS
Bobbili Jn 50 C1 VBL
Bochasan Jn 29 H4 BCHN
Bodarwar 23 F1 BBW
Bodarwas 21 E5
Bodavara 50 C2 BDVR
Bodearapur 43 E6 BDXX
Bodeli 30 A4 BDE
Bodhan 48 B1 BDHN
Bodhani Bujrug 41 G5 BHBK
Bodhwal Majri 12 D2 BDMJ
Bodma BH 35 G2 BM
Bodinayakkanur 60 D2 BDN
Bodwad 40 C2 BDWD
Bogada 54 B2 BGDA
Bogapani 17 G5 BGPI
Bogolu 53 H2 BVO
Bogri Rd 35 H3 BGO
Bohali 47 E3 BHLI
Bohani 32 B4 BNE
Boinda 44 C2 BONA
Boisar 39 F4 BOR
Bojawas Halt 12 C3 BJWS
Bokajan 27 G2 BXJ
Bokaro Steel City Jn 35 F2, 45 inset BKSC
Bokaro Thermal 35 F2 BKRO
Boko 26 C2 BOKO
Bolai 31 F2 BLX
Bolangir 43 H3 BLGR
Bolangir Rd 43 H2 BNRD
Bolanikhadan 35 E5 BYX
Bolarum 48 C3, 51 inset BMO
Bolarum Bazar 51 inset BOZ
Bolda 41 E5 BLC
Bolenahalli 52 D5 BLNH
Bolina Doaba 8 D3 BLND
Bolpur 36 A2 BHP
Bolsa 41 F6 BLSA
Bolwad 46 D4 BLWD
Bomadra 19 F3 BOM
Bommagundanakere 53 F4 BDMN
Bommasamudram 58 C1 BUM
Bommidi 58 A4 BQI
Bommidi BH 58 A4 BLBH
Bonakalu 49 F4 BKL
Bondamunda 34 D5 BNDM
Bongaigaon 26 B2 BNGN
Bongaon Jn 36 C3 BNJ
Bonidanga 25 E5 BDAG
Boparai Halt 8 C3 BXO
Borabanda 51 inset BRBD
Boraki Halt 13 E3 BRKY
Borawar 11 H6 BOW
Bordhai 32 A5 BXY
Bordi 30 B3 BIO
Bordi Rd 39 F3 BRRD
Bordoloni Halt 17 E5 BDLN
Bordubi Rd 17 F5 BDT
Borgaon 41 E2 BGN
Borhat 17 F5 BFD
Boribial 46 D1 BRB
Boridand Jn 33 G3 BRND
Boridara 29 H5 BII
Borigaon 17 E6 -
Borivali 39 F5, 38 inset BVI
Boroti 47 G3 BOT
Borraguhalu 50 C2 BGHU
Borsad 29 H4 BO
Bortalao 42 C1 BTL
Borvihir 40 B2 BRVR
Botad Jn 29 F4 BTD
Bowaichandi 36 A3, 63 E3 BWGN
Boxirhat 26 A2 *
Brace Bridge 37 inset BRJ
Brahmajan 16 D6 BJL
Brahmanagudem 49 H5 BMGM
Brahmanapalli 48 C3 BMPL
Brahmanwada 29 G1 BMDI
Brahmapur 44 C5 BAM
Brahmapuri 42 B3 BMP
Brahmavart 22 A2 BRT
Brajkishore H 23 H2
Brajrajnagar 34 C6 BRJN
Bral Square 15 inset BRSQ
Bridgmanganj 15 F6 BMJ
Brijnagar 12 D5 BINR
Brindabanpur 35 H3 BDPR
Brundamal 34 C6 BXQ
Buchanan 60 C2 -
Budalur 58 B6 BAL
Budaun 13 G4 BEM
Buddireddipatti 58 A3 BDY
Buddireddipatti BH 58 A4 BBBH
Budge Budge 36 B4, 37 inset BGB
Budh Singhwala Halt 8 B6 BDSW
Budha Khera 12 D1 BKDE
Budhai Balamgarh Halt 8 B4
Budhapank 44 C2 BDPK
Budhapank Junction Cabin 44 C2 -
Budhdev Chak Yadav Nagar 25 inset -
Budhel 29 F5 BUDL
Budhgaon 46 D4 -
Budhi 7 G6 BDHY
Budhlada 8 D6 BLZ
Budhma 24 D3 BDMA
Budipuram 60 D2 BDPM
Budni 31 H4 BNI
Budora H 45 inset BDQ
Budvel 48 C4, 51 inset BDVL
Bugganipalli Cement Nagar 54 A2 BEY
Bugia Halt 11 F1 BUGY
Buglanwali Halt 8 B6 BUGL
Bulandshahr 13 E3 BSC
Bulanpur Halt 23 E4 BHLP
Bulbulchandi 25 F5 BBCE
Bundi 20 B4 BUDI
Bundki 13 F1 BEK
Buniadpur 25 F4 -
Burah Bharthara Halt 13 F6 BUBT
Burakayalakota 54 A5 BYKT
Buramara 35 G5 BWO
Burgula 48 C4 BRGL
Burhanpur 40 D1 BAU
Burhar 33 F3 BUH
Burhpura 21 F4 BPW
Burhwal Jn 14 C6 BUW
Burimara 25 G2 BWO
Burmi Halt 14 B5 BRMX
Burnihat 26 D3
Burnpur 35 G2 BURN
Burrabazar 37 inset BZB
Burwadag 35 E3 BWJ
Butari 8 D2 BTR
Butewala 8 C3 BWF
Buti Bori Jn 42 A2 BTBR
Buxa Rd 25 H1 BXD
Buxar 23 G4 BXR
Byadarahalli 57 F2 BDRL
Byadgi 52 D3 BYD
Byatrayanahalli 57 H2 BFW
Byculla 38 inset BY
Byndoor 52 C5 BYNR
Byree 44 D3 BYY
BYPL Yard 57 H1 -

C

Calicut 56 D5 CLT
Campierganj 23 F1 CM
Canacona 52 B2 CNO
Cannanore 56 D4 CAN
Cannanore South 56 D4 CS
Canning 36 C5 CG
Cansaulim 52 A2 CSM
Capper Quarry 58 C4 CQS
Caranzol 52 B2 CRZ
Carron 25 G1 CRX
Carterpuri 12 D3, 15 inset CRPI
Castle Rock 52 B2 CLR
Cauvery 57 H5 CV
Cavalry Barracks 51 inset CVB
Chabua 17 F4 CHB
Chachaura Binaganj 31 G1 CBK
Chacher 42 A1 CHCR
Chaddotar Rd 18 D6 CDQ
Chaf Halt 23 G1 CHAF
Chagallu 49 H5 CU
Chaibasa 35 F4 CBSA
Chailaha H 24 A2
Chainpur 35 E2 CNPR
Chainwa 23 H3 CW
Chak Banawala 8 B4 CKLA
Chak Dayala 7 G6 CKDL
Chak Kalan 8 D1 CKKN
Chak Pakhewala 8 B4 CKA
Chak Safaura Halt 13 H4 CKSR
Chakai 24 C6 *
Chakand 24 A5 CKH
Chakardha 24 D2 CRDA
Chakarlapalli 53 G5 CPL
Chakarwaha 7 G5 *
Chakdaha 36 B3 CDH
Chakeri 22 A2 CHK
Chakia 24 A2 CAA
Chakia Thermal 24 C4
Chakicherla 54 D3 CKC
Chakiting 27 G1 CFG
Chakkali Lait Halt 13 F2 CKLT
Chakki Bank Jn 8 D1 CHKB
Chakmakrand 24 B3, 25 inset CKRD
Chakra 23 H2 CKY
Chakra Rd Halt 23 G3 CKYD
Chakrabhata 33 G6 CHBT
Chakradharpur 35 E4 CKP
Chakrajmal 13 F2 CAJ
Chakrapur Halt 14 A2 CKK
Chakrod 31 F3 CKOD
Chaksikandar 24 B4 CSR
Chaksu 20 B1 CKS
Chakulia 35 G4 CKU
Chakur 47 H1 CKX
Chalakudi 60 B1 CKI
Chalala 29 E6 CLC
Chalgeri 52 D4 CLI
Chalisgaon Jn 40 B3 CSN
Chalkhoa 17 F5 CKW
Challakere 53 F4 CHKE
Challavaripalle 54 A3 CLPE
Chalsa 25 G1 CLD
Chalthan 39 F1 CHM
Chamagram 25 F5 CMX
Chamak 41 F1 CMK
Chamaraj 29 F3 CJR
Chamarajanagar 57 F4 CMNR
Chamarajapuram 57 F3 CMJ
Chamardighi 36 A3, 63 E3 CMDG
Chamarua 13 G3 CHRU
Champa Jn 33 H5 CPH
Champadanga 36 A4, 63 E5 CDX
Champahati 36 B5 CHT
Champajharan 34 D5 CJQ
Champaner Rd Jn 30 A4 CPN
Champapukur 36 C4 COR
Champapur 24 B4 CPPR
Champion 58 A2 CHU
Chamrail 63 F5 CMRL
Chamrola 13 F5 CMR
Chamua 15 H6 CAMU
Chamunda Marg Halt 9 F1 CMMG
Chanakh 41 G4 -
Chanakyapuri 15 inset CNKP
Chananwala 8 B5 CNW
Chanasma Jn 29 G1 CSMA
Chanchai 36 A3 CHC
Chanchapar 28 D3 CHNP
Chanchelav 30 A3 CCL
Chand Bhan 8 C5 CBX
Chand Siau 13 F2 CPS
Chanda Fort 42 A4 CAF
Chanda Halt 22 D3 CHDA
Chandagiri-Koppal Halt 57 F2 CGKP
Chandameta 32 B5 CAE
Chandan Chauki 14 B3 CDC
Chandanagar 51 inset CDNR
Chandanattop Halt 60 B4 CTPE
Chandannagar 36 B4, 37 inset CGR
Chandanpur 36 B4, 37 inset CDAE
Chandar 35 H3 CNR
Chandargao 52 B2 CNRG
Chandari Jn 22 A2 CNBI
Chandarwa 29 F4 CDV
Chandauli Majhwar 23 F4 CDMR
Chandauna Halt 24 B2 CNX
Chandausi Jn 13 G3 CH
Chandawal 19 G2 CNL
Chander Nagar Halt 15 inset CNJ
Chandera Halt 56 C3 CDRA
Chanderiya 19 H5 CNDY, cna
Chandeshwar Asthan 24 C2 CDNA
Chandi Mandir 9 F4 CNDM
Chandia Rd 33 E2 CHD
Chandigarh 9 F4 CDG
Chandil Jn 35 F3 CNI
Chandiposi 34 D5 CPE
Chandisar Rd 18 D6 CDS
Chanditala [Kol] 4 inset *
Chanditala Jn 63 F5, 37 inset CLL
Chandkheda Rd 28 inset CDK
Chandkhirabagan 27 E5 CHBN
Chandlodiya Jn 29 G3, 28 inset CLDY
Chandok 13 F1 CNK
Chandni 40 D1 CDI
Chandod 30 A5 CDD
Chandpara 36 C3 CDP
Chandragiri 54 C6 CGI
Chandrakona Rd 35 H4 CDGR
Chandrampalem 50 B4 CRPM
Chandranathpur 27 E4 CNE
Chandrapur 42 A4 CD
Chandrapura Jn 35, 45 inset CRP
Chandresal 20 B4 CDSL
Chandsara Halt 13 E2 CXA
Chandur 41 G2 CND
Chandur Bazar 41 F1 *
Chanethi 13 H4 CHTI
Changanacheri 60 B3 CGY
Changrabandha 25 G2 CBD
Changsari 26 D2 CGS
Channani 20 D2 CHNN
Channapatna 57 G2 CPT
Channasandra 57 H1 CSDR
Channi Halt 11 E4 -
Chanol 28 D4 CX
Chanpatia 23 H1 CAI
Chapar 26 B2 *
Chaparmukh Jn 27 E2 CPK
Chhapi 18 D6 CHP
Chaprakata 26 B2 CPQ
Chapramari 25 G1 CPY
Charadu 29 G2 CARD
Charamula Kusumi 43 F6 CJS
Charaud 12 B2 CRW
Charbatia 44 D3 CBT
Charbhuja Rd 19 G4 CBG
Charduar 16 B6 CHOD
Charegaon 32 D5 CRN
Charewan Halt 8 C4 CWN
Charghatpiparia 32 D3 CGE
Chargola 27 E5 CGX
Chariali 17 F5 CGF
Charil 7 G3 *
Charkhari Rd 21 H4 CRC
Charkheda Khurd 31 F5 CKKD
Charkhera 31 G5 CRK
Charkhi Dadri 12 C3 CKD
Charlapalli 48 C3, 51 inset CHZ
Charmal 44 B1 CHAR
Charmuria 43 E2 CHMA
Charni Rd 38 inset CYR
Charodiya 39 D1 CHRD
Charpokhri 23 H4 CRQ
Charup 29 G1 CHRP
Charvattur 56 C3 CHV
Chas 45 inset CHAS
Chas Rd 35 F3 CAS
Chatar 24 B5 CHJ
Chataud 43 E2 CATD
Chatouli 9 F4 CTLI
Chatra 25 F6 CTR
Chatra 34 D1 *
Chatrappati 60 D1 CHPT
Chatrapur 44 C5 CAP
Chatrapur Court 44 C5 CAPC
Chattarhat 25 F2 CAT
Chattriput 43 G6 CTS
Chau Mahla 31 E1 CMU
Chaube 35 E1 CBH
Chaubepur 22 A2 CBR
Chaubisi 22 C2 CHBS
Chaudhuribandh 35 F1 CDB
Chauhani 31 F2 CAZ
Chowk 38 inset
Chaukhandi 23 E4 CHH
Chauki Man 8 D4 CKM
Chaunrah 21 H3 CNH
Chauntra Behetrah 9 F2 CTZ
Chaupale 30 B6 CUE
Chaura 24 C5 CUX
Chauradano 24 A1 CAO
Chaurai 32 C5 CHUA
Chaurakheri 20 D6 CRKR
Chaurashi 35 G2 CRS
Chaure Bazar 22 D2 CHBR
Chauri Chaura 23 F2 CC
Chausa 23 G4 CSA
Chautara 26 A2 CROA
Chauth ka Barwara 20 B2 CKB
Chavadipalaiyam 57 H5 CVD
Chavaj 29 H5 CVJ
Chaval Kheda 40 B2 CHLK
Chawapail 9 E4 CHA
Chaygaon 26 C2 CGON
Chebrol 49 H5 CEL
Chedhabanni H 24 D4
Chegro BH 35 F1 CEME
Chegunta 48 A5 CGTA
Cheharta 8 C2 CIA
Chelama 54 B2 CMZ
Chemancheri Halt 56 D5 CMC
Chembur 38 inset CMBR
Chengail 37 inset CGA
Chengalpattu Jn 58 D2 CGL
Chengannur 60 B3 CNGR
Chengmari 25 G1 CNM
Chennai Beach 59 inset MSB
Chennai Central 59 inset MAS
Chennai Egmore 59 inset MS
Chennai Fort 59 inset MSF
Chennai region 58 D1, 59 inset
Chepauk 59 inset MCPK
Cheppad 60 B4 CHPD
Cheragram BH 36 B3 CRAE
Cheranmahadevi 60 D5 SMD
Cheriyanad 60 B4 CYN
Cherrapunji 26 D4 -
Cherukara Halt 57 E6 CQA
Cherukuvada 49 H5 CKV
Cheruvu Madhavaram 49 F5 CVV
Chetar 34 D2 CTQ
Chetpet 59 inset MSC
Chettinad 61 F2 CTND
Chettipalaiyam 57 F6 CIM
Chettiyapatti 61 E1 CII
Cheyyar 58 C2 *
Chhabra Gugor 20 C5 CAG
Chhachhar 38 C1 CCHR
Chhada 33 F3 CHDX
Chhaderiya 19 H5
Chhajawa 20 C5 CJW
Chhajli 8 D5 CJL
Chhalesar 13 F6 CHLR
Chhan Arorian 7 G6 CHNR
Chhandrauli 22 C2 CDRL
Chhannera 31 F5 CAER
Chhansara 29 E1 CASA
Chhanua 35 F5 CHNU
Chhapra Jn 23 H3 CPR
Chhapra Kacheri Jn 23 H3 CI
Chhaprawat Halt 13 E3 CHWT
Chharodi 29 G3 CE
Chharrah 35 F3 CHRA
Chhata 13 E5 CHJ
Chhata Aschaura H 23 G3 CATA
Chhatapur Rd 24 D2 CTU
Chhateni 33 F1 CTJ
Chhatna 35 G3 CJN
Chhatral 29 G2 CTRL
Chhatrapati Shhahu Maharaj T. 46 C5 KOP
Chhatrapati Shivaji Terminus 38 inset CSTM
Chhayapuri 29 H4 CYI
Chheoki 22 D4 COI
Chhidgaon 31 G4 CGO
Chhina 8 D2 CHN
Chhindwara Jn 32 B5 CWA
Chhintanwala 9 E5 CTW
Chhipadohar 34 C2 CPDR
Chhota Ambona 35 G2, 45 inset CAM
Chhota Gudha 12 B5 COD
Chhota Udepur 30 B4 CTD
Chhoti Odai 20 C2 COO
Chhuchhapura Jn 30 A4 CCP
Chhulha 33 G3 CLF
Chianki 34 C1 CNF
Chichaki 35 F1 CCK
Chicholi 42 B1 CCO
Chicholi Buzurg 42 B3 CCBZ
Chichonda 32 A6 CCD
Chichpalli 42 A4 CIP
Chidambaram 58 C5 CDM
Chigicherla 53 H4 CCA
Chiheru 8 D3 CEU
Chikale 38 inset
Chikalthan 40 B4 CTH
Chikballapur 53 H6 CBP
Chikbanavar 57 G1 BAW
Chikhli Rd 39 F2 CIO
Chikjajur Jn 53 E5 JRU
Chikkandavadi Halt 53 E5 CKVD
Chikmagalur 52 D6 CMG
Chikna 24 C2 CKNA
Chikni Rd 41 H3 CKNI
Chikodi Rd 46 D5 CKR
Chiksana 13 E6 CIK
Chiksugur 48 A6 CK
Chil Kahar 23 G3 CHR
Chilakalapudi 49 G6 CLU
Chilbila Jn 22 D3 CIL
Chilh 23 E5 CHIL
Chilhia 15 F6 CIH
Chilka 44 C4 CLKA
Chilo 11 F5 CLO
Chiluvur 49 F6 CLVR
Chilwaria 14 D5 CLW
Chimalpahad 49 F3 CMW
Chimidipalli 50 C2 CMDP
Chinchli 46 D5 CNC
Chinchpada 39 H1 CPD
Chinchpokli 38 inset CHG
Chinchuriya 35 G2 CCR
Chinchwad 39 G6 CCH
Chindadripet 59 inset MCPT
Chingavanam 60 B3 CGV
Chink Hill 47 F2 CNHL
Chinna Salem 58 B4 CHSM
Chinnababu Samudram 58 C4 CBU
Chinnadagudihundi Halt 57 F3 CGHD
Chinnaganjam 54 D2 CJM
Chinnaravuru 49 G6 CIV
Chinnekuntapalle 53 H4 CCI
Chinpai 35 H2 CPLE
Chintakani 49 F4 CKN
Chintalapalli 49 E3 CLE
Chintaman Ganesh 31 E3 CNN
Chintamani 53 H6 CMY

Chintaparru 50 A6	CTPR
Chintapatri 54 B6	CTY
Chiplun 46 B3	CHI
Chipurupalli Rd 50 D2	CPP
Chipyana Buzurg 13 E3, 15 inset	CYZ
Chirai 28 D2	CHIB, CHI
Chiraidongri 32 D5	CID
Chirakkal Halt 56 D4	CQL
Chirala 55 E1	CLX
Chiralla Pauthu BH 23 G5	**CPBH**
Chirawa 12 B4	CRWA
Chirayinkil 60 B5	CRY
Chirgaon 21 G4	CGN
Chirimiri 33 H3	CHRM
Chitahara 22 B5	CTHR
Chital 29 E5	CTL
Chitalda 30 A6	CHLD
Chitali 40 A4	CIT
Chitbaragaon 23 G3	CBN
Chitgidda 48 B4	CTF
Chitoda 41 H2	CHJC
Chitora Renwal 20 B1	CHRW
Chitra 13 F2	-
Chitradurg 53 E4	CTA
Chitrakootdham Karwi 22 B4	CKTD
Chitrapur 52 B5	CTTP
Chitrasani Rd 18 D6	CTT
Chitravad 28 D6	CTRD
Chitrod 28 D2	COE
Chitta 48 A3	CHTT
Chittapur 47 H4	CT
Chittaranjan 35 G2	CRJ
Chittauni 15 G6	CTE
Chittauni Ghat 15 G6	CIG
Chittaurgarh Jn 19 H5	COR
Chitteri 58 C1	CTRE
Chittoor 58 C1	CTO
Chityala 48 D4	CTYL
Chodiala 9 G6	CDL
Choka 31 H4	CHQ
Choki Sorath 28 D5	CKE
Chola 13 E4	CHL
Cholang 8 D2	CGH
Cholapuram 60 D3	CPM
Chomu-Samod 12 B6	COM
Chondi 41 E5	CWI
Chongajan 27 G2	CJA
Chopan 23 F6	CPU
Chorvadodra 29 G3	COV
Choral 31 E4	CRL
Choranda Jn 29 H5	CRND
Chorepura 21 E3	CPV
Chorgi 47 F4	CHRG
Chorwad Rd 38 B1	CVR
Chosla 20 B2	CSL
Chotila 29 E4	COW
Choti Padoli 42 A4	CPW
Chotti Khatu 11 G6	CTKT
Chovvara 60 B2	CWR
Chowhatta 36 A2, 63 E1	CWT
Chowka Ghat 14 C6	CKG
Chowrigacha 36 B1	CWLE
Chromepet 59 inset	CMP
Chuchela Kalan Halt 13 F2	CLKN
Chuchura 37 inset	CNS
Chuda 29 F4	CDA
Chudawa 41 E5	CRU
Chulheta 32 A1	CHULHETA
Chuli 29 E3	CUL
Chullimada 57 F6	CLMD
Chun Bhati 25 F1	CHF
Chunabhatti 38 inset	CHF
Chunar Jn 23 E5	CAR
Churaibari 27 E6	CBZ
Churaman Nagri 13 E5	CRG
Churaru Takrala 9 E3	
Churchgata Halt 25 F1	
Churchgate 39 F5, 38 inset	CCG
Chureb 23 E1	CRV
Churk 23 F6	CUK
Churu Jn 12 A3	CUR
Churulia 35 G2	CMA
Chutlinkpur 25 F1	
Chuva Rd 29 H4	-
Cinnamara 17 E6	CMA
Clutterbuckganj 13 G3	CBJ
Coalfields region 45 inset	
Cochin Harbour Terminus 60 B2	CHTS
Cochin Pier 60 B2	CNP
Coimbatore Jn 57 F6	CBE
Coimbatore North Jn 57 F6	CBF
Colaba 38 inset	-
Collectorate 60 D2	-
Collectorganj 22 A2	-
Colonelganj 14 D6	CLJ
Companyganj 26 D4	-
Contai Rd 35 H5	CNT
Cooch Behar 25 H2	COB
Coonoor 57 F5	ONR
Coromandel 58 A2	COL
Cossimbazar 36 B1	CSZ
Cossye Halt 35 H4	CSY
Cotton Green 38 inset	CTGN
Cuddalore Port Jn 58 D4	CUPJ
Cuddapah 54 B4	HX
Cumbum 54 C2	CBM
Currey Rd 38 inset	CRD
Cuttack Jn 44 D3	CTC
D	
Dabasang 28 C4	DBSN
Dabhau 29 H4	DBOU
Dabhaura 22 C5	DBR
Dabhli Rathan 11 G1	DBI
Dabhoda 29 G2	DBO
Dabhoi Jn 30 A5	DB
Dabilpur 48 C3	DBV
Dabirpura 51 inset	DQR
Dabka 41 E1	DBKA
Dabla Jn 12 B4	DBLA
Dabolim 52 A2	DBM
Dabpal 43 E6	DPF
Dabra 21 F3	DBA
Dabtara 13 G4	DUB
Dachna 25 F3	DHNA
Dadar 39 F5, 38 inset	DDR, DR
Dadgaon 41 F3	DDZ
Dadgaon 41 F3	DDZ
Dadhal Inam 29 H5	DHM
Dadhapara 33 G5	DPH
Dadhdevi 20 B4	DDV
Dadhera Halt 27 E1	-
Dadpur 24 C5	DPX
Dadri 13 E3	DER
Dagaon 27 E2	DGX
Dagarkhedi 31 F5	DGRI
Daghora 34 B6	DAO
Dagmagpur 23 E5	DAP
Dagori 33 G6	DGS
Dagru 8 D4	DAU
Dahanu Rd 39 F3	DRD
Dahapara Dham 36 B1	DHPD
Daharka Balaji 12 B6	DKBJ
Dahegaon 41 G2	DAE
Dahej 29 G5	DHF
Dahina Zainabad 12 C4	DZB
Dahinsara Jn 28 D3	DAC
Dahisar 38 inset	DIC
Dahod 30 B3	DHD
Daijar 19 E1	DJJ
Dailwara 21 F5	DWA
Dainhat 36 B2	DHAE
Daitari 44 D2	DTR
Dakaniya Talav 20 B4	DKNT
Dakor 29 H3	DK
Dakshin Barasat 36 B5	DBT
Dakshin Durgapur 36 B5	DKDP
Dakshin Maju 63 F5, 37 inset	DJU
Dakshinbari 63 F5, 37 inset	DKB
Dakshineshwar 37 inset	DAKE
Daladi 29 E3	DL
Dalan 25 E4	DLF
Dalapathisamudrarn 60 D5	DYS
Dalauda 30 D1	DLD
Dalbhumgarh 35 G4	DVM
Dalchhapra Halt 23 H3	DCP
Daldali 27 G3	DLDE
Dalelnagar 14 B6	DLQ
Dalgaon 25 G1	DLO
Dalhousie Rd 9 E1	DLSR
Daliganj Jn 22 B1	DAL
Dalimgaon 25 F3	DLX
Dalkhola 25 E3	DLK
Dallirajhara 42 D3	DRZ
Dalmau Jn 22 C3	DMW
Dalpat Singhpur Halt 8 A5	DPT
Dalpatpur 13 G3	DLP
Dalsanur 58 A1	DNU
Dalsingpara 25 H1	-
Dalsingh Sarai 24 B4	DSS
Daltonganj 34 C1	DTO
Damalcheruvu 54 B6	DCU
Damanjodi 50 C1	DMG
Damanpur 25 H2	DPO
Damchara 27 F4	DCA
Damdim 25 G1	DDM
Damlai 29 H5	DMLI
Damnagar 29 E5	DME
Damodar Jn 35 G2	DMA
Damoh 32 C2	DMO
Damoy 33 E2	DMYA
Damrughutu 35 F2	DRGU
Danapur 24 A4, 25 inset	DNR
Dandeli 52 C2	DED
Dandimal 44 D2	DNDL
Dandirhat 63 H5	-
Dandkhora 25 E4	DNQ
Dandu Gopalpuram 51 E1	DGB
Dandupur 22 D3	DND
Danea 35 E2	DNEA
Dangari 17 F4	DNGI
Dangarwa 29 G2	DNW
Dangidhar 32 B2	DGD
Dangoaposi 35 E5	DPS
Dangtal 26 B2	DTX
Danishpet 58 A4	DSPT
Daniawan H 24 A4	DNWN
Daniawan Bazar H 24 A4	DNWN
Dankaur 13 E3	DKDE
Dankuni Jn 36 B4, 37 inset	DKAE
Dansi 37 inset	DNI
Dantan 35 H6	DNT
Dantewara 42 D6	DWZ
Dantia 12 D6	DTF
Dantra 20 A1	DTRA
Danwar 13 E4	DAR
Daotuhaja 27 F4	DJA
Dapodi 46 C1	DAPD
Dapsaura 22 A3	DPSR
Dara 20 B5	DARA
Daraganj 22 D4	DRGJ
Darasuram 58 C6	DSM
Darauli BH 23 F4	**DRV**
Darazpur 9 G5	DZP
Darbari Halt 11 F4	DBK
Darbhanga Jn 24 B3	DBG
Darekasa 42 C1	DKS
Darimeta 32 B6	DDMT
Darjeeling 25 F1	DJ
Darlaghat 9 F3	*
Darliput 50 B2	DPC
Daroji 53 F2	DAJ
Darritola Jn 33 H3	DTL
Darshannagar 22 D2	DRG
Darwa Motibagh 41 F3	DWM
Daryabad 22 C1	DYD
Daryaoganj 13 G5	DRO
Daryapur Jn 22 C3	DYP
Dasalwada A Rd 29 H3	DTD
Dasampatti 58 A3	DST
Dasarah BH 25 E1	**DSME**
Dasarathpur 24 C4	DRTP
Dasghara 36 A3	-
Daskalgram 36 A2, 63 E1	DLM
Dasna 13 E3	DS
Dasnagar 37 inset	DSNR
Dasua 8 D2	DZA
Datarda Kalan 20 C3	DTQ
Datewas 8 D6	DTW
Datha Rd 29 F6	DTH
Datia 21 F4	DAA
Dativli 38 inset	
Dativli Chord Cabin 38 inset	**DCC**
Daud Khan 13 F5	DAQ
Daudpur 23 H3	DDP
Daulakot Bhai Halt 8 C5	DQB
Daulatabad 40 B4	DLB
Daulatpur 25 F4	-
Daulatpur H 24 C4	DLTR
Daulatpur Haryana 12 B1	DULP
Daulta 21 F5	DLA
Daund Jn 46 D1	DD
Daundaj 46 C2	DNJ
Daurai 19 H2	DOZ
Daurala 13 E2	DRLA
Dauram Madhepura 24 D3	DMH
Dausa 20 C1	DO
Dausni 9 H6	DSNI
DAV College Jalalabad 8 B4	DAVC
DAV College Jalandhar H 8 D3	DAVJ
Davangere 53 E4	DVG
Davol 29 H4	DOW
Dayabasti 12 D3, 15 inset	DBSI
Dayadara 29 H5	DAY
Dayalpur 22 D4	DLPR
Dayanandnagar 51 inset	DYE
DCOP 35 H2	**DCOP**
Debagram 36 B2	DEB
Debari 19 F5	DRB
Debiganj 24 D2	DGZ
Debipur 36 B3	DBP
Deedarganj 25 inset	DDGJ
Deedarganj Rd 23 E3	DJD
Deeg 12 D5	DEEG
Deenapatti Halt 24 D3	DEPI
Deepnagar 24 B5	DPNR
Degana Jn 11 G6	DNA
Deganga 63 G6	-
Dehare 40 A5	DIH
Dehit 20 B4	DEIT
Dehradun 9 H5	DDN
Dehri City23 G5	DTY
Dehri On Sone 23 G5	DOS
Dehu Rd 39 G6	DEHR
Dekapam Halt 17 F4	DKPM
Dekargaon 27 E1	DGTB
Dekpura 24 B4	DKR
Delaji-ka-Khera 19 F4	DJKR
Delang 44 D4	DEG
Delhi Azadpur 15 inset	DAZ
Delhi Cantt 12 D3, 15 inset	DEC
Delhi Inderpuri 15 inset	DLPI
Delhi Jn 12 D3, 15 inset	DLI
Delhi Kishanganj 15 inset	DKZ
Delhi region 12 D3, 15 inset	
Delhi Safdarjang 15 inset	DSJ
Delhi Sarai Rohilla 15 inset	DEE
Delhi Shahdara Jn 12 D3, 15 inset	DSA
Delvada 38 C1	DVA
Demai 29 H3	DIE
Demu 34 C2	DEMU
Dendukur 49 F5	DNDK
Denduluru 49 G5	DEL
Deoband 13 E1	DBD
Deogaon Rd 43 H3	DFR
Deojhar 35 E5	DJHR
Deokali 14 B4	DEO
Deonagar 45 inset	DNH
Deoragram 33 H1	DRGM
Deorahwababa Rd 23 G2	DRBR
Deoranian 13 H3	DRN
Deo Rd BH 23 H5	**DORD**
Deori 32 D3	DEO
Deori Halt 14 A3	DYU
Deoria Sadar 23 G2	DEOS
Deotala 25 F4	-
Depa 26 B3	*
Depalsar 12 A3	DEP
Dera Baba Jaimal Singh 8 D2	DBCA
Dera Baba Nanak 8 D1	DBNK
Derdi 29 E5	DRX
Dergaon 24 B5	DRGN
Derol 30 A4	DRL
Derowan 35 E4	DRWN
Desang Siding 17 E5	DSX
Desar Rd 30 A3	DSRD
Desari 24 B4	DES
Deshalpur 28 B2	DSLP
Deshapran Shashmal (Bajkul) 36 A5	DSPN
Deshnok 11 F4	DSO
Desur 52 B1	DUR
Deswal Halt 11 G6	DSL
Det 19 H4	DET
Dethli 29 G2	DHLI
Detroj 29 G2	DTJ
Deula 36 B5	D
Deulti 36 A4	DTE
Devakottai Rd 61 F2	DKD
Devalgaon Avchar 40 D5	DAV
Devalia Rd 28 C2	DVRD
Devaliya 29 E2	DVY
Devanahalli 57 H1	DHL
Devangonthi 57 H2	DKN
Devanur 53 E6	VNR
Devarapalle 53 G5	DPE
Devarayi 52 C2	DEV
Devargudda 52 D3	DAD
Devarkadra 48 B5	DKC
Devbalodacharoda 43 E2	DBEC
Devgadh Baria 30 B4	DVB
Devgam 18 C6	DVGM
Devgarh Madariya 19 F3	DOHM
Devi 32 B6	DVH
Devlali 39 H4	DVL
Devpura 20 C3	DPZ
Devrakot 22 D1	DELO
Devsana 29 G2	DEU
Devthana 41 F5	DVN
Dewa 29 G4	DEWA
Dewalgaon 42 C2	DEW
Dewanganj 31 H2	DWG
Dewanhat 25 H2	DWT
Dewas Jn 31 E3	DWX
Dhaban 8 B6	DABN
Dhabla 31 E2	DHB
Dhablan 9 E5	DBN
Dhaka 24 A2	*
Dhakia Tiwari Halt 14 A4	DOT
Dhakuria 37 inset	DHK
Dhalaibil 16 B6	DQL
Dhalgaon 47 E4	DLGN
Dhalpukhuri 27 F2	DHRY
Dhamalgaon 17 E5	*
Dhamangaon 41 G2	DMN
Dhamara 45 F2	*
Dhamara Ghat 24 D4	DHT
Dhamarda 30 B3	DHMA
Dhamdaha 24 D3	*
Dhamdhamia 25 E5	DDX
Dhamni 41 E4	DNE
Dhamora 13 G3	DAM
Dhampur 13 F2	DPR
Dhamtan Sahib 9 E6	DTN
Dhamtari 43 E2	DTR
Dhamuah 36 B5	DMU
Dhana Kherli 21 E1	DXK
Dhana Ladanpur Halt 12 C3	DZL
Dhanaichha 23 F4	DCX
Dhanakwada 18 C6	DKW
Dhanala 29 E2	DHNL
Dhanapur 43 F6	DIR
Dhanari 13 F3	DN
Dhanauli Phulwaria 24 C4	DPL
Dhanauri 24 C5	DNRE
Dhanauti 23 H4	DAT
Dhanawada 18 D6	DHVR
Dhanbad Jn 35 F2, 45 inset	DHN
Dhandari Kalan 9 E4	DDL
Dhandhera 9 H6	DNRA
Dhandhuka 29 F4	DCK
Dhanera 18 C5	DQN
Dhaneta 13 G3	DAN
Dhang 24 B2	DAG
Dhangaria 35 H3	DGF
Dhaniakhali H 36 B3	
Dhani-Kasar 20 B5	DKQ
Dhankya 12 B6	DNK
Dhankuria G Garden 63 H5	-
Dhanmandal 45 E2	DNM
Dhanoli 42 C1	DNL
Dhanora (Deccan) 41 G5	DHNR
Dhanori 41 G2	DNZ
Dhanpura 29 G2	DNPR
Dhansar H 45 inset	DQS
Dhansimla 35 H3	DIM
Dhansiri 27 G3	DSR
Dhansu 12 B2	DNX
Dhansura 29 H2	DNUA
Dhantola 25 F2	-
Dhanushkodi Halt 61 G4	
Dhanushkodi Pier 61 G4	DSY
Dhanuvachapuram Halt 60 C5	DAVM
Dhanvala Wada 28 B2	DHVR
Dhapdhapi 36 B5	DPDP
Dhapewara 32 D6	DPW
Dhappar 9 F4	DHPR
Dharamkundi 31 H4	DKI
Dharampur (Himachal) 9 F4	DMP
Dharampur 13 F4	DMPR
Dharamtul 27 E2	DML
Dharangaon 40 B2	DXG
Dhareshwar 19 F3	DRS
Dharewada 29 G1	DRW
Dharhara 24 C4	DRH
Dhari 29 E6	DARI
Dhariwal 8 D2	DHW
Dharmabad 41 F6	DAB
Dharmadam Halt 56 D4	DMD
Dharmaj 29 H4	-
Dharmanagar 27 E6	DMR
Dharmapuram 57 H6	*
Dharmapuri 58 A3	DPJ
Dharmavaram Jn 53 H4	DMM
Dharminia Halt 23 H1	DRQ
Dharnoda 20 D6	DHR
Dharodi 9 E6	DHY
Dharuadih 34 C5	DIH
Dharur 48 B4	DRR
Dharwad 52 C2	DWR
Dhasa Jn 29 E5	DAS
Dhatrigram 36 B3	DTAE
Dhatura Alipur 32 D5	DTAP
Dhaulimuhan 44 D4	DLMH
Dhaulpur Jn 21 E1	DHO
Dhauni 24 D5	DWLE
Dhaura 21 F6	DUA
Dhaurmui Jaghina 13 E6	DUM
Dhaursalar Halt 22 A1	DUO
Dhavalas 47 E2	DHS
Dheena 23 F4	DHA
Dhekiajuli 27 E1	-
Dhekiajuli Rd 16 B6	DKJR
Dhekiajuli TE Siding 27 E1	-
Dhekvad 30 B6	DWD
Dhelana 11 E6	DLNA
Dhemaji 17 E5	DMC
Dhengli Pimpalgaon 40 D5	DGPP
Dhenkanal 44 D2	DNKL
Dherai Siding 27 E1	-
Dhigawara 12 C5	DGW
Dhilwan 8 D2	DIW
Dhindha 12 A6	DHND
Dhindhora Hukmikheda 20 D1	DNHK
Dhindsa Halt 8 C4	DDK
Dhing 27 E2	DIU
Dhing Bazar 27 E2	DBZ
Dhinoj 29 G1	DHJ
Dhirera 11 F3	DHRR
Dhirganj 22 D3	DHRJ
Dhirpur 9 F5	DPP
Dhoda Kheri 9 F5	DHKR
Dhodhar 30 D1	DOD
Dhodra Mohar 31 H5	DOH
Dhogri H 8 D3	DRE
Dhoki 47 G2	DKY
Dhola Jn 29 F5	DLJ
Dhola Mazra 9 F5	DHMZ
Dholbaja Halt 25 E2	DLZ
Dholi (Bhal) 29 F4	DIBL
Dholi 24 B3	DOL
Dholikuva 39 G2	DOLK
Dholipal 8 B6	DPK
Dholka 29 G3	DOK
Dhondhadih 23 G4	DDD
Dhondi 41 E6	DNDI
Dhone Jn 53 H2	DHNE
Dhoraji 28 D5	DJI
Dhorakhoh 31 H5	DHQ
Dhosawas 30 D2	DHWS
Dhrangadhra Jn 29 F3	DHG
Dhrol 28 D3	DHRI
Dhuankheri 20 B6	DKRA
Dhubri 26 A3	DBB
Dhubri Ghat 26 A3	DYG
Dhubulia 36 B2	DHU
Dhulabari 25 F2	DBQ
Dhule 40 B2	DHI
Dhulghat 41 E1	DGT
Dhulian Ganga 25 F6	DGLE

Dhulkot 9 F5 DKT
Dhumdangi 25 F2 DMZ
Dhupdhara 26 C3 DPRA
Dhupguri 25 G2 DQG
Dhurana Halt 12 D2 DHRN
Dhurant Jwas 24 C4 DJS
Dhuri Jn 9 E5 DUI
Dhurwasin 33 G3 DRSN
Dhutra 34 C6 DTV
Dhuva 29 E3 DV
Dhuwala 19 H3 DWL
Diamond Harbour 36 B5 DH
Diara 37 inset DEH
Dibai 13 F4 DIB
Dibnapur Halt 13 H3 DBNR
Dibru Darrang Siding 27 E1 -
Dibrugarh Town 17 F5 DBRT
Dibrumukh 17 F5 DBMK
Dichpalli 48 C1 DHP
Didwana 11 H5 DIA
Digaru 26 D2 DGU
Digboi 17 G5 DBY
Diggi 20 A2 DIGI
Digha 36 A6 *
Digha Ghat 24 A4, 25 inset DDG
Digha Wani 32 B5 -
Dighe 38 inset
Dighirpar 63 F6 -
Dighori Buzurg 42 A2 DGY
Dighwa Dubauli 23 H2 DWDI
Dighwara 24 A3, 25 inset DGA
Dignagar 36 B3, 63 G3 DTG
Digod 20 B4 DXD
Digsar 29 F3 DXR
Diguvametta 54 B2 DMT
Dihakho 27 F3 DKE
Dihor 29 F6 DIO
Dijaobra 27 F3 DJB
Dikom 17 F5 DKM
Diksal 47 E1 -
Dilaram Halt 25 F1 DALM
Dilawarnagar 22 B1 DIL
Dildarnagar Jn 23 F4 DLN
Dilkusha Cabin 22 B1 LBH
Dilli Dewanganj 25 E4 DVJ
Dilmili 43 E6 DMK
Dilwa 24 B6 DLW
Dimapur 27 G2 DMV
Dimow Halt 17 E4 DM
Dinagaon 40 C4 DIQ
Dinanagar 8 D1 DNN
Dindigul Jn 61 E1 DG
Ding 12 A1 DING
Dingania 14 B3 DNY
Dingwahi 22 A4 DWI
Dinhata 25 H2 DHH
Dinhata College Halt 25 H2 DCH
Dipa Halt 17 E4 DIPA
Diphu 27 G3 DPU
Diplana 12 A2 DPLN
Dipore 41 G2 DIP
Disa 18 D6 DISA
Ditokcherra 27 F4 DTC
Diva Jn 39 F5, 38 inset DW
Divine Nagar Halt 60 B1 DINR
Divitipalli 48 B5 DTP
Diwan Khauti 46 B2 DWV
Diwana 12 D1 DWNA
Diyawan H 24 A4 DYW
Diyodar 18 C6 DEOR
Dobbspet Halt 57 G1 DBS
Dobh Bahali 12 C2 DBHL
Dobhi 23 E4 DHE
Dockyard Rd 38 inset DKRD
Doda 7 H5 *
Dodballapur 57 G1 DBU
Dodbele 57 G1 DBL
Doddampatti 58 A3 DPI
Doddanetta 54 A6 DTT
Doddappanayakkanur 60 D2 DODP
Doddasiddavanahalli 53 F4 DSHI
Dodh 8 C4 DODH
Dodjala Halt 57 H1 DJL
Dohna 13 H3 DOX
Dohrighat 23 F2 DIT
Dohru 22 A3 DOH
Doikallu 43 H4 DKLU
Doiwala 9 H5 DWO
Dokra 35 F2, 45 inset DOKRA
Dokwa 12 A3 DKWA
Dolavli 39 F6, 38 inset DLV
Domahalli 57 E3 DOY
Dombivli 39 F5, 38 inset DI
Dombivli CTL Cabin 38 inset DICTL
Domingarh 23 F1 DMG
Domjur 36 B4, 37 inset, 63 F5 DJR
Domjur Rd 37 inset DJRR
Domohani 25 G2 DOI
Donakonda 54 C1 DKD
Dondaicha 40 C4 DDE
Dongargaon 31 F6 DGN
Dongargarh 42 D1 DGG
Dongri Buzurg 42 B1 DGBZ
Donigal 56 D1 DOGL
Donkinavalsa 50 C2 DNV
Doraha 9 E4 DOA
Doravarichattram 54 D5 DVR
Dornakal Jn 49 F3 DKJ
Dosapadu 49 G6 DPD
Dosvada 39 G1 DSD
Donta 31 E3 DON
Dr. Radhakrishnanagar 30 D2 DRRN
Duan Mouza 36 A5 DUAN
Duankalan 9 E5 DOC
Dubaha 24 B3 DUBH
Dubia 16 D6 DBW
Dubrajpur 35 H2 DUJ
Dubri Kalan 33 F1 BARD
Dudahi 23 G1 DUE
Dudda 57 E1 DUH
Dudhani 47 G3 DUD
Dudhaunda Halt 23 F4 DDNA
Dudhia Khurd 14 A3 DYK
Dudhinagar 34 A1 DXN
Dudhnoi 26 B3 DDNI
Dudhrej 29 F3 DEJ
Dudhsagar 52 B2 DDS
Dudhsagar Falls 52 B2 DWF
Dudhwa Khara 12 A3 DKX
Dudia 19 E2 DUK
Dudwa Jn 14 B3 DDW
Dudwindi 8 D3 DDY
Duganpur 13 G3 DUN
Dugda 35 F2, inset DDGA
Dugdol 18 D5 DGQ
Duggalapura 52 D5 -
Duggirala 49 G6 DIG
Duhai Halt 13 E3 DXH
Dukheri 9 F5 DOKY
Dukhlangia 17 E6 DLGS
Dukhnawaran 8 C2 DUQ
Dulakhapatna 45 E2 DLPT
Dulariya 31 H4 DRA
Duliajan 17 F5 DJG
Dullabcherra 27 E5 DLCR
Dullahpur 23 F3 DLR
Dulmera 11 F3 DLC
Dulrasar Halt 11 H3 DUS
Dum Dum Cantt 37 inset DDC
Dum Dum Jn 36 B4, 37 inset DDJ
Dumari Juwara Halt 24 A3 DRI
Dumariya 20 D1 DY
Dumduma Town 17 F4 DUT
Dumetra 34 D5 DMF
Dumiyani 28 D5 DUY
Dumka 35 H1 *
Dumraon 23 G4 DURE
Dumri 24 C4 DRI
Dumri Bihar 35 E2 DMBR
Dumri Khurd 42 A1 DKU
Dumurdaha 36 B3 DMLE
Dumuriput 50 C1 DMRT
Dundara 19 E2 DOR
Dundi 32 D2 DDCE
Dundlod Mukundgarh 12 4A DOB
Dungar 38 D1 DGJ
Dungarda 39 G2 DNGD
Dungarpur 30 B1 DNRP
Dungarpur Quarry 28 D6 DUV
Dungri 39 F2 DGI
Dungripali 43 H2 DJX
Dupadu 54 A1 DUU
Duraundha Jn 23 H3 DDA
Durg Jn 42 D1 DURG
Durg Link Cabin 42 D2 DLC
Durgachak 36 B5 DZK
Durgachak Town 36 B5 DZKT
Durgada Gate 50 B4 DGDG
Durganagar 37 inset DGNR
Durgapur 35 H2 DGR
Durgapura 20 B1 DPA
Durgapuri 20 C3 DGPI
Durgauti 23 F4 DGO
Dusi Rd 50 D2 DSI
Duskheda 40 C2 DSK
Duttapukur 36 B4 DTK
Duvvada 50 C3 DVD
DV Block Hut 57 H4 DVBH
Dwarapudi 50 A5 DWP
Dwarka 28 B4 DWK
Dwarkaganj 22 D2 DWJ

E

Echanuggurree 63 F5 ENG
Edamann 60 C4 EDN
Edapalayam Halt 60 C4 EDP
Edavai 60 B5 EVA
Edduladoddi 53 H2 EDD
Eden Gardens 37 inset EDG
Egattur 58 D1 EGT
Ekambarakuppam 58 C1 EKM
Ekangar Sarai 24 A4 EKR
Ekchari 24 D4 EKC
Ekdill 21 G1 EKL
Eklakhi Jn 25 F4 EKI
Ekma 23 H3 EKMA
Eksari 24 B5 EKH
Ekshara 63 F5 EKS
Elamanchili 50 C3 YLM
Elamanur 58 A6 EL
Elangakurichi 61 E1 ELG
Elantangudi 58 C6 EGD
Elattur 56 D5 ETR
Elavur 54 D6 EVR
Elimala 56 C3 ELM
Ellenabad 11 H1 ENB
Elphinstone Rd 38 inset EPR
Eluru 49 G5 EE
Ennore 58 D1, 59 inset ENR
Eraligul 27 E5 ELL
Eraniel 60 C6 ERL
Erich Rd 21 G3 ERC
Eriodu 61 E1 EDU
Ernakulam Goods 60 B2 ERG
Ernakulam Jn 60 B2 ERS
Ernakulam Town 60 B2 ERN
Erode Jn 57 H5 ED
Errupalem 49 F5 YP
ERS C Cabin 60 B2 ERSC
ERS D Cabin 60 B2 ERSD
Erumeli 60 C3 *
Etah 13 F5 ETAH
Etakkot 56 D4 ETK
Etawah 21 G1 ETW
Etmadpur 13 F6 ETUE
Ettapur Rd 58 A4 ETP
Ettimadai 57 F6 ETMD
Ettumanur 60 B3 ETM
Ezhukone 60 B4 EKN
Ezhuppunna 60 B2 EZP

F

Fagunagaon 26 B2 FGN
Faizabad Jn 22 D1 FD
Faizullahpur 22 B3 FYZ
Fakharpur Halt 12 D2 FAP
Fakhrabad 41 G6 FKB
Fakiragram Jn 26 A2 FKM
Falakata 25 H2 FLK
Falaknuma 48 C4, 51 inset FM
Falimari 25 H3 FLM
Falna 19 E4 FA
Falta 63 F6, 36 B5 -
Faqarsar 8 C5 FSR
Farah 13 E6 FAR
Farah Town 13 E6 FHT
Fareni 28 D5 FRN
Farhat Nagar Halt 22 A1 FRH
Farhedi Halt 13 G3 FRD
Faridabad 12 D3, 15 inset FDB
Faridabad New Town 12 D3 FDN
Faridaha Halt 23 F4 FRDH
Faridkot 8 C4 FDK
Fariha 23 F3 PHY
Faringepetta Halt 56 C1 FRG
Farrukhabad Jn 13 H5 FKD, FBD
Farukhnagar 12 D3 FN
Fateh Singhpura 20 D1 FSP
Fateh Singhwala Halt 8 B6 FSW
Fateha H 24 B4
Fatehbad 21 F1 *
Fatehbad 12 B1 *
Fatehabad Chandrawatiganj Jn 31 E3 FTD
Fatehgarh 13 H6 FGR
Fatehgarh Churian 8 C2 FGCN
Fatehgarh Haryana Halt 12 C3 FGH
Fatehgarh Sahib 9 E4 FGSB
Fatehnagar 19 G5 FAN
Fatehnagar 51 inset FAN
Fatehpur 22 B3 FTP
Fatehpur Chaurasi Halt 22 A1 FTC
Fatehpur Shekhawati 12 4A FPS
Fatehpur Sikri 13 E6 FTS
Fatuha Jn 24 A4, 25 inset FUT
Fatuhi 8 B5 FTH
Fazalpur 13 F1 FZL
Fazilka Jn 8 B4 FKA
Fedusar 19 E2 FDR
Fedusar Quarry Siding 19 E2 FDR
Fernhill 57 F5 FER
Ferok 56 D5 FK
Ferozpur 13 F3 -
Fichal 29 G1 FHL
Firozabad 13 F6 FZD
Firozpur Cantt Jn 8 C3 FZR
Firozpur City Jn 8 C3 FZP
Firozshah 8 C4 PHS
Forbesganj Jn 24 D2 FBG
Fraserganj 36 B6 *
Fulgram 29 F3 FLG
Fungo 24 D3
Furkating Jn 27 G1 FKG
Fursatganj 22 C2 FTG

G

Gachhipura 11 G6 GCH
Gad Chiroli 42 B4 *
Gadadharpur 36 A1 GHLE
Gadag Jn 52 D2 GDG
Gadarwara 32 B4 GAR
Gadchandur 42 A5 GDCR
Gadhada Swaminarayan 29 F5 GDSN
Gadhakda 29 E6 GKD
Gadhwala 11 F4 GDW
Gadiganuru 53 F2 GNR
Gadra Rd 18 A2 GDD
Gadwal 48 B6 GWD
Gagariya 18 B3 GGY
Gahmar 23 G4 GMR
Gahndran Halt 8 D3 GNZ
Gainjahwa 14 D5 GAW
Gainoori Jn 15 E5 GIR
Gaipura 22 D5 GAE
Gaisal 25 F2 GIL
Gaj Singhpur 8 6A GJS
Gajapathinagaram 50 C2 GPI
Gajara Bahra 33 G1 GAJB
Gajjelakonda 54 C1 GJJ
Gajner Halt 11 E4 GJN
Gajraula Jn 13 F3 GJL
Gaju Halt 14 B6 GAJU
Gajulagudem 49 G3 GLE
Gajuwal Halt 12 B1 GJW
Galan 40 B2 GAA
Galgalia 25 F2 GAGA
Galpadar 28 D2 W
Galsi 36 A3 GU
Galudih 35 F4 GUD
Galvav 28 C5 GVV
Gamani 16 B6 GAMN
Gambhir Br. Cabin 31 E3 GRF br
Gambhiri Rd 19 H5 GRF
Gambhirpura 30 A5 GHI
Gamharia Jn 35 F4 GMH
Ganapathiipalaiyam 57 H5 GNM
Ganaur 12 D2 GNU
Gandevi 39 F2 GNV
Gandhi Halt 24 A4 GNHI
Gandhi Smriti 39 F1 GNST
Gandhidham C Cabin 28 C2 GIMC
Gandhidham Jn 28 C2 GIMB, GIM
Gandhigram 29 G3, 28 inset GG
Gandhinagar Capital 29 G2 GNC
Gandhinagar Jaipur 20 B1 GADJ
Gandhipuram Halt 49 F3 GHPU
Ganeshganj 32 B2 GAJ
Gangadham 14 D6 GADM
Gangadharpur 44 C4 GNGD
Gangadhra 39 F1 GGAR
Gangaganj 22 C2 GANG
Gangaghat 35 E3 GAG
Gangagrah Halt 13 F5 GGG
Gangaikondan 60 D5 GDN
Gangajhari 42 B1 GJ
Gangakher 41 E6 GNH
Ganganiyan 24 D4 GNNA
Gangapur City 20 C2 GGC
Gangapur City North Cabin 20 C2 GGNC
Gangapur Rd 47 G3 GUR
Gangapara 25 G4 -
Ganga Sahai 24 C4 -
Gangatikuri 36 B2 GGLE
Gangatola 32 D5 GNGT
Gangayapalle 54 B4 GPY
Gangineni 49 F5 GNN
Gangiwara Halt 32 B5 GNW
Gangiwara Town 32 B5 GNW
Gangnapur 36 B3 GGP
Gangpur 36 A3 GRP
Gangrar 19 H4 GGR
Gangraul 13 E4 GNRL
Gangsar Jaito 8 C5 GJUT
Ganguvada 51 E1 GVA
Gangwapur Halt 22 A1 GWP
Gani Dham 24 D5 GDF
Ganj Basoda 32 A2 BAQ
Ganj Dundwara 13 G5 GWA
Ganj Muradabad 22 A1 GJMB
Ganjam 44 C5 GAM
Ganjkhwaja 23 F4 GAQ
Gankar 25 F6 GALE
Gankhera 42 C1 GKT
Gannavaram 49 G5 GWM
Ganpatpura 29 H5 GNPT
Garbeta 35 H4 GBA
Garea Bihar BH 25 F1 GRBH
Garh Banaili 25 E3 GBN
Garh Baruwari 24 D3 GEB
Garh Nokha 23 G5 GNK
Garhani 23 H4 GQN
Garhara 24 C4 GHZ
Garhdhrubeswar 35 G2 GRB
Garhi Bhagi H 8 C5 GHB
Garhi Harsaru Jn 12 D3 GHH
Garhi Manikpur 22 C3 GRMR
Garhi Sandra 21 E1 GIS
Garhmau 21 F4 GRM
Garhmukteshwar 13 F3 GMS
Garhmukteshwar Br 13 F3 GGB
Garhpura 24 C4 GRPA
Garhshankar 9 E3 GSR
Garhwa 34 B1 GHQ
Garhwa Rd Jn 34 B1 GHD
Garia 37 inset GIA
Garifa 37 inset GFAE
Gaigaon 41 E2 GAO
Garividi Rd 50 D2 GVI
Garjaipur 35 F3 GUG
Garkha 13 G5 GRAK
Garkha 24 A3 *
Garla 49 F3 GLA
Garladinne 53 H3 GDE
Garmadi 29 E1 GM
Garna Sahib 8 D2 GSB
Garubigha H 24 B5
Garopara 25 H1 GRU
Garot 20 B6 GOH
Garposh 34 C5 GPH
Garra 32 D6 GRHX
Garsanda 24 C5 GSDH
Garudabilli 50 C2 GRBL
Gatora 33 G5 GTW
Gatra 32 D6 GRJ
Gauchari Gopalpur Halt 24 D4 GPPA
Gaudgaon 47 G3 GDGN
Gauntra Halt 14 A6 GNTR
Gaur 23 E1 GAU
Gaura 22 D3 GRX
Gaurangdi 35 G2 GNI
Gauri Bazar 23 F2 GB
Gauri Sriram Halt 23 G1 GSRM
Gauriamau 22 D1 GMU
Gauribidanur 53 G6 GBD
Gauriganj 22 C2 GNG
Gauriphanta 14 B3 GPF
Gauripur 26 A2 GUP
Gaushala 13 G2 GWS
Gautam Asthan 23 H3 GTST
Gautamdhara 35 E3 GATD
Gautampura Rd 30 D3 GPX
Gavadka 29 E5 GAV
Gawada Malosan 29 H2 MLNR
Gawnaha 15 H6 GAH
Gaya Jn 24 A5 GAYA
Gayabari 25 F1 GBE
Gazole 25 F4 GZL
Gazulapalli 54 B2 GZL
Gede 36 C2 GEDE
Gegal Akhri 19 H1 GEK
Gehlota 19 H1 GLTA
Genoli Rd 20 A4 GNRD
Geong Halt 9 E6 GXG
Geratpur 29 G3 GER
Gerita-Kolvada 29 G2 GTKD
Getor Jagatpura 20 B1 GTJT
Gevra Rd 33 H5 GAD
Gevrai 40 C4 GOI
Ghadela 32 B6 GELA
Ghaggar 9 F4 GHG
Ghaghara Ghat 14 C6 GHT
Ghagwal 7 G6 GHGL
Ghal Kalan 8 C4 GKX
Ghanauli 9 F4 GANL
Ghanpur 48 D3 GNP
Ghansoli 38 inset GNSL
Ghanta 30 A4 GTH
Ghantikal Nidipur 44 D3 GHNH
Ghantila 29 E2 GHM
Ghantoli 30 A5 GHTI
Gharani 47 G1
Gharaunda 12 D1 GRA
Gharyala 8 C3 GYL
Ghasara Halt 21 G1 GHSR
Ghaso 12 C1 GSO
Ghat Pindrai 32 C3 GPC
Ghatala 12 C5 GAL
Ghatampur 22 A3 GTM
Ghatera 32 C2 GEA
Ghatia 31 E2 GIH
Ghatigaon 21 E3 GHAI
Ghat-ka-Varana 20 B4 GKB
Ghatkesar 48 C3, 51 inset GT
Ghatkopar 39 F5, 38 inset GC
Ghatnandur 40 D6 GNU
Ghatprabha 46 D6 GPB
Ghatpuri 13 G4 GTP
Ghatsila 35 G4 GTS
Ghatwad 38 C1 GTWD
Ghaunspur 8 D2 GPW
Ghausganj Halt 14 A6 GSGJ
Ghaziabad Jn 13 E3, 15 inset GZB
Ghazipur City 23 F4 GCT
Ghazipur Ghat 23 F4 GZT
Ghelda 29 G2 GLD
Gher 21 E1 GHER
Ghevra 12 D3 GHE
Ghiala Halt 8 D1 GILA
Ghoga 24 D4 GGA
Ghoghardiha 24 C2 GGH
Ghograpar 26 D2 GOE
Ghoksadanga 25 H2 GDX
Gholeshapur 63 G6 -
Gholvad 39 F3 GVD
Ghoradongri 31 H5 GDYA
Ghoraghata 36 A4 GGTA
Ghoraras Ghona 36 C4 GGV
Ghorasahan 24 A1 GRH

Ghorawadi 39 G6 GRWD
Ghori Halt 14 B6 GHRI
Ghorparan BH 24 C5 GHN
Ghorpuri 46 C1 GPR
Ghoshi 23 F3 GSI
Ghosipura 21 F2 GOPA
Ghosla 31 E2 GSH
Ghosrana 12 D6 GOS
Ghosunda 19 G5 GSD
Ghotgewadi 52 B2 GWE
Ghoti 39 G4 GO
Ghudankhapa 32 A6 GDKP
Ghughali 15 G6 GH
Ghughus 42 A4 GGS
Ghum 25 F1 GHUM
Ghumasan 29 G2 GUS
Ghunas Halt 8 D5 GUNS
Ghunghuti 33 F3 GGT
Ghungrana Halt 9 E4 GUA
Ghunsor 32 D4 GNS
Ghuriadhor Mines 34 C5 -
Ghusia Kalan 23 G5 GSK
Ghutai 21 G4 GTI
Ghutiari Shariff 36 B4 GOF
Ghutku 33 G5 GTK
Giani Zail Singh Sandhwan 8 C4 GZS
Gidam 43 E6 GIZ
Gidda Pahar 25 F1 GDS
Giddalur 54 B2 GID
Giddarbaha 8 C5 GDB
Giddarpindi 8 D3 GOD
Gidhaur 24 C5 GHR
Gidhni 35 G4 GII
Gidnahalli 53 H6 GDH
Giellekhola 25 F1 -
Gill 9 E4 GILL
Ginigera 53 E2 GIN
Gir Gadhara 38 C1 GEG
Girdharpur 20 C3 GIW
Gir-Hadmatiya 38 B1 GRHM
Giri Maidan 35 H5 GMDN
Giridih 35 F1 GRD
Girwar 32 B2 GW
Gitaldaha Jn 25 H3 GTG
Goalpara Town 26 B2 GLPT
Gobardanga 36 C3 GBG
Gobarsanda 13 H4 GBRS
Goberwahi 42 B1 GBRI
Gobra 37 inset GBRA
Gocharan 36 B5 GCN
Godamgura 48 B4 GDQ
Godapiasal 35 H4 GSL
Godavari 50 A4 GVN
Godbhaga 44 A1 GBQ
Godha 13 F4 GDHA
Godhaneswar 29 G3 GS
Godhani 42 A2 GNQ
Godhra Jn 30 A3 GDA
Goethal's Halt 25 F1
Gogameri 12 A2 GAMI
Gogamukh 17 E5 GOM
Gogipothia Halt 25 E2 GPE
Gognaposh 34 D6 GAX
Gohad Rd 21 F2 GOA
Gohana 12 D2 GHNA
Gohlwar Varpal 8 C2 GRV
Gohpur 16 D6 GPZ
Goilkera 35 E4 GOL
Goindwal Sahib 8 D3 GWSP
Gojhariya 29 G2 GJR
Gojpur Sankheda 30 A5 GPS
Gokak Rd 46 D6 GKK
Gokarna Rd 52 B3 GOK
Gokhula 15 H6 GKA
Gokulpur 35 H4 GKL
Gola Gokarannath 14 B4 GK
Gola Rd 35 E2 GRE
Golabai 44 D4 GLBA
Golabari 63 G5 -
Golaghat 27 G1 GLGT
Golaka Mandir 21 F2 GLK
Golakganj 26 A2 GKG
Golana 12 C6 GLNA
Golanthara 44 B5 GTA
Golapatti 32 D2 GTY
Goldinganj 24 A3 GJH
Gole 18 D2 GOLE
Golehwala 8 C4 GHA
Golhalli 57 G1 GHL
Gollapalli 48 B5 GLY
Gollapeta 50 C1 GTY
Gollaprolu 50 B4 GLP
Golsar Halt 11 H4 GOZ
Gomangalam 60 C1 GMGM
Gomia 35 E2 GMIA
Gomoh Jn 35 F2, 45 inset GMO
Gomta 28 D5 GTT
Gomti Nagar Halt 22 B1 GTNR
Gonda Bihar 35 F3 GDBR
Gonda Jn 14 D6 GD
Gonda Kutcheri 14 D6 GDK
Gondal 28 D5 GDL
Gondia Jn 42 C1 G
Gondumri 42 C2 GMI
Gondwali 33 H1 GNDI
Goner Rd 20 B1 GONR
Gonglee 42 C1 GNL
Goniana 8 C5 GNA
Gooty Jn 53 H3 GY
Gooty Jn Cabin53 H3 -
Gop (Jamnagar) 28 C4 GPP
Gopalapatnam BH 50 C3 GPT
Gopalganj 23 H2 GOPG
Gopalnagar 36 C3 GN
Gopalpur-Balikuda 44 D3 GBK
Gopalpurgram 36 A2, 63 E1 GPLG
Gopalpuri 28 C2 GPPR
Gopalpur-on-Sea 44 C5 *
Gopinathpur FS 36 A3, 63 E3 GOR
Gopnath Rd 29 F6 GPO
Gora Ghuma 29 G3 GGM
Gorakhnath 45 E3 GRKN
Gorakhpur Cantt Jn 23 F1 GKC
Gorakhpur City 23 F1 GKY
Gorakhpur Jn 23 F1 GKP
Goramghat 19 F3 GGO
Gorapur 50 C2 GPJ
Goratia 29 H5 GRTA
Goraul 24 B3 GRL
Goraya 9 E3 GRY
Goregaon 38 inset GMN
Goregaon Rd 46 B2 GNO
Goreswar 26 D1 GVR
Gorinja 28 B4 GRJA
Gorintada 50 A6 GOTD
Goriyan 12 A5 GIO
Gorphar 25 E4 GRR
Gosaigaon 17 E6 GSN
Gosaingaon Hat 26 A2 GOGH
Gosaingram 36 B1 GSGB
Gosalpur 32 D3 GSPR
Goshainganj 23 E2 GGJ
Got 13 G2 GOT
Gotan 19 F1 GOTN
Gothaj 29 H3 GTE
Gothangam 29 H6 GTX
Gotlam 50 C2 GTLM
Gotra Halt 12 D2 GTRA
Gour Malda 25 F5 GZM
Gourdaha 36 B4 GOD
Gourinathdham 35 F3 GTD
Govandi 38 inset GV
Goverdhan 12 D5 GDO
Govindgarh 12 D5 GVH
Govindgarh Khokhar 8 D6 GGKR
Govindgarh Malikpur 12 B6 GND
Govindi Marwar 12 A6 GVMR
Govindnagar 23 E1 GOVR
Govindpur Dugauli Halt 23 G3 GOX
Govindpur Rd 35 E3 GBX
Govindpuri 22 A2 GOY, GOV
Gowdavalli 48 C3, 51 inset GWV
Grant Rd 38 inset GTR
Greenways Rd 59 inset
Gua 35 E5 GUA
Guabari 26 A2 GBY
Guagachha H 26 C2 GSA
Gubbi 53 F6 GBB
Gudaparti 50 A4 GDPT
Gudgeri 52 D2 GDI
Gudha 12 A6 GA
Gudimetta 54 B2 GMA
Gudipudi 49 F6 GPDE
Gudivada Jn 49 G6 GDV
Gudiyattam 58 B2 GYM
Gudlavalleru 49 G6 GVL
Gudma 42 C1 GDM
Gudru 32 D5 GDU
Gudupulli 58 A2 GDP
Gudur Jn 54 D5 GDR
Guduvancheri 58 D2 GI
Gugalwa Kirtan H 12 B3 GLKN
Guhagar 46 B3 *
Guindy 58 D2, 59 inset GDY
Guirsaranga 36 A3, 63 E3 GSQ
Gujhandi 24 B6 GJD
Gujjangivalasa 50 D2 GUL
Gujran Balwa Halt 12 D1 GLBN
Gulabganj 31 H2 GLG
Gulabpura 19 H3 GBP
Gulaothi 13 E3 GLH
Gularbhog 13 G2 GUB
Gulbarga 47 H4 GR
Guldhar 13 E3 GUH
Guledagudda Rd 47 F6 GED
Guler 9 E1 GULR
Gullaguda 48 B3 GGD
Gullipadu 50 B4 GLU
Gulma 25 F1 GLMA
Gulvanchi 47 E4 GLV
Gulyapalem 53 G3 GPU
Gulzarbagh 24 A4, 25 inset GZH
Guma 36 B4 GMA
Gumada 43 H6 GMDA
Gumandev 29 H5 GME
Gumani 25 E5 GMAN
Gumani Hat 25 H2 GMZ
Gumgaon 42 A2 GMG
Gumman 9 F4 GMM
Gummidipundi 54 D6 GPD
Gumtali Halt 8 D3 GTQ
Gumthal 13 G3 GTF
Guna Jn 20 D5 GUNA
Gunadala 49 F5 GALA
Gunatitnagar 28 D3 GAT
Gunda Rd Jn 53 F3 GDJ
Gunderdehi 42 D1 GDZ
Gundla Pochampalli 51 inset GDPL
Gundlakamma 54 D1 GKM
Gundratimadugu 49 F3 GUU
Guneru Bamori 21 E6 GVB
Gungauli Halt 23 E4 GNGL
Gunja 29 G1 GUJ
Gunjaria 25 F2 GEOR
Gunji 52 B1 GNJ
Guntakal Jn 53 G3 GTL
Guntakal West 53 G3 GTLW
Guntakoduru 49 G5 GUA
Guntur Jn 49 F6 GNT
Gunupur 44 A6 GNPR
Guptipara 36 B3 GPAE
Guramkhedi 32 A4 GMD
Gurap 36 B3 GRAE
Guraru 23 H5 GRRU
Gurdaspur 8 D1 GSP
Gurgaon 12 D3, 15 inset GGN
Gurha Kemla 12 C3 GRKA
Gurhanwa Halt 24 A1 GRNA
Gurhi 31 F6 GUX
Guriya 19 G2 GRI
Gurla Jn 20 B4 GQL
Gurla North Cabin 20 B4 GOLN
Gurli Ramgarhwa 15 G6 GRRG
Gur Market 46 D5 GRMY
Gurmura 23 F6 GMX
Gurnay 8 D6 GRN
Guroli 46 D1 GUO
Gurpa 24 A6 GAP
Gurra 31 H4 GRO
Gurrah Bridge 14 A5 GRH
Gursahaiganj 13 H6 GHJ
Gurthari Halt 9 E6 GRZ
Guru Harsahai 8 B4 GHS
Guru Teg Bahadur Nagar 38 inset GTBN
Gurudas Nagar 36 B5 GURN
Gurudijhatia 44 D3 GJTA
Gurujala 49 E5 GZA
Gurumahisani 35 F5 GUMI
Gurusar Sahnewala 8 C5 GSW
Gurusar Sutlani 8 C2 GRS
Guruvayur 60 A1 GUV
Guskara 36 A2 GKH
Guwahati 26 D2 GHY
Guwarighat 32 D3 GRG
Gwalior Jn 21 F2 GWL
Gyanpur Rd 23 E4 GYN
Gypsum Halt 18C2 GYP

H

Habaipur 27 F3 HWX
Habanghatta 57 E1 HHT
Habibganj 31 G3 HBJ
Habibpur 36 B3 HBE
Habibwala 13 F2 HBW
Habra 36 B3 HB
Hadaiya 8 D5 HYA
Hadala 29 E5 HAK
Hadala Bhal 29 F4 HLB
Hadapsar 46 C1 HDP
Haddinagundu 53 F3 HDD
Hadgaon Rd 41 F5 HDGR
Hadmatiya 28 D4 HM
Hadobanghi 50 D1 HBF
Hadyal 12 A3 HYL
Hafizpeta 48 C3, 51 inset HFZ
Hafizpur 13 E3 HZR
Haflong Hill 27 F4 HFG
Hagari 53 G3 HGI
Hagari Bommanahalli 53 E3 HBI
Haibargaon 27 E2 HBN
Haidar Nagar 23 G6 HDN
Haidergarh 22 C2 HGH
Hailakandi 27 E5 HKN
Hajipur Jn 24 A3, 25 inset HJP
Hakimpur 13 F2 HKP
Halbarga 48 A2 HBU
Haldaur 13 F2 HLDR
Haldharpur 23 G3 HLP
Haldi Rd 13 H2 HLDD
Haldia 36 B5 HLZ
Haldia Bihar Halt 25 E2 HDB
Haldibari 25 G2 HDB
Haldipada 35 G6 HIP
Haldwani 13 H2 HDW
Halisahar 37 inset HLR
Haliyuru 53 E4 HLV
Hallakatta 47 H4 -
Hallakatta H 47 H4 HLKT
Halol 30 A4 HLL
Halt No.1 63 F6 -
Halt No.2 63 F6 -
Halt No.3 63 F6 -
Halt No.4 63 F6 -
Haludpukur 35 F4 HLD
Halvad 29 E2 HVD
Hamarapur 39 F6, 38 inset HMRR
Hamiltonganj 25 H1 HOJ
Hamira 8 D3 HMR
Hamirgarh 19 H4 HMG
Hamirhati 35 H3 HAM
Hamirpur Rd 22 A3 HAR
Hampapatam Halt 53 E3 HPM
Hampapura 57 E2 HPA
Hamre 7 F2 *
Hamsavaram 50 B4 HVM
Hanakere 57 F2 HNK
Handapa 44 C2 HNPA
Handia Khas 22 D4 HDK
Hangarahalli Halt 57 E2 HNG
Hansapore 39 F1 HXR
Hansara 17 F4 HNR
Hansi 12 B2 HNS
Hansiawas Halt 12 A2 HSWS
Hanspura 31 E1 HNU
Hanumanahalli Halt 53 E4 HNH
Hanumangah Jn 8 B6 HMH
Hanumangarh Town 8 B6 HMO
Hanumapura 53 G1 HPH
Hanwant 19 E2 HWT
Hapa 28 C3 HAPA
Hapa Rd 29 H2 HPRD
Hapur Jn 13 E3 HPU
Harangajao 27 F4 HJO
Harangul 47 G1 HGL
Haranyakheri 31 E4 HKH
Haraokhal 63 G5 -
Harauni 22 B1 HRN
Harchandpur 22 C2 HCP
Harda 31 G5 HD
Hardasbigha 24 A4, 25 inset HDE
Hardattpur 23 E4 HDT
Hardoi 14 A5 HRI
Hardorawal 8 C2 HDWL
Hardua 32 D2 HDU
Harduaganj 13 F4 HGJ
Hargaon 14 B5 HA
Hari Nagar 15 H6 HIR
Haridanga 63 F6 -
Haridaspur 45 E2 HDS
Haridranadhi 61 G1 HNI
Haridwar 9 H6 HW
Harihar 53 E4 HRR
Harij 29 F1 HRJ
Haripad 60 B4 HAD
Haripal 36 B4 HPL
Haripur 19 G2 HP
Haripur Gram 44 D4 HPGM
Harish Dadpur 36 B4, 63 F5, 37 inset HDC
Harishankar Rd 43 G3 HSK
Harishchandrapur 25 E4 HCR
Harishchandrapuram 51 E1 HCM
Harishnagar 36 C2 HRSR
Harisingha 26 D1 HRSN
Harkia Khal 19 H6 HKL
Harlapur 53 E2 RLP
Harmadiya 38 C1 HRM
Harmuti 16 D5 HMY
Harnahalli 52 D5 HNHL
Harnaut 24 B4 HRT
Harpalganj 23 E3 HRPG
Harpalpur 21 G4 HPP
Harpalu 12 B3 HR
Harpanahalli 53 E3 HNHL
Harpur 13 F2 -
Harpur Bachaha 24 B4 HBP
Harpur Nag Halt 24 A2 HRNG
Harrad 33 G3 HRV
Harrawala 9 H5 HRW
Harri 33 G4 HRB
Harsana Kalan Halt 12 D2 HNN
Harsar Dehri 9 E1 HRDR
Harsauli 12 C4 HSI
Harsawa 12 4A ASW
Harsingpur Goba 13 H5 HSY
Harsud 31 F5 HRD
Harthala 13 G2 HRH
Harua Rd 36 C4 HRO
Harubera 35 E2 HRBR
Harwada 52 B3 HAA
Hasanbazar 23 H4 HSB
Hasanparti Rd 49 E2 HSP
Hasanpur Rd 24 C3 HPO
Hasimara 25 H1 HSA
Hasnabad 36 C4, 63 H5 HNB
Hassan Jn 57 E1 HAS
Hastavaramu 54 C5 HAQ
Hastings 37 inset *
Hat-Karota H 34 C4 HTR
Hat Puraini 24 D5 HPLE
Hathbandh 33 G6 HN
Hathigadh 29 E5 HTGR
Hathras City 13 E5 HTC
Hathras Jn 13 F5 HRS
Hathras Qilah 13 F5 HRF
Hathras Road 13 F5 HTJ
Hathuran 29 H6 HAT
Hathuwa 23 H2 HTW
Hati 22 B6 HATI
Hatia 35 E3 HTE
Hatiali Ground Siding 17 F5 HEG
Hatiara 63 G5 -
Hatibari 44 A1 HATB
Hatidah Jn 24 B4 HTZ
Hatighisa 25 F1 HTA
Hatikhali 27 F3 HTL
Hatkanagale 46 D5 HTK
Hatnapur 32 A6 HTN
Hatta Rd 32 D6 HTT
Hatundi 19 H2 HTD
Hatwar 25 F3 HWR
Haur 36 A5 HAUR
Hausnagar 25 F6 HSM
Hautly 27 G1 HAY
Haveri 52 D3 HVR
Hawakhana 36 A4, 63 F5 HWK
Haya Ghat 24 B3 HYT
Hazaratpur 35 H2 HZH
Hazaribagh 35 E1 HZME
Hazaribagh Rd 35 F1 HZD
Hazigarh 36 B3 HIH
Hazira Port 29 G6 *
Hazrat Nizamuddin 12 D3, 15 inset NZM
Hazratnagar Halt 13 F3 HZN
Hebbal 57 H1 HEB
Hebbe 52 D5 -
Hebsur 52 D2 HBS
Heelalige 57 H2 HLE
Heggere Halt 53 G6 HEI
Hehegara 34 C2 HHG
Hejjala 57 G2 HJL
Helak 12 D6 HK
Helem 16 D6 HML
Hempur Halt 14 B5 HMP
Hendegir 34 D2 HNDR
Henrya 36 A6 HEN
Her 47 H1 HER
Heslabera 35 E3 HBZ
Heslang 35 F3 HNSL
Hetampur 21 E1 HET
Hijiguri 17 F4 -
Hijli Jn 35 H5 HIJ
Hilara 27 E4 HLX
Hillgrove 57 F5 HLG
Hilli 25 G4 *
Hilsa 24 A4 HIL
Himatnagar Jn 29 H2 HMT
Himayatnagar (Deccan) 41 F5 HEM
Himgir 34 B6 HGR
Himmatana 9 E5 HMI
Himmatpura 9 E6 HMQ
Hinauta Ramban 22 B6 HNM
Hind 13 E1 HIND
Hindaun City 20 D1 HAN
Hindmotor 37 inset HMZ
Hindol Rd 44 C2 HND
Hindon Cabin 9 G6 HNC
Hindu College 59 inset HC
Hindumalkote 8 B5 HMK
Hindupur 53 G5 HUP
Hinganghat 41 H3 HGT
Hingoli Deccan 41 E4 HNL
Hirakud 44 A1 HKG
Hiranagar 7 G6 HRNR
Hirangaon 13 F6 HNG
Hiranwali Halt 8 B6 HLW
Hirapur 40 B3 HPR
Hirdagarh 32 B5 HRG
Hirdamali 42 C1 HDM
Hirehalli 57 G1 HHL
Hirenanduru 47 H4 HQR
Hirnoda 12 A6 HDA
Hirodih 24 B6 HRE
Hisar Jn 12 B2 HSR
Hissam Gunj 51 inset -
Hisua 24 B5 *
Hisvahal 40 A3 HSL
Hi-tec City 51 inset HTCY
Hitnal 53 E2 HTNL
Hiwarkhed 41 E1 HKR
Hodal 12 D4 HDL
Hogla 36 B5 HGA
Hojai 27 F2 HJI
Hol 40 B1 HOL
Holalkere 53 E5 HLK
Holambi Kalan 12 D2 HUK
Hole-Alur 52 D1 HLAR
Hole-Narsipur 57 E2 HLN
Hole-Narsipur Town 57 E2 HLT
Holipura 21 F1 -
Hombal 52 D2 HBL
Honaganahalli 47 F5 HOH
Honnavalli Rd 57 E1 HVL
Honnavar 52 B4 HNA
Hooghly 37 inset HGY
Hooghly Ghat 37 inset HYG
Hosa-Agrahara 57 E2 HAH
Hosdurga Rd 53 E5 HSD
Hoshahalli 52 D5 -
Hoshangabad 31 H4 HBD

Hoshiarpur 9 E2 HSX
Hospet Jn 53 F2 HPT
Hosur 57 H2 HSRA
Hotar 36 B5 HT
Hotgi Jn 47 F3 HG
Howbagh 32 D3 HBG
Howrah 36 B4, 37 inset HWH
Howrah Jn Cabin 37 inset HJN
Howrah Ghat 63 F5 -
Howrah Maidan 63 F5 HWM
Hridaypur 37 inset HHR
Hubli East Cabin 52 D2 HBQ
Hubli Jn 52 D2 UBL
Hudera 11 H4 HDO
Hudukula 58 A1 HUD
Hugrajuli 27 E1 HJLI
Hugrajuli Siding 27 E1 -
Hulkoti 52 D2 LKT
Humma 44 C5 HMA
Hunsenahalli 53 H6 HUN
Hunsi-Hadgil 47 G3 HHD
Huppuguda 51 inset HPG
Hurmujpur Halt 23 F3 HMPR
Husainiwala 8 C3 HSW
Husainpur 8 D3 HSQ
Hussainsagar Jn 48 C3, 51 inset HSJ
Hyderabad 48 C4, 51 inset HYB

I

Ib 34 C6 IB
IBP No. 3 35 F2, 45 inset IB3
IBP No. 9 24 B6 IBP9
IBP No. 10 24 A6 IBP10
Ibrahimpur 47 F5 IMR
Ichauli 22 A4 ICL
Ichchangadu 58 C5 ICG
Ichchangadu Halt 58 C5 ICGH
Ichchapuram 44 B6 IPM
Ichchiputtur 58 C1 IPT
Ichhapur 37 inset IP
Ichchapuri 12 C3 ICPR
Idaiyar 61 F2 IDYR
Idalhond 52 B1 IDJ
Idapalli 60 B2 IPL
Idar 29 H1 IDAR
Idgah Agra Jn 13 E6 IDH
Igatpuri 39 G4 IGP
Ikarchala 25 F2 IKC
Ikdori 20 D3 IKD
Ikkar 9 H6 IKK
Iklehra 32 B5 IKR
Ikra Jn 35 H2 IKRA
Ikran 13 E6 IK
Ilavelangal 60 D4 IVL
Illoo 35 F3 ILU
Imamganj 23 H6 *
Imli 24 C4 IMLI
Imlibigha 24 B4 IPBG
Imphal 27 G5 IMP
Imphal Rd 27 G5 *
Indalvai 48 C1 IDL
Indamau Halt 22 B2 IDM
Indapur 46 B2 INP
Indara Jn 23 F3 IAA
Indargarh 21 E3 IDG
Indi Rd 47 F4 IDR
Indira Nagar 28 D2 -
Indira Nagar 59 inset -
Indore G Cabin 31 E4 -
Indore Jn 31 E4 INDB, INDM
Indrabil 35 G3 IBL
Indragarh Sumerganj Mandi 20 C3 IDG
Indrapuri 23 G5 INI
Indupalli 49 G5 IDP
Indus 35 H3 INS
Ingohta 22 A3 IGTA
Ingorala 29 F5 IGRL
Ingur 57 G5 IIG
Innanje 52 C6 INJ
Intekanne 49 E3 INK
Intiathok 14 D6 ITE
Ippaguda 48 D3 IPG
Ipurupalem 55 E1 IPPM
Iqbal Gadh 18 D6 IQG
Iqbalpur 9 G6 IQB
Iradatganj 22 D4 IDGJ
Iranagallu 53 G1 EGU
Iravipuram Halt 60 B4 IRP
Irgaon 34 D3 IRN
Iringal Halt 56 D4 IGL
Irinjalakuda 60 B1 IJK
Irki 24 A5 -
Irugur 57 F6 IGU
Irulapatti 58 A3 -
Isand 29 G2 EN
Isarda 20 B2 ISA
Isharwara 32 B1 ISH
Isivi 53 G2 ESV
Islampur 24 A5 IPR
Ismaila Haryana 12 D2 ISM
Ismailpur 23 H5 IMGE
Ispatnagar 45 inset IPTN
Israna 12 D2 IRA
Itahar 25 F4 *
Itanagar 16 D5 *
Itarsi Jn 31 H4 ET
Itaunja 14 B6 IJ
Itayakalan 31 H3 ITAYA
Itehar 21 F2 AAH
Itikyala 48 B6 IKI
Itki 34 D3 ITE
Itlamvaripalle 54 B6 IM
Itola 29 H4 ITA
Ittittanam 60 B3 ITM
Itwandundail 22 B5 EDA
Itwari Jn 42 A2 ITR
Izzatnagar 13 H3 IZN

J

Jabalpur Jn 32 D3 JBP
Jabli 9 F4 JBL
Jabri 31 G3 JBX
Jabugam 30 A4 JBU
Jadabpur 37 inset JDP
Jadar 29 H1 JADR
Jadcherla 48 B5 JCL
Jadoli ka Bas 12 D5 JBS
Jadudih 35 E1 YDD
Jafarganj 23 E2 JFG
Jagabor 30 A1 JO
Jagaddal 37 inset JGDL
Jagadhri 9 G5 JUD
Jagadhri Town 9 G5 JGT
Jagadhri Workshop 9 G5 JUDW
Jagadishpur 35 G1 JGD
Jagalur 53 E4 *
Jagannathji Rd 18 D4 JNX
Jagannathpur 44 C5 JNP
Jagannath Temple Gate 56 D4 JGE
Jagatballabpur 63 F5 JGB
Jagatbela 23 F1 JTB
Jagdalpur 43 F6 JDB
Jagdeowala 11 F3 JDL
Jagdishpur Baluhati 63 F5 JBT
Jagesharganj 22 D3 JGJ
Jageswar Bihar 35 E2 JGBR
Jaggambhotla Krishnapuram 54 C2 JBK
Jaggayyapet Town 49 F5 JPTM
Jagi Rd 27 E2 JID
Jagjivan 23 H4 JGWL
Jagraon 8 D4 JGN
Jagtial 41 H6 *
Jagudhan 29 G2 JDN
Jahanabad 24 A4 JHD
Jahanabad Court 24 A4 JHDC
Jahangirabad Raj 22 C1 JBR
Jahanikhera 14 A5 JKH
Jai Jai Wanti 12 C2 JJT
Jaicholi 12 D6 JCU
Jaijon Doaba 9 E3 JJJ
Jaimurtinagar Halt 24 A1 JMM
Jainti 25 H1 JNI
Jaintipura 8 D2 JNT
Jaiprakash (Mahuli) 24 B4 JPML
Jaipur Jn 12 B6 JP
Jairamnagar 33 G5 JRMG
Jais 22 C2 JAIS
Jaisalmer 10 B6 JSM
Jaisingder 18 A2 JSD
Jaithari 33 G3 JTI
Jaitipur 22 B2 JTU
Jaitsar 11 F1 JES
Jaitwar 22 B5 JTW
Jaiwa 28 D3 JAV
Jajan Patti 13 E5 JJA
Jajau 21 E1 JJ
Jajiwal 19 F2 JWL
Jajpur Keonjhar Rd 45 E2 JJKR
Jakalabandha 27 F1 JKD
Jakanur 52 D1 JAK
Jakhal Jn 8 D6 JHL
Jakhanian 23 F3 JKN
Jakhapura Jn 45 E2 JKPR
Jakhaura 21 F5 JHA
Jakhim 23 H5 JHN
Jakhlaun 21 F6 JLN
Jakhod Khera 12 B2 JKHI
Jakhvada 29 G3 JKA
Jakkalacheruvu 53 H3 JKO
Jakolari 8 D1 JK
Jakpur 35 H5 JPH
Jaksi 29 F2 JKS
Jalalabad 8 B4 JBD
Jalalganj 23 E4 JLL
Jalalgarh 25 E3 JAG
Jalalkhali 36 B3 JKL
Jalalpur 23 G2 JGP
Jalalpur H 23 G2 -
Jalalpur Dhai 22 C3 JPD
Jalalpur Panwara Halt 14 A6 JPP
Jalalsi 63 F5, 37 inset JLI
Jalamb Jn 40 D2 JM
Jalandhar Cantt Jn 8 D3 JRC
Jalandhar City Jn 8 D3 JUC
Jalesar City 13 F5 JSC
Jalesar Rd 13 F5 JLS
Jaleswar 35 H6 JER
Jalgaon Jn 40 C2 JL
Jalila Rd 29 F4 JIL
Jalindri 20 A4 JNRI
Jaliya 29 F5 JA
Jaliya Devani 28 D4 JALD
Jaliya Math 29 H2 JLM
Jalna 40 C4 J
Jaloda-Shajapur 31 F2 JASR
Jalor 18 D3 JOR
Jalpaiguri 25 G2 JPG
Jalpaiguri Rd 25 G2 JPE
Jalpur Halt 13 G2 JLQ
Jalsu 11 C6 JAC
Jalsu Nanak 11 G6 JACN
Jam Jodhpur 28 C5 JDH
Jam Khambaliya 29 E4 -
Jam Wanthali 28 D4 WTJ
Jamadoba H 45 inset JBO
Jamai Osmania 51 inset JOO
Jamalpur Jn 24 C4 JMP
Jamalpurganj 36 A3 -
Jamalpur Sheikhan 8 D6 JPS
Jambara 32 A5 JMV
Jambhali 41 F5 JMBL
Jambrung 39 G6 JBC
Jambur 38 B1 JBB
Jambusar City 29 G5 JMBC
Jambusar Jn 29 H5 JMB
Jambusar Rd 29 H5 JBSR
Jamdha 40 B2 JMD
James Street 51 inset JET
Jamga 34 B6 JMG
Jamgaon 32 D5 JGZ
Jamguri 27 G1 JMI
Jamikunta 49 E2 JMKT
Jamir Ghata 25 F5 JMQ
Jamira 27 E6 JMRA
Jamira Halt 23 H4 JMIR
Jammu Cantt 7 G5 -
Jammu Tawi 7 G5 JAT
Jamnagar 28 C3 JAM
Jamner 40 C2 JMNR
Jamsar 11 F3 JMS
Jamsher Khas 8 D3 JME
Jamsole 35 G6 JSE
Jamtara 35 G1 JMT
Jamtara Paraswara 32 D3 JPV
Jamuawan 24 A5 JMN
Jamui 24 C5 JMU
Jamunamukh 27 E2 JMK
Jamuni 45 inset JMX
Jamuniatanr 35 F2, 45 inset JNN
Jamuniya Kalan 19 H6 JMKL
Jamuria 35 G2 JMA
Jamwala 38 C1 JVL
Janai 63 F5, 37 inset -
Janai Rd 37 inset JOX
Janakideipur 44 D4 JKPD
Janakinagar 24 D3 JNKR
Janakpur Rd 24 B2 JNR
Jandiala 8 D2 JNL
Jandoke 8 C3 JDK
Jandrapeta 55 E1 JAQ
Jangalpara 63 F5 JAP
Jangaon 48 D3 ZN
Janghai Jn 22 D4 JNH
Jangiganj 22 D4 JGG
Jangipara 36 A4, 63 F5, 37 inset JNG
Jangipara 37 inset JNG
Jangipur Rd 25 F6 JRLE
Janiyana 18 D3 JNE
Jankampet Jn 48 B1 JKM
Jankampet Rd 48 B1 JKMR
Jannaghatta 58 A1 GJT
Janwal 47 H1 JOA
Jaora 30 D2 JAO
Japla 23 G6 JPL
Japog 20 A1 -
Jaradih 34 A5 JDI
Jaraikela 34 D5 JRA
Jarod 30 A4 JD
Jarandeswar 46 C2 JSV
Jarangdih 35 F2 JAN
Jarapada 44 C2 JRPD
Jarati 43 G6 JRT
Jarauda Nara 13 E1 JDW
Jarauna 23 E4 JUA
Jargaon 13 G3 JRJ
Jari 18 C5 JARI
Jariagarh 34 D3 JGX
Jaruli 35 E6 JRLI
Jarwa 15 E5 JAW
Jarwal Rd 14 C6 JLD
Jasai 18 B3 JSA
Jasai 39 F5, 38 inset -
Jasali 18 C6 JSI
Jasdan 29 E4 JAS
Jashapar 28 C5 JSPR
Jasia 12 C2 JSS
Jasidih Jn 24 D6 JSME
Jasoda 13 H6 JDA
Jaspalon 9 E4 JSPN
Jasra 22 D4 JSR
Jassowal 9 E4 JSL
Jaswantgarh 11 H5 JSH
Jaswantnagar 21 G1 JGR
Jataula Jauri Sampka 12 D3 JSKA
Jatdumri 24 A4 JTDM
Jath Rd 47 E4 JTRD
Jatinga 27 F4 JTG
Jatkanhar 42 D1 JTR
Jatpipli 29 F3 JTX
Jatusana 12 C3 JTS
Jatwara 20 C1 JW
Jaugram 36 B3 JRAE
Jaulka 41 E3 JUK
Jaulkhera 32 A6 JKR
Jaunpur City 23 E3 JOP
Jaunpur Jn 23 E3 JNU
Jaunpur Kuchery 23 E3 JNUK
Javale 47 E3 JVA
Jawad Rd 19 H5 JWO
Jawaharpur Kamsen 13 F5 JWK
Jawai Bandh 19 E4 JWB
Jawalamukhi Rd 9 E1 JMKR
Jawali 19 F3 JAL
Jawanwala Shahr 9 E1 JWLS
Jay Samand Rd 19 F6 JYM
Jayasingpur 46 D5 JSP
Jaynagar 24 C2 JYG
Jaynagar Majilpur 36 B5 JNM
Jegani Khas Halt 23 G3 JGKS
Jejuri 46 C1 JJR
Jekot 30 B3 JKT
Jenal 18 C6 JNZ
Jenapur 45 E2 JEN
Jenapur Rd 44 D4 JERD
Jeonara 32 D4 JONR
Jeonathpur 23 F4 JEP
Jerthi Dadia12 A5A JDD
Jeruwa Khera 32 A1 JRK
Jessore Rd 37 inset *
Jetalsar Jn 28 D5 JLR
Jetalvad 28 D6 JTV
Jetha 34 A5 JDDA
Jetha Chandan 10 C5 JCH
Jethantri H 18 D3 JTHR
Jethi 18 D6 JTY
Jethuke 8 D5 JHK
Jetpur 28 D5 JTP
Jetpur Machchhu Kantha 29 E2 JTM
Jeur 47 E2 JEUR
Jeypore Rd 43 F6 JYP
Jhabelwale Halt 8 C4 JBW
Jhadupudi 44 B6 JPI
Jhagadiya Jn 29 H5 JGI
Jhajha 24 C5 JAJ
Jhajjar 12 C3 *
Jhalawar 20 B6 *
Jhalawar Rd 20 B6 JHW
Jhalda 35 F3 JAA
Jhalra Halt 13 F1 JHH
Jhaluarber 37 inset -
Jhalwara 33 E2 JLW
Jhamat Halt 15 F6 JLT
Jhamatpur Baharan 36 B2 JHBN
Jhanjharpur Bazar Halt 24 C2 JJPR
Jhanjharpur Jn 24 C2 JJP
Jhankad Sarala Rd 45 E3 JSRD
Jhankhvav 29 H6 ZKV
Jhansi Jn 21 F4 JHS
Jhantipahari 35 G3 JPH
Jhapandanga 36 B3 JPQ
Jhapater Dhal 36 A3 JTL
Jhar 29 E6 JHAR
Jharekhapur 14 B5 JKP
Jhargram 35 G4 JGM
Jharia 35 F2, 45 inset JRI
Jharkhandi Halt 14 D5 JKNI
Jharli 12 C3 JRL
Jharokhas 34 A1 JRQ
Jharsuguda Jn 34 C6 JSG
Jharwasa 19 H2 JWS
Jhaua 25 E4 JAU
Jhawar Halt 8 D1 JHWR
Jhilahi Flag H 14 D6 JLHI
Jhilimili 32 B5 JLY
Jhilo 12 B4 JILO
Jhimri 35 F3 JHMR
Jhingura 23 E5 JHG
Jhinjhak 21 H2 JJK
Jhinkpani 35 E5 JNK
Jhir 20 C1 JHIR
Jhitkia Halt 25 F3 JTK
Jhok Tahal Singh 8 C4 JTH
Jhotana 29 G2 JTN
Jhulasan 29 G2 JUL
Jhund Jn 29 F2 JN
Jhunjhunu 12 4A JJN
Jhunpa 12 B2 JUP
Jhusi 22 D4 JI
Jiabharali 16 B6 JBH
Jiadhal Halt 17 E5 JFD
Jiaganj 36 B1 JJG
Jibanti 36 B1 JVT
Jibdharpur 35 H2 JDQ
Jigna 22 D5 JIA
Jijhavadar 29 F5 -
Jimidipeta 43 H6 JMPT
Jind City 12 C1 JCY
Jind Jn 12 C1 JIND
Jinti Rd 47 E1 JNTR
Jintoda 29 G1 JED
Jira Rd 29 E6 JIR
Jiradei 23 G2 ZRD
Jirat 36 B3 JIT
Jiribam 27 F5 JRBM
Jirighat 27 F5 JRGT
Jiron 21 F6 JRO
Jirona 41 G5 JXN
Jiwajigunj 21 F2 JWGJ
Jirwan 31 F6 JRWN
Jita Kheri 12 C2 JKZ
Jite 39 F6, 38 inset JITE
Jiwa Arain 8 B4 JWN
Jiwajinagar 31 E3 JWR
Jiwdhara 24 A2 JDR
Jiyapuram Halt 58 A6 JPM
Jnanabharathi (BU Campus) 57 G2 GNB
Jnandas Kandra 36 A2, 63 E1 GNND
JNPT 39 F5, 38 inset JNPT
Joba 33 G1 JOBA
Jodhka Halt 12 A1 JOK
Jodhpur Jn 19 E2 JU
Jodhpuriya 19 H4 JUYA
Jodiya 28 D3 JYA
Jodiya Bandar 28 D3 JYAB
Jogal 35 G6 JOL
Jogbani 24 D2 JBN
Jogeshwari 38 inset JOS
Jogi Magra 19 F1 JOM
Jogiara 24 B2 JGA
Jogidih 34 A1 JGF
Jogighopa 26 B2 JPZ
Jogindernagar 9 F2 JDNX
Jogiwala 8 D3 JGW
Jojwa 30 A4 JJW
Jolarpettai A Cabin 58 B2 JTJA
Jolarpettai B Cabin 58 B2 JTJB
Jolarpettai Jn 58 B2 JTJ
Jonekareng Halt 17 F4 JYK
Jonha 35 E3 JON
Jora Alapur 21 E2 JPO
Jora Vasan 39 F2 JRS
Jorai 26 A2 JOQ
Joramow 35 G1 JRW
Joranda Rd 44 D3 JRZ
Joravarnagar 29 F3 JVN
Jorebunglow 25 F1 JBY
Jorekhola Siding 25 F1 -
Jorhat 17 E6 JT
Jorhat Town 17 E6 JTTN
Jorkian Halt 8 B6 JRKN
Joychandipahar 35 G2 JOC
Juchandra 39 F5, 38 inset JCNR
Jugaur 22 C1 JRR
Jugijan 27 F2 JGJN
Jugpura 35 G6 JRG
Juharpura 11 H4 JOH
Juhi Cabin 22 A2 JUI
Jui Nagar 38 inset JNJ
Jujharpur 31 H4 JHP
Jujomura 44 B1 JUJA
Jukehi 33 E2 JKE
Julagaon (Deccan) 41 F5 JLG
Julana 12 C2 JNA
Jumapatti 38 inset JTT
Jumnal 47 F5 JML
Juna Rajuvadia 30 A5 JRV
Junagadh Jn 28 D5 JND
Junagarh 43 G4 *
Junction Cabin 12 D3, 15 inset JNC
Junction Point 13 G4 JNPT
Junehta 32 B4 JHT
Jung Bahadurganj 14 A5 JBG
Juniar H 24 A4 -
Junichavand 28 D6 JCN
Junnor Deo 32 B5 JNO
Junona 41 E5 JUNX
Juriagaon 27 E2 JRX
Jurtara 32 D5 JRTR
Jutogh 9 F3 JTO
Juturu 53 H3 JUR
Jwalapur 9 H6 JWP

K

Kabakaputtur 56 C2 KBPR
Kabrai 22 A4 KBR
Kachchanavilai 61 E5 KCHV
Kachchhidhana 32 B6 -
Kacheguda 48 C4, 51 inset KCG
Kachera 12 B5 KHRA
Kachewani 42 B1 KWN
Kachhiyana H 24 C5
Kachhla 13 G4 KCU
Kachhla Bridge 13 G4 KCO
Kachhpura 32 D3 KEQ
Kachhwa Rd 23 E4 KWH
Kachna 25 F3 KAU
Kachnara 30 D1 KHNR

Kachnara Rd 30 D1 KCNR
Kachnaria 31 G2 KNRA
Kachujor 35 H2 KOX
Kadabari Halt 25 G2 KDX
Kadakavur 60 B5 KVU
Kadakola 57 F3 KDC
Kadalundi 56 D5 KN
Kadambagachi 63 G5 -
Kadambankulam Halt 61 E3 KMBK
Kadambattur 58 D1 KBT
Kadambur 60 D4 KDU
Kadampur Halt 24 D2 KDRA
Kadamtala 63 F5 -
Kadaramkondan H 58 C6 KAKO
Kadavakuduru 54 D2 KVDU
Kadayanallur 60 C4 KDNL
Kaderpur 29 G1 KDYA
Kadhethan 46 D1 KDTH
Kadi 29 G2 KADI
Kadimbala Halt 56 D2 KDBA
Kadipur 23 F4 KDQ
Kadipur Sani Halt 14 B5 KDPS
Kadiri 54 A5 KRY
Kadiyadra 29 H1 KADR
Kadiyam 50 A5 KYM
Kadlimatti 47 F6 KLM
Kadur 53 E6 DRU
Kaduturutti Halt 60 B3 KDTY
Kafurpur 13 F2 KFPR
Kagankarai 58 B3 KEY
Kagmala H 18 D5 KXC
Kahalgaon 25 E4 CLG
Kahangarh 8 D6 KAGR
Kaher 39 G1 KRAI
Kahilia 14 A5 KH
Kaichar 36 A2, 63 F2 KCY
Kaikala 36 B4 KKAE
Kaikaluru 49 H5 KKLR
Kaikoram 49 H5 KKRM
Kailahat 23 E5 KYT
Kailaras 21 E2 KQS
Kailasapuram 61 E5 KLPM
Kaili 13 E3 KALI
Kailsa 13 F2 KIV
Kaima 22 B6 KMA
Kaimarakalan 20 D2 KAKN
Kaimganj 13 G5 KMJ
Kaipadar Rd 44 D4 KPXR
Kairla 19 E3 KAI
Kairon 8 C3 KCZ
Kaithal 9 E6 KLE
Kaithalkuchi 26 C2 KTCH
Kaiyal Sedhavi 29 G2 KYSD
Kaiyar 36 A3, 63 E3 KYB
Kajgaon 40 B2 KJ
Kajgoan Terhwan 23 E4 KJTW
Kajoragram 35 H2 KJME
Kajra 24 C4 KJH
Kajrat Nawadih 23 G6 KYF
Kajri 34 C1 KET
Kakar Ghatti 24 C3 KKHT
Kakapora 7 G3 *
Kakdwip 36 B5 KKDP
Kakilamukh 16 D6 -
Kakinada Port 50 B5 COA
Kakinada Town 50 B4 CCT
Kaklur 43 E6 KKLU
Kakori 22 B1 KKI
Kakoshi Metrana Rd 18 D6 KKSI
Kakraha Rest House 14 C4 KARH
Kakrala Halt 9 E5 KKRL
Kakrigumma 43 G6 KKGM
Kala Amba 39 G2 KMB
Kala Bakra 8 D2 KKL
Kalachand 27 F4 KQI
Kalachara 63 F5 KLC
Kalajhari BH 44 D3 KJR
Kalaakher 31 H5 KQE
Kalaikunda 35 H5 KKQ
Kalakund 31 E4 KKD
Kalamalla 54 B4 KMH
Kalamasseri 60 B2 KLMR
Kalamb Rd 47 G2 KMRD
Kalambha 41 H1 KLBA
Kalamboli 39 F5, 38 inset KLMG
Kalana 12 A2 KALN
Kalanad Halt 56 C2 KLAD
Kalanaur 9 G5 KNZ
Kalanaur Kalan 12 C2 KLNK
Kalanwali 8 C6 KNL
Kalapipal 31 F3 KPP
Kalas Halt 52 D2 KALS
Kalasamudram 54 A4 KCM
Kalasapakkam 58 B3 KSPM
Kalasar 29 E4 KLSR
Kalasur 52 D3 KVS
Kalavur Halt 60 B3 KAVR
Kalayat 9 E6 KIY
Kalchini 25 H1 KCF
Kaldhari 49 H5 KLDI
Kalediya 30 A5 KLDA
Kaleh Majra Halt 9 E5 KLMJ
Kalem 52 B2 KM
Kalgupur 48 A2 KCP
Kalhar 32 A1 KAH
Kalighat 63 G5 KLGH
Kali Rd 28 inset KLRD
Kalisindh 31 F2 KSH
Kalianpur 22 A2 KAP
Kalighat 37 inset -
Kalijai 44 C4 KLJI
Kalijhora 25 F1 KJF
Kalikapur 36 B4, 37 inset KLKR
Kalikiri 54 B6 KCI
Kalinarayanpur Jn 36 B3 KLNP
Kalipahari 35 G2 KPK
Kalipatti Rd 57 H5 KLPT
Kalipur 63 F5 KLPR
Kalitalawadi 29 G4 KLWD
Kaliyaganj 25 F3 KAJ
Kalka 9 F4 KLK
Kalkalighat 27 E5 KKGT
Kalladaka 56 C1 KLKD
Kallagam 58 B5 KLGM
Kallakkudi Palanganatham 58 B6 KKPM
Kallal 61 F2 KAL
Kallar 57 F5 QLR
Kallayi 56 D5 KUL
Kallidaikurichi 60 D5 KIC
Kalligudi 61 E3 KGD
Kallur Yedahalli Halt 57 F3 KLYH
Kalluru 53 H3 KLU
Kalmeshwar 41 H1 KSWR
Kalmitar 33 G5 KLTR
Kalol Jn 29 G2 KLL
Kalpaganur 58 A4 KPGN
Kalpattichatram 61 E1 KFC
Kalpi 21 H3 KPI
Kalsur 52 D3 KVS
Kalthuruthy Halt 60 C4 KTHY
Kalubathan 35 G2 KAO
Kalumna 42 A2 KAV
Kalunga 34 D5 KLG
Kaluparaghat 44 D4 KAPG
Kalva 38 inset KLVA
Kalwan Halt 9 E6 KLWN
Kalyan Jn 39 F5, 38 inset KYN
Kalyanchak 25 E5 KXE
Kalyandurg 53 G4 *
Kalyani Ghoshpara 37 inset KLYG
Kalyani Jn 36 B3, 37 inset KYI
Kalyani Silpanchal 37 inset KLYS
Kalyani Simanta 36 B3, 37 inset KLYM
Kalyankot 11 F1 KYNT
Kalyanpur 36 B5, 37 inset KYP
Kalyanpur Rd 24 D4 KPRD
Kamakhya Jn 26 D2 KYQ
Kamakhyaguri 26 A2 KAMG
Kamalapuram 54 B4 KKM
Kamalganj 13 H6 KLJ
Kamaliyapur 30 A4 -
Kamalnagar 48 A2 KMNR
Kamalpur H 13 E4 KAMP
Kamalur 42 D6 KMLR
Kaman 38 inset, 39 F5 KMN
Kamarbandha Ali 27 G1 KXL
Kamareddi 48 C2 KMC
Kamarkundu 36 B4, 37 inset KQU
Kamasamudram 58 A2 KSM
Kamathe 46 B3 KMAH
Kambaraganvi 52 C2 KBI
Kambarasampettai 58 B6 KPT
Kambol 29 F1 KAMI
Kamlabad Barhauli 22 B1 KMBH
Kamlapur 14 B6 KMP
Kamli 29 G1 KMLI
Kamnara 36 A3, 63 E3 KMRA
Kampil Rd 13 G5 KXF
Kamptee 42 A1 KP
Kampur 27 F2 KWM
Kamranga 27 F5 KMNG
Kamrup Khetri 26 D2 KKET
Kamshet 39 G6 KMST
Kamtaul 24 B2 KML
Kamudakkudi 61 F3 KMY
Kanad 29 F5 KNAD
Kanai Bazar 27 E5 KNBR
Kanakkanpatti 60 D1 KNPT
Kanakot 28 D4 KNKT
Kanakpura 12 B6 KKU
Kanale Halt 52 C4 KNLF
Kanalus East BH 28 C4 KNLSBH
Kanalus Jn 28 C4 KNLS
Kanalus South BH 28 C4
Kanamalopalle 54 B4 KNLP
Kanarona 34 D4 KNRN
Kanas Rd 44 D4 KASR
Kanasar 11 F3 KNSR
Kanauta 20 B1 KUT
Kanchanpur Rd 33 F1 KNC
Kanchausi 21 H2 KNS
Kanchipuram 58 D2 CJ
Kanchipuram East 58 D2 CJE
Kanchrapara 36 B3, 37 inset KPA
Kanchrapara Workshop 37 inset -
Kandaghat 9 F4 KDZ
Kandambakkam 58 C4 KDMD
Kandanur Puduvayal 61 F2 KNPL
Kandari 29 H5 KNDR
Kandarpur 44 D3 KDRP
Kandel Rd 43 H4 KDLR
Kandhla 12 D1 KQL
Kandhran Halt 12 B3 KDHN
Kandi 36 A1 *
Kandikuppam 58 A2
Kandivli 38 inset KILE
Kandla 28 C2 KAND
Kandla Port 28 C2 KDLP
Kandra Jn 35 F4 KND
Kandrori 8 D1 KNDI
Kandwal Halt 9 E1 KAWL
Kang Khurd 8 D3 KGKD
Kangali Halt 23 H1 KNLI
Kangam 29 G5 KNGM
Kanginhal 53 E2 KGX
Kangra 9 E1 KGRA
Kangra Mandir 9 E1 KGMR
Kanhadgaon 32 D6 KNDG
Kanhaipur 24 B4 KNHP
Kanhan Jn 42 A1 KNHN
Kanhangad 56 C3 KZE
Kanhargaon Naka 41 E4 KNRG
Kanhe 39 G6 KNHE
Kanhegaon 40 A4 KNGN
Kanhiwara 32 C5 KWB
Kanij 29 G3 KANJ
Kanimahuli 35 G4 KNM
Kanimangalam H 60 B1 KNGL
Kanina Khas 12 C3 KNNK
Kaniuru Halt 56 D2 KNYR
Kaniyambadi 58 C2 KNB
Kaniyapuram 60 C5 KXP
Kanjara 41 E4 KAJR
Kanjari 30 A4 KJE
Kanjari Boriyavi Jn 29 H4 KBRV
Kanjh 29 G2 KNU
Kanjia 21 E6 KXB
Kanjikode 57 F6 KJKD
Kanjiramittam 60 B2 KPTM
Kanjurmarg 38 inset KJMG
Kankaha 22 B2 KKAH
Kankanadi Jn 56 C1 KNKD
Kankariya Cabin 28 inset KKEC
Kankather 13 F3 KHE
Kankavli 46 B6 KKW
Kanki 25 F3 KKA
Kankinara 37 inset KNR
Kankra Mirzanagar 36 C4 KMZA
Kankret 21 E2 KAS
Kankroli 19 F4 KOL
Kankurgachi Rd Jn 37 inset KGK
Kannamangalam 58 C2 KMM
Kannapuram 56 D3 KPQ
Kannauj 22 A1 KJN
Kannauj City 22 A1 KJNC
Kanniyakumari 60 D6 CAPE
Kanoh 9 F4 KANO
Kanor 19 G6 KFN
Kanpur Anwarganj 22 A2 CPA
Kanpur Bridge Left Bank 22 A2 CPB
Kanpur Central Jn 22 A2 CNB
Kansbahal 34 D5 KXN
Kansiya Nes 28 D6 KANS
Kanspur Gugauli 22 B3 KSQ
Kansrao 9 H5 QSR
Kansudhi 30 A3 KIZ
Kantabanji 43 G3 KBJ
Kantadih 35 F3 KTD
Kantakapalli 50 C2 KPL
Kantalia 63 F5 KNTL
Kanth 13 F2 KNT
Kanthalia Rd 36 B1 KTLR
Kanthariya 29 H5 KNTR
Kanthi 36 A6 KATI
Kanwalpura 20 B5 KIW
Kanwat 12 B5 KAWT
Kaotha 41 G2 KAOT
Kapadvanj 29 H3 KVNJ
Kapali Rd 45 E2 KPLD
Kapan 33 H5 KPNA
Kaparpura 24 B3 KVC
Kapasan 19 G5 KIN
Kapilas Rd Jn 44 D3 KIS
Kappalur 61 E2 KFL
Kappil 60 B5 KFI
Kapren 20 B4 KPZ
Kapsethi 23 E4 KEH
Kaptanganj Jn 23 G1 CPJ
Kapurdah 32 C5 KPDH
Kapurthala 8 D3 KXH
Kapustalni 41 F2 KTNI
Karaboh 32 C5 KRBO
Karachiya Yard 29 H4 KRCA
Karad 46 C3 KRD
Karahdih H 24 B5
Karahia 23 G4 KKRH
Karaikal 58 D6 KIK
Karaikkudi Jn 61 F2 KKDI
Karai-Kovilpathu 58 D6 KVPT
Karaikurichchi Halt 60 D5 KARK
Karaila Rd Jn 33 H1 KRLR
Karaimadai 57 F5 KAY
Karamanikkuppam 58 C4 KRPM
Karmelaram 57 H2 CRLM
Karainthi 12 C2 KHV
Karajgi 52 D3 KJG
Karakad 57 E6 KRKD
Karakavalasa 50 C2 KVLS
Karakbel 32 C3 KKB
Karambeli 39 F3 KEB
Karamgarh Sardargarh Halt 8 C5 KRSH
Karamnasa 23 F4 KMS
Karampada 35 E5 KMPD
Karamsad 29 H4 KRYR
Karamtola 25 E4 KRMA
Karan Nagar 29 G2 KANG
Karanahali Halt 53 E5 KRNH
Karanja 41 F3 KRJA
Karanja Town 41 F3 KRJT
Karanjadi 46 B2 KFD
Karanjali 36 B5 -
Karanpura 12 D6 KPO
Karanpurato 25 E5 KPTO
Karapgaon 32 B4 KFY
Karari 21 F4 KRQ
Karasangal 58 D3 KSGL
Karatwadi 41 E2 KTWD
Karauta 24 B4 KWO
Karavadi 54 D2 KRV
Karbigwan 22 B2 KBN
Karchana 22 D4 KCN
Karchha 31 E3 KDHA
Karchhui 23 G2 KYW
Karchiya 29 H4 KCHA
Kardi 57 F1 RDI
Karea Kadambagachhi 36 B4, 37 inset KBGH
Kareli 32 B4 KY
Karengi 13 G4 KEG
Karepalle Jn 49 F3 KRA
Karepur 47 H1 KRPR
Kargaon 42 A2 KG
Kargi Rd 33 G5 KGB
Karhagola Rd 25 E4 CRR
Karhiya Bhadoli 32 C2 KYX
Katra 7 G5 *
Kariganuru 53 F2 KGW
Kariha Halt 9 E3 KYY
Karimganj Jn 27 E5 KXJ
Karimnagar 48 D1 KRMR
Karimuddinpur 23 G3 KMDR
Karisath 23 H4 KRS
Karivalam Vandanallur 60 D4 KVNR
Kariyapattinam 61 H1 KXY
Karjana 36 A3, 63 E3 KJRA
Karjangram 36 A3, 63 E3 KJRM
Karjara 24 A5 KRJR
Karjat 39 G5, 38 inset KJT
Karjoda 18 D6 KRJD
Karkatta 23 G6 KRTA
Karkeli 33 E2 KKI
Karkend 45 inset KRKN
Karkheli 41 F6 KEK
Karlgurki 47 F5 KDGI
Karmabad BH 35 F1 KRMB
Karmad 40 C4 KMV
Karmahat 35 E2 KMHT
Karmali 52 A1 KRMI
Karna 14 A6 KAR
Karna Subarna 36 B1 KNSN
Karnal 9 F6 KUN
Karnauti 24 B4 KRNN
Karod 32 A1 KTD
Karona 24 A4 KRON
Karonda 21 F6 KOA
Karong 27 G4 *
Karonji Jn 34 A3 KJZ
Karota Patri 24 C5 -
Karpurigram 24 B3 KPGM
Karra 35 E3 KRRA
Karsindhu 12 D1 KSDE
Kartarpur 8 D3 KRE
Kartauli Halt 13 G4 KRTL
Karu Khirhar Nagar H 24 D3 KKNH
Karukutty 60 B2 KUC
Karumathur Halt 61 E2 KAMU
Karunagapalli 60 B4 KPY
Karunguzhi 58 D3 KGZ
Karupatti 61 E2 KYR
Karuppur 58 A4 KPPR
Karur Jn 57 H6 KRR
Karuvalli Halt 57 H4 KVLR
Karuvatta Halt 60 B3 KVTA
Karwandiya 23 G5 KWD
Karwar 52 B3 KAWR
Kasap 23 H4 KAC
Kasara 39 G4, 38 inset KSRA
Kasaragod 56 C2 KGQ
Kasarwadi 39 G6 KSWD
Kasba 25 E3 KUB
Kasbe Sukene 39 H3 KSBN
Kaseetar 35 G1 KEE
Kasganj City 13 F5 KJC
Kasganj Jn 13 F5 KSJ
Kashi 23 F4 KEI
Kashiabari 25 G2 KSBI
Kashinagar H 36 B5 KHGR
Kashinagar 44 A6 KNGR
Kashipur Jn 13 G2 KPV
Kashipura 29 H3 KSUA
Kashipura Sarar 29 H5 KSPR
Kashti 46 D1 KSTH
Kasi Chak 24 B5 KSC
Kasimkota 50 C3 KCH
Kasimpur Halt 22 C2 KCJ
Kasrak Halt 13 H4 KSRK
Kastar Mahadev 23 H4 -
Kastha 24 A5 KSTA
Kastla Kasmabad Halt 13 E3 KKMB
Kasturbai Nagar 59 inset
Kasturi 14 D6 KSR
Kasu 39 F6 KASU
Kasu Begu 8 C4 KBU
Kata Rd 41 E3 KXX
Katahri 23 E2 KTHE
Kataiya Dandi 22 C5 KTDD
Katakhal Jn 27 E5 KTX
Katalpur Halt 23 H2 KTLP
Katangi 32 C6 KGE
Katangi Khurd 33 E2 KTKD
Katareah 25 E4 KTRH
Katariya 28 D2 KATR
Katarnian Ghat 14 C4 KTG
Katea 23 G2 *
Katepurna 41 E2 KTP
Kateli Halt 14 B5 KATA
Kateri Rd 57 F5 KXR
Kathajori 44 D3 KJH
Kathalpukhuri 16 D5 KTPR
Kathaltali H 27 E6 KTLI
Kathana 29 G4 KTNA
Kathara Rd 22 A2 KTRR
Kathghar 13 G2 KGF
Kathgarh Left Bank 13 G3 KGFLB
Kathgarh Right Bank 13 G3 KGFRB
Kathgodam 13 H2 KGM
Kathivakkam 59 inset KAVM
Kathkuiyan 23 G1 KKT
Kathlal 29 H3 KTAL
Kathleeghat 9 F3 KEJ
Kathola 14 D6 KTHL
Kathua 7 H6 KTHU
Kathunangal 8 D2 KNG
Kathuwas 12 C4 KTWS
Kati 24 B3 KATI
Katihar Jn 25 E4 KIR
Katihar 25 E4 KIRB
Katka 23 E4 KFK
Katkola 28 C5 KTLA
Katlicherra 27 E5 KTCR
Katni Jn 33 E2 KTE
Katni Murwara 33 E2 KMZ
Katni South 33 E2 KTES
Katoghan 22 B3 KTCE
Katol 41 H1 KATL
Katora 33 H3 KTO
Katosan Rd Jn 29 G2 KTRD
Katpadi Jn 58 C2 KPD
Katphal 46 D2 KFH
Katra 22 D1 KEA
Katra 7 G5 *
Katraj 47 E1 KZ
Katrasgarh Jn 35 F2, 45 inset KTH
Kattangulathur 58 D2 CTM
Kattar Singh Wala 8 C5 KZW
Kattukottai 58 B4 KTKT
Kattur 58 B6 KTTR
Katuda 29 F3 KTDA
Katuria 24 D5 *
Katwa Jn 36 B2, 63 F2 KWAE
Kaukuntla 48 B5 KQO
Kauli 9 F5 KLI
Kaulseri 9 E5 KLSX
Kaunriya 19 G4 KXA
Kaurara 13 F6 KAA
Kaurha 14 A5 KUF
Kauria Jungle 23 F1 JKI
Kauriala Ghat 14 C4 KGT
Kauriya 23 H4 KYA
Kausika Halt 57 E1 KSKA
Kauwapur 14 D5 KPE
Kavalande Halt 57 F3 KVE
Kavali 54 D3 KVZ
Kavalkinaru H 60 D6 KVLK
Kavanur 58 B2 KVN
Kavaraipettai 58 D1 KVP
Kavas 18 C2 KVA
Kavathe Mahankal 47 E4 KVK
Kavi 29 G4 KAVI
Kavi Bunder 29 G4 KVBD
Kavutaram 49 G6 KVM
Kawargaon 43 E6 KWGM
Kawas Jn Cabin 29 G6
Kayalpattinam 61 E5 KZY
Kayamsar 12 4A QMRS
Kayankulam Jn 60 B4 KYJ
Kayasthagram 27 E5 KTGM
Kayavarohan 29 H5 KV
Kaydi 32 D6 KAYI
Kazhakuttam 60 C5 KZK
Kazipara 36 B1, 63 G5 KZPR

Kazipet Jn 49 E2 KZJ
KBCS Siding 29 G6 KBCS
Kechki 34 C2 KCKI
Kedgaon 46 D1 KDG
Keeranur 61 F1 KRUR
Kekatumar 41 E4 KKG
Keladevi 12 D6 KEV
Kelamangalam 57 H2 KMLM
Kelanpur 29 H4 KEP
Kelavli 39 F6, 38 inset KLY
Kelod 41 H1 KLOD
Kelve Rd 39 F4 KLV
Kelzar 42 B4 KEZ
Kem 47 E2 KEM
Kemari Halt 13 G3 KEMR
Kemmanugundi 52 D6 -
Kempalsad 42 A2 KEM
Kenchanalu Halt 52 D5 KCLA
Kendposi 35 E5 KNPS
Kendrapara Rd 44 D3 KNPR
Kendri 43 E2 KDRI
Kenduapada 45 E2 KED
Kendujhargarh 44 D1 *
Kendukana 26 D2 KDKN
Kengeri 57 G2 KGI
Keolari 32 D5 KLZ
Kerakat 23 E4 KCT
Kerejanga 44 C2 KPJR
Keruganj 13 H5 CWJ
Kesamudram 49 E3 KDM
Kesariya Rd 29 F3 KXZ
Kesavaram 50 A5 KSVM
Keshabpur 36 A5 KSBP
Keshav Nagar H 11 F1 KSVR
Keshavganj 19 E5 KVJ
Keshod 28 C6 KSD
Kesholi 20 C5 KOLI
Keshorai Patan 20 B4 KPTN
Keshwari BH 25 F1 KSHR
Kesimpa 29 G1 KEC
Kesinga 43 H4 KSNG
Kesla 31 H4 KSLA
Kesri 9 F5 KES
Kesri Singhpur 8 A5 KESR
Ketohalli Halt 57 G2 KHLL
Kettandapatti 58 B2 KDY
Ketti 57 F5 KXT
Keutuguda 43 H5 KTGA
Kevdi 30 A6 KR
Kevdi Rd 39 G2 KVO
Khabra Kalan Halt 12 B1 KBKN
Khachrod 30 D2 KUH
Khadapa 43 F6 KDPA
Khadavli 39 F5, 38 inset KDV
Khadda 15 G6 KZA
Khadeen 18 B3 KOF
Khaderpet 53 G3 KDT
Khadki 46 C1 KK
Khadki Bazar 41 F5 KDBR
Khadoor Sahib 8 D3 KDSB
Khaga 22 B3 KGA
Khagaria Jn 24 C4 KGG
Khagraghat Rd 36 B1 KGLE
Khai Phameki 8 C4 KIQ
Khairabad Awadh 14 B5 KB
Khairah 24 A3 KYH
Khairahi 23 E5 KHRY
Khairar Jn 22 A4 KID
Khairatabad 48 C4, 51 inset KQD
Khairatia Bandh Rd 14 B4 KYBR
Khairee 32 D5 KHR
Khairtal 12 C5 KRH
Khajauli 24 C2 KJI
Khajpur Naya 12 B4 KJNY
Khajraha 21 F4 KHJ
Khajuraho 21 H5 *
Khajurhat 22 D2 KJA
Khajuri 21 E4 KAW
Khajwana 11 G6 KJW
Khakhariya 28 D5 KKK
Khakhrala Rd 28 D3 KKR
Khakhrechi 29 E2 KXH
Khakhi Jalia 28 C5 KAK
Khalari 34 D2 KLRE
Khalgaon 31 F5 KHA
Khaliapali 43 H2 KHPL
Khalilabad 23 F1 KLD
Khalilpur 12 C4 KIP
Khalipur 29 G1 KHPR
Khalispur 23 E4 KSF
Khallikot 44 C5 KIT
Khaltipur 25 F5 KTJ
Khamargachi 36 B3 KMAE
Khambel 29 F1 KVH
Khambhada 29 F3 KBG
Khambhaliya Jn 28 C4 KMBL
Khambhat 29 G4 CBY
Khambli Ghat 19 F3 KBK
Khamgaon 40 D2 KMN
Khamgaon Burti 40 D2 KJL
Khamkhed 40 D2 KMKB
Khammam 49 F4 KMT
Khana Jn 36 A3 KAN
Khanalampura Goods Yard 9 G6 KJGY
Khanalampura West 9 G6 KWT
Khanapur 52 B1 KNP
Khanapur 48 A2 KHNP
Khan Bhankri 12 C6 KBV
Khandala 39 G6 KAD
Khandbara 30 B6 KBH
Khandel 12 A6 KNDL
Khanderi 28 D4 KHDI
Khandeshwar 38 inset KNDS
Khandi Halt 19 E2 KNDX
Khandikar 26 D2 KYO
Khandip 20 D1 KNDP
Khandiya 30 A3 KHDA
Khandrawali H 12 D1 KZI
Khandwa Jn 31 F5 KNW
Khanja Halt 23 E3 KHJA
Khanna 9 E4 KNN
Khanna Banjari 33 E2 KHBJ
Khanoodih 35 F2, 45 inset KNF
Khanpur 28 D3 KNAR
Khanpur Ahir 12 C4 KNAR
Khantapara 45 F1 KHF
Khanyan 36 B3 KHN
Khapa 41 H1 KHPA
Khaparkheda 42 A1 KPKD
Khapri 42 A2 KRI
Khar Rd 38 inset KHAR
Khara 32 D6 KRXA
Kharadih 23 G5 KAE
Kharaghoda 29 F2 KOD
Kharagpur Jn 35 H5 KGP
Kharahat 17 E5 KRHT
Kharak 12 C2 KHRK
Khara Kameri 19 F4 KRKM
Kharaon 7 G3 *
Kharhand 12 C2 KRZ
Kharbao 39 F5, 38 inset KHRB
Khardaha 37 inset KDH
Khardi 39 G4, 38 inset KE
Khareshwar Rd 29 F3 KHRS
Kharghar 38 inset KHAG
Khargone 30 D5 *
Khargpur 24 C5 *
Khari Amrapur 29 H2 KIA
Khari Jhalu 13 F1 KILU
Kharia-Khangarh 19 F1 KXG
Kharia-Pipra H 24 B4
Khari Rohar Rd 28 C2 KRIR
Khariar Rd 43 F2 KRAR
Kharibaria 63 G5 -
Kharida 35 H5 KAF
Kharik 24 D4 KHQ
Kharika Halt 24 B4 KHQ
Kharikatia 27 H1 KOY
Khario 45 inset KARO
Kharkhari F 45 inset KHRI
Kharkhauda 13 E3 KXK
Kharpokhra 15 G6 KPB
Kharsaliya 30 A3 KRSA
Kharsia 34 A5 KHS
Kharuara 24 B4 -
Kharwa 19 G2 KRW
Kharwa Chanda 19 F5 KRCD
Khasa 8 C2 KSA
Khat 42 B1 KHAT
Khatauli 13 E2 KAT
Khatgaon 39 H1 KHTG
Khatima 14 A2 KHMA
Khatipura 20 B1 KWP
Khatkar Kalan Jhandalji 9 E3 KHHJ
Khatkura 35 G4 KATB
Khatu 11 G6 KHTU
Khed 46 B2 KHED
Khed Brahma 29 H1 KDBM
Khed Temple 18 D2 KHTX
Kheduli 19 G1 KOW
Khejuria Ghat 25 F5 KGU
Khekra 12 D2 KEX
Khelmati 17 E6 -
Khem Karan 8 C3 KEMK
Khemasuli 35 H5 KSO
Khemli 19 F5 KLH
Khempur 25 F3 KHMP
Khera Kalan 12 D3 KHKN
Khera Sandhan Halt 13 E6 KHSN
Kheralu 29 G1 KRU
Kheri Salwa 19 F1 KSW
Kherkabari 26 B2 KRBK
Kherli 12 D6 KL
Kheroda 19 G5 KHW
Kherol 29 H2 KOY
Kherua 36 A1 KVF
Kherwadi 39 H3 KW
Kherwakocha 35 E3 KWKC
Kheta Sarai 23 E3 KS
Khetia 36 A3, 63 E3 KSHT
Khidirpur 37 inset C
Khijadiya Jn 29 E5 KJV
Khileriyan Halt 11 H3 KKYN
Khimei 19 E4 KQZ
Khinaniyan 11 H1 KNNA
Khinchan H 10 D5 KHCN
Khirai 36 A5 KHAI
Khirerkot 25 G2 KRKT
Khiri Town 14 B4 KITN
Khiriakhurd Halt 14 A4 KIE
Khirkiya 31 F5 KKN
Khirsadoh 32 B5 KUX
Khodiyar Jn 29 G2, 28 inset KHD
Khodiyar Mandir 29 F5 KDMR
Khodri 33 G4 KOI
Khodseoni 42 C2 KSIH
Khoh 22 B4 KHOH
Khoirabari 26 D1 KBY
Khojeepura 20 D3 KJP
Khojewala 8 D3 KWJ
Kholadiad 29 F3 KLDD
Kholapota 63 H5 -
Khongsara 33 G4 KGS
Khonkar 21 E4 KCR
Khopoli 39 F6, 38 inset KHPI
Khorampur H 24 A5 KRMP
Khorana 28 D4 KHC
Khorasan Rd 23 E3 KRND
Khori 12 C4 KORI
Khotar 14 A4 -
Khotkhoti 27 G2 KHKT
Khowang 17 F5 *
Khubagaon 41 G2 KBGN
Khudaganj 13 H6 KDJ
Khudda Kurala 8 D2 KZX
Khudi Ram Bose Pusa 24 B3 PUV
Khudlapur 13 H6 KHDP
Khukrana 12 D1 KKRE
Khumtai 27 G1 KUTI
Khun Khuna 11 H5 KKNA
Khurai 32 A1 KYE
Khurda Rd Jn 44 D3 KUR
Khurdpur 8 D3 KUPR
Khurhand 22 B4 KHU
Khurhat 23 F3 KRT
Khurial 25 E4 KWE
Khurja City 13 E4 KJY
Khurja Jn 13 E4 KRJ
Khusropur 24 B4 KOO
Khusta Buzurg 41 F1 KSBG
Khutaha 22 B5 KTHA
Khutauna 24 C2 KHTN
Khutbhav 46 D1 KTT
Khutwansa 31 H4 KTZ
Kichha 13 H2 KHH
Kidiyanagar 28 D2 KYG
Kikakui Rd 39 G1 KKRD
Kila Raipur 9 E4 QRP
Kila Zafargarh 12 C2 KZH
Kilakkadaiyam 60 C5 KKY
Kilanwalli Punjab 8 B5 KLWL
Kilikollur 60 B4 KLQ
Kille 58 C5 KII
Kim 29 H6 KIM
Kinana 12 C2 KIU
Kinattukadavu 57 F6 CNV
King's Circle 38 inset KCE
Kinharapur 23 G3
Kinkhed 41 F3 KQV
Kinwat 41 G4 KNVT
Kirandul 49 H1 KRDL
Kiraoli 13 E6 KLB
Kiratgarh 31 H4 KRTH
Kiratpur Sahib 9 F3 KART
Kiriburu 35 E5 KRBU
Kirloskarwadi 46 D4 KOV
Kirnahar 36 A2, 63 E1 KNHR
Kiroda 11 G6 KRC
Kirodimalnagar 34 B6 KDTR
Kirti Nagar 15 inset KRTN
Kirtimenda 42 B3 KMMD
Kishan Manpura 12 B5 KMNP
Kishanganj 25 F3 KNE
Kishanganj City 25 F3 -
Kishangarh 19 H1 KSG
Kishangarh Balawas H 12 C4 KGBS
Kishanpur 24 B3 KSP
Kisoni 31 F2 KONY
Kistam Settipalli 54 B2 KSTE
Kita 35 E3 KITA
Kitham 13 E6 KXM
Kiul Jn 24 C5 KEU
Kivarli 19 E5 KWI
Kizha Ambur Halt 60 C5 KIB
Kizhapuliyur 60 C4 KYZ
Kizhvelur Halt 58 C6 KVL
KM 13/7 24 D4 -
Kobdi 29 F5 KOBD
Kochewani 32 D6 KFX
Kochugaon 26 A1 -
Kochuveli 60 C5 KCVL
Kodaganur 53 E4 KAG
Kodaikanal Rd 60 D2 KQN
Kodambakkam 59 inset MKK
Kodavaluru 54 D4 KJJ
Koderma 24 B6 KQR
Kodi 40 C4 KODI
Kodigehalli 57 G1 KDGH
Kodikkalpalayam Halt 58 C6 KOM
Kodikkarai 61 H2 PTC
Kodinar 38 C1 KODR
Kodumudi 57 H5 KMD
Kodumunda Halt 57 E6 KODN
Koduru 54 C5 KOU
Koelwar 23 H4 KWR
Kohand Halt 12 D1 KFU
Kohar Singh Wala 8 B4 KRSW
Kohdad 31 F6 KDK
Kohima 27 H3 *
Kohir (Deccan) 48 B3 KOHR
Kohli 41 H1 KOHL
Kohndaur 22 D3 KDF
Koiripur 22 D3 KEPR
Koka 42 B1 KUKA
Kokalda 41 F2 KXD
Kokkalanjeri 61 E3 KOJ
Kokpara 35 G4 KKPR
Kokrajhar 26 B2 KOJ
Kolad 46 B1 KOL
Kolagallu 53 F2 KOG
Kolaghat 36 A4 KIG
Kolaigram 25 G2 KLGR
Kolakalur 49 G6 KLX
Kolanalli 57 H5 CNY
Kolanukonda 49 F6 KAQ
Kolanur 49 E1 KOLR
Kolar 58 A1 KQZ
Kolaras 21 E4 KLRS
Kolatur 61 F1 KLS
Kolayat 11 E4 KLYT
Kolde 39 H1 KFF
Kole BH 34 D2 KOLE
Kolhadi 40 D2 KHLD
Kolhana H 24 A5
Kolianur 58 C4 COU
Koliapani 17 E6 -
Kolida Beri 12 4A KLBR
Kolikad 30 A2 KLKD
Kolkata Airport 37 inset *
Kolkata region 36 B4, 37 inset
Kollengode 60 B1 KLGD
Kollidam 58 C5 CLN
Kollikhutaha 24 D5 KKTA
Kollumangudi 58 C6 KLMD
Kolvagram 12 C6 KVGM
Kolwihir 41 F1 *
Komakhan 43 F2 KMK
Komali 53 H3 KMQA
Komarpur 36 A2, 63 E1 KMPR
Komatipalli 50 C2 KMX
Kona 37 inset, 63 F5 KONA
Konagavalli Halt 52 D5 KGV
Konanur Halt 57 F3 KRNU
Konark 45 C4 *
Konch 21 G3 KNH
Kondagaon 43 E5 KDGN
Kondagunta 54 D5 KQA
Kondapalli 49 F5 KI
Kondapuram 54 A3 KDP
Kondrapol 49 E5 KDGL
Konnagar 37 inset KPG
Konnur 48 B5 KONN
Kopa Samhota 23 H3 KPS
Kopaganj 23 F3 KPJ
Kopai 36 A2 KPLE
Kopar Lahar 9 E1 KPLR
Kopar Khairane 38 inset KPHN
Kopar Rd 38 inset *
Kopargaon 40 A4 KPG
Koparia 24 D3 KFA
Koppal 53 E2 KBL
Kora 29 G5 KORA
Koradacheri 58 C6 KDE
Koradih 42 A1 KRDH
Korahiya Halt 24 C2 KRHA
Korai 45 E2 KRIH
Koranwas 31 F2 KNWS
Koraput Jn 50 B1 KRPU
Korari 22 B2 KURO
Koratti Angadi Halt 60 B1 KRAN
Korattur 59 inset KOTR
Koravangala Halt 57 E1 KRVL
Korba 33 H5 KRBA
Koregaon 46 C3 KRG
Korukkupet 59 inset KOK
Korukkupet Goods Terminal 59 inset KOKG
Korukonda 50 C2 KUK
Kosa Rd 29 G1 KSRD
Kosad 29 H6 KSE
Kosadi 29 H6 KSAI
Kosai 41 G5 KSAE
Kosamba 29 H6 KSB
Kosgi 53 G1 KO
Kosi Kalan 13 E5 KSV
Kosiara 23 G6 KVQ
Kosli 12 C3 KSI
Kosma 13 G6 KOZ
Kot Fateh 8 C5 KTF
Kot Kapura Jn 8 C4 KKP
Kota C Cabin 20 B4 KOTAC
Kota City 20 B4 KTCY
Kota Jn 20 B4 KOTA
Kota Jn South Cabin 20 B4 KTSC
Kotabommali 51 E1 KBM
Kotakadra 48 B5 KTKA
Kotala 54 C6 KEN
Kotalpukur 25 E5 KLP
Kotana 30 B1 KTOA
Kotapalle 50 A5 *
Kotarlia 34 B6 KRL
Kotdwara 9 H6 KTW
Kotegangur 52 D5 KGH
Koteshwar 29 G5 KOH
Koteshwar 28 A1 *
Kotgaon 42 B3 KTGO
Koth Gangad 29 G3 KTGD
Kothandaramankoil 61 D4 -
Kotha Pakki 8 B5 KTPK
Kothapalli 48 D1 *
Kotha Pandillapalli 55 E1 KPLL
Kothar 19 E4 KTR
Kothara 28 B2 QTR
Kothari Rd 33 H5 KTHD
Kothariya 28 D4 RYK
Koti 9 F4 KOTI
Kotikulam 56 C2 KQK
Kotla Gujran 8 C2 KTGN
Kotlakheri 31 E5 KTKH
Kotli Kalan 8 D5 KKL
Kotma 33 G3 KTMA
Kotmisonar 33 H5 KTSH
Kotpar Rd 43 F6 KPRR
Kotra 21 F3 KTRA
Kotshila Jn 35 F3 KSX
Kottacheruvu 53 H4 KTCR
Kottaiyur 61 F2 KTYR
Kottakota 58 B1 KOHA
Kottapalam BH 50 C3 KAPM
Kottapalli 49 E1 KYOP
Kottarakara 60 B4 KKZ
Kottavalasa Jn 50 C3 KTV
Kottayam 60 B3 KTYM
Kottekkad 57 F6 KTKU
Kottur 48 C4 KTY
Kotturpuram 59 inset
Kottur 53 E3 KTY
Kovilpalaiyam 57 F6 CVM
Kovilpatti 60 D4 CVP
Kovvur 50 A4 KVR
Koyilvenni Halt 58 C6 KYV
Krishna 48 A5 KSN
Krishna Canal Jn 49 F5 KCC
Krishnagiri 58 A2 -
Krishnamohan 36 B5 KRXM
Krishnaballabh Sahay Halt 35 F1 KBSH
Krishnachandrapur 35 G6 KCV
Krishnai 26 B3 KRNI
Krishnammakona 54 A2 KEF
Krishnanagar 29 F5 KRSN
Krishnanagar City Jn 36 B3, 63 G2 KNJ
Krishnanagar Road 63 G2 KJD
Krishnapatnam Port 54 D4
Krishnapur 25 F6 KRP
Krishnapuram 54 B4 KPU
Krishnaraja Nagar 57 E3 KRNR
Krishnarajapuram 57 H2 KJM
Krishnarajasagara 57 F3 KJS
Krishnarampur 63 F5
Krishna Shila 33 H1 KRSL
Krityanandnagar 25 E3 KTNR
Kuakhera Halt 13 G3 KZS
Kuarmunda 34 D5 KRMD
Kuberpur 13 F6 KBP
Kuchai 35 G5 KUHI
Kuchaman City 11 H6 KMNC
Kuchavaram H 48 C3
Kuchesar Rd 13 E3 QXR
Kuchman 23 F4 KCA
Kuda Salt Siding 29 E2 KDR
Kudachi 46 D5 KUD
Kudal 46 B6 KUDL
Kudal Nagar 61 E2 KON
Kudala Sangama Rd 47 F6 KSAR
Kudatini 53 F2 KDN
Kudchade (Sanvordem) 52 B2 SVM
Kudgi 47 F5 KDG
Kudikadu 58 C6 KXO
Kudni Halt 8 D6 KUDN
Kudra 23 G5 KTQ
Kudsad 29 H6 KDSD
Kuhi 42 A2 KUHI
Kuhuri 44 C4 KUU
Kujibali 17 E6 -
Kukar 20 A2 KKAR
Kukarvada 29 G2 KKRV
Kukma 28 C2 KEMA
Kukrakhapa 32 B6 KFP
Kukurmara 26 C2 KKMA
Kulali 47 G3 KUI
Kulasekharapatnam 61 E5 -
Kuldiha 35 F5 KIJ
Kulem 52 B2 QLM
Kulgachia 36 A4 KGY
Kulha Halt 22 B2 KULH
Kulharia 23 H4 KUA
Kulikarai 58 C6 KU
Kulipalaiyam 57 G5 KUY
Kulitalai 58 A6 KLT
Kulitturai 60 C6 KZT
Kulitturai West Halt 60 C6 KZTW

Kullanchavadi 58 C4 KLNC
Kulpahar 21 H4 KLAR
Kulpi 36 B5 KUL
Kultham Abdullah Shah Halt 9 E3 KASH
Kulti 35 G2 ULT
Kulti Link Cabin 35 G2 ULT L/C
Kulukkalur Halt 57 E6 KZC
Kulwa 13 E4 KLA
Kumaramangalam 58 B6 KRMG
Kumaranallur Halt 60 B3 KFQ
Kumarapatnam 53 E4 KMPS
Kumarapuram 60 D4 KPM
Kumarbagh 23 H1 KUMB
Kumardanga 36 A2, 63 E1 KMDG
Kumardubi 35 G2 KMME
Kumarganj 25 F4 KMRJ
Kumarghat 37 H1 KUGT
Kumarhatti Dagshai 9 F4 KMTI
Kumahu 23 G5 KMGE
Kumaripara Halt 25 E4 -
Kumarmaranga 43 E6 KMEZ
Kumbakonam 58 C6 KMU
Kumbalam 60 B2 KUMM
Kumbhawas Mundhalia Dabri H 12 C4 KWMD
Kumbhraj 20 D6 KMRJ
Kumbla 56 C2 KMQ
Kumedpur 25 E4 KDPR
Kumendi 34 C2 KMND
Kumhari 43 E1 KMI
Kumharsodra 43 E6 KMSD
Kumirmora 63 F5 KUMR
Kumki 35 F4 KZU
Kumrabad Rohini 24 D6 KBQ
Kumrul 35 H3 KMRL
Kumsa 34 A3
Kumsi 52 D5 KMSI
Kumta 52 B4 KT
Kumthakurd 47 H1 KTKR
Kund 12 C4 KUND
Kunda Harnamganj 22 C3 KHNM
Kundala 60 C2 -
Kundalgarh 30 B1 KDLG
Kundanganj 22 C2 KVG
Kundapura 52 C6 KUDA
Kundara 60 B4 KUV
Kundara East Halt 60 B4 KFV
Kundarkhi 13 G3 KD
Kunder 24 C5
Kundgol 52 D2 KNO
Kundhela 30 A4 KDHL
Kundli 29 F4 KDI
Kundwa Chainpur 24 A1 KWC
Kuneru 43 H6 KNRT
Kunkavav 29 E5 KKY
Kunkavav Town 29 E5 KVT
Kunnattur Halt 58 A3 KNNT
Kuntighat 36 B3 KJU
Kunuri 35 H1 KNRI
Kunwar 22 C3 KUW
Kunwar Chintawanpur H 24 A2 KPCB
Kup 9 E4 KUP
Kupgal 53 G1 KGL
Kuppam 58 A2 KPN
Kupwara 7 F1 *
Kurabalakota 54 A6 KBA
Kuraiya 14 A3 KRYA
Kural 29 H5 KORL
Kurali 9 F4 KRLI
Kuram 41 F2 KUM
Kuranga 28 B4 KRGA
Kurasti Kalan 22 B3 KKS
Kuravapulam 61 H1 KVV
Kurawan 31 F5 KRO
Kurduvadi Jn 47 F2 KWV
Kurebhar 22 D2 KBE
Kuretha 25 E4 KUO
Kurgunta 48 A4 KQT
Kurhni 24 B3 KHI
Kuri Halt 60 C4 KIF
Kuria Halt 24 A2 KXR
Kurichchi 60 D5 KRCH
Kurichedu 54 C1 KCD
Kurikad Halt 60 B2 KFE
Kurinjipadi 58 C4 KJPD
Kurkura 34 D4 KRKR
Kurla Jn 39 F5, 38 inset CLA
Kurlasi 20 B6 KRLS
Kurmabad Rd BH 23 G5 KVD
Kurnool Town 54 A1 KRNT
Kursela 25 E4 KUE
Kurseong 25 F1 KGN
Kurud 43 E2 KRX
Kurukshetra Jn 9 F6 KKDE
Kurumalai 60 D4 KRML
Kurumbur 61 E5 KZB
Kurumurti 48 B5 KXI
Kuruppantara 60 B3 KRPP
Kurwai Kethora 32 A1 KIKA
Kusagal 52 D2 KUG
Kusarna H 23 E4 KSRN
Kushal Nagar Halt 23 G1 KSNR
Kushalpura Halt 12 B3 KSLP
Kusheshwar Asthan 24 C3 *
Kushmi 23 F2 KHM
Kushtala 20 C3 KTA
Kusiargaon 25 E3 KSY
Kuslamb 47 F2 KCB
Kustaur 35 G3 KSU
Kusumba Bihar 24 B5 KSMB
Kusumbhi 22 B2 KVX
Kusumkasa 42 D3 KYS
Kusunda 45 inset KDS
Kuswaha 13 F5 KWW
Kuthur Halt 58 C6 KOQ
Kutralam 58 C6 KTM
Kuttakudi 58 C4 KKTI
Kuttipuram 57 E6 KTU
Kuwandih H 22 D4
Kuwanthal 19 F4 KUTL
KWAE Siding 29 G6 KWAE
Kyarkop 52 C2 KRKP
Kyatanakeri Rd 47 F4 KTK
Kyatsandra 57 G1 KIA
KZJ E Cabin 49 E2 -
KZJ F Cabin 49 E2 -

L

Laban 20 C3 LBN
Laban Satyagraha Smarak 36 A5
Labha 25 E4 LAV
Labpur 36 A2, 63 E1 LBP
Labutala 36 C4 LBTL
Lachakheri 33 E2 LEK
Lachhmangarh Sikar 12 4A LNH
Lachhmanpur 22 C3 LMN
Lachhmanpur Rd 35 G2 LCME
Lachipura 19 H2 LAC
Lachyan 47 F4 LHN
Ladda 43 H6 LDX
Ladhowal 9 E4 LDW
Ladhuka 8 B4 LDK
Ladkhed 41 G3 LDD
Ladnun 11 G5 LAU
Ladpura 19 H1 LR
Lagargawan 22 B6 LGCE
Lahabon 24 D6 LHB
Lahavit 39 G4 LT
Laheria Sarai 24 B3 LSI
Lahing 17 E6 LH
Lahli 12 C2 LHLL
Lahoal 17 F5 LHL
Laiburwa Halt 15 E5 LBW
Lailakh Mamalkha 24 D4 LMM
Laimekuri Halt 17 F4 LMY
Lain Bazar 23 G2 *
Lajai 28 D3 LJAI
Lajkura Cabin 34 B6 LJKR
Lajpat Nagar 15 inset LPNR
Lakadiya 28 D2 LKZ
Lakdi-ka-pul 51 inset
Lake Gardens 37 inset LKF
Lakhabawal 28 C4 LKBL
Lakhamanchi 29 E3 LMC
Lakhannath Rd 35 H6 LXD
Lakhanpuri 41 F2 LPU
Lakhanwara 32 D6 LNW
Lakheri 20 C3 LKE
Lakhewali 8 B4 LKW
Lakhimpur 14 B4 LMP
Lakhmapur 52 D1 LKY
Lakhminia 24 C4 LKN
Lakhna 43 G3 LKNA
Lakhnauria Halt 14 A5 LNO
Lakho 24 C4 LAK
Lakholi 43 E2 LAE
Lakhpat 29 E1 LAA
Lakhpat Nagar 22 D1 LKNR
Lakhtar 29 F3 LTR
Lakkadkot 39 G1 LKKD
Lakkavalli 52 D5 -
Lakkiti 57 E6 LDY
Lakodra 29 H5 LKD
Laksar Jn 9 H6 LRJ
Lakshmanpur Halt 14 D5 LHNR
Lakshmibai Nagar 31 E4 LMNR
Lakshmikantapur 36 B5 LKPR
Lakshminarayanapuram 49 H5 LKSX
Lakshmipur 36 B2 LKK
Lakshmipur Rd 43 G6 LKMR
Lakwa 17 E6 LXA
Lalabazar 27 E5 LLBR
Lalaghat 27 E5 LAG
Lalapet 58 A6 LP
Lalauri Khera 13 H3 LUA
Lalbagh BH 24 B6 LBZ
Lalbagh Court Rd 36 B1 LCAE
Lalganj 22 B3 LLJ
Lalgarh Bihar 34 C1 LBT
Lalgarh Jn 11 F4 LGH
Lalgola 25 F6 LGL
Lalgola Ghat 25 F6 LGG
Lalgopalganj 22 C3 LGO
Lalgudi 58 B6 LU
Lalit Lakshmipur Halt 24 C2 LLPR
Lalitgram 24 D2 LLP
Lalitpur 21 F5 LAR
Lalkua Jn 13 H2 LKU
Lallaguda 51 inset LGD
Lallaguda Gate 51 inset LGDH
Lalpur (Jamnagar) 28 C4 LPJ
Lalpur 22 A2 LLR
Lalpur Umri 20 C2 LRU
Lalru 9 F5 LLU
Lalwadi 32 A5 LLD
Lamana 19 G2 LNA
Lambhua 22 D3 LBA
Lambiya 19 H3 LMA
Lamsakhang 27 F3 LKG
Lamta 32 D5 LTR
Landhaura 9 H6 LDR
Langai 27 E5 LGI
Langal Pota 63 G5 -
Langcholiet 27 F3 LCT
Langerpeth 47 E4 LNP
Langhnaj 29 G2 LNJ
Langting 27 F3 LGT
Lanja 46 C4 *
Lanjigarh Rd 43 H4 LJR
Lanka 27 F3 LKA
Lankalakoderu 50 A6 LKDU
Laole 7 G4 *
Laopani 27 E2 LPN
Lapanga 34 C6 LPG
Lar Rd 23 G2 LRD
Larabad BH 24 B6 LRB
Lasalgaon 39 H3 LS
Laseri Halt 12 B2 LSE
Lasina 41 G3 LSN
Lasur 40 B4 LSR
Latabor 42 D1 LBO
Lataguri 25 G1 LTG
Latehar 34 C2 LTHR
Latemda 35 F3 LTMD
Lathi 29 E5 LAT
Lathidad 29 F4 LTD
Lathikata 34 D5 LTK
Latipura 29 H4 LPA
Latteri 58 B2 LTI
Lattipur 24 D4 LTP
Latur 47 G1 LUR
Latur Rd 47 H1 LTRR
Laukaha Bazar 24 C2 LKQ
Laul 47 F2 LL
Lawa Sardargarh 19 G4 LSG
Lawanpur 28 D3 LUN
Laxmiganj 23 G1 LIJ
Laxmipur 15 F6 LIR
Laxmipur Bhorang 25 E4 LKB
Layabad 45 inset LYD
Ledarmer 18 D4 LDM
Ledo 17 G5 LEDO
Lehgaon 41 F2 LGN
Lehra Flag 15 F6 LER
Lehra Gaga 8 D6 LHA
Lehra Muhabbat 8 D5 LHM
Lekhapani 17 G5 LKPE
Lekoda 31 E3 LOD
Lelligumma 43 H5 LLGM
Lemuabad 24 B4 LEB
Level Crossing No 3 H 24 C4 -
Lidhora Khurd 32 B2 LDA
Lighthouse 59 inset MLHS
Lihuri 44 A6 LRI
Likhma 43 E4 -
Lilabari 16 D5 LBI
Lilapur Rd 29 F3 LPR
Liliya Mota 29 E5 LMO
Lilma 18 A2 LIL
Liluah 37 inset LLH
Lilwan 29 F6 LLV
Limarua 32 D4 LMU
Limbare 29 H6 LMB
Limbdi 29 F4 LM
Limbgaon 41 E5 LBG
Limbodra 29 G2 LBD
Limkheda 30 B3 LMK
Linch 29 G2 LGH
Ling 41 G3 LING
Linga 32 B5 LIG
Lingamguntla 49 F5 LIM
Lingampally 48 C3, 51 inset LPI
Linganenidoddi 53 H2 LMD
Lingaraj Temple Rd 44 D3 LGTR
Lingiri 48 A5 LGRE
Link Jn Cabin 22 D4 LKJN
Lodhi Colony 15 inset LDCY
Lodhikhera 32 B6 LDE
Lodhipur Bishanpur 13 G2 LDP
Lodhma 35 E3 LOM
Lodna 45 inset LDJE
Lodra 29 H2 LRA
Loha 11 H4 LOHA
Lohagad 41 E3 LHD
Lohgarh Abub Halt 8 B6 LGB
Lohanda H 24 A4 LOR
Lohapur 25 F6 LAP
Lohardaga 34 D3 LAD
Loharpurwa Halt 15 F6 LPW
Loharu Jn 12 B3 LHU
Loharwara 12 B6 LHW
Lohgara 22 C4 LOG
Lohian Khas Jn 8 D3 LNK
Lohna Rd 24 C2 LNO
Lohta 23 E4 LOT
Loisingha 43 H2 LSX
Lokmanyanagar 31 E4 LKMN
Lokmanya Tilak Ter. 39 F5, 38 inset LTT
Loknath 36 A4 LOK
Lokur 58 A4 LCR
Lokvidyapithnagar 15 F6 LVR
Loliya 29 G4 LO
Lonand 46 C2 LNN
Lonavla 39 G6 LNL
Londa Jn 52 B2 LD
Longadi 39 E1 LOE
Longpatia 17 F5 LPTA
Longrangajao 27 F4 LJO
Loni 46 C1 LONI
Lorha 33 E2 LOA
Lorwada Rd 18 D6 LW
Lotana 30 A4 LAN
Lotapahar 35 E4 LPH
Lotarva 39 G1 LTV
Lothal Bhurkhi 29 G4 LHBK
Lottegolahalli 57 G1 LOGH
Lovedale 57 F5 LOV
Lower Haflong 27 F4 LFG
Lower Parel 38 inset PL
Lowjee 39 F6, 38 inset LWJ
Luckeesarai Jn 24 C5 LKR
Lucknow 22 B1 LJN
Lucknow City 22 B1 LC
Lucknow Jn (Charbagh) 22 B1 LKO
Lucknow West 22 B1 ALH
Ludhiana Jn 9 E4 LDH
Lukwasa 21 E4 LWS
Lumding Jn 27 F3 LMG
Lumding South 27 F3 LMG(S)
Lunavada 30 A3 LNV
Luni Jn 19 E2 LUNI
Luni Richha 30 D2 LNR
Lunidhar 29 E5 LDU
Lunkaransar 11 G3 LKS
Lunsariya 29 E3 LXR
Lunsu Halt 9 E1 LNS
Lusa 23 E5 LUSA
Lusadiya 30 A2 LSD
Lushala 28 C6 LAL
Lyalpur Khalsa Coll. Jalandhar H 8 D3 LKK

M

Mabbi H 24 C3 MABB
Machapur Jn BH 44 D3 MZY
Macharya 13 G3 MCV
Machavaram 55 E1 MCVM
Macherla 48 D5 MCLA
Machhakund Rd 50 B1 MKRD
Machhriawan H 24 A4, 25 inset -
Machhrowal Halt 8 D2 MHWL
Machiala 29 E5 MAC
Machilipatnam 49 G6 MTM
Machilipatnam Port 49 G6 MTP
Machlandapur 36 C3 MSL
Madanapalle Rd 54 B6 MPL
Madanapur 41 G5 MDPJ
Madankata 35 G1 MNC
Madanmahal 32 D3 MML
Madanpur 36 B3, 37 inset MPJ
Madanthukulam H 60 D1
Madar 19 H2 MD
Madaraha 22 D4 MFX
Madarihat 25 H1 MDT
Maddikera 53 G2 MKR
Maddur 57 G2 MAD
Madgaon Jn 52 B2 MAO
Madha 47 F2 MA
Madhabpur 36 B5 MDBP
Madhada 29 F5 MDHA
Madhapur Rd 28 C2 MADP
Madhav Nagar Rd 32 D2 MDRR
Madhavnagar 46 D4 MDVR
Madhi 39 G1 MID
Madhira 49 F5 MDR
Madho Singh Jn 23 E4 MBS
Madhoganj 14 A6 MAH
Madhopur Punjab 7 H6 MDPB
Madhubani 24 C2 MBI
Madhugiri 53 G6 *
Madhukunda 35 G2 MDKD
Madhupur Jn 35 G1 MDP
Madhusudanpur 37 inset MDSE
Madhyamgram 37 inset MMG
Madhyampur 36 C4 MPN
Madikere 56 D3 MKR
Madimangalam 58 C2 MCL
Madlauda 12 D1 MLDE
Madpur 35 H5 MPD
Madukarai 57 F6 MDKI
Madurai Bridge 57 F6 MEB
Madurai East 61 E2 MES
Madurai Jn 61 E2 MDU
Madurantakam 58 D3 MMK
Madure 52 A1 MADR
Madwarani 33 H5 MWRN
Mael 35 E2 MAEL
Magardah 23 E6 MWF
Magardoh 31 H5 MGRD
Magarpur 21 G4 MGRR
Magarwara 22 B2 MGW
Maghar 23 F1 MHH
Magnad 29 H5 MGND
Magnesite Jn 58 A4 MGSJ
Magra 36 B3, 37 inset MUG
Magra Hat 36 B5 MGT
Magudanchavadi 57 H5 DC
Mahabalipuram 58 D2 *
Mahabuang 34 D4 MCZ
Mahadanapuram 58 A6 MMH
Mahadeokhedi 32 A1 MDVKI
Mahadeopur Ghat 24 D4 MGP
Mahadeopuri Bhadara 23 G6 MHDR
Mahadeopara 29 H1 MHDP
Mahadevsal 35 E4 MXW
Mahadewa 14 C6 -
Mahadewa Buzurg 15 E5 MHBG
Mahadiya 33 H1 MHDA
Mahajan 11 G2 MHJ
Mahalam 8 C3 MFM
Mahalaxmi 38 inset MX
Mahali Marup 35 F4 MMV
Mahamandir 19 E2 MMC
Mahanadi 25 F1 MHN
Mahanagar 25 F4 -
Mahananda Bridge H 25 F4 MBC
Mahansar 12 4A MWR
Maharajganj 23 H3 MGZ
Maharani Paschim 22 D3 MWP
Mahasamund 43 F2 MSMD
Mahavankhor Halt 23 F1 MVKR
Mahbubabad 49 E3 MABD
Mahbubnagar 48 B5 MBNR
Mahbubnagar Town 48 B5 MHBT
Mahe 56 D4 MAHE
Maheji 40 C2 MYJ
Mahendergarh 12 C4 MHRG
Mahendra Nath Halt 23 H3 MHRN
Mahendralalnagar 36 B4, 37 inset MHLN
Mahendravadi 58 C2 MDVE
Mahesana Jn 29 G2 MSH
Mahesh Khunt 24 D4 MSK
Maheshari Sandhuan 8 C4 MSSD
Maheshganj 36 B3, 63 G2 MSGJ
Maheshi 24 D4 MVV
Maheshleta 24 C5 MHLT
Maheshmunda 35 F1 MMD
Maheshpur 36 A2, 63 E1 MHSP
Mahesra 13 F2 MHHR
Mahilabad 22 B1 MLD
Mahim Jn 38 inset MM
Mahimba 41 G5 MHMB
Mahinpurwa 14 C4 MIN
Mahipal 25 F6 MPLE
Mahipal Rd 25 F6 MPLR
Mahisgaon 47 F2 MGO
Mahishadahari 36 A1 MWZ
Mahishadal 36 A5 MSDL
Mahiyapur 25 E4 MHPR
Mahjgawan 22 B5 MJG
Mahjgawan Phatak 32 D2 MJGP
Mahmudabad (Awadh) 14 C6 MMB
Mahnar Road 24 B4 MNO
Mahngarwal Doaba 9 E3 MGWD
Mahoba 21 H4 MBA
Maholi Halt 14 B5 MAHO
Mahpur 23 F4 MHO
Mahrail 24 C2 MHRL
Mahrauli 13 E3 MFH
Mahrawal 13 E4 MWUE
Mahroi 33 E2 MFQ
Mahrufganj 25 inset *
Mahtha Bazar Halt 15 E6 MHBZ
Mahua Milan 34 D2 MMLN
Mahuariya 34 B1 MXY
Mahuawa Khurd Halt 23 F1 MUVA
Mahudha 29 H3 MHUA
Mahugarha 20 D6 MUGA
Mahul 38 inset *
Mahuli 42 A2 MZB
Mahur 27 F4 MXR
Mahutgaon 17 E6 MUGN
Mahuva 38 D1 MHV
Mahuva Bunder 38 D1 MHVB
Mahwa 12 C5 MWW
Mahwal 24 A2 MHL
Maibong 27 F4 MBG
Maigalganj 14 A5 MINJ
Maihar 33 E1 MYR
Maijapur 14 D6 MIR
Maika Mandir 9 H5 -
Mailam 58 C3 MTL
Mailani Jn 14 A4 MLN
Mailaram 48 B4 MLRM
Mailongdisa 27 F4 MGX
Mainarbandh 27 F5 MNBD
Mainpuri 13 G6 MNQ
Mainpuri Kutchery 13 G6 MPUE
Mairabari 27 E2 MBO
Mairwa 23 G2 MW

Station	Code
Maisar Khana 8 C5	MASK
Maishashan 27 E5	MSSN
Maitha 22 A2	MTO
Maitrabagan 63 H5	-
Maivadi Rd 60 D1	MVRD
Majbat 27 E1	MJBT
Majerhat 63 G5, 37 inset	MJT
Majgaon Assam 26 B2	MZQ
Majhari Ghat 24 C2	-
Majhaula Halt 13 F3	MJHL
Majhdia 36 B2	MIJ
Majheran Himachal 9 F1	MNHL
Majhergram 36 B3	MAJ
Majhiari 22 C5	MJHR
Majbola Pakaria 14 A3	MJZ
Majholi 33 H1	MZHL
Majhwalia 23 H1	MJL
Majitha 8 C2	MJTA
Majorda Jn 52 A2	MJO
Majri Jn 42 A4	MJRI
Majri Khadan 42 A4	MJKN
Maju 63 F5	MAJU
Makakhad 29 H2	MAYA
Makalidurg 53 G6	MKL
Makansar 29 E3	MU
Makardaha 63 F5, 37 inset	MDC
Makarpura 29 H4	MPR
Maker 24 A3	*
Makhanpur 13 F6	MNR
Makhdumpur Gaya 24 A5	MDE
Makhepar Rd 32 C6	MKZ
Makhi 22 B2	MKHI
Makhu 8 C3	MXH
Makkajipalli 53 H5	MKJ
Makoria-am 31 E3	MKAM
Makrana Jn 11 H6	MKN
Makrandpur 13 G4	MQP
Makrauli 12 C2	MKLI
Makrera 19 H2	MKRA
Makronia 32 B2	MKRN
Maksi Jn 31 E3	MKSI
Makudi 42 A5	MKDI
Makum Jn 17 F4	MJN
Mala 14 A3	MALA
Malad 38 inset	MDD
Malad-Gaon 46 D1	MDDG
Malahar Halt 25 F4	MFZ
Malakavemula 54 A4	MVA
Malakhera 12 C5	MKH
Malakpet 51 inset	MXT
Malanpur 21 F2	MLAR
Malarna 20 C2	MLZ
Malasa 21 H2	MLS
Malatipatpur 44 D4	MLT
Malatipur 36 C4	MPE
Malavi Halt 53 E3	MVY
Malavli 39 G6	MVL
Malbazar 25 G1	MBZ
Malda Court 25 F5	MLFC
Malda Town 25 F5	MLDT
Malegaon 41 H1	MGVK
Malegaon 40 A2	*
Malerkotla 9 E4	MET
Malethu Kanak 22 D2	MEQ
Malhargarh 19 H6	MLG
Malhaur 22 C1	ML
Maligaon Halt 26 D2	
Maligura 43 G6	MVG
Malihati Talibpur Rd 36 B2	MHTR
Malikpeth 47 F2	MKPT
Malikpur 25 G4	MLKP
Malikpur Halt 13 H6	MLKP
Malipur 23 E2	MLPR
Maliya 36 B4	MLYA
Maliya Hatina 28 C6	MLHA
Maliya Miyana 28 D2	MALX
Maliya Miyana Jn 28 D2	MALB
Malkajgiri 51 inset	MJF
Malkangiri 50 A2	*
Malkapur 40 D2	MKU
Malkapur Rd 31 H5	MALK
Malkapuram 53 H2	MLK
Malkera 45 inset	MLQ
Malkhaid Rd 48 A4	MQE
Malkhed 41 F2	MLR
Malkhedi 32 A1	MAKR
Malkisar 11 G2	MLC
Mallan Nagar Halt 13 G4	MQW
Mallankinar H 61 E3	MNKR
Mallanwala Khas 8 C3	MWX
Mallanwan 22 A1	MLW
Mallappa Gate 53 G2	MLGT
Mallapur 52 D1	MLP
Mallarpur 36 A1	MLV
Mallasandra 53 F6	MLSA
Mallavaram 50 B4	MVRM
Mallemadugu 49 F4	MLMG
Malleswaram 61 G1	MWM
Mallikpur 37 inset	MAK
Mallividu 50 C2	MVW
Malliyala 53 H2	MYL
Malliyam 58 C6	MY
Malod 29 F3	MLDP
Maloncha 25 G4	-
Malout 8 B5	MOT
Malpura 20 A2	MLA
Malsar 30 A5	MLSR
Malsian Shahkot 8 D3	MQS
Malthan 46 D1	MLM
Malugur 53 G5	MLU
Maluka 35 E5	MLKA
Malupota 9 E3	MXP
Malur 57 H2	MLO
Malwan 22 B3	MWH
Malwara 18 D5	MBW
Maman 13 E4	MOM
Mamanduru 54 C6	MRM
Mambalam 58 D2, 59 inset	MBM
Mamhalapattu 60 C4	MMP
Mamdapur 48 D4	MMPR
Mana 41 F2	MUN
Mana 43 E2	MANA
Manabar 50 B1	MVF
Manaklao 19 E1	MLH
Manaknagar Jn 22 B1	MKG
Manaksar 8 B6	MNSR
Manali Halt 61 H1	MNLI
Manamadurai East 61 E3	MNME
Manamadurai Jn 61 E3	MNM
Manani 9 G6	MNZ
Mananpur 24 C5	MNP
Mananwala 8 C2	MOW
Manaparai 61 E1	MPA
Manauri 22 C4	MRE
Manavadar 28 C5	MVR
Manavasi 58 A6	MVS
Manavur 58 D1	MAF
Mancheswar 44 D3	MCS
Manchili 49 H5	MCLE
Manchiryal 42 A6	MCI
Mandagadde 52 D5	-
Mandagere 57 E2	MGF
Mandah Rd 22 D5	MNF
Mandal 19 H4	MDL
Mandalgarh 19 H4	MLGH
Mandalghat 25 G2	MDG
Mandamari 42 A6	MMZ
Mandan Mishra Halt 24 C2	MNMA
Mandapadu 49 F6	MDPD
Mandapam 61 G4	MMM
Mandapam Camp Halt 61 G4	MC
Mandar Hill 24 D5	MDLE
Mandar Vidyapith 24 D5	MDVH
Mandardisa 27 F3	MYD
Mandasa Rd 44 B6	MMS
Mandavalli 49 G5	MDVL
Mandawali Chander Vihar H 15 inset	MWC
Mandavariya 19 H1	MNDV
Mandavelli 59 inset	MDVL
Mandawar Mahwa Rd 12 D6	MURD
Mandhali Halt 9 E3	MYE
Mandhana Jn 22 A2	MDA
Mandhar 43 E1	MDH
Mandi Adampur 12 B1	ADR
Mandi Bamora 32 A1	MABA
Mandi Dabwali 8 C6	MBY
Mandi Dhanaura 13 F2	MNDR
Mandidip 31 H3	MDDP
Mandi Gobindgarh 9 E4	GVG
Mandirhasaud 43 E1	MNDH
Mandiyai Kalan 19 E1	MKDL
Mandla Fort 32 D4	MFR
Mandor 19 E2	MDB
Mandpiya 19 H4	MDPA
Mandrak 13 F5	MXK
Mandsor 30 D1	MDS
Manduadih 23 E4	MUV
Mandura 41 F2	MNDA
Mandurai Halt 58 B6	MAND
Mandwa 31 F6	MWA
Mandya 57 F2	MYA
Manekwadi 29 F5	MKV
Manendragarh 33 G3	MDGR
Maneswar 44 A1	MANE
Mangal Mahudi 30 B3	MAM
Mangalagiri 49 F6	MAG
Mangalampeta 54 B6	MPT
Mangaliyawas 19 H2	MLI
Mangalore 56 C1	MAQ
Mangalore Harbour 56 C1	-
Manganallur H 58 C6	MNX
Mangaon 46 B2	MNI
Mangapatnam 54 A3	MUM
Mangapuram 54 C6	MGPM
Mangela 29 F6	MGL
Manglajhora Halt 26 A2	MONJ
Mangli 42 B3	MNGL
Mangliya Gaon 31 E4	MGG
Mangolpuri 15 inset	MGLP
Mangra 34 C2	MAZ
Mangrolia 39 G1	MGRL
Mangudi 61 G1	MAX
Manguli Chawdwar 44 D3	MACR
Mangurjan 25 F2	MXJ
Manguru 49 G2	MUGR
Manheru 12 C3	MHU
Manhgupur H 22 D4	
Mani Kala Halt 23 E3	MNKN
Mania 21 E1	MIA
Manigachhi 24 C2	MGI
Manigram 25 F6	MGLE
Manihari 25 E4	MHI
Manihari Ghat 25 E4	MNG
Manik Chouree 43 E2	MCF
Manikgarh Jn 42 A4	MAGH
Manikpur Jn 22 C5	MKP
Manikui 35 F3	MIK
Manimau 22 A1	MNMU
Maninagar 29 G3, 28 inset	MAN
Manipuram Block Cabin 49 F6	MIX
Manipurbagan 27 E6	MOAR
Maniram 23 F1	MIM
Manjari Budruk 46 C1	MJBK
Manjattidal 58 B6	MCJ
Manjeshwar 56 C2	MJS
Manjhagarh 23 H2	MJV
Manjhauligram 24 B4	MJM
Manjhi 23 H3	MHT
Manjhlepur Halt 22 C3	MNJR
Manjhra Purab 14 C4	MJPB
Manjhwe 24 B5	MZW
Manjri Nangal 12 C4	MJNL
Manjrol 30 A5	MJRL
Manjuri Rd 45 E2	MZZ
Mankapur Jn 22 D1	MUR
Mankar 35 H2	MNAE
Mankara 57 E6	MNY
Mankatha 24 C4	MKB
Mankhurd 38 inset	MKND
Manki 52 B4	MANK
Mankundu 37 inset	MUU
Manmad Jn 40 A3	MMR
Mannampandal 58 C6	MNMP
Mannanur 57 E6	MNUR
Mannargudi 61 G1	MQ
Manoharabad 48 C3	MOB
Manoharganj 22 C4	MNJ
Manopad 53 H1	MOA
Manpur Jn 24 A5	MPO
Manpur Nagaria 13 G4	MPG
Mansa 8 D5	MSZ
Mansahi 25 E4	MNS
Mansapooran 21 E4	MNPN
Mansarovar 38 inset	MANR
Mansi Jn 24 C4	MNE
Mansurpur 13 E1	MSP
Mantapampalle 54 C4	MMPL
Mantatti 48 A4	MVH
Mantralayam Rd 53 G1	MALM
Manu 37 H1	MANU
Manubolu 54 D5	MBL
Manund Rd Jn 29 G1	MRD
Manvat Rd 40 D5	MVO
Manwa Halt 14 B6	MANW
Manwal 7 G5	MNVL
Manwala Kot Bakhtu H 8 C5	MKBH
Manyamkonda 48 B5	MQN
Manzurgarhi 13 F4	MZGI
Maonda 12 B4	MADA
Marahra 13 F5	MHA
Maraimalai Kamarajar Nagar 58 D2	MMNK
Maralahalli 58 A2	MZV
Maramjhiri 31 H5	MJY
Marampalli 49 H5	MPL
Marandahalli 57 H3	MZU
Mararikulam 60 B3	MAKM
Marauda 42 D1	MXA
Maravakkadu 61 G2	MVK
Margherita 17 G5	MRG
Marhaura 24 A3	MEW
Mariahu 23 E4	MAY
Mariamman Kovil H 58 C6	MAV
Mariani Jn 27 H1	MXN
Marichethal 48 A6	MRC
Maridhal Halt 17 E4	MDHL
Marikuppam 58 A2	MKM
Marine Lines 38 inset	MEL
Maripalem 50 C3	MPM
Maripat 13 E3, 15 inset	MIU
Mariyal Gangavadi Halt 57 F4	MRLA
Mariyammanahalli 53 F3	MMI
Marjadwa 23 H1	MRJD
Markadhana 32 B5	MKDN
Markandi Udadon 32 C5	MOG
Markapur Rd 54 C2	MRK
Markona 45 F1	MKO
Markundi 22 B5	MKD
Maroli 39 F1	MRL
Marpalli 48 B3	MRF
Marsul 41 E5	MRV
Martur 47 H4	MR
Marudalam 58 C2	MRLM
Marudur Halt 58 A6	MUQ
Marwar Bagra 18 D4	MBGA
Marwar Balia 11 H5	MBSK
Marwar Bhinmal 18 D4	MBNL
Marwar Bithri 10 D5	MBT
Marwar Chhapri 19 G1	MCPE
Marwar Jn 19 F3	MJ
Marwar Khara 10 D5	MKHR
Marwar Kori 18 D4	MOF
Marwar Lohawat 11 E6	MWT
Marwar Mathaniya 19 E1	MMY
Marwar Mundwa 11 G6	MDW
Marwar Musuria Siding 19 E2	MMSA
Marwar Ranawas 19 F3	MRWS
Marwar Ratanpur 18 D5	MSQ
Marwasgram 33 G1	MWJ
Masagram 36 A3	MSAE
Masaipet 48 C3	ME
Masanadih 23 H1	MSDH
Masangaon 31 G5	MUO
Masani 13 E5	MSE
Masaniwal Halt 11 F1	MOWA
Masarahalli 52 D5	MSS
Masaudhi Court H 24 A4	
Masit 14 A6	MST
Masjid 38 inset	MSD
Maskanwa 23 E1	MSW
Masodha 22 D1	MSOD
Masor Rd 29 H5	MXD
Masudan 24 C4	MSDN
Masur 46 C3	MSR
Matalila 21 F5	MZH
Matalkunta 48 A3	MTV
Matana Buzurg 31 E3	MABG
Matari 35 F2, 45 inset	MRQ
Mataundh 22 A4	MTH
Matera 14 C5	MT
Mathabhanga 25 G2	*
Mathela 31 F5	MTA
Matheran 39 F5	MAE
Mathiabar Ghat 23 G1	MTBG
Mathur 58 C5	MTUR
Mathura Cantt 13 E5	MRT
Mathura Jn 13 E5	MTJ
Mathurapur 24 D6	MUW
Mathurapur Rd 36 B5	MPRD
Matiali 25 G1	-
Matigara 25 F1	MTRA
Matlabpur 13 G2	MTB
Matmari 53 G1	MTU
Matoda 29 G3	MQA
Mattagazpur 44 D3	MTND
Mattancheri Halt 60 B2	MTNC
Mattupetti 60 C2	-
Matunga 38 inset	MTN
Matunga Rd 38 inset	MRU
Matyakheri 19 H6	MYKR
Mau Aimma 22 D3	MEM
Mau Jn 23 F3	MAU
Mauhari 33 G3	MZH
Maula Ali 48 C3, 51 inset	MLY
Mauli BH 9 E3	MAULI
Maur 8 D5	MAUR
Mau-Ranipur 21 G4	MRPR
Maval 19 E5	MAA
Mavelikara 60 B4	MVLK
Mavelipalaiyam 57 H5	MVPM
Mavinahalli 47 F4	MVHL
Mavinkere 57 E2	MVC
Mavli Jn 19 F5	MVJ
Mavur Rd 61 G1	MARD
Mayakonda 53 E4	MYK
Mayanoor 58 A6	MYU
Mayar Halt 12 B2	MAYR
Mayavaram Town 58 C6	MVM
Mayiladuturai Jn 58 C6	MV
Maynaguri Rd 25 G2	MYGD
Mayurhat 36 B3	MYHT
Mayyanad 60 B4	MYY
Mccluskieganj 34 D2	MGME
Mechcheri Rd 57 H4	MCRD
Mecheda 36 A5	MCA
Medaksara 53 G5	*
Medapadu 50 A4	MPU
Medchal 48 C3, 51 inset	MED
Medra 29 G2	MDRA
Meenambakkam 59 inset	MN
Meenapur 25 E4	MENP
Meerut Cantt 13 E2	MTC
Meerut City Jn 13 E2	MUT
Megh Rajpura Halt 9 E1	MGRP
Meghnagar 30 C3	MGN
Meghpur 28 C5	MGHP
Meghpur Titodi 28 B4	MGTD
Mehemadabad & Kheda Rd 29 H3	MHD
Mehidpur Rd 30 D2	MEP
Mehgawan 23 E3	MGNW
Mehpani 32 B4	
Mehrawan 23 E3	MIH
Mehsi 24 A2	MAI
Mehuwala Halt 12 A1	MHUL
Meja Rd 22 D4	MJA
Mekliganj 25 G2	*
Mekra Memerakhabad 24 B4	
Mekkudi Halt 58 A6	MKY
Melakallur 60 D5	MKQ
Melakkonnakulam 61 E3	MEKM
Melathur 58 B2	MEH
Melamarudhur 61 H1	MLDR
Melappalayam Halt 60 D5	MP
Melattur Halt 57 E5	MLTR
Meleng 17 E6	MEG
Melmaruvathur 58 D3	MLMR
Melnariyappanur Halt 58 B4	MLYR
Melpakkam 58 C1	MLPM
Melpattambakkam 58 C4	MBU
Melpatti 58 B2	MPI
Melusar Halt 11 H3	MELH
Memari 36 B3	MYM
Mendu 13 F5	MEU
Meodala 42 B3	MWG
Meppuliyur 58 C4	MPLY
Meralgram 34 B1	MQX
Meriyana 29 E6	MRYA
Mermandoli 44 C2	MHDL
Merppanaikkadu 61 G2	MPX
Merta City 19 G1	MEC
Merta Rd Jn 19 G1	MTD
Mertala Phaleya 36 B2	MTFA
Methai 24 D3	MEE
Methi Tikur Halt 22 B1	METR
Metpanjra 41 H1	MER
Mettupalaiyam 57 F5	MTP
Mettur 60 C5	MTE
Mettur Dam 57 H4	MTDM
Metyal Sahar 35 G2	MYX
Mevli 30 A4	MVLI
Mewa Nawada 13 F2	MWE
Mezenga 17 E6	MZA
Mhasawad 40 C2	MWD
Mhow 31 E4	MHOW
Miangram 36 B2	MIAN
Mianpur 9 F4	MNPR
Midghat 31 H4	MIG
Midnapur 35 H4	MDN
Mighauna Halt 13 H4	MIW
Migrendisa 27 F4	MGE
Milak 13 G3	MIL
Milakpur H 13 H4	-
Milangarh 25 F4	MQG
Milavali 21 E2	MIAL
Milavittan 61 E5	MVN
Mile 5B Cabin 37 inset	M5B
Minatchipuram 60 C1	MXM
Minchnal 47 F4	MNL
Mindha 12 A6	MNHA
Minjur 58 D1, 59 inset	MJR
Minnampalli 58 A4	MPLI
Mira Rd 38 inset	MIRA
Miraj Jn 46 D4	MRJ
Miraj North Cabin 46 D4	-
Miranpur Katra 13 H4	MK
Miran Sahib 7 G6	-
Mirchandhori 33 H1	MCQ
Mirkhal 41 E5	MQL
Mirthakur 13 E6	MIQ
Mirthal 8 D1	MRTL
Miryalaguda 49 E5	MRGA
Mirza 26 C2	MZRA
Mirzacheuki 25 E4	MZC
Mirzapalli 48 C2	MZL
Mirzapur 23 E5	MZP
Mirzapur Bachhod 12 C4	MBV
Mirzapur Bankipur 37 inset	MBE
Mirzapur Ghat 23 E5	MZT
Misamari 16 B6	MSMI
Misrauli 22 D3	MFL
Misrikh Tirath 14 B5	MSTH
Misrod 31 G3	MSO
Mitawali 13 F6	MTI
Mitewani 42 B1	MTWN
Mitha 18 C6	MITA
Mithapur 28 A3	MTHP
Mithila Deep Halt 24 C2	MTLP
Miyagam Karjan Jn 29 H5	MYG
Miyana 20 D5	MYN
Miyon ka Bara 19 E2	MNKB
Moabund 27 G1	MOBD
Mobha Rd 29 H4	MBH
Mochia 25 F5	MCE
Modasa 30 A2	MDSA
Model Gram 9 E4	MG
Modinagar 13 E2	MDNR
Modlimb 47 F2	MLB
Modpur 28 C4	MDPR
Modran 18 D4	MON
Modukuru 49 F6	MDKU
Moga 8 D4	MOGA
Mohadara 42 A2	MXZ
Mohadc Pargane Laling 40 B2	MAHD
Mohalbani 45 inset	MLBN
Mohammad Khera 31 F2	MQE
Mohammadganj 23 G6	MDJ
Mohammadi 14 A4	*
Mohammadpur 27 E5	NPRA
Mohan Nagar 11 F1	MNGR
Mohana 21 E3	MYZ
Mohanlalganj 22 B1	MLJ
Mohanpura Halt 8 B5	MOPR
Moharajpur 25 E4	MJP
Mohari Jn 21 E1	MHF
Mohasa 21 F6	MXS
Mohibullahpur 22 B1	MBP
Mohini Mandal Halt 24 B2	MMDL
Mohishila 35 G2	MOH
Mohitnagar 25 G2	MOP
Mohiuddin Nagar 24 B4	MOG
Mohkhuti 17 E5	MHKT

Mohol 47 F3 MO
Mohope 38 inset
Mohri 9 F5 MOY
Mohuda Jn 35 F2, 45 inset MHQ
Mokalsar 18 D3 MKSR
Mokama Ghat 24 B4 MKG
Mokama Jn 24 B4 MKA
Mokhampura 19 H3 MAKH
Mokhasakalavapudi 49 G5 MVP
Mokholi 20 C2 MXL
Molagavalli 53 G2 MGV
Molakalmuru 53 F3 MOMU
Molakarampatti 53 F3 MOLK
Molisar 11 H4 MIO
Monabari 16 C6 MFC
Monacherra 27 E5 MNCR
Mondh 23 E4 MOF
Monghyr 24 C4 MGR
Monghyr Ghat 24 C4 MHG
Monkey Hill Cabin 39 G6 MHC
Monmohinipur Rd Siding 27 E1 -
Monoharpur 35 E5 MOU
Mor 24 B4 MOR
Moradabad City 13 G3 MBCT
Moradabad Jn 13 G3 MB
Moradabad West Cabin 13 G3 MBWC
Moraiya 29 G3 MORA
Morak 20 B5 MKX
Morampudi 49 F6 MOD
Moran 17 F5 MOX
Moranhat 17 F5 MRHT
Morappur 58 A3 MAP
Morbi 28 D3 MVI
Mordad Tanda 40 B2 MWK
Mordar 31 F6 MRDD
Morena 21 E2 MRA
Morgram 25 F6 MGAB
Mori Bera 19 E4 MOI
Morinda 9 F4 MRND
Mormugao Harbour 52 A2 MRH
Morshi 41 G1 *
Morthala 19 E5 MXO
Morwani 30 E3 MRN
Mosale Hosahalli Halt 57 E2 MLHL
Moshat 63 F5 MOS
Mosur 58 D1 MSU
Mota 13 G6 MOTA
Mota Jadra 38 D1 MOZ
Mota Miya Mangrol 29 H6 MNGV
Mota Surka 29 F5 MTSK
Motari 44 D4 MWQ
Moterjhar 26 A2 MTJR
Moth 21 G3 MOTH
Mothala 28 B2 MTLA
Mothala Halt 28 B2 MTHH
Motichur 9 H6 MOTC
Moti Khavdi 28 C4 MTKD
Moti Koral 29 H5 MKRL
Moti Zari 30 B3 MZI
Motibagh 42 A2 MIB
Motiganj 14 D6 MOTG
Motihari 24 A2 MKI
Motihari Court H 24 A2 MCO
Motijheel 21 F2 MTJL
Motipur 24 A2 MTR
Motipura Chauki 20 D5 MTPC
Motumari Jn 49 F4 MTMI
Moturu 49 G5 OTR
Mourigram 37 inset MRGM
Mowad 41 G1 *
Muazzampur Narain Jn 13 F1 MZM
Mudaria 33 F3 MDXR
Muddalinganahalli Halt 57 G1 MDLL
Muddanuru 54 A4 MOO
Mudigubba 53 H4 MGB
Mudkhed Jn 41 F5 MUE
Mudlana 12 D2 MDLA
Mududi Halt 57 E1 MUDI
Muftiganj 23 E3 MFJ
Mugad 52 C2 MGD
Mugaiyur Halt 58 C4 MUY
Mugalolli 47 F6 MGL
Mugat 41 F5 MGC
Mughal Sarai Jn 23 F4 MGS
Mugma 35 G2 MMU
Muhammadabad 23 F3 MMA
Muhammadpur 24 B2 MHP
Muhiuddinpur 13 E2 MUZ
Muirpur Rd 34 A1 MPF
Mujnai 25 H1 MJE
Mukerian 8 D2 MEX
Mukhasa Parur 58 C5 MKSP
Mukkali Halt 56 D4 MUKE
Muktapur 24 B3 MKPR
Muktapuram 53 H4 MPM
Mukteswarpuri 44 D4 MKTP
Muktiara Balwada 31 E4 MKT
Muktsar 8 C4 MKS
Mukundarayapuram 58 C2 MCN
Mukundawadi 40 B4 MKDD
Mukuria 25 F4 MFA
Mukutban 41 H4
Mukutmanipur 35 G3 *
Mulagunnathukavu 60 B1 MGK
Mulakala Cheruvu 54 A5 MCU
Mulanturutti 60 B2 MNTT
Mulanur 58 A2 MAR
Mulewal Khaira 8 D3 MLKH
Muli Rd 29 E3 MOL
Mulki 56 C1 MULK
Mullanpur 8 D4 MLX
Mullurcarai Halt 57 E6 MUC
Mulmarora 42 B4 MME
Mulshi 46 C1 *
Multai 32 A6 MTY
Mulund 38 inset MLND
Mulvad 47 F5 MVD
Mumbai Central 39 F5, 38 inset MCT
Mumbai region 39 F5, 38 inset
Mumbra 38 inset MBQ
Munabao 18 A2 MBF
Munda Gopal Ashram 14 C6 MGPA
Mundalaram 30 D2 MDLM
Munderwa 23 E1 MND
Mundha Pandey 13 G3 MPH
Mundhewadi 47 F3 MVE
Mundikota 42 B1 MNU
Mundiyambakkam 58 C4 MYP
Mundka Halt 12 D3 MQC
Mundra 28 C2
Mundra Port 28 C2 MDPT
Mungaoli 21 E6 MNV
Muniguda 43 H5 MNGD
Munirabad 53 F2 MRB
Munnar 60 C2
Munrothuruttu Halt 60 B4 MQO
Munsirhat 37 inset, 63 F5 MNH
Munumaka 49 E6 MUK
Mupa 27 F4 MUPA
Muradih 35 G2 MDF
Muradnagar 13 E3 MUD
Muradpur Halt 23 F2 MRDP
Muragachha 36 B2 MGM
Muraitha Halt 24 B2 MRTA
Murarai 25 F6 MRR
Murarpur 24 D4 MPY
Murdeshwar 52 B4 MRDW
Murga Mahadev Rd 35 E5 MMVR
Murhari H 24 B4
Murhesi Rampur 13 E5 MSRP
Murhipar 42 D1 MUP
Muri Jn 35 F3 MURI
Muribahal 43 G3 MRBL
Murkong Selek 17 F4 MZS
Murliganj 24 D3 MRIJ
Murli Halt 25 E5 MRLI
Mursan 13 E5 MSN
Murshadpur 13 F1 MSDR
Murshidabad 36 B1 MBB
Murtazapur Jn 41 F2 MZR
Murtazapur Town 41 F2 MZRT
Murthipalaiyam 57 H6 MPLM
Murti 40 D6 MRTY
Murtiha 14 C4 MUH
Murud 47 G1 MRX
Murukkampuzha 60 B5 MQU
Musafirkhana 22 D2 MFKA
Musahibpur 8 D1 MSBR
Musharwa Halt 23 H1 MSHW
Mushrakh 24 A3 MHC
Musra 42 D1 MUA
Mustabada 49 G5 MBD
Mustafabad 9 F5 MFB
Musunur 54 D2 MSNR
Muthalamada 60 C1 MMDA
Muthani 23 F5 MTGE
Muttampatti 58 A4 MPC
Muttanendal 61 E3 MTZ
Muttarasanallur 58 B6 MTNL
Mutupet 61 G1 MTT
Muval Tank 30 A4 MUVL
Muzaffarnagar 13 E1 MOZ
Muzaffarpur Jn 24 B3 MFP
Mysore New Goods Ter. 57 F3 MNGT
Mysore Jn 57 F3 MYS

N

N Panakudi Halt 60 D6 NPK
Naba Ray Nagar 36 B3 NRBN
Nabadwip Dham 36 B3 NDAE
Nabadwip Ghat 36 B3, 63 G2 NDF
Nabagram 36 A3 NBAE
Nabagram Kakurhati 36 B2 NBKH
Nabha 9 E5 NBA
Nabinagar Rd 23 G6 NBG
Nabipur 29 H5 NIU
Nachinda 36 A6 NCN
Nachlana 7 G4 *
Nada 30 A5 NADA
Nadapuram Rd Halt 56 D4 NAU
Nadaul 24 A4 NDU
Nadbai 12 D6 NBI
Nadgam 29 H3 NDG
Nadiad Jn 29 H3 ND
Nadiapur 27 E6 NPU
Nadikudi Jn 49 E5 NDKD
Nadwan 24 A4 NDW
Nagal 9 G6 NGL
Nagalapalli 48 C3 NPL
Nagalwancha 49 F4 NVC
Nagamalai West Halt 61 E2 NGMW
Naganahalli 57 F3 NHY
Nagansur 47 G3 NGS
Nagapattinam 58 D6 NGT
Nagapattinam Beach 58 D6 NPB
Nagar 33 H3 NGE
Nagar Untari 34 B1 NUQ
Nagardevla 40 B2 NGD
Nagargali 52 C2 NAG
Nagari 58 C1 NG
Nagaria Sadat 13 G3 NRS
Nagarnabi 25 F6 NGF
Nagarsol 40 A3 NSL
Nagarur 53 G2 NRR
Nagarwada 32 D5 NWA
Nagasamudram 53 H4 NGM
Nagaur 11 F5 NGO
Nagaur Mela 11 F5 NF
Nagavangala 53 E5 NVF
Nagda Jn 30 D2 NAD
Nagercoil Jn 60 D6 NCJ
Nagercoil Town Halt 60 C6 NJT
Nageshwadi 47 H1 NGHW
Naghbir Jn 42 B3 NAB
Nagina 13 F1 NGG
Naginimora 17 E6 NOM
Nagireddipalli 48 D4 NRDP
Nagjua 34 D3 NJA
Nagla Tula 21 E1 NGLT
Naglavi 52 C2 NGV
Nagnath Cabin 39 G6 NAG
Nagore 58 D6 NCR
Nagothane 46 B1 NGTN
Nagpur Jn 42 A2 NGP
Nagrakata 25 G1 NKB
Nagri 41 H3 NGI
Nagrota 9 F1 NGRT
Nagrota Suriyan 9 E1 NGRS
Nagsar Halt 23 F4 NXR
Nagshankar H 16 C6 NSK
Nahargarh 30 C3 NRH
Naharkatia 17 F5 NHK
Nahiyar 29 H5 NAH
Nahorani Siding 16 B6 -
Nahorbari 27 H1 -
Nahur 38 inset NSBD
Naigaon 38 inset NIG
Naihati Jn 36 B4, 37 inset NH
Naikheri 31 E3 NKI
Naikot 15 F6 NIT
Naila 33 H5 NIA
Nailalung 27 F3 NLN
Naimisharanya 14 B6 NM
Nainaragaram 60 D4 NRGM
Naini Jn 22 D4 NYN
Nainpur Jn 32 D5 NIR
Najibabad Jn 13 F1 NBD
Nakaha Jungle 23 F1 JEA
Nakardei 24 A1 NKU
Nakchari 17 E6 NCH
Nakkanadoddi 53 G3 NKDO
Nakodar Jn 8 D3 NRO
Naksalbari 25 F1 NAK
Naktisemra 43 F6 NKX
Nal Halt 11 F4 NX
Nalanda 24 B5 NLD
Nala Sopara 38 inset NSP
Nalattinputtur 60 D4 NLT
Nalbari 26 C2 NLV
Nalgonda 48 D4 NLDA
Nalhati Jn 25 E6 NHT
Nalikul 36 B4, 37 inset NKL
Naliya 28 A2 NLY
Naliya Cantt 28 A2 NLC
Nalkata H 37 H1 NLKT
Nallacheruvu 54 A5 NCU
Nallacheruvu East 54 A5 NCE
Nallapadu 49 F6 NLPD
Nallattipalaiyam 57 F6 NLPM
Nalli 60 D4 NLL
Nallur Rd 61 E5 NLU
Naloi Barwa 12 B2 BVZ
Nalpur 37 inset NALR
Nalukody 60 B3 NAY
Nalwar 47 H4 NW
Namakkal 58 A5 NMOA
Namanasamudram 61 F2 NMN
Namburu 49 F6 NBR
Namdong Wharf 17 G5 NDWF
Namkhana 36 B6 -
Namkom 35 E3 NKM
Namli 30 D2 NLI
Namrup 17 F5 NAM
Namtiali 17 E6 NMT
Nana 19 E4 NANA
Nanadi Halt 17 E5 NOD
Nanaksar 8 D4 NNKR
Nanauta 9 G6 NNX
Nancherla 53 G2 NLA
Nand Ganj 23 F4 NDJ
Nandaigajan 36 A5 NDGM
Nandakumar 36 A5 NDKR
Nandalur 54 C4 NRE
Nandapur 41 E5 NDPR
Nandarkha 29 G5 NDKH
Nanded 41 F5 NED
Nandesari 29 H4 NDR
Nandgaon 40 A3 NGN
Nandgaon Rd 46 B5 NAN
Nandi Halt 53 H6 NDY
Nandini Lagunnia 24 B4 NNNL
Nandiyambakkam 58 D1, 59 inset NPKM
Nandkhas 21 G3 NDK
Nandol Dahegam 29 H2 NHM
Nandpur Bhatauli 9 E1 NDBT
Nandre 46 D4 NDE
Nandura 40 D2 NN
Nandurbar 30 B6 NDB
Nandyal 54 B2 NDL
Nangal Dam 9 F3 NLDM
Nangal Degrota Halt 12 C3 NDRT
Nangal Mundi 12 C4 NNU
Nangal Pathani Halt 12 C3 NLO
Nangaon 21 F2 NGON
Nangi 37 inset NAI
Nangloi 12 D3, 15 inset NNO
Nanguneri 60 D5 NNN
Nani Baral 28 D2 NBRL
Nanjangud Town 57 F3 NTW
Nannilam 58 C6 NNM
Nanpara Jn 14 C5 NNP
Nanwan 12 B3 NWN
Naojan 27 G2 NJN
Napasar 11 F4 NPS
Nar 29 G4 NAR
Nar Town 29 G4 NTN
Narah 12 D1 NARA
Naraikkinar 60 D5 NRK
Naraina 20 A1 NRI
Naraina Vihar 15 inset NRVR
Narainpur Anant 24 B3 NRPA
Narainpur Colony 63 G5 -
Narainpur Murti 24 D2 NRPM
Naraj Marthapur 44 D3 NQR
Narangi 26 D2 NNGE
Naranjipur 31 E3 NRGR
Naranpura 11 H6 -
Narasambudhi Halt 57 F3 NBU
Narasapur 49 H5 NS
Narasaraopet 49 F6 NRT
Narasimhapura 44 C5 NRSP
Narasimharajupuram 52 D5 -
Narasinganpet 58 C6 NPT
Narasingapalli 50 C3 NASP
Narauna Jodhpur Romana H 8 C5 NJM
Narayan Pakuria Murail 36 A5 NPMR
Narayanappavalasa 50 C1 NGJA
Narayanapura 53 H5 NRYP
Narayangarh 35 H5 NYA
Narayanpet Rd 48 A5 NRPD
Narayanpur 24 D4 NNR
Narayanpur Tatwara 20 C2 NNW
Nardana 40 B1 NDN
Narela 12 D2 NUR
Narendrapur 37 inset NRPR
Nareshwar Rd 29 H5 NRUR
Narganjoo 24 C5 NRGO
Narhan 24 C3 NRN
Nari Khetri 12 B4 NRKE
Nariaoli 32 B2 NOI
Narikkudi 61 E3 NKK
Narimogaru 56 D2 NRJ
Narinderpura 8 D6 NPX
Nariyar Halt 24 A2 NRV
Narkatia Bazar 23 H2 NKBR
Narkatiaganj Jn 15 H6 NKE
Narkhed 41 H1 NRKR
Narkopi 34 D3 NRKP
Narmada Br. 31 H4 NRNDB
Narnaul 12 C4 NNL
Naroda 29 G3, 28 inset NRD
Narpatganj 24 D2 NPV
Narshipuram 50 D1 NSX
Narsingpur 32 C4 NU
Narsipatnam Rd 50 B4 NRP
Narthamalai 61 F1 NTM
Narthar Halt 13 G5 NHX
Narwana Jn 12 C1 NRW
Narwasi 12 B2 NRWI
Nashik Rd 39 H3 NK
Nashipur Rd 36 B1 NSO
Nashkal 48 D3 NSKL
Nasibpur 37 inset NSE
Nasirabad 19 H2 NSD
Nasrala 9 F2 NAS
Naswadi 30 A5 NSW
Natesar 24 B5 *
Nathapettai 58 D2 NTT
Nathdwara 19 F5 NDT
Nathganj BH 24 B6 NGY
Nathnagar 24 D4 NAT
Nathpura 30 A4 NT
Nathu Kheri 31 E1 NKH
Nathwana 11 G3 NTZ
Nattarasankottai 61 F2 NTS
Nature Cure Hospital 51 inset NCHS
Naugachia 24 D4 NNA
Nauganwan 30 D3 NGW
Naugarh 15 F6 NUH
Naulatha 12 D1 NLH
Naunanda 21 E3 NUN
Naupada Jn 51 E1 NWP
Nautanwa 15 F6 NTV
Nautar 15 G6 NVR
Navabpalem 49 H5 NBM
Navade Rd 39 F5, 38 inset NVRD
Navagadh 28 D5 NUD
Navalgaon 41 E4 NLVN
Navalgund Rd 52 D2 NVD
Navalpura 29 H2 NVP
Navalur 52 C2 NVU
Navapur 39 G1 NWU
Navipet 41 G6 NVT
Navlakhi 28 D3 NLK
Navsari 39 F1 NVS
Nawa City 12 A6 NAC
Nawabganj 22 D1 NGB
Nawada 24 B5 NWD
Nawada H 24 B4
Nawagaon 34 D5 NXN
Nawalgarh 12 4A NWH
Nawan Halt 8 B6 NAWN
Nawandgi 48 A4 NAW
Nawapara Rd 43 G2 NPD
Nawa Patra BH 24 D6 NPZ
Nawarangpur 43 F5 *
Nawashahr Doaba Jn 9 E3 NSS
Nawegaon 32 A5 NVG
Naya Azadpur 12 D3, 15 inset NDAZ
Naya Ghaziabad 13 E3, 15 inset GZN
Naya Khardia 11 H6 NYK
Naya Nagar 24 C3 NWC
Naya Nangal 9 F3 NNGL
Nayabhagirathipur 44 C2 NBT
Nayadongri 40 B3 NI
Nayagaon 24 A3, 25 inset NYO
Nayakanali 45 inset NKZ
Nayakdih Halt 23 F3 NAKD
Nayandahalli 57 G2 NYH
Nayatola 25 E4 NYT
Nayudupetta 54 D5 NYP
Nazarbagh 29 E3 NZG
Nazareth 61 E5 NZT
Nazira 17 E6 NZR
Nazirganj 24 B3 NAZJ
Neamati Ghat 17 E6 NEMT
Near Tunnel 9 H6 -
Necklace Road 51 inset NLRD
Nedimoliyanur 58 C3 NMO
Nedumbalam 61 G1 NMB
Nedungulam 61 E3 NDGM
Neema H 24 A4
Negun 36 A2, 63 F2 NGX
Nekonda 49 E3 NKD
Nekurseni 35 H5 NSI
Nelaballi 54 D5 NLB
Nelamangala 57 G2 *
Nellayi 60 B1 NYI
Nellikuppam 58 C4 NPM
Nellimarla 50 D2 NML
Nellore 54 D4 NLR
Nellore South 54 D4 NLS
Nemam Halt 60 C5 NEM
Nemaththanpatti 61 F2 NMI
Nenpur 29 G3 NEP
Neoli 47 G1 NEI
Neora 24 A4 NEO
Neoranadi 25 G1 NOR
Neoria Husainpur 14 A3 NRY
Nepa Nagar 40 D1 NPNR
Nepalganj Rd 14 D4 NPR
Ner 24 A5 NERH
Neral Jn 39 G5, 38 inset NRL
Neralakatte Halt 56 C1 NRF
Nergundi Jn 44 D3 NRG
Neri Halt 14 B5 NE
Nerul 38 inset NEU
Netawal 19 G5 NTWL
Netra 36 B5 NTA
Netranahalli 53 F4 NEHL
Netravathi H 56 C1 NTVT
Netrang 30 A5 NET
Neura O Grande 52 B2 *
New Alipore 37 inset NACC
New Alipurduar 25 H2 NOQ
New Balarampur 36 B1 NBPH
New Baneswar 25 H2 NBS
New Barrackpore 37 inset NBE
New Bongaigaon Jn 26 B2 NBQ
New Coochbehar Jn 25 H2 NCB
New Delhi 12 D3, 15 inset NDLS
New Dibrugarh Town 17 F5 *
New Domohani 25 G2 NOH
New Farakka Jn 25 F5 NFK
New Garh Madhpur 45 E2 NGMP
New Gitaldaha 25 H3 NGTG
New Guntur 49 E6 REP
New Guwahati 26 D2 NGC
New Jalpaiguri Jn 25 F1 NJP

New Katni 33 E2 NKJ
New Mal Jn 25 G1 NMZ
New Maynaguri 25 G2 NMX
New Misamari 16 B6 NMM
New Silchar 27 F5 NSCL
New Sisibargaon 17 E5 *
New Tinsukia Jn 17 F4 NTSK
Neyamatpur 24 A5 NYM
Neykkarapatti Halt 57 H4 NEA
Neyveli 58 C5 NVL
Neyvilakku 61 H1 NVK
Neyyattinkara 60 C5 NYY
Nibhapur 22 D4 NBP
Nibkarori 13 H6 NBUE
Nichitpur Jn 35 F2, 45 inset NPJE
Nidadavolu Jn 49 H6 NDD
Nidaghatta Halt 57 G2 NZH
Nidamangalam Jn 58 C6 NMJ
Nidamanuru 49 G5 NDM
Nidhani 32 D4 NN
Nidi 46 B1 NIDI
Nidigallu 54 C5 NDZ
Nidubrolu 55 E1 NDO
Nidur 58 C5 NID
Nidvanda 57 G1 NDV
Nigatpur 23 E4 NTU
Nigaura 33 G3 NIQ
Nigohan 22 C2 NHN
Nigohi 13 H4 NOH
Nihalgarh 22 C2 NHH
Nihastha Halt 22 B2 NHF
Nijbari 25 F2 NJB
Nilaje 39 F5, 38 inset NILJ
Nilambazar 27 E5 NLBR
Nilambur Rd 57 E5 NIL
Nileshwar 56 C3 NLE
Nilgiri 45 F1 -
Nilgiri Rd 45 F1 NGRD
Nilokheri 9 F6 NLKR
Nimach 19 H6 NMH
Nimarkheri 31 E5 NKR
Nimbahera 19 H5 NBH
Nimbal 47 F4 NBL
Nimbalak 40 A5 NNB
Nimbhora 40 C1 NB
Nimcha BH 35 G2 NMC
Nimdanri 36 C4 NMDR
Nimdih 35 F3 NIM
Nimera 20 B2 NMR
Nimhat 23 G6 NIMT
Nimiaghat 35 F2, 45 inset NMG
Nimka Khera 20 A4 NIMA
Nim-ka-Thana 12 B5 NMK
Nimo 36 A3 NMF
Nimoda 20 C2 NMD
Nimpura Jn 35 H5 NMP
Nimshirgaon Tamdalge 46 D5 NMGT
Nimtita 25 F6 NILE
Nindhar Benar 12 B6 NDH
Nindra BH 34 D2 NVA
Ningala 29 F5 NGA
Nipani Vadgaon 40 A4 NPW
Nipania 33 G6 NPI
Niphad 39 H3 NR
Nira 46 C2 NIRA
Nirakarpur 44 D4 NKP
Nirmali 24 C2 NMA
Nirol 36 A2, 63 F1 NXL
Nirolgram 36 A2, 63 F1 NRLM
Nischindapur 36 B5 NCP
Nischindapur Market H 36 B5 NCPM
Nishangara 14 C4 NSA
Nishatpura 31 G3 NSZ
Nisoi Halt 13 G4 NSU
Nittur 57 F1 NTR
Nityananddham 30 D2 NTDM
Nivasar 46 B4 NIV
Niwar 32 D2 NWR
Niwari 21 G4 NEW
Niwarkhed 41 G1 *
Niwas Rd 33 G1 NWB
Niyalishpara 36 B1 NLSF
Niyol 39 F1 NOL
Nizamabad 48 B1 NZB
Nizampur 12 B4 NIP
Nizbargaon 16 C6 NBX
Nizchetia 16 C6 NCA
Nizsariha Halt 26 C2 NSHR
Noadar Dhal 36 A2 NRX
Noamundi 35 E5 NOMD
Noapara Mahishasur 25 F6 NWMS
Nobanda 35 H3 NOB
Nogawan 9 F4 NGWN
Nohar 11 H2 NHR
Nohbachhamadi 13 E6 NHB
Nokha 11 F5 NOK
Noli 12 D3 NOLI
Nonapar Halt 23 G2 NNPR
Nonar 23 H4 NON
Nonera 21 F2 NNE
Noonmati 26 D2 NMY
Norla Rd 43 H4 NRLR
North Lakhimpur 16 D5 NLP
Nosaria Halt 11 H4 NOA
Nowbagh 41 F1 NBGH
Nowgong Assam 27 E2 NOG
Nowrozabad 33 E3 NRZB
Noyal 57 H5 NOY
NPA Shivarampalli 51 inset NSVP
NTPC BH 44 C2 NTPC
Nua 12 4A NUA
Nuagaon Mayurbhanj Rd 35 H6 NMBR
Nudurupadu 49 F6 NDPU
Nujella 49 G6 NUJ
Nulenuru Halt 53 E5 NLNR
Numaligarh 27 G1 NMGY
Nungambakkam 59 inset NBK
Nunkhar 23 G2 NRA
Nurahad 21 E2 NUB
Nurmahal 8 D3 NRM
Nurnagar Halt 13 E2 NRNR
Nurpur Rd 9 E1 NUPR
Nurpura 21 E1 NPH
Nusratabad Kharkhari 12 D3 NTG
Nuzvid 49 G5 NZD
Nyoli Kalan Halt 12 B2 NKN

O

Oating 27 G1 OTN
Obaidulaganj 31 H3 ODG
Obalapuram Halt 53 F3 OBM
Obra Dam 23 E6 OBR
Obulavaripalle 54 C5 OBVP
Ochira 60 B4 OCR
Odara 60 B3 ODA
Oddanchatram 60 D1 ODC
Oddarahalli 57 G1 ORH
Ode 29 H3 ODE
Odela 49 E1 OEA
Odha 39 H3 ODHA
Odhaniya Chacha 10 C6 OCH
Odur 54 D5 ODUR
Oel 14 B5 OEL
Ohan 22 B5 OHAN
Okha 28 B3 OKHA
Okha Madhi 28 B4 OKD
Okhla 12 D3, 15 inset OKA
Olakur 58 D3 OLA
Olapur 24 C4 OLP
Old Malda 25 F5 OMLF
Ollur 60 B1 OLR
Omalur Jn 57 H4 OML
Omkareshwar Rd 31 E5 OM
Ondagram 35 H3 ODM
Ongole 54 D2 OGL
Onnupuram 58 C2 OPM
Ontimitta 54 B4 VNM
Oodlabari 25 G1 ODB
Oorgaum 58 A2 OGM
Ootwar 12 D5 OTD
Orai 21 H3 ORAI
Orchha 21 F4 ORC
Ordi 19 H5 ORDI
Orga 34 D5 ORGA
Orki 8 B5 ORK
Orr 21 E6 ORR
Orwara 23 E1 ORW
Oshiwara 38 inset *
Osian 19 E1 OSN
Osmanabad 47 F2 *
Osra 31 E3 OSRA
Otha Rd 38 D1 OTH
Ottakkal 60 C4 OKL
Ottakovil 58 B5 OTK
Ottankadu 61 G2 TCT
Ottapalam 57 E6 OTP
Ottivakkam 58 D2 OV

P

Pabai 31 H2 PAI
Pabli Khas 13 E2 POY
Pabnawa Jasmahinder Halt 9 F6 PBJM
Pachandi 36 A2, 63 F1 PNDI
Pachawan 31 G3 PNWN
Pachar Malikpura 12 A6 PCMK
Pachchakuppam 58 B2 PCKM
Pachchapur 46 D6 PCH
Pachegaon 41 G2 PCGN
Pachor Rd 31 F2 PFR
Pachora Jn 40 B2 PC
Pachpadra City 18 D2 PBRY
Pachpadra Salt Depot 18 D2 PCB
Pachpahar 20 B6 PPO
Pachperwa 15 E5 PPW
Pachpokharia Halt 24 A1 PPK
Pachrukhi 23 H3 PCK
Padadhari 28 D4 PDH
Padalam 58 D2 PTM
Padampur 29 E1 PDF
Padampur 43 G2 *
Padapahar Jn 35 E5 PDPH
Padhegaon 40 A5 PDGN
Padi 59 inset PADI
Padiya Nagla 13 G2 PAQ
Padla 19 F6 PDQ
Padli 39 G4 PDL
Padmapukur 37 inset PDPK
Padnur 47 F3 PDNR
Padra 29 H4 PDRA
Padrauna 23 G1 POU
Padriganj 32 D5 PNJ
Padsali 47 F2 PSS
Padse 40 B1 PDP
Padua 50 B2 PFU
Padubidri 56 C1 PDD
Padugupadu 54 D4 PGU
Padur 58 C4 PADR
Padwania 29 H5 PWI
Pagara 20 D5 PGA
Pagdhal 31 G4 PGL
Pagidipalli Jn 48 D3, 51 inset PGDP
Pagidirai 53 H2 PGDI
Paglachandi 36 B2 PCX
Pahara 23 E5 PRE
Paharaja Gangur H 24 C4 PRGA
Paharpur 24 A6 PRP
Paharsar Halt 12 B2 PRSR
Pahleza 23 G5 PHE
Pahur 40 C2 PHU
Pailan 63 G6 -
Paimar 24 A5 PMI
Paintipur 14 C6 PPE
Pajian 8 D3 PJA
Pakala Jn 54 B6 PAK
Pakalpatti 57 H4 PKTH
Pakaria Rd 33 E1 PKRD
Pakhajan 29 G5 PKJ
Pakhna 13 G6 PKNA
Pakhrauli 22 D2 PKX
Pakkam 58 D3 PQM
Pakki 8 B5 PKK
Pakni 47 F3 PK
Pakra 34 D4 PKC
Pakri Dayal 24 A2 *
Pakur 25 E5 PKR
Palachuri 32 B5 PCLI
Palaiyam 57 H6 PALM
Palakkanuthu H 60 D1 PLKN
Palakkodu 57 H3 PCV
Palakollu 50 A6 PKO
Palam 12 D3, 15 inset PM
Palampur Himachal 9 F1 PLMX
Palana 11 F4 PAE
Palani 60 D1 PLNI
Palanpur Jn 18 D6 PNU
Palappuram Halt 57 E6 PLPM
Palari 32 D5 PUE
Palasa 51 E1 PSA
Palasdhari 39 G5, 38 inset PDI
Palasin 41 G1 *
Palasingi 44 A6 PLSG
Palasner 31 G5 PAL
Palasthali 35 G2 PSME
Palayankottai 60 D5 PCO
Palayasivaram 58 D2 PYV
Paldhi 40 C2 PLD
Palej 29 H5 PLJ
Paleza Ghat 24 A4, 25 inset PZT
Palghar 39 F4 PLG
Palghat Jn 57 F6 PGT
Palghat Town 57 F6 PGTN
Pali 12 C4 PALI
Pali Garh Halt 23 F3 PLGH
Pali Marwar 19 F3 PMY
Palia 31 E3 PLA
Paliakalan 14 B3 PLK
Paliba 50 B1 PBV
Palitana 29 F6 PIT
Paliyad Rd 29 E4 PAC
Palla Rd 36 A3 PRAE
Pallavaram 59 inset PV
Pallevada 49 H5 PLVA
Pallikere 56 C3 PKP
Pallikona 55 E1 POA
Pallinellianur 58 C4 PYN
Pallipattu 58 C1 *
Pallipuram 57 E6 PUM
Palliyadi Halt 60 C6 PYD
Palpara 36 B3 PXR
Palsana 12 A5 PLSN
Palsap 47 G1 PCP
Palsi 46 C2 PLV
Palsit 36 A3 PLAE
Palsora Makrawan 30 D3 PSO
Palta 37 inset PTF
Palur 58 D2 PALR
Palwal 12 D4 PWL
Paman 22 A2 PMN
Pambakovil Shandy 60 D4 PBKS
Pamban 61 G4 PBM
Pamidi 53 H3 PMD
Pampore 7 G3 *
Panagarh 35 H2 PAN
Panambur 56 C1 PNMB
Panangudi 61 F2 PNGI
Panapakam 54 C6 PAM
Panbari 26 D2 PNB
Panchnoi 27 E1 -
Panch Piplia 30 C3 PCN
Panch Rukhi 9 F1 PHRH
Panchalam 58 C3 PCLM
Panchanai 25 F1 -
Panchanandatala 63 F5 -
Pancharatna 26 B2 PNVT
Panchberia 36 B3 PNCB
Panchgachia 24 D3 PGC
Panchgam 7 G3 *
Panchgram 27 E5 PNGM
Panchot 29 G1 PHC
Panchra 35 H2 PCR
Panchtalavda Rd 29 E5 PCT
Pandabeswar 35 H2 PAW
Pandaravadai 58 C6 PDV
Pandaul 24 C2 PDW
Pandavapura 57 F3 PANP
Pandharpur 47 E3 PVR
Pandhurna 32 A6 PAR
Pandi Halt 61 G1 PNY
Pandikanmoi Halt 61 F3 PDM
Pandillapalli 49 F4 PNDP
Pandiyapuram Halt 60 D5 PYM
Pandoli 19 G5 PMO
Pandooah 36 B3 PDA
Pandori 29 G4 PNDR
Pandu 26 D2 PNO
Pandu Ghat 26 D2 PNGT
Pandu Mewas 30 A3 PME
Pandu Pindara 12 C1 PPDE
Pandurangapuram 49 G3 PGP
Pandur Pawani 42 A4 PRPI
Paneli Moti 28 C5 PLM
Panewadi 40 A3 PNV
Pangaon 47 H1 PNF
Pangara Shinde 41 E5 PNSD
Pangri 47 F2 PJR
Panhai 22 C5 PNHI
Pani Mines 30 B4 PNN
Paniajob 42 C2 PJB
Paniara Halt 23 F3 PNRA
Panihar 21 E3 PNHR
Panikhaiti 26 D2 PHI
Panipat Jn 12 D1 PNP
Panisagar 27 E6 PASG
Panitola 17 F4 PNT
Paniyahawa 15 G6 PNYA
Panjhan 40 A3 PJN
Panjipara 25 F2 PJP
Panj-Kosi 8 B5 PJK
Panjwara Rd 24 D5 PJLE
Panki 22 A2 PNK
Panna 22 A6 *
Panoh 9 E3
Panoli 29 H6 PAO
Panpali 34 C6 PNPL
Panpana 45 F1 PNPN
Panposh 34 D5 PPO
Panpur 63 F5, 37 inset PNZ
Panruti 58 C4 PRT
Pansar 29 G2 PN
Panskura Jn 36 A5 PKU
Panskura East Outer 36 A5
Pantihal 63 F5, 37 inset PTHL
Pantnagar 13 H2 PBW
Panvel Jn 39 F5, 38 inset PNVL
Panyam 54 A2 PNM
Papanasam 58 C6 PML
Papatapalli 49 F4 PPY
Papinayaka Halli 53 F2 PKL
Pappinisseri 56 D3 PPNS
Paprakund 23 E6 PPRK
Paprera 12 D6 PPEA
Paradeep 45 F3 PRDP
Paradgaon 40 D4 PDG
Paradol 33 G3 PRDL
Paradsinga 32 B6 PSK
Paraiya 24 A5 PRY
Paraj 36 A3 PAJ
Parajani Halt 21 H2 PJY
Parakanahatti 46 D6 PRKH
Parakheda 21 E3
Paramakkudi 61 F3 PMK
Parambikulam 60 C1 -
Parangipettai 58 C5 PO
Parannavalasa 50 C1 -
Paranur 58 D2 PWU
Parao Mahna 8 D4 PMH
Paras 41 E2 PS
Paraspani 23 F6 PRPN
Parasia 32 B5 PUX
Parasnath 35 F1 PNME
Parassala 60 C5 PASA
Parauna 21 G3 PRN
Paravur 60 B4 PVU
Parbati 31 G3 PRB
Parbatonia 34 D4 PBB
Parbhani Jn 41 E5 PBN
Pardhade 40 B2 PHQ
Pardi 39 F2 PAD
Parel 38 inset PR
Paresneu 11 G4 PSV
Parewadi 47 E1 PRWD
Pargaon Sudrik 48 D1 PRSK
Pargothan 41 G2 PRGT
Parhanamau 31 F2 PQU
Pariawan Kalankakar Rd 22 C3 PQN
Paricha 21 F4 PIC
Paricha Thermal Siding Cabin 21 F4 PTSC
Parihara 11 H4 PIH
Parikha 29 H5 PRKA
Parikkal 58 C4 PRKL
Parisal 12 C5 PSL
Park 59 inset MPK
Park Circus 37 inset PQS
Park Town 59 inset MPKT
Parkham 13 E6 PRK
Parlakimidi 51 E1 PLH
Parli 57 F6 PLL
Parli Vaijnath 40 D6 PRLI
Parlu 18 D3 PRU
Parma Nand 8 D1 PMQ
Parmalkasa 42 D1 PMS
Parmanandpur 24 A3, 25 inset PMU
Parminia H 24 D3 PMYA
Paror Halt 9 F1 PRAR
Parpanangadi 56 D5 PGI
Parsa 15 E5 PRZ
Parsa Bazar 24 A4, 25 inset PRBZ
Parsa Khera 13 G3 PKRA
Parsa Nagar Halt 23 H1 PRSN
Parsabad 35 E1 PSB
Parsadpur 14 A3 PRSP
Parsanavly Halt 24 C2 PRNL
Parsauni 24 B2 PSZ
Parsipur 23 E4 PRF
Parsoda 40 B4 PSD
Parsoli 19 H4 PSLI
Parsumalai 61 E2 -
Partabpura 8 D3 PPB
Partapur 13 E2 PRTP
Partur 40 D4 PTU
Parvatipuram 50 D1 PVP
Parvatipuram Town 50 D1 PVPT
Parvatsar City 11 H6 PBC
Parvatsar Mela 11 H6 PRCY
Parvezpur 12 B3 PVZ
Parwakhurd 41 F5 -
Parwanoo 9 F4 *
Pasalapudi 49 G5 PSLP
Paschamvahini 57 F3 -
Pashwashraya 25 F1 PSRY
Pasivedala 50 A4 PSDA
Pasraha 24 D4 PSR
Pasupathikoil 58 C6 PVL
Pasur 57 H5 PAS
Pat 31 E2 PTX
Pata 21 H1 PATA
Patakattacherruvu 53 G3 PLU
Patal Pani 31 E4 PTP
Patan 29 G1 PTN
Patan Saongi 42 A1 PTS
Patan Saongi Town 42 A1 PSX
Patancheru 48 C3 PTCR
Patapatnam 51 E1 PRM
Patara 22 A2 PTRE
Patas 46 D1 PAA
Patasahi 34 D5 PSJ
Pataudi Rd 12 D3 PTRD
Patchur 58 A2 PU
Patdi 29 F2 PTR
Patecouddy 58 D6 PCD
Patel 24 A4 PATL
Patel Nagar 15 inset PTNR
Paterhi 24 A3 PEE
Pathakpur Halt 13 F3 PHX
Pathankot Jn 8 D1 PTK
Pathardih Bazar H 45 inset PHQ
Pathardih Jn 35 F2, 45 inset PEH
Patharia 32 C2 PHA
Patharkhandi 27 E5 PTKD
Patharkhola 27 F3 PKB
Pathauli 13 E6 PTLI
Pathrad 41 F5 PARD
Pathrala Halt 8 C5 PTRL
Pathri 9 H6 PRI
Pathrot 41 F1 PTRT
Pathshala 26 C2 PBL
Patia 44 D3 PTAB
Patiagaon 17 E6 PTON
Patiala 9 E5 PTA
Patiala Cantt 9 E5 PTE
Patiali 13 G5 PTI
Sanjeevaiah Park 51 inset SJVP
Patiladaha 26 C2 PTLD
Patipukur 37 inset PTKR
Patiyara 22 B2 PTYR
Patli 12 D3 PT
Patna Ghat 24 A4, 25 inset PTG
Patna Jn 24 A4, 25 inset PNBE
Patna Sahib 24 A4, 25 inset PNC
Patohan 32 D2 PTHD
Patranga 22 C1 PTH
Patrasayer 35 H3 PSF
Patratu 35 E2 PTRU
Patsul 41 E2 PTZ
Pattabiram 58 D1, 59 inset PAB
Pattabiram East Siding 59 inset PRES
Pattabiram E Depot 59 inset
Pattabiram Military Siding 59 inset PTBS

Pattabiram West Siding 59 inset	PRWS
Pattambi 57 E6	PTB
Pattan 7 F2	*
Pattaravakkam 59 inset	PVM
Patti 8 C3	PAX
Patti Rajpura Halt 9 F1	PATTI
Pattikkad Halt 57 E5	PKQ
Pattipooker 63 G5	-
Pattukottai 61 G1	PKT
Patuli 36 B2	PTAE
Patuwas Maharana Halt 12 C3	PUW
Patwara 33 E2	PTWA
Paulaha 14 B3	PLX
Pauni Rd 42 B2	PNRD
Pauta Halt 13 H3	PUF
Pauwara 42 D1	PUWA
Pavagarh 30 A4	PVG
Pavdiyari 29 E3	PDYR
Pavi 30 B4	PAVI
Pavthi 29 F6	pvt
Pavurchutram 60 C4	PCM
Pawai Brahmasthan H 24 C5	PWBN
Pawani Kamarpur 23 G4	PWKP
Pawapuri Rd 24 B5	POE
Payagpur 14 D6	PDR
Payangadi 56 C3	PAZ
Payli 11 H4	PYI
Payradanga 36 B3	PDX
Payyanur 56 C3	PAY
Payyoli 56 D4	PYOL
Pazhavanthangal 59 inset	PZA
Pedakakani 49 F6	PDKN
Pedakurapadu 49 F6	PKPU
Pedana 49 G6	PAV
Pedapariya 54 D5	PYA
Pedda Avutapalli 49 G5	PAVP
Peddabrahmadevam 50 A4	PRD
Peddadinne 48 B6	PDNA
Peddampet 42 A6	PPZ
Peddanayakkanpalayam 58 A4	PDKM
Peddapalli Jn 48 D1	PDPL
Peddasan 51 E1	PDSN
Peddavadlapudi 49 F6	PVD
Pehowa Road 9 F6	PHWR
Pelluru 54 D2	PLRU
Pembarti 48 D3	PBP
Pen Jn 39 F6, 38 inset	PEN
Pencharthal 27 E6	PEC
Penchi 31 G1	PCG
Pendekallu Jn 53 H2	PDL
Pendra Rd 33 G4	PND
Pendrasali 35 F4	PRSL
Pendurti 50 C3	PDT
Penganga 41 E4	PGG
Pennada Agraharam 49 H5	PAGM
Pennadam 58 C5	PNDM
Pennathur 58 C2	PNTR
Pentikhera 21 F1	-
Penukonda Jn 53 G5	PKD
Penumarru 49 G6	PUMU
Peokol 23 G2	POKL
Peralam Jn 58 C6	PEM
Perambdur 58 B5	*
Perambur 59 inset	PER
Perambur Carriage Works 59 inset	PCW
Perambur Loco Works 59 inset	PEW
Perani 58 C3	PEI
Perashshannur Halt 57 E6	PEU
Peravurani 61 G2	PVI
Perecherla 49 F6	PRCA
Pergaon 40 D5	PG
Periagaram 58 A2	-
Peria Kandili 58 A2	-
Perinad 60 B4	PRND
Periyakottai Rd 61 F2	PRKR
Periyanaikanpalaiyam 57 F5	PKM
Periyangathuni 57 H2	PRNT
Pernem 52 A1	PERN
Persehramal Halt 14 B5	PHM
Persendi 14 B5	PSN
Perugamani 58 A6	PGN
Perumanur H 60 B2	PRMN
Perundurai 57 G5	PY
Perungalattur 58 D2, 59 inset	PRGL
Perunguzhi Halt 60 B5	PGZ
Petlad Jn 29 H4	PTD
Petrapole 36 C3	PTPL
Pettai 60 D5	PEA
Pattaivaytalai 58 A6	PLI
Peyanapalli 58 C1	PYX
Phagi 20 B1	PYE
Phagwara Jn 9 E3	PGW
Phakoagram 27 E5	PKGM
Phalodi 10 D5	PLC
Phaltan 46 D2	*
Phanda 31 G3	PUD
Phaphamau Jn 22 D4	PFM
Phaphund 21 H2	PHD
Phardhan 14 B4	PD
Phephna Jn 23 G3	PEP
Phesar 23 H5	PES
Phiding 27 F4	PDJ
Phillaur Jn 9 E3	PHR
Phirangipuram 49 F6	PPM

Phulad 19 F3	PLD
Phulaguri 27 E2	PUY
Phulbani 44 B3	PLBO
Phulera Jn 12 A6	FL
Phuleswar 37 inset	FLR
Phulia 36 B3	FLU
Phulpur 22 D4	PLP
Phulsar 29 F6	PLR
Phul Singha 13 F3	-
Phulwaria 23 G2	*
Phulwari Sharif 24 A4, 25 inset	PWS
Phulwaria Phanta 14 B3	PBF
Phulwartanr 45 inset	PLJE
Phursungi 46 C1	PSG
Phusro 35 F2	PUS
Piali 36 B4	PLF
Piardoba 35 H3	PBA
Pichchandarkovil 58 B6	BXS
Pichkurir Dhal 36 A2	PCQ
Piduguralla 49 E5	PGRL
Pij 29 H3	PIJ
Pilamedu 57 F5	PLMD
Pilanshat 25 F1	PNS
Piler 54 B6	PIL
Pilibanga 11 G1	PGK
Pilibhit Jn 13 H3	PBE
Pilibhit Kacheri 13 H3	PBK
Pilkhani 9 G6	PKY
Pilkhua 13 E3	PKW
Piloda 20 D2	PDZ
Pilol 29 H4	PIO
Piludra 29 G2	PLDR
Pilu Khera 12 C1	PKDE
Pilwai Rd 29 H2	PWR
Pimpalgaon 40 C2	PMGN
Pimpalkuti 41 H4	PMKT
Pimparkhed 40 A3	PKE
Pimplachauri 41 E5	PPLC
Pimpri 39 G6	PMP
Pinahat 21 F1	-
Pindarsi 9 F6	PDS
Pindial 49 E3	PQL
Pindkepar 42 C1	PQH
Pindra Rd Halt 23 E4	PDRD
Pindrai 32 D4	PDE
Pingleshwar 31 E3	PLW
Pingli 41 E5	PIZ
Pingora 12 D6	PNGR
Pinjrapole BH 35 H2	POL
Pipalda Rd 20 C5	POR
Pipali 29 E3	-
Pipalsana 13 G2	PLS
Pipalwali Chowki 20 D2	PPCK
Pipar City 19 F2	PCY
Pipar Rd Jn 19 F1	PPR
Pipardahi 32 C5	PED
Pipardi 29 E4	PID
Pipariya 32 A4	PPI
Pipariya Kalan 33 E2	PWK
Piparpur 22 D3	PPU
Pipar Sand 22 B1	POF
Pipavav 38 D1	PPBR
Pipavav Port 38 D1	PPSP
Piperan 11 G1	PPN
Pipiganj 23 F1	PJ
Pipla 42 A1	PQA
Piplaj 19 G2	PPF
Piplani 31 F5	PLN
Piplee 29 F1	PLE
Pipli 28 C4	PPLI
Pipli- Ka-Bas 12 A6	PKBS
Pipli Pakhi Kalan 8 C4	PKZ
Piplia 19 H6	PIP
Piplia Rd 28 D3	PPS
Piplod Jn 30 B3	PPD
Piploda Bagla 30 D2	PPG
Pipra 24 A2	PPA
Pipraha Halt 24 A2	PPRH
Pipraich 23 F1	PPC
Pipraigaon 21 E6	PIA
Piprala 29 E1	PFL
Pipridih 23 F3	PPH
Piprithan 25 F2	PPTN
Pir Dhule-Shah Halt 19 E2	PRDH
Pir-Jhalar 30 D3	PJH
Pirappamvalasai 61 G4	PPVL
Piravam Rd 60 B2	PVRD
Pirpainti 25 E4	PPT
Pirtala 25 F6	PRTL
Pirthala Lalauda 9 E6	PLT
Pirthiganj 22 D3	PHV
Piru 23 H4	PRO
Pirumdara Halt 13 G2	PRM
Pir Umrod 31 F3	PUO
Pirwa 11 H5	PW
Piska 34 D3	PIS
Pitambarpur 13 H4	PMR
Pithapuram 50 B4	PAP
Piyasara 36 A4 , 63 E5	PYS
Plassey 36 B2	PLY
Pocharam 49 F3	PCZ
Podanur Jn 57 F6	PTJ
Pohe 41 F3	POHE
Poisar 38 inset	*

Pokhani Narasimha 41 E5	PKNS
Pokhran10 D6	POK
Pokhrayan 21 H2	PHN
Pokla 34 D4	PKF
Polapathar 31 H5	POX
Polireddipalem 54 D5	PEL
Pollachi Jn 60 C1	POY
Polur 58 C3	PRL
Pomalwadi 47 E1	PMW
Pondicherry 58 D4	PDY
Pondicherry Port 58 D4	PPPS
Pondugula 49 E5	PDGL
Ponduru Rd 50 D2	PDU
Ponmalai (Golden Rock) 58 B6	GOC
Ponneri 58 D1, 59 inset	PON
Ponpadi 58 C1	POI
Poodoor 48 B6	PDO
Poonamallee 59 inset	*
Poonch 7 F3	*
Pophalaj 47 E2	PPJ
Pora 13 F5	PORA
Pora H 24 A5	-
Porabazar 36 B3	PBZ
Poradanga 25 F6	PRDG
Poraiyar 58 D6	PRYR
Porbandar 28 B5	PBR
Porbandar Dock 28 B5	PBRD
Porda Bhatera 29 H3	POD
Port Albert Victor 38 D1	VCT
Posoita 35 E5	PST
Pothahi 24 A4	PFT
Potheri 58 D2	POTI
Pothia 25 F2	POT
Potkapalli 49 E2	PTKP
Potlapadu 54 C1	POO
Potul 40 B4	POZ
Powai 17 G5	PWA
Powayan 14 A4	-
Powerkheda 31 H4	PRKD
Powerpet 49 G5	PRH
Prachi Rd Jn 38 C1	PCC
Pradhankhunta Jn 35 F2, 45 inset	PKA
Pragati Maidan 15 inset	PGMD
Prajapati 23 H1	PJPT
Pranpur Rd 25 E4	PQD
Prantij 29 H2	PRJ
Prantik 36 A2	PNE
Pratapbagh 42 C1	PRBG
Pratapganj 24 D2	PPV
Pratapgarh Jn 22 D3	PBH
Pratapkhata 26 A2	POK
Pratapnagar 29 H4	PRTN
Prattipadu 49 H5	PTPU
Prayag 22 D4	PRG
Prayag Ghat 22 D4	PYG
Prayagpura 30 A4	PYQ
Prempur 22 B2	PMPR
Princep Ghat 37 inset	PPGT
Pritamnagar 30 D3	PRNG
Prithvirajpur 8 A5	PRUR
Prosadpur 63 F5	PSP
Point Calimere 61 H2	PTC
Pudgam Ganeshpura 29 G1	PDGP
Pudi 54 C6	PUDI
Puduchattiram 58 C5	PUC
Pudukkad 60 B1	PUK
Pudukkottai 61 F1	PDKT
Pudunagaram 57 F6	PDGM
Pudur 58 B6	PDUR
Pugalur 57 H6	PGR
Pujali 37 inset	*
Pukkiravari 58 B4	PRV
Pulakurthi 53 F3	PLQ
Pulankinar 60 C1	PLKR
Pulgaon Jn 41 G2	PLO
Pulicherla 54 B6	PCL
Puliyamangalam 58 C1	
Puliyur 57 H6	PUR
Pulla 49 H5	PUA
Pullambadi 58 B6	PMB
Pullampeta 54 C5	PMT
Pulliarpatti 58 B6	-
Punalur 60 C4	PUU
Punarakh 24 B4	PHK
Pundag 35 F2	PNW
Pundi 51 E1	PUN
Pundibari 25 H2	PQZ
Pune Jn 46 C1	PUNE
Punggudi 58 B6	PUG
Puniyavant 30 B4	PQT
Punkunnam 60 B1	PNQ
Punnapra 60 B3	PNPR
Punpun 24 A4, 25 inset	PPN
Punpun Ghat 25 inset	PNUG
Punsia 24 D5	PNSA
Puntamba 40 A4	PB
Punthottam 58 C6	POM
Purab Sarai 24 C4	PBS
Puraini 13 F1	PNI
Puranderpur 15 F6	PDPR
Puranigudam 27 F2	PUQ
Puranpur 14 A3	PP
Purbasthali 36 B2	PSAE
Puri 44 D4	PURI

Purna Jn 41 E5	PAU
Purnapani 34 D5	PUZ
Purnia Court 25 E3	PRNC
Purnia Jn 25 E3	PRNA
Purulia Jn 35 F3	PRR
Purwa Khera 13 G3	PRKE
Pusad 41 F4	PUB
Pusauli 23 G5	PSE
Pushkar 19 H2	PUH
Pushpattur 60 D1	PPTR
Pusla 41 G1	*
Putalapattu 58 B1	PTT
Putlacheruvu 49 G5	PCU
Puttlur 59 inset	PTLR
Puttur 54 C6	PUT
Puvanur 58 C4	PVN
Puzhuthivakkam 59 inset	*

Q

Qabarwala 8 B5	QBW
Qadian 8 D2	QDN
Qasimpur Khetri 12 D2	KPKI
Qazigund 7 G3	*
Quarry Siding 34 D5	QRS
Quilandi 56 D5	QLD
Quilon Jn 60 B4	QLN
Qutabpur Halt 9 E6	QTP

R

R Block H 25 inset	
Rabale 38 inset	RABE
Rachagunneri 54 C6	RCG
Radhabalampur H 22 C3	RDV
Radhagaon 35 F2, 45 inset	RDF
Radhakishorepur 44 D3	RQP
Radhamohanpur 36 A5	RDU
Radhanagar 35 G2	RDR
Radhanpur 29 F1	RDHP
Radhikapur 25 F3	RDP
Rae Bareli Jn 22 C2	RBL
Rafaleshwar 29 E3	RF
Rafiganj 23 H5	RFJ
Rafinagar 22 C1	RFR
Ragaul 22 A4	RGU
Raghavapuram 48 D1	RGPM
Raghogarh 20 D6	RGG
Raghopur 24 D2	RGV
Raghubans Nagar 24 D3	RBN
Raghunathbari 36 A5	RGX
Raghunathgarh 11 F1	RGNH
Raghunathpalli 48 D3	RGP
Raghunathpur 23 G4	RPR
Raghunathpur 45 E3	RCTC
Raghuraj Singh 22 B2	RRS
Raha 27 E2	RAHA
Rahama 45 E3	RHMA
Raharia 24 C2	-
Rahenbata 43 G3	RNBT
Rahimabad 22 B1	RBD
Rahimatpur 46 C3	RMP
Rahiyod 29 H2	RYL
Rahmatnagar 22 C1	RMNR
Rahon 9 E3	RHU
Rahui Rd 24 B4	RRE
Rahuri 40 A5	RRI
Rai Ka Bag Palace Jn 19 E2	RKB
Rai Mehatpur 9 F3	MTPR
Rai Singh Nagar 8 A6	RSNR
Raibha 13 E6	RAI
Raibojha 14 C4	RBJ
Raichur 48 A6	RC
Raigadh Rd 29 H2	RGQ
Raiganj 25 F4	RGJ
Raigarh 34 B6	RIG
Raigir 48 D3	RAG
Raila Rd 19 H3	RLR
Railey English 24 B4	RLE
Rainagar (Rayna) 36 A3, 63 E3	RNGR
Raipatan Rd 46 C5	*
Raipur BH 43 E1	RVH
Raipur City 43 E2	RCT
Raipur Haryana Jn 12 B2	RPHR
Raipur Jn 43 E1	R
Rairakhol 44 B1	RAIR
Rairangpur 35 F5	RRP
Raiserjagir 20 D5	
Raishree 21 E4	
Raisi 9 H6	RSI
Raiwala Jn 9 H6	RWL
Raj Kharsawan Jn 35 F4	RKSN
Raj Narainpur 14 B4	RNIR
Raja Ganj 14 B4	RZJ
Raja Ka Sahaspur Jn 13 G3	RJK
Raja Rammohunpur 25 F1	RRM
Rajabera BH 35 F2, 45 inset	RJB
Rajabhatkhowa 25 H2	RBK
Rajagambiram Halt 61 E3	RAGM
Rajahmundry 50 A4	RJY
Rajakhera 21 F1	-
Raja-ki-Mandi 13 E6	RKM
Rajaldesar 11 H4	RJR
Rajaluka 35 G5	RJLK

Rajamatam Rd 61 G1	RJMT
Rajankunti 57 G1	RNN
Rajapalayam 60 D3	RJPM
Rajapatti 24 A3	RPV
Rajappayyan Chavadi 61 G1	RJV
Rajapur 48 B5	RJAP
Rajapur Rd 46 B5	RAJP
Rajarhat Bishnupur 63 G5	-
Rajatalab 23 E4	RTB
Rajatgarh Jn 44 D3	RJGR
Rajbandh 35 H2	RBH
Rajchandrapur 37 inset	RCD
Rajendranagar 24 A4, 25 inset	RJPB
Rajendranagar 31 E4	RJQ
Rajendrapul 24 B4	RJO
Rajewadi 46 C1	RJW
Rajgangpur 34 D5	GP
Rajgarh 12 C6	RHG
Rajghat 35 H6	RGT
Rajghat Narora 13 F4	RG
Rajgir 24 B5	RGD
Rajgoda 36 A5	RGA
Rajgram 25 F6	RJG
Rajhura 34 C1	RHR
Rajiasar 11 G2	RJS
Rajim 43 E2	RIM
Rajiv Nagar H 25 inset	
Rajkiawas 19 F3	RKZ
Rajkot City 28 D4	RJTC
Rajkot Jn 28 D4	RJT
Rajkot Town 28 D4	-
Rajlu Garhi Halt 12 D2	RUG
Rajmahal 25 E5	RJL
Rajmalpur Rd 23 G3	RJMP
Rajmane 40 B2	RM
Rajnagar 24 C2	RJA
Rajnandgaon 42 D1	RJN
Rajoli 42 B3	ROL
Rajomajra Halt 8 D5	RJMA
Rajoshi 19 H2	ROS
Rajpar 28 D3	RJPR
Rajpardi 29 H5	RJD
Rajpipla 30 A5	RAJ
Rajpur 29 E3	
Rajpura Jn 9 F5	RPJ
Rajsitapur 29 F3	RJC
Rajula City 38 D1	RJU
Rajula Rd Jn 38 D1	RLA
Rajur 41H4	RAJR
Rajwari 23 F4	RJI
Rajwiansher 7 F2	*
Rakha Mines 35 F4	RHE
Rakhi Halt 18 D3	RHI
Rakhitpur 35 F2, 45 inset	RKJE
Rakhiyal 29 H2	RKH
Rakshi 34 D5	ROXY
Ralapet 42 A5	RLI
Ram Bisanpur 24 D2	RBQ
Ramdàs 8 C1	RDS
Ram Garhwa 23 H1	RGH
Ram Govind Singh (Mahuli) 25 inset	-
Ram Kola 23 G1	RKL
Ramnathpur 22 D4	RTR
Ram Singhpur 11 F1	RMSR
Ramagiri 53 E5	RGI
Ramagundam 49 E1	RDM
Ramaipur Halt 14 B5	RAMR
Ramakona 32 B6	RMO
Ramakrishnapuram 60 D3	RKP
Raman 8 C6	RMN
Ramanagaram 57 G2	RMGM
Ramanand Tiwari H 23 H4	
Ramanathapuram 61 F4	RMD
Ramannapet 48 D4	RMNP
Ramanujampalle 53 H4	RLX
Ramapuram 58 C1	RAM
Ramarajupalli 53 H3	RRJ
Ramavarappadu 49 G5	RMV
Ramavarappadu Gate 49 G5	RMVG
Rambha 44 C5	RBA
Rambhadrapur 24 B3	RBZ
Rambhawan H 24 A4	RBWM
Ramchandrapur 22 C3	RCP
Ramchandrapuram 48 C3	RCP
Ramchaura Halt 23 F1	RCRA
Ramchaura Rd 22 C4	RMC
Ramdevra 10 D6	RDRA
Ramdhira-on-Sone 23 G5	RMDS
Ramdyalunagar 24 B3	RD
Rameshwar Nagar Halt 23 H1	RSWN
Rameshwaram 61 G4	RMM
Rameshwaram Port 61 G4	RMMP
Rameshwaram Rd 61 G4	ROD
Ramgad 53 F3	RMGD
Ramganga 13 G4	RGB
Ramganga Bridge 13 H4	RGBD
Ramganga South Cabin 13 H4	RSC
Ramganj 22 D3	RMGJ
Ramganj Mandi 20 B5	RMA
Ramgaon Rameshwar 41 F3	RMRS
Ramgarh 12 D5	RAH
Ramgarh 10 A5	*
Ramgarh Shekhawati 12 A4	RSWT
Ramgarh Town 35 E2	RMT

Ramghat H 22 D1
Ramkanali 35 G2 RKI
Ramakistapuram Gate 51 inset RKO
Ramkot 14 B5 RAK
Ramkrishnabati 63 F5 RKBT
Ramling 47 F2 RANG
Ramna 34 B1 RMF
Ramnagar 13 G1 RMR
Ramnagar 36 A6
Ramnagar Rd 7 G5 RNJK
Ramnathpur 27 F6 RTR
Rampahari 20 D2 RMPH
Rampara 29 F3 RMPR
Ramparda 29 E RA
Rampur Dumra 24 B4 RDUM
Rampur 25 G4 -
Rampur H 24 C5
Rampur Jn 13 G3 RMU
Rampur Maniharan 9 G6 RPMN
Rampura Beri 12 B3 RMB
Rampura Phul 8 D5 PUL
Rampurhat 36 A1 RPH
Rampuri 32 D5 RAMP
Ramrajatala 37 inset RMJ
Ramramatola 32 D6 -
Ramri 31 G1 RMQ
Ramsagar 35 H3 RSG
Ramsan 18 C5 RXN
Ramsar 18 B3 RMX
Ramshai 25 G1 RMS
Ramtek 42 A1 RTK
Ramva 22 B3 RAMA
Rana Bordi 28 C5 RNBD
Rana Pratap Nagar 19 F5 RPZ
Ranaghat Jn 36 B3 RHA
Ranala 30 C6 RNL
Ranapura 21 E1 RNB
Ranavav 28 C5 RWO
Ranbirsinghpura 7 F6 -
Ranchi Jn 35 E3 RNC
Ranchi Rd 35 E2 RRME
Randala 29 G1 RLD
Randheja 29 G2 RDJ
Rangajan 27 H1 -
Rangaliting 27 G1 RNGG
Rangapahar 27 G3 RXR
Rangapahar Crossing 27 G2 RXRX
Rangapani 25 F1 RNI
Rangapara 16 B6 -
Rangapara North Jn 16 B6 RPAN
Rangapuram 54 A2 RGM
Rangareddi Guda 48 B4 RRGA
Rangbhul Siding 25 F1 RGBS
Rangenhali 52 D5 -
Rangiya Jn 26 D2 RNY
Rangjuli 26 C2 RJGI
Rangmahal 11 G1 RMH
Rangpur 29 E3 -
Rangra 35 E5 RGZ
Rangtong 25 F1 RTG
Rani 19 E4 RANI
Ranibennur 52 D3 RNR
Raniganj 35 G2 RNG
Ranigaon 27 F5 RNPO
Ranikund Rarah 13 E6 RKR
Ranimukkanur 58 A3 -
Raninagar Jalpaiguri Jn 25 G2 RQJ
Ranipatra 25 E3 RNX
Ranippettai 58 C2 RPT
Ranipur Rd 21 G4 RNRD
Ranital 45 E2 RNTL
Raniwara 18 D5 RNV
Ranjangaon Rd 40 A6 RNJD
Ranjani 40 D4 RNE
Ranjitpura 53 F3 RNJP
Rankuva 39 F2 RW
Ranoli 29 H4 RNO
Ranoli Shishu 12 A5 RNIS
Ranpur 29 F4 RUR
Rantej 29 G2 RTJ
Ranthambhor 20 C2 RNT
Ranu Pipri 29 H4 RPP
Ranuj Jn 29 G1 RUJ
Ranyala Jasnia 31 E3 RCJ
Raoli Jn 38 inset RVJ
Raoti 30 C3 RTI
Raparla 54 D2 RPAR
Ras 29 G4 RAS
Rasana Rd 18 D6 RSNA
Rasauli 22 C1 RES
Rasayani 39 F5, 38 inset RSYI
Rashidpura Khori 12 4A RDK
Rasipuram 58 A5 *
Rasmara 42 D1 RSM
Rasra 23 G3 RSR
Rasuiya 13 H4 RYS
Rasulabad 22 B3 RUB
Rasulpur 36 A3 RSLR
Rasulpur Gogamau 22 A2 RPGU
Raswan 35 H2 RSME
Ratabari 27 E5 RTBR
Ratangaon 32 D2 RTGN
Ratangarh Jn 11 H4 RTGH
Ratangarh Kankawal 8 C6 RKK
Ratangarh West Jn 11 H4 RXW
Ratanpur 24 C4 RPUR
Ratanpura 23 G3 RTP
Ratansarai 23 H2 RTU
Ratanshahar 12 B4 RSH
Rath 21 H4 RATH
Rathdhana 12 D RDDE
Rati-ka-Nagla 13 F5 RKN
Ratlam A Cabin 30 D2 RTD
Ratlam E Cabin 30 D2 RTM'E'
Ratlam Jn 30 D2 RTM
Ratnagiri 46 B4 RN
Ratnal 28 C2 RUT
Ratona 32 B2 RTZ
Rattar Chhattar Halt 8 D1 RCR
Rattoke Gurdwara 8 C3 RKG
Rau 31 E4 RAU
Rau Khedi 32 A1 RAU
Rauli 43 G5 RUL
Rautabagan 26 D1 RWTB
Rautara 25 E3 RWA
Rauzagaon 22 C1 RZN
Rayalapalli Kalan 48 B3 RPK
Ravanasamudram 60 C5 RVS
Raver 40 D1 RV
Ravikampadu 50 B4 RVD
Ravindrakhani 42 A6 RVKH
Ravtha Rd 20 B5 RDT
Rawanjna Dungar 20 C3 RWJ
Rawangaon 46 D1 RWN
Rawatganj 23 F1 RJ
Rawatpur 22 A2 RPO
Raxaul Jn 24 A1 RXL
Ray 34 D2 RAY
Raya 13 E5 RAYA
Rayadurg 53 F3 RDG
Rayagada 43 H5 RGDA
Rayaka 29 F4 RY
Rayakkottai 57 H3 RYC
Rayalacheruvu 53 H3 RLO
Rayanapadu 49 F5 RYP
Rayanapadu WS 49 F5 RYPS
Rayaru 21 F2 RRU
Rayatpura 21 F2 RYT
Raybag 46 D5 RBG
Razampeta 54 C5 RJP
RCF Halt 8 D3 RCF
Reay Rd 38 inset RRD
Rechni Rd 42 A5 RECH
Reddiarchatram 60 D1 RED
Reddigudem 49 F6 REM
Reddipalayam 58 D2 RDY
Reddipalli 54 C5 RPL
Regadipalli 54 A3 RLL
Regupalem 50 C4 REG
Rehatwas 21 E6 RTW
Rehta 14 B3 RTS
Rejinagar 36 B2 REJ
Relangi 49 H5 RLG
Remount Rd 37 inset *
Ren 19 G1 REN
Rengali 34 C6 RGL
Renhat 21 E3 RAT
Renigunta Jn 54 C6 RU
Rentachintala 49 E5 RCA
Rentia 30 B3 RET
Renukut 34 A1 RNQ
Renwal 12 A6 RNW
Reoti 23 H3 ROY
Reoti Behora Khera Halt 13 G4 RBK
Repalle 55 E1 RAL
Repalliwada 42 A5 RLW
Retang 44 D3 RTN
Rethora Kalan 21 F2 RAKL
Retreat Halt 25 F1 RTC
Revelganj 23 H3 RVG
Revelganj Ghat 23 H3 RVT
Rewa 22 C6 REW
Rewaghat 24 A3 *
Rewari Jn 12 C4 RE
Rewral 42 B1 RRL
Riasi 7 G5 *
Ribada 28 D4 RBR
Richha Rd 13 H3 RR
Richughuta 34 D2 RCGT
Riga 24 B2 RIGA
Rikhab Dev Rd 30 B1 RDD
Rilli 25 F1 -
Ringas Jn 12 B5 RGS
Risama 42 D1 RSA
Rishikesh 9 H5 RKSH
Rishra 37 inset RIS
Risia 14 C5 RS
Rithi 32 D2 REI
Riyang 25 F1 -
Robertsganj 23 F5 RBGJ
Robertson 34 A5 ROB
Rohla 46 B1 ROHA
Rohalkhurd 30 D2 RLK
Rohana Kalan 13 E1 RNA
Rohand Nagar Halt 12 D3 ROHN
Rohat 19 E2 RT
Rohini 40 B3 RHNE
Rohira Gallughara 9 E4 RHW
Rohna 41 G2 RHO
Rohna Town 41 G2 RHOT
Rohtak Jn 12 C2 ROK
Rohtas 23 G6 RHS
Rohtas Fort 23 G6 RHSF
Romana Albel Singh 8 C4 RLS
Rompalli 50 C1 RMPL
Rooma 22 B2 RXM
Roorkee 9 H6 RK
Rora 21 G4 RORA
Roranwala 8 B4 RRW
Roshan Mau Halt 22 A2 RMW
Roshanpur 13 G2 RHN
Rotegaon 40 A4 RGO
Rourkela Jn 34 D5 ROU
Routhpuram 51 E1 RMZ
Rowriah 16 D6 RWH
Royapuram 59 inset RPM
Roza Jn 14 A5 ROZA
Rozi 28 C3 ROZ
Rozi Block Hut 28 C3 RZB
Rudain 13 G5 RDN
Rudauli 22 D1 RDL
Rudrapur City 13 H2 RUPC
Rukadi 46 D5 RKD
Rukhi Halt 12 C2 RKX
Rukmapur 48 B4 RMY
Rukni 35 G2 RUI
Rundhi 12 D4 RDE
Runija 30 D3 RNJ
Runkhera 30 D2 RNH
Runkuta 13 E6 RNKA
Runneymede 57 F5 RME
Rup Nagar 9 F4 RPAR
Rupaheli 19 H3 RPI
Rupahigaon 27 E2 RUP
Rupai 17 G4 RPY
Rupamau 22 C2 RUM
Rupasibari 27 E5 RPB
Rupauli Halt 24 D3 RPLA
Rupaund 33 E2 RPD
Rupbas 13 E6 RBS
Rupnarayanpur 35 G2 RNPR
Rupra Rd 43 H4 RPRD
Rupsa Jn 35 G6 ROP
Rura 21 H2 RURA
Rure Asal 8 C3 RRAL
Rusera Ghat 24 C3 ROA
Ruthiyai Jn 20 D6 RTA

S

Sabalgarh 20 D2 SBL
Sabarimalai 60 C3 *
Sabarmati A Cabin 28 inset SBIA
Sabarmati D Cabin 28 inset SBID
Sabarmati Jn 29 G3, 28 inset SBI
Sabaur 24 D4 SBO
Sabira 45 E1 SZZ
Sabli Rd 29 F3 SR
Sabrum 37 G3 *
Sachin 39 F1 SCH
Sachiwalaya 25 inset SCY
Sadala 29 F2 SADL
Sadanapura 29 H4 SNA
Sadar Bazar 15 inset DSB
Sadashibpur 44 D2 SSPR
Sadashivpeth Rd 48 B3 SSPD
Sadat 23 F4 SDT
Sadda Singh Wala 8 D5 SSZ
Sadhli 30 A5 SHL
Sadhoo Garh 9 F4 SDY
Sadipur 24 B5
Sadisopur 24 A4 SDE
Sadulpur Jn 12 B3 SDLP
Sadulshahr 8 B6 SDS
Sadura 7 G3 *
Safdarganj 22 C1 SGJ
Safedabad 22 C1 SFH
Safiasarai 24 C4 SFS
Safidon 12 D1 SFDE
Safilguda 51 inset SFX
Safipur 22 A1 SFQ
Safrai 17 F5 SFR
Sagar 32 B2 SGO
Sagar Jambagaru 52 C4 SRF
Sagar Sangam 38 inset *
Sagarakatte 57 3 STE
Sagardighi 25 F6 SDJ
Sagarpali 23 G3 SVI
Sagauli Jn 23 H1 SGL
Sagma 22 B6 SAGM
Sagoni 32 D2 SAO
Sagphata 31 F6 SXA
Sahajipur Halt 22 D3 SHJP
Sahamatganj 13 H3 SMG
Saharanpur Jn 9 G6 SRE
Sahari 24 B4 SAHR
Saharsa Jn 24 D3 SHC
Saharsa Kacheri 24 D3 SHOK
Sahaspur Rd 36 A3, 63 E3 SHJ
Sahasrakund 41 G5 SHSK
Sahatwar 23 H3 STW
Sahawar Town 13 G5 SWRT
Sahdei Buzurg 24 B4 SDG
Sahebtala 36 B2 SHBA
Saheli 31 H4 SALI
Saheri Halt 23 F4 SAHR
Sahibabad Jn 13 E3, 15 inset SBB
Sahibganj 25 E4 SBG
Sahibganj Ghat 25 E4
Sahibpur Kamal Jn 24 C4 SKJ
Sahid Matangini 36 A5 SMTG
Sahijpur 29 G3, 28 inset SAHP
Sahja Halt 25 E4 SAJH
Sahjanwa 23 F1 SWA
Sahuwala Halt 11 G1 SHWL
Saidabad 22 D4 SDC
Saidanwala 8 C4 SWX
Saidapet 59 inset SP
Saidkhanpur 22 C1 SYK
Saidpur Jalalabad 8 D2 SPJB
Saidraja 23 F4 SYJ
Saij Sertha Rd 29 G2, 28 inset SHRD
Saikhoa Ghat 17 G4 SIKG
Saila Khurd 9 F3 SOJ
Saintala 43 H3 SFC
Sainthal 13 H3 STH
Sainthia Jn 36 A1 SNT
Saiyed Sarawan 22 C4 SYWN
Saiyedpur Bhitari 23 F4 SYH
Sajanvav Rd 38 D1 SJF
Sajerpar 25 H2 SJRR
Sajiavadar 29 E6 SVJ
Sajuma 9 E6 SJM
Sakaldiha 23 F4 SLD
Sakchura 63 H5 -
SakherBazar 63 G6 -
Sakhigopal 44 D4 SIL
Sakhoti Tanda 13 E2 SKF
Sakhpur 28 C5 SKR
Sakhun 20 A1 SK
Sakleshpur 57 E1 SKLR
Sakri Jn 24 C2 SKI
Sakrigali 25 E4 SLJ
Sakrigali Ghat 25 E4 SGK
Saktesgarh 23 E5 SKGH
Sakti 34 A5 SKT
Saktigarh Jn 36 A3 SKG
Salabad 12 D6 SABD
Salagaon 44 D3 SQQ
Salai Banwa BH 23 F6 -
Salaia 32 D2 SYA
Salal A 7 G5 *
Salal B 7 G4 *
Salakati 26 B2 SLKS
Salamatpur 31 H2 SMT
Salanpur 35 G2 SLS
Salar 36 B2 SALE
Salarkhurd 23 G2 *
Salarpur 22 D1 SLRP
Salauna 24 C4 SLNA
Salawas 19 E2 SZ
Salaya 28 B4 SLYA
Salbari 25 G2 SXX
Salboni 35 H4 SLB
Salchapra 27 F5 SCA
Salekasa 42 C1 SKS
Salem East 58 A4 SLME
Salem Jn 58 A4 SA
Salem Market 58 A4 SAMT
Salem Town 58 A4 SXT
Salemgarh Masani Halt 11 H1 SJSM
Salempur Gosain 13 F2 -
Salempur Jn 23 G2 SRU
Salesian College 25 F1 SCX
Salgajhari 35 F4 SLJR
Salhana 33 E2 SLHA
Sali 20 A1 SALI
Salichauka Rd 32 B4 SCKR
Salimpur Bihar 24 B4 SMBG
Saliyamangalam 58 C6 SMM
Salka Rd 33 G5 SLKR
Salkhapur 23 E4 SAF
Salmari 25 E4 SRI
Salogra 9 F4 SLR
Salona 27 F1 SLQ
Salpa 46 C2 SLP
Salpura 20 C5 SYL
Salsalabari 25 H2 SLBS
Salt Cotaurs 59 inset SO
Salur 50 C1 SALR
Salwa 42 A1 SAL
Samaguri 27 E2 SMGR
Samalkha 12 D2 SMK
Samalkot Jn 50 B4 SLO
Samalpatti 58 A3 SLY
Samar Gopalpur 12 C2 SMF
Samastipur Jn 24 B3 SPJ
Samayanallur 61 E2 SER
Samba 7 G6 SMBX
Sambalpur City Jn 44 A1 SBPY
Sambalpur Jn 44 A1 SBP
Sambalpur Rd 44 A1 SBPD
Sambanarkoil 58 C6
Sambhal Hatim Sarai 13 F3 SHTS
Sambhar Lake 12 A6 SBR
Sambheti 29 G5 SBTI
Sambhu 9 F5 SMU
Sambre 52 C1 SXB
Samdari Jn 18 D3 SMR
Samhon 21 G1 SHW
Samkhiali Jn 28 D2 SIOB, SIO
Samlaya Jn 30 A4 SMLA
Samloti 9 E1 SMLT
Samnapur 32 D5 SMC
Samni Jn 29 H5 SAZ
Sampige Rd 57 F1 SPGR
Sampla 12 D3 SPZ
Samrala 41 F6 SQE
Samrau 11 6 SRK
Samsi 25 F4 SM
Samudragarh 36 B3 SMAE
Samudram 61 F1 SMDM
Samuktala Rd 25 H2 SMTA
Sanala 28 D3 SNLA
Sanand 29 G3 SAU
Sanappiratti 57 H6 SYP
Sanathal 29 G3 SNTI
Sanatnagar Jn 48 C3, 51 inset SNF
Sanaura 8 D2 SWU
Sanawad 31 E5 SWD
Sanchi 31 H2 SCI
Sandal Kalan 12 D2 SLKN
Sandalpur 21 F3 SLV
Sandasal 30 A4 SDSL
Sandei Halt 14 A3 SNDY
Sandhanidhar 38 C1 SDHR
Sandhia 30 A5 SNDA
Sandhurst Rd 38 inset SNRD
Sandila 14 B6 SAN
Sandispur 24 C4 SNDP
Saneh Rd 13 F1 SNX
Sanehwal 9 E4 SNL
Sangaldan 7 G4 *
Sangameshwar 46 B4 SGR
Sangamjagarlamudi 49 F6 SJL
Sanganer 20 B1 SNGN
Sangannapur 41 E5 SNGR
Sangar 7 G5 SGR
Sangat 8 C5 SGF
Sangaria 8 C6 SGRA
Sangli 46 D4 SLI
Sangola 47 E3 SGLA
Sangrampur 36 B5 SNU
Sangrana Sahib H 8 C2 SBS
Sangrur 9 E5 SAG
Sangwi 41 F3 SWQ
Sanha 24 C4 SXW
Sanhati H 36 C4 SNHT
Sanichara 21 F2 SAC
Saniyad 29 H5 SNAD
Sanjali 29 H6 SNJL
Sanjan 39 F3 SJN
Sanjha 24 D5 SJJ
Sanjharpur Halt 23 F3 SJER
Sanjoygram 25 F3 SJGM
San Juje da Areyal 52 B2 SJDA
Sank 21 E2 SANK
Sanka 35 G2 SNKR
Sankaragummanur 53 G3 SNKG
Sankarankovil 60 D4 SNKL
Sankaridurg 57 H5 SGE
Sankarilingapuram 60 D3 SLGM
Sankarpur Halt 24 D6 SNQ
Sankaval 52 A2 SKVL
Sankhalpur 29 F2 SNKP
Sankhari 29 G1 SNHR
Sankheda Bahadurpur 30 A4 SAK
Sankopara 25 F5 SXP
Sankra 43 E2 SNKX
Sankrail 36 B4, 37 inset SEL
Sanodiya 12 A6 SFE
Sanosara 29 F5 SOA
Sanosara 28 B2 SNSR
Sanpada 38 inset SNCR
Sansarpur 32 D2 SNRR
Sant Rd 30 B3 SAT
Santa Cruz 38 inset STC
Santaldih 35 G2, 45 inset SNTD
Santalpur 29 E1 SNLR
Santmagulur 49 E6 SAB
Santak 17 E6 SQC
Santoshpur 37 inset SSP
Santragachi Jn 36 B4, 37 inset SRC
Sanvatsar 40 A4 SNVR
Sanvrad 11 H5 SVO
Sanwara Halt 23 G3 SNRA
Saoner 41 H1 SONR
Saonga 41 H1 SZH
Saongi 32 D6 SGC
Saota 36 A2, 63 E2 SOF
Sapada 28 C2 SPDA
Sapar 29 E3 SPAR
Sapatgram 26 A2 SPX
Sapekhati 17 F5 SPK
Sape Wamne 46 B2
Saphale 39 F4 SAH
Sapoi Siding 27 E1 -
Saradhana 19 H2 SDH
Saradiya 28 C5 SRDA
Saragaon Rd 33 H5 SDRD

Saragbundia 33 H5 SRBA
Saragipalli 44 B1 SRGP
Sarahula Halt 23 F4 SAHA
Sarai 24 B3, 25 inset SAI
Sarai Banjara 9 F4 SBJ
Sarai Bhopat 21 G1 SB
Sarai Chandi 22 D4 SYC
Sarai Gopal Halt 22 D4 SPGL
Sarai Harkhu 23 E3 SVZ
Sarai Jagdish H 22 D4 SJGH
Sarai Kansrai 23 E4 SQN
Sarai Mir 23 E3 SMZ
Sarai Rani 23 F3 RKS
Sarai Rohilla 12 D3 DEE
Saraigram 33 G1 SGAM
Sarangpur 31 F2 SFW
Sarangpur Rd 29 F4 SAPR
Sararbat 63 F6 -
Saraswatinagar 43 E1 SRWN
Sarayan 14 C6 SYU
Saraygarh 24 D2 SRGR
Sarbahara 33 G4 SBRA
Sardar Nagar 23 F2 SANR
Sardar Patel Marg 15 inset SDPR
Sardargarh Halt 11 G1 SRZ
Sardargram 29 G3, 28 inset SDGM
Sardarshahr 11 H3 SRDR
Sardiha 35 H5 SUA
Sareri 19 H3 SSR
Sargachhi 36 B1 SGV
Sarju 14 C6 SUJ
Sarkantra BH 44 D3 SRKT
Sarkara 13 G2 SKX
Sarkhej 29 G3, 28 inset SEJ
Sarkoni 23 E4 SIQ
Sarla Jn 44 A1 SLRA
Sarmatanr 24 B6 SMND
Sarna 8 D1 SRM
Sarnath 23 F4 SRNT
Sarobag 24 C4
Sarojini Nagar 15 inset SOJ
Sarola 40 A6 SRL
Sarona 43 E1 SZB
Sarotra Rd 18 D5 SZA
Sarpeswar 44 D3 SPSR
Sarsadh Halt 12 D2 SRDH
Sarsanpuri 43 E2 SPY
Sarsawa 9 G6 SSW
Sarsi 25 E3 SRSI
Sarupathar 27 G2 SZR
Sarupeta 26 C2 SPQ
Sarupnagar 63 H5 -
Sarupsar Jn 11 G1 SRPR
Sarvay 58 B4 SRVY
Sarvodaya H 23 H4
Sarwari 40 C4 SVD
Sasa Musa 23 H2 SSU
Sasalu 53 E4 SLU
Sasan Gir 28 D6 SASC
Sasaram 23 G5 SSM
Sasni 13 F5 SNS
Sason 44 A1 SSN
Sasthankotta 60 B4 STKT
Sasvad Rd 46 C1 SSU
Satadhar 28 D6 STDR
Satanwara 21 E4 STV
Satar Halt 25 E3 STAR
Satara 46 C3 STR
Satbahini 23 G6 SZF
Satberia 36 C3 STBR
Satellite Goods Terminal 57 H2 SGWF
Sathgawan 24 B5 *
Sath Naraini 22 B3 SNIE
Sathajagat 24 B4 STJT
Sathi 23 H1 SAHI
Sathiaon 23 F3 SAA
Sathin Rd 19 F1 SWF
Satish Samanta 36 A5 SSPH
Satlana Halt 19 E2 SUT
Satna Jn 22 B6 STA
Satnali 12 B3 STNL
Satnarain Temple 9 H6 -
Satnaur Badesron Halt 9 E3 SNB
Satorda 52 A1 *
Satraon 23 G2 STZ
Satrod 12 B2 STD
Satsangnagar 24 D6 SSNR
Sattenapalli 49 F6 SAP
Sattirakkudi 61 F3 SQD
Satulur 49 F6 STUR
Satuna 40 D5 SCO
Satur 60 D4 SRT
Satyamangalam 57 G4 STYM
Satyanarayanapuram 49 G5 STPM
Satyavada 49 H5 STVA
Saunshi 52 D2 SNH
Sausar 32 B6 SASR
Savalgi 47 H4 SVG
Savalyapuram 49 E6 SYM
Savanur 52 D3 SVNR
Savarde 46 B3 SVX
Savarkundla 29 E6 SVKD
Savda 40 C1 SAV
Savli 29 H4 SVLI
Savni 38 B1 SVB
Sawai Madhopur D Cabin 20 C3 SWM'D'
Sawai Madhopur Jn 20 C3 SWM
Sawantwadi Rd 52 A1 SWV
Sayama 29 G4 SAY
Sayan 29 H6 SYN
Sayla 29 F3 SYX
Scindia-ka-Chhaoni 21 F2 -
Sealdah 36 B4, 37 inset SDAH
Seawoods-Darave 38 inset
Secunderabad Jn 48 C3, 51 inset SC
Secunderabad region 48 C3, 51 inset
Sedarampattu Halt 58 C2 SDPT
Sefinagar 31 E4 SFNR
Sehal 13 G2 SEW
Seharabazar 36 A3, 63 E3 SRBZ
Sehore 31 G3 SEH
Sehra Mau 14 A4 SW
Sekha 8 D5 SEQ
Selavi 29 G1 SHLV
Seleng Hat 17 E6 SLX
Seloa Rd 41 H2 SLOR
Selu 40 D5 SELU
Semali 21 E2 SYF
Semandapatti Halt 57 H4 SMDT
Semapur 25 E4 SMO
Semari 19 F6 SES
Semarkheri 21 E6 SRKI
Semdanur 58 C4 SXR
Semla 28 D4 SE
Semmanahalli 58 A3 -
Semra 23 H1 SRA
Semraon 23 H4 SRMN
Senapura 52 C5 SEN
Senchoa 27 E2 SCE
Sendhwa 30 D6 *
Sendra 19 G2 SEU
Sendurai 58 C5 SNDI
Sengottai 60 C4 SCT
Sengulam 60 D5 SGLM
Senjipanambakkam 58 D1 SPAM
Seohara 13 F2 SEO
Seoni 32 C5 SEY
Seoraphuli Jn 36 B4, 37 inset SHE
Sepon 17 E5 SEPN
Sepoydhura 25 F1 SFD
Seram 48 A4 SEM
Seroni Rd 20 D3 SEX
Seshanchavadi 58 A4 SNVD
Sessa 27 E1 SETB
Settigunta 54 C5 SF
Settihalli 57 G2 SET
Sevaliya 30 A3 SVL
Sivok 25 F1 SVQ
Sevur 58 C2 SVUR
Sevvapet Rd 59 inset SVR
Sewa Nagar 15 inset SWNR
Sewagram 41 H2 SEGM
Sewapuri 23 E4 SWPR
Sewar 13 E6 SWAR
Sewri 38 inset SVE
Seydunganallur 60 D5 SDNR
Shadnagar 48 C4 SHNR
Shadoragon 21 E5 SHDR
Shahabad 47 H4 SDB
Shahabad Markand 9 F5 SHDM
Shahad 39 F5, 38 inset SHAD
Shahbad Mohammadpur 12 D3, 15 inset SMDP
Shahbazkuli 23 G4 SBK
Shahbaznagar 14 A4 SZN
Shahdol 33 F3 SDL
Shaheed Ishwar Chowdhury H 24 A5 -
Shaheed SN Singh Halt 24 C2 -
Shahganj Jn 23 E3 SHG
Shahgarh 14 A3 SG
Shahi 13 H3 SSC
Shahibag B Cabin 28 inset SHB
Shahjahanpur Jn 14 A5 SPN
Shahjahanpur Kutcheri 14 A5 SXK
Shahnagar Timarua 13 F5 SWW
Shahpur 28 D5 SHH
Shahpur Patoree 24 B4 SPP
Shahzad Nagar 13 G3 SAR
Shaitan Singh Nagar 10 D6 STSN
Shajapur 31 F2 SFY
Shakar Nagar 48 B1 SKNR
Shakti Para 28 D3 SKTP
Shaktinagar 33 H1 SKTN
Shakurbasti 12 D3, 15 inset SSB
Shalap 63 F5 SHLP
Shalashah Thana 30 A1 SHLT
Shalimar 36 B4, 37 inset SHM
Sham Chaurasi 9 E3 SCQ
Sham Kauria 24 A3 SMKR
Shambazar 63 G5 -
Shambhua 22 A2 SMBA
Shambhupura 19 H5 SMP
Shamgarh 20 B6 SGZ
Shamlaji Rd 30 A2 SJS
Shamli 12 D1 SMQL
Shampur Halli 47 H4 SPHL
Shamsabad 13 H5 SSD
Shamshabad 21 F1 *
Shankar 8 D3 SQK
Shankargarh 22 C5 SRJ
Shankarpalli 48 B3 SKP
Shankarpur Bhadoura 33 G1 SKBR
Shankerpur Halt 14 B5 SKLP
Shankrul 36 A3, 63 E3 SHKL
Shantipur Jn 36 B3, 63 G3 STB
Sharma Halt 14 A5 SHRM
Shasan H 24 C3 SSRH
Shashan Rd 36 B5, 37 inset SSRD
Sheakhala 36 A4, 63 F5, 37 inset SEK
Shedbal 46 D5 SED
Sheela Kheri 31 E3 SKBN
Shegaon 41 E2 SEG
Shehera 30 A3 SHRA
Sheikhpura 24 B5 SHK
Shelarwadi Cabin 39 G6 SLRW
Shelavi 29 G1 SHLV
Shelgaon 41 F6 SLGH
Shelu 39 G5, 38 inset SHLU
Shendri 47 F2 SEI
Shendurni 40 C2 SDRN
Shenoli 46 C4 SNE
Sheo Prasad Nagar 33 H3 SPDR
Sheodaspura Padampura 20 B1 SAS
Sheopur Kalan 20 C3 SOE
Sheosinghpura 12 B6 SHNX
Sher Halt 23 H2 SHER
Sherekan 8 B6 SRKN
Sherganj 13 H3 SNZ
Shergarh 8 C5 SGA
Sherpur Halt 13 F2 SEPR
Sherpurdhipura 24 B4 SPPA
Shertalai 60 B3 SRTL
Shewbabudih 45 inset SBW
Shiblun 36 B2 SHBL
Shibpur 34 D1 *
Shikara 32 D4 SKY
Shikarpur 32 B5 SKPR
Shikhpura 13 G4 SKW
Shikohabad Jn 13 F6 SKB
Shikra Kulingram 63 H5 -
Shimiliguda 50 C2 SMLG
Shimla 9 G3 SML
Shimoga 52 D5 SME
Shimoga Bidare Halt 52 D5 BEI
Shimoga Town 52 D5 SMET
Shindawane 46 D1 SHIV
Shingatgeri 52 C2 SXH
Shingnali 30 A3 SNGI
Shirakola 63 F6 -
Shirala 41 F2 *
Shiravade 46 C3 SIW
Shirawata Dam 39 G6
Shirdi 40 A4 SSBA
Shirgur 52 C2 SHOR
Shiroor 52 C5 SHMI
Shirpur 40 B1 *
Shirsai 46 D1 SSI
Shirsoli 40 C2 SS
Shirsuphal 46 D2 SSF
Shirud 40 B2 SHF
Shirva 28 C2 SRVA
Shisho Halt 24 B2 SHEO
Shitalpur 24 A3, 25 inset STLR
Shitala Rd 20 B1 STRD
Shiu Sagar Rd 23 G5 SSR
Shivaji Bridge 15 inset CSB
Shivaji Nagar 46 C1 SVJR
Shivalingapuram 50 C2 SLPM
Shivani 53 E5 SHV
Shivanipur 63 F6 -
Shivhar 24 A2 *
Shivlakha 28 D2 SIA
Shivnagar 22 D2 SHNG
Shivnar 24 B4 -
Shivnarayanpur 25 E4 SVRP
Shivpur 23 E4 SOP
Shivpura 31 E3 SVT
Shivpuri 21 E4 SVPI
Shivrajpur 30 A4 SVU
Shivrampur 22 B4 SWC
Shiwala Telu 13 F5 SWT
Shobhasan 29 G2 SXS
Shoghi 9 F3 SGS
Shohrathgarh 15 E6 SOT
Sholaka 12 D4 SHLK
Sholavandan 61 E2 SDN
Sholingur 58 C2 SHU
Shoranur East Cabin 57 E6
Shoranur Jn 57 E6 SRR
Shoranur South Cabin 57 E6
Shravanabelagola 57 F2 *
Shreesharada Nagar H 57 F1 SSNR
Shri Amirgadh 18 D5 SIM
Shri Balaji 11 F5 SBLJ
Shri Bhadriya Lathi 10 C5 SBLT
Shri Bhavnath 30 A1 SBHN
Shri Ghasi Nagar 12 C6 SHGN
Shri Kalyanpura 20 B4 SKPA
Shri Khetra Nagihari 41 E2 NGZ
Shri Krishna Janmasthan 13 E5 SKJS
Shri Madhopur 12 B5 SMPR
Shri Mahabirji 20 D1 SMBJ
Shri Rajnagar 22 C2 SAGR
Shri Vijayanagar 11 F1 SBNR
Shribagilu 56 D2 SVGL
Shridham 32 C3 SRID
Shrigonda Rd 46 D1 SGND
Shrimad Dwaraka Puri Halt 13 H6 SRDW
Shrirampur 36 B4, 37 inset SRP
Shrirangapattana 57 F3 S
Shudnipur 23 E4 SPPR
Shujalpur 31 F3 SJP
Shujatpur 22 C4 SJT
Shukarullahpur Halt 13 H5 SHX
Shyamacharanpur 44 D3 SCPR
Shyamchak 35 H5 SMCK
Shyamnagar 37 inset SNR
Shyampura 20 A4 SMPA
Shyampura 9 H5 -
Shyamsundar 36 A3, 63 E3 SHMR
Siajuli 16 D5 SWJ
Sibaichandi 36 B3 SHBC
Sibsagar Town 17 E6 SRTN
Siddampalli 58 C1 SIE
Sidhapur 29 G1 SID
Sidhari Halt 23 F3 SDHA
Sidhauli 14 B6 SD
Sidheswar 48 A2 SIX
Sidhmukh 12 A2 SDMK
Sidhwalia 23 H2 SQW
Sidhwan 8 D3 SWG
Sidlaghatta 53 H6 IDT
Siduli 35 H2 SXD
Sigadam Rd 50 D2 SGDM
Sigsigi 34 B1 SQS
Sihapar Halt 23 F1 SIPR
Sihari Baharatpur 13 G3 -
Siho 24 B3 SIHO
Sihor Jn 29 F5 SOJN
Sihora 31 F5 SWZ
Sihora Rd 32 D3 SHR
Sijua 45 inset SJA
Sikandarpur 13 E4 SKQ
Sikandra 13 E6 SKD
Sikandra Rao 13 F5 SKA
Sikar Jn 12 A5 SIKR
Sikaria 23 H4 SKRI
Sikir 43 H3 SFK
Sikka 28 C3 SIKA
Sikkal 58 D6 SKK
Sikkampatti 60 D2 SIK
Sikosa 42 D1 SKSO
Sikroda 21 E2 SKU
Sikroda Kwari 21 E2 SIKD
Sikroda Mina 20 D1 SKDM
Sikta 23 H1 STF
Sila Kheri Halt 12 D1 SXR
Silaiman 61 E2 ILA
Silakjhori 43 E6 SZY
Silanibari 16 D5 SOB
Silao 24 B5 SILO
Silapathar 17 E4 SPTR
Silari H 19 F2 SILR
Silaut 24 B3 SLT
Silawar 13 E1 SLWR
Silchar 27 F5 SCL
Silghat Town 27 F1 SHTT
Siliguri Jn 25 F1 SGUJ
Siliguri Rd 25 F1 -
Siliguri Town 25 F1 SGUT
Sillakkudi 58 B5 SLTH
Silli 35 E3 SLF
Sillipur 20 D3 SPRA
Silpa Prabesh 36 B5 SLPR
Silyari 43 E1 SLH
Simaiaya Kajarwada 32 D5 SAKA
Simaluguri Jn 17 E6 SLGR
Simaria 24 C4 SAE
Simariatal 21 F3 SMTL
Simbhaoli 13 E3 SMBL
Simenchapari Halt 17 F4 SMCP
Simhachalam 50 C3 SCM
Simhachalam North Jn 50 C3 SCMN
Simlagarh 36 B3 SLG
Simodra 29 H6 SMDR
Simraha 25 E2 SMH
Simri Bakhtiarpur 24 D3 SBV
Simultala 24 C5 STL
Simurali 36 B3 SMX
Sindewahi 42 B3 SYE
Sindhar 8 D3 SDZ
Sindhavadar 29 E3 SDD
Sindhudurg 46 B6 SNDD
Sindi 41 H2 SNI
Sindkheda 40 A1 SNK
Sindpan 19 H6 SDPN
Sindri BH 35 F2, 45 inset SDBH
Sindri Marshalling Yard 35 G2, 45 inset SNMY
Sindri Town 35 G2, 45 inset SNDT
Sinduria Kachari 31 G1 SFZ
Sindurwa 22 C2 SYW
Singaji 31 F5 SJ
Singanallur 57 F5 SHI
Singaperumal Kovil 58 D2 SKL
Singara 26 C2 SNCA
Singaram 43 G6 SNGM
Singarayakonda 54 D3 SKM
Singareni Collieries 49 F3 SYI
Singarpur 13 E6 SNPR
Singhabad 25 F5 SOB
Singhana 12 B4 SNNA
Singhapuram Rd Jn 43 H5 SPRD
Singhirampur Halt 13 H6 SGRP
Singhpokharia 35 F4 SIPA
Singhpur 33 F3 SNGP
Singiyawan H 24 A4 SIWN
Singoli Shyam 19 H4 SISM
Singrauli 33 H1 SGRL
Singri Ghat 27 E1 SIT
Singur 37 inset SIU
Singwal 19 H2 SGW
Sinhan 28 C4 SYQ
Sini Jn 35 F4 SINI
Sinor 30 A5 SINR
Sinthal Halt 11 F4 STHL
Sion 38 inset SIN
Sipaya Halt 23 H2 SPYA
Sipra Br. 31 E3 SPBG
Sir Gurudas Banerjee Halt 37 inset SGBA
Sirajnagar 36 B2 SRJN
Sirajuli Siding 27 E1 -
Sirari 24 C5 SRY
Siras 20 B2 SRAS
Sirathu 22 C3 SRO
Sircarpalayam 58 B6 -
Sirhind Jn 9 E SIR
Sirhitara 22 A2 SIRA
Sirjam 35 G3 SRJM
Sirkazhi 58 C5 SY
Sirlli 41 E5 SIF
Sirmuttra 20 D2 SRMT
Sirnapalli 48 C1 SCP
Sirohi Rd 19 E5 SOH
Siroliya 31 E3 SYO
Sirpur Kaghaznagar 42 A5 SKZR
Sirpur Town 42 A5 SRUR
Sirran 31 E5 SIRN
Sirri 43 E2 SIY
Sirsa 12 A1 SSA
Sirsa Inayatpur 13 G3 -
Sirsala Halt 12 A3 SRSL
Sirsaul 22 B2 SSL
Sirsi Makhdumpur 13 F3 SRMP
Sirugamani H 58 A6 SGMN
Siruvattur Halt 58 B4 SRVT
Sisai Gulab Rai Halt 23 G2 SSGR
Sisarka 13 G3 SSKA
Sisauna 13 F2 SISN
Sisibargaon 17 E4 SBGN
Sisvinahalli 52 D2 SVHE
Siswa Bazar 15 G6 SBZ
Sitafalmandi 51 inset STPD
Sital Nagar Halt 11 G4 STNR
Sitamarhi 24 B2 SMI
Sitampet 49 G5 STPT
Sitanagaram 50 C1 SNP
Sitapur Cantt Jn 14 B5 SCC
Sitapur City Jn 14 B5 STP
Sitapur Kutcheri 14 B5 STPK
Sitapuram 44 A6 SPRM
Sitapurhat 63 F5 STPH
Sitarampur Jn 35 G2 STN
Sitarampur Link Cabin 35 G2 STN L/C
Sithalavai 58 A6 SEV
Sitalpur 24 A3, 25 inset STLR
Sithouli 21 F2 STLI
Sitimani 47 F6 SII
Siuri 35 H2 SURI
Sivadevunichikkala 50 A5 SVDC
Sivadi 58 A3 SZV
Sivaganga 61 F3 SVGA
Sivakasi 60 D3 SVKS
Sivapur 53 E5 SPV
Sivarakottai 61 E3 SVK
Sivni Shivpuri 41 E2 SVW
Sivungaon 41 F6 SVN
Siwaha 12 C1 SWDE
Siwaith 22 D4 SWE
Siwan Jn 23 H2 SV
Siwan Kacheri 23 H2 SVC
Siwani 12 B2 SWNI
Sleemanabad Rd 32 D2 SBD
Sobhapur 32 A4 SXF
Sodpur 37 inset SEP
Sogaria Cabin 20 B4 SOGARIA
Sogra 34 C5 SOGR
Sohagpur 32 A4 SGP
Sohal 8 D1 SOHL
Sohansara 12 B3 SAWN
Sohawal 22 D1 SLW
Sohsarai 24 B4 SOW
Sojat Rd 19 F3 SOD
Sojitra 29 G4 SJTR
Solagampatti 58 B6 SGM
Solan 9 F4 SOL
Solan Brewery 9 F4 SBY
Solapur Jn 47 F3 SUR
Solari 44 C4 SLZ
Soldi 29 E3 SOZ
Soledevanhalli 57 G1 SDVL
Somaguddu 53 F4 SOMA

Somalapuram 53 F3 SLM
Somanayakkanpatti 58 A2 SKPT
Somankatti 52 D1 SMKT
Somanur 57 G5 SNO
Somaswara 32 C5 SMSR
Somatne 39 F5, 38 inset SMTN
Somesar 19 F3 SOS
Somidevipalli 54 B2 SDV
Somna 13 E4 SOM
Somnath 38 B1 *
Sompeta 44 B6 SPT
Sompur Rd 53 E2 SOQ
Somra Bazar 36 B3 SOAE
Somthan 41 F3 SMTN
Sona Arjunpur 9 G6 SNAP
Sonachara 35 H2 SCH
Sonada 25 F1 SAD
Sonadanga 36 B2 SVH
Sonagir 21 F3 SOR
Sonai 13 E5 SYZ
Sonaili 25 E4 SI
Sonakhan 34 C5 SXN
Sonamukhi 35 H3 SONA
Sonardih H 45 inset SZE
Sonaripur 14 B3 SOI
Sonarpur Jn 36 B4, 37 inset SPR
Sonasan 29 H2 SNSN
Sonaulim 52 B2 LIM
Sonbarsa H 24 B5
Sonbarsa Kacheri 24 D3 SBM
Sondad 42 C2 SNV
Sondalia 36 B4 SXC
Sondha Rd 21 F2 SCN
Sondimra 35 E2 SND
Sonegaon 41 H3 SNN
Sonekpur H 13 F3 SNK
Songadh 29 F5 SGD
Songir 30 A5 -
Soni 21 F2 SONI
Soniana 19 H4 SNYN
Sonik 22 B2 SIC
Sonipat 12 D2 SNP
Sonipur Rupal 29 G2 SNAP
Soniyana Mewar 19 F4 SNMR
Sonkhamb 41 H1 SNKB
Sonma Pranpur Halt 24 C4 SOPR
Sonnagar Jn 23 G5 SEB
Sono 24 C5 SONO
Sonpur 24 A3, 25 inset SEE
Sonshelu 40 A1 SNSL
Sontalai 31 H4 SOL
Sonthaliya 12 B5 SNTH
Sonua 35 E4 SWR
Sonwara 9 F4 SWQ
Sookerating 17 F4 STT
Soorothee 21 E1 SRTE
Sopore 7 F2 SXZ*
Sorai 31 H2 SORI
Sorbhog 26 C2 SBE
Soro 45 F1 SORO
Soron Shukarshetra 13 F4 SRN
Sorta 41 G2 SRTA
Sovabazar Ahiritola 37 inset SOLA
Sravanur Halt 57 E2 SRVN
Sreepur 35 G2
Sri Dungargarh 11 G4 SDGH
Sri Ganganagar Jn 8 B5 SGNR
Sri Jhadeswar 44 D3 SJDR
Sri Karanpur 8 A6 SRW
Sri Krishan Nagar 23 E3 SKN
Sri Makrinath Nagar Halt 11 H4 SMNN
Sri Ramgarh Halt 12 A2 SHRG
Sri Satya Sai Prasanti Nilayam 53 H5 SSPN
Sri Venkateswarapalem 54 D3 SVPM
Sribar 27 F5 SIPC
Srikakulam Rd 50 D2 CHE
Srikalahasti 54 C6 KHT
Srikhanda 36 A2, 63 F2 SIZ
Srikona Halt 27 F5 SXO
Srinagar 20 A4 SNAR
Srinagar 7 G3 SIGP
Sringavruksham 49 H5 SGKM
Srinivasanagar 48 C3 SHAN
Srinivasa Udasipuram H 54 C6 SUPM
Srinivaspur 58 A1 SVS
Sripani Halt 17 E4 SRPN
Sripat Srikhanda 36 B2, 63 F2 SPS
Sriperumbudur 58 D2, 59 inset *
Sripur Halt 25 F4 SRPU
Sripuram 49 F6 SRPM
Sripuriagaon 17 F5 SPGN
Srirampur 48 B6 SRNR
Srirampur 35 H3 SMR
Srirampur Assam 26 A2 SRPB
Srirampuram 48 D4 SRMR
Srirangam 58 B6 SRGM
Srivaikuntam 60 D5 SVV
Srivilliputtur 60 D3 SVPR
Srungavarapukota 50 C2 SUP
St Thomas Mount 59 inset STM
Stuartpuram 55 E SPF
Suaheri Halt 13 F1 SXQ
Subansiri 17 E5 SUZ
Subarnamrigi 25 F6 SBNM
Subedarganj 22 D4 SFG
Subhagpur 14 D6 SUBR
Subhasgram 37 inset SBGR
Subramanya Rd 56 D2 SBRD
Subzi Mandi 15 inset SZM
Suchan Kotli 12 A1 SHN
Suchetgarh 7 F6 -
Suchi Pind 8 D3 SCPD
Suchia Halt 63 F5 -
Suchindram H 60 D6 SCUH
Sudamdih 35 F2, 45 inset SDMD
Sudhani 25 F3 SUD
Sudiyur 61 F3 SUX
Sudrana 12 C3 SDRA
Sudsar 11 G4 SDF
Sui Halt 12 C2 SUI
Suisa 35 F3 SSIA
Sujalpur 36 A6
Sujangarh 11 H4 SUJH
Sujanpur 8 D1 SJNP
Sujatapuram Halt 57 F3 SJPM
Sujhauli 23 G5 SJV
Sujnipara 25 F6 SPLE
Sujra Halt 12 D2 SUJR
Sukh Chain Halt 8 C6 SCV
Sukhasan Kothi Halt 24 D3 SKHK
Sukhi-Siwaniya 31 H3 SUW
Sukhpur 28 C2 SUKP
Sukhpur Roha 28 B2 SRHA
Sukhra 34 A1 SUKR
Sukhshena Halt 24 D3 SKEN
Sukinda 44 D2 SKND
Sukli 32 C6 SKLI
Sukna 25 F1 SN
Sukrimangela 32 D4 SOY
Sukritipur 27 E5 SOF
Suku 50 B1 SXV
Sulah Himachal 9 F1 SLPH
Sulakarai 61 E3 SUQ
Suldhal 46 D6 SUL
Sulebhavi 46 D6 SBH
Sulehalli 47 H4 SUH
Sulerjavalge 47 F3 SLGE
Sulgare 47 E4 SGRE
Sulhani 8 C4 SULH
Sullurupeta 54 D6 SPE
Sultanabad 48 D1 STBD
Sultanganj 24 D4 SGG
Sultanpur Jn 22 D2 SLN
Sultanpur Kaliwas Halt 12 D3 STRW
Sultanpur Lodi 8 D3 SQR
Sulur Rd 57 F5 SUU
Sumaoli 21 E2 SMV
Sumer 31 H2 SUMR
Summadevi 51 E1 SUDV
Summer Hill 9 G3 SHZ
Summit 39 H3 SUM
Sumreri 32 A1 SMRR
Sunak 30 A2 SUC
Sunam 8 D5 SFM
Sunamai Halt 13 F4 SUNM
Sundaram 61 G2 SUN
Sundaram Benchi Siding 53 F3 SDMG
Sundaraperumal Koil 58 C6 SPL
Sundarna 29 H4 SUND
Sunderabad 30 D3 SNBD
Sundhia Mau 14 C6 SDAM
Sundlak 20 C4 SDLK
Sunhera Halt 12 D2 SFA
Sunheti Kharkhari Halt 9 G6 SNKE
Supaul 24 D3 SOU
Supedi 28 D5 SPD
Suprakandi H 27 E5 SAKD
Suradhenupura 57 G1 SRUP
Sura Nussi 8 D3 SRX
Suraimanpur 23 H3 SIP
Suraincha Halt 14 B6 SUIR
Surajdevi 29 E4 SIK
Surajgarh 12 B3 SRGH
Surajkund 22 C3 SRJK
Surajpur Rd 34 A3 SJQ
Surajpur 9 F4 SUPR
Surapur 23 E2 SU
Surareddipalem 54 D2 SDM
Surasaraighat Jhara 33 G1 SSGJ
Surat 39 F1 ST
Suratgarh Jn 11 G1 SOG
Suratkal 56 C1 SL
Suratpura Jn 12 B3 SURP
Suravali 52 A2 SRVX
Surbari 28 D2 SRBR
Surdia 35 H5 SUA
Sureli 20 B2 SURL
Surendranagar Camp 29 F3 SRNG
Surendranagar East Cabin 29 F3 SUNRE
Surendranagar Gate 29 F3 SRGT
Surendranagar Jn 29 F3 SUNR
Surera Halt 11 H1 SURR
Surergoth 12 C6 SRRG
Surgaon Banjari 31 F5 SGBJ
Suriawan 23 E4 SAW
Surjakamal 25 F3 SJKL
Surjyapur 36 B5 SJPR
Surkhand-ka-Khera 19 F6 SZK
Surla Rd 44 B5 SLRD
Surnera-Pirkheri 31 F2 SFF
Surpura 11 F4 SPO
Sur Rd 29 H1 SORD
Surukote 7 G4 *
Suskal 30 B4 SSKL
Sutarpete Halt 56 C1 SOTE
Suwansa 22 D4 SWS
Suwasra 31 E1 SVA
Swadinpur 36 A1 SDLE
Swami Narain Chhapia 23 E1 SNC
Swamihalli 53 F3 SMLI
Swamimalai 58 C6 SWI
Swarupganj 19 E5 SRPJ
Sycotta 27 H1 -

T

T Sakibanda H 53 G3 TKBN
Tada 54 D6 TADA
Tadasa 52 D5
Tadalapusapalli 49 E3 TPY
Tadali Jn 42 A4 TAE
Tadepalligudem 49 H5 TDD
Tadikalapudi 49 F3 TPY
Tadipatri 53 H3 TU
Taduku 54 C6 TDK
Tadwal 47 F3 TVL
Tagdi 29 F4 TID
Taherpur 36 B3 THP
Tahsil Fatehpur 14 C6 TSF
Taiabpur 25 F2 TBR
Tajpur 31 E3 TJP
Tajpur Dehama 23 G3 TJD
Takal 31 F6 TAKL
Takari 46 D4 TKR
Takarkheda 40 B2 TKHE
Takazhi 60 B3 TZHI
Takha 13 G6 TKHA
Takhrau 13 G6 TKRU
Takhteshwar 29 F5 TIWF
Taki Rd 36 C4, 63 H5 TKF
Takia 22 B2 TQA
Takipur 25 F6 TKP
Takkolam 58 C2 TKO
Takli 41 F2 TKI
Takli Bhansali 41 H1 TKLB
Taklimiya 40 A5 TKMY
Taksal 9 F4 TSL
Taku 31 H4 TAKU
Tala 37 inset TALA
Talaburu 35 E5 TABU
Talaivasal 58 B4 TVS
Talaiyuthu 60 D5 TAY
Talaja 29 F6 TJA
Talakhajuri 22 D2 TLKH
Talala Jn 38 B1 TAV
Talamadugu 41 G4 TLMG
Talamanchi 54 D4 TMC
Talanallur 58 C5 TLNR
Talandu 36 B3 TLO
Talap 17 F4 TLL
Talara 9 E1 TLRA
Talavli 31 E1 TLZ
Talbahat 21 F5 TBT
Talbandh 35 F5 TND
Talcher 44 C2 TLHR
Talcher Junction Cabin 44 C2 -
Talcher Rd 44 C2 TLHD
Talcher Thermal 44 C2 TLTM
Talchera Baraoli Ran 12 D6 TBL
Talchhapar 11 H4 TLC
Taldi 36 B5 TLX
Talegaon 39 G6 TGN
Talgajarda 38 D1 TGJ
Talgoria Jn 35 F2, 45 inset TLE
Talguppa 52 C4 TLGP
Talheri Buzurg 9 G6 THJ
Talit 36 A3 TIT
Taljhari 25 E5 TLJ
Tall Jn BH 24 B4 TALL
Talli Saida Sahu 8 C3 TSS
Talmadla 48 C2 TMD
Talni 41 G2 TLN
Talod 29 H2 TOD
Talodi Rd 42 B3 TUD
Taloja Panchanand 38 inset TPND
Talshahi 21 E1 TSH
Talvadiya 31 F5 TLV
Talwandi 8 C4 TWB
Talwara 9 E2 TWTS*
Tamaraipadi 61 E1 TMP
Tambadmal IBS 39 G4 TMM
Tambaram 58 D2, 59 inset TBM
Tambaram Sanatorium 59 inset TBMS
Tamkuhi Rd 23 G1 TOI
Tamlor 18 A2 TMO
Tamluk 36 A5 TMZ
Tamluk Jn Cabin 36 A5
Tamna 35 F3 TAO
Tamrakulam H 60 D6 TMJ
Tamuria 24 C2 TMA
Tanakallu 54 A5 TKU
Tanakpur 14 A2 TPU
Tanasa 29 F6 TNS
Tancha 29 H5 TCA
Tanda 23 E2 TD
Tanda Urmar 8 D2 TDO
Tandarai 58 C3 TNI
Tandavapura Halt 57 F3 TXM
Tandur 48 B4 TDU
Tandwal 9 F5 TDW
Tangarmunda 34 C5 TGQ
Tangerbansli 34 D3 TGB
Tangla 26 D1 TNL
Tangni 17 E5 *
Tangra 8 D2 TRA
Tanguturu 54 D2 TNR
Tanijan 16 D5 TUJ
Tanisandra 57 H1 THSA
Tankara 28 D3 TNQ
Tankari Rd 29 G5 TKRD
Tankhala 30 A5 TNKA
Tankuppa 24 A5 TKN
Tannirpandalpalayam 57 H5 TPLM
Tanodia 31 E2 TIO
Tantpur 21 E1 TPO
Tanuku 49 H5 TNKU
Tanur 56 D5 TA
Tapa 8 D5 TAPA
Tapang 44 D4 TAP
Tapasi Jn 35 H2 TOP
Tapaswi Narayan Nagar H 24 B2 TNNR
Tappa Khajuria Halt 14 B5 TKUR
Tapri Jn 9 G6 TPZ
Tapuna 41 F3 TPN
Tar Sarai 24 C2 TRS
Tarabari 27 E2 TRBE
Taradevi 9 F3 TVI
Tarakeshwar 36 A4 TAK
Taraknagar 36 B3 TNX
Taramani 59 inset *
Tarana Rd 31 E3 TAN
Taranga Hill 29 H1 TRAH
Tarangambadi 58 D6 TQB
Taraon 23 F4 TRN
Taraori 9 F6 TRR
Tarapith Rd 36 A1 TPF
Tarapur 29 G4 TRP
Tarapur 24 D5 *
Tarawata 20 D5 TRWT
Taraya Sujan 23 G2 TRJ
Taregna 24 A4 TEA
Targaon 46 C3 TAZ
Tarighat 23 F4 TRG
Tarigoppula 49 G5 TGU
Tarikere 52 D5 TKE
Tarlupadu 54 C2 TLU
Tarn Taran 8 C3 TTO
Taropa 30 A5 TRF
Tarrakalan 20 D3 TKLN
Tarsai 28 C5 TRSR
Tarur 40 A3 TR
Tarva 29 H5 TRV
Tatanagar Jn 35 F4 TATA
Tatasijua 45 inset TSAH
Tatasijua Valatand 45 inset TSBD
Tati 34 D4 TATI
Tatibahar 16 D6 TBH
Taticherla 53 H3 TAC
Tatsilwai 35 E3 TIS
Tattaparai 61 E5 TIP
Tavargatti 52 C2 TVG
Teegaon 32 A6 TEO
Teghra 24 C4 TGA
Teharka 21 G4 TKA
Tehsil Bhadra 12 A2 TSD
Tehta 24 A5 THA
Tejgadh 40 B4 TJH
Tejpurwa Halt 24 A3 TJW
Tekanwas 23 H3 TKV
Tek Bigha 24 B4 TKBG
Tekkali 51 E1 TEK
Tektar Halt 24 B2 TQR
Telaprolu 49 G5 TOU
Telapur 48 C3 TLPR
Telem 17 F4 TQM
Teli Halt 58 C4 TEI
Tellicherry 56 D4 TLY
Telo 35 F2, 45 inset TELO
Telpung 17 H5
Telta 25 F3 TETA
Temburu 51 E1 TMB
Tempa 42 B3 TEP
Tenali Jn 49 G6 TEL
Teneri H 24 A4 -
Tengenmanda 33 G5 TGQ
Teni 60 D2 TENI
Tenkasi Jn 60 C4 TSI
Tenmalai 60 C4 TML
Tennampalam 61 H1
Tenneru 49 G5 TNRU
Ten Talav 30 A5 TV
Tentulia 45 inset TNJE
Tenya 36 B2 TYAE
Terban 41 F5 TBU
Tetelia 26 D2 TTLA
Tettu 54 D3 TTU
Tetulmari 35 F2, 45 inset TET
Tetunbari Halt 16 D6 TOB
Teznarayanpur 25 E4 TNPR
Tezpur 27 E1 TZTB
TGR Cabin 1 39 G4
TGR Cabin 2 39 G4
TGR Cabin 3 39 G4
Thabalke 8 D3 TYK
Thadi 50 C3 THY
Thalaku 53 F4 THKU
Thair 47 G2 TER
Thaiyat Hamira 10 B5 THKM
Thakurbari 16 B6 TKTB
Thakurganj 25 F2 TKG
Thakurkuchi 26 D2 TKC
Thakurli 38 inset THK
Thakurnagar 36 C3 TKNG
Thakurpukur 63 G6 -
Thakurtala 35 G6 TKII
Thakurwadi 39 G6 TKW
Thal 39 F6 THAL
Thalangai 58 C2 TUG
Thalera 20 B4 THEA
Thalwara 24 B3 TLWA
Tham 29 H5 THAM
Thambawati Nagari 19 H5 TVTN
Thambikkottai 61 G2 TKK
Thamla Mogana 19 F5 TMGN
Than 29 E3 THAN
Thana Bhawan 13 E1 THBN
Thana Bhawan Town 13 E1 THBT
Thana Bihpur Jn 24 D4 THB
Thandla Rd 30 C3 THDR
Thane 39 F5, 38 inset TNA
Thanesar City 9 F6 TMDE
Thangachimadam 61 G4 TCM
Thangamapatti 61 E1 TGPT
Thangundi 47 H5 TGDE
Thanjavur Jn 58 B6 TJ
Thansit 39 G4 THS
Thaparnagar 35 G2 TNW
Thara 21 E2 THR
Tharbitia 24 D2 TB
Thariaghat 26 D4 -
Tharsa 42 A1 TAR
Tharwai 22 D4 THW
Thasra 29 H3 TAS
Thathana Mithri 11 H6 THMR
Thathankulam 60 D5 TTQ
Thawe Jn 23 H2 THE
Theh Qalandar Halt 8 B4 TQL
Thekeraguri 27 E2 TGE
Therai 13 F6 -
Therubali 43 H5 THV
Thipparthi 48 D4 TPPI
Thirumangalam 61 E3 TMQ
Thirumayilai 59 inset TMYL
Thiruppachetti 61 E3 TPC
Thiruthuraiyur Halt 58 C4 TUY
Thiruvalangadu 58 D1 TO
Thiruvallur 58 D1, 59 inset TRL
Thiruvanmiyur 59 inset *
Thiruvarur Jn 58 C6 TVR
Thivim 52 A1 THVM
Thokur 56 C1 TOK
Thondebhavi 53 G6 TDV
Thonganur Halt 58 A3 TNGR
Thuraiyur 58 A5
Thuravur 60 B2 TUVR
Thuria 30 D1 THUR
Thuwavi 30 A4 TWV
Tibi 11 H1 TIBI
TIDEL Park 59 inset *
Tiger Hill 33 H3 TGG
Tihu 26 C2 TIHU
Tik 9 F6 TIQ
Tikamgarh 21 F5 *
Tikani 24 D5 TKLE
Tikaria 22 B5 TKYR
Tikauli Rawatpur 22 B2 TKRP
Tikekarwadi 47 F3 TKWD
Tikiapara 37 inset TPKR
Tikirapal 45 F1 TKPL
Tikiri 43 G6 TKRI
Tikkoti 56 D4 TKT
Tikri Halt 22 D1 TRE
Tikunia 14 B4 TQN
Tilaiya 24 B5 TIA
Tilak Bridge 15 inset TKJ
Tilak Nagar 38 inset TKNG
Tilaru 51 E1 TIU
Tilati 47 G3 TLT
Tilaunchi 22 A2 TLNH
Tilbhita 25 E5 TBB
Tilbhum 27 E5 TBX
Tilda 33 G6 TLD
Tildanga 25 F5 TDLE
Tilhar 13 H4 TLH
Tillaivilagam 61 G1 TAM
Tillaiyadi 58 D6 TYD
Tiloniya 19 H1 TL
Tilothu 23 G5 THI
Tilothu Bazar 23 G5 THIB
Tilrath 24 C4 TIL

Tilwara 18 D2 TWL
Tilwara Mela 18 D2 TWF
Timarni 31 G4 TBN
Timba Rd Jn 30 A3 TBA
Timbarva 39 F1 TBV
Timmachipuram Halt 58 A6 TIC
Timmancherla 53 G3 TIM
Timmapur 48 C4 TMX
Timmapuram 50 B4 TMPM
Timtala 41 F2 TMT
Tin Mile Hat 25 F2 TMR
Tinaighat 52 B2 TGT
Tindauli 13 G6 TNUE
Tindharia 25 F1 TDH
Tindivanam 58 C3 TMV
Tingrai 17 G4 TII
Tinich 23 E1 TH
Tinkheda 41 H1 TNH
Tinnapatti 58 A4 TNT
Tinpahar Jn 25 E5 TPH
Tinpheriya Halt 23 G2 TPV
Tinsukia Jn 17 F4 TSK
Tintoda 29 G2 TIRA
Tipkai 26 A2 TPK
Tipling H16 D5 TPG
Tipongpani Wharf 17 G5 TGWF
Tippampatti 60 C1 TPMP
Tiptur 57 F1 TTR
Tirap Siding 17 G5 TPWF
Tirka 36 A6
Tirodi 32 C6 TRDI
Tirora 42 B1 TRO
Tiruchanur 54 C6 TCNR
Tiruchchi Palakkarai 58 B6 TPE
Tiruchchipalli Goods 58 B6 TPGY
Tiruchchirapalli Jn 58 B6 TPJ
Tiruchchirapalli Fort 58 B6 TP
Tiruchchirapalli Town 58 B6 TPTN
Tiruchchittrambalam 61 G2 TCT
Tiruchchuli 61 E3 TCH
Tiruchendur 61 E5 TCN
Tirukkadaiyur 58 D6 TKDR
Tirukkovilur 58 C4 TRK
Tiruldih 35 F3 TUL
Tirumalpur 58 C2 TMLP
Tirumani 58 D2 TRX
Tirumathikkunam 58 C6 TMU
Tirumayam 61 F2 TYM
Tirumayiladi 58 C5 TMU
Tirumullaivoil 59 inset TMVL
Tirunageswaram 58 C6 TRM
Tirunalar 58 D6 TXR
Tirunellikaval 61 H1 TNK
Tirunelveli Jn 60 D5 TEN
Tirunelveli Town 60 D5 TYT
Tirunettur 60 B2 TNU
Tiruninravur 59 inset TI
Tirunnavaya 57 E6 TUA
Tiruparankundram 61 E2 TDN
Tirupati 54 C6 TPTY
Tirupati West 54 C6 TPW
Tiruppachetti 61 E3 TPC
Tirupattur 58 B3 TPT
Tiruppadirippuliyur 58 D4 TDPR
Tirupparaithurai H 58 A6 TRPT
Tiruppur 57 G5 TUP
Tiruppuvanam 61 E3 TVN
Tirur 56 D6 TIR
Tiruttani 58 C1 TRT
Tirutthangal 60 D3 TTL
Tirutturaipundi Jn 61 H1 TTP
Tiruvalam 58 C2 THL
Tiruvalla 60 B3 TRVL
Tiruvallur 58 D1 TRL
Tiruvannamalai 58 B3 TNM
Tiruvellikeni 59 inset MTCN
Tiruvennainallur Rd 58 C4 TVNL
Tiruverumbur 58 B6 TRB
Tiruvidaimarudur 58 C6 TDR
Tiruvizha 60 B3 TRVZ
Tiruvottiyur 59 E1, 59 inset TVT
Tisaiyanvilai 60 D6 TSOA
Tisi 30 B6 TISI
Tisua 13 H4 TSA
Titabar 27 H1 TTB
Titagarh 37 inset TGH
Titlagarh Jn 43 G3 TIG
Titte 58 C6 TT
Titur 42 A2 TOR
Titwa 32 D5 TTW
Titwala 39 F5, 38 inset TLA
Tiura Pipardih 23 G6 TUPR
Tiwari 19 E1 TIW
Toda Rai Singh 20 B3 TDRS
Todarpur 14 A5 TDP
Todiyappulam Halt 57 E5 TDPM
Tohana 9 E6 TUN
Tokisud 35 E2 TKS
Tokopal 43 E6 TPQ
Tokuttu Halt 56 C2 TKOT
Tolahunse 53 E4 THN
Tolasampatti 57 H4 TOS
Tolewahi 42 B4 TWI
Tollygunge 37 inset TLG
Tolra 34 B1 TRZ
Tondalagopavaram 49 F5 TNGM
Tondaman Nallur 61 F1 TNLR
Tondamanpatti 58 B6 TOM
Tondiarpet 59 inset TNP
Toppur 57 H4 TPP
Topputhurai 61 H1 TOY
Top Station 60 C2
Toranagallu Jn 53 F2 TNGL
Torang 35 F3 TRAN
Tordi Sagar 20 A2 TDSR
Tori 34 D2 TORI
Torna 29 H3 TRNA
Torniya 28 D6 TORA
Totiyapalam 57 H5 TPM
Tovalai 60 D6 THX
Tozhupedu 58 D3 TZD
TP-14/9 24 D5 -
TP 345.14 24 C5 -
TP 362.29 24 C5 -
TP 6/3 35 G1 -
TP 61/2 36 B3 -
TP 7/11 35 G1 -
TP-23 24 D5 TP-23
Tralsamadh 29 H5 TSM
Transport Nagar 22 B1 TPNR
Trapaj 29 F6 TPS
Trapaj Bungalow 29 F6 TPSB
Tribediganj 22 C2 TEG
Tribeni 36 B3, 37 inset TBAE
Tribeni Ghat 36 B3, 37 inset -
Trichur 60 B1 TCR
Trikarpur 56 C3 TKQ
Trilochan Mahadev 23 E4 TLMD
Trilokpur Halt 15 E5 TPB
Tripal Halt 9 E1 TRPL
Tripunittura 60 B2 TRTR
Trisulam 59 inset tlm
Trivandrum Central 60 C5 TVC
Trivandrum Pettah 60 C5 TVP
Trivikramdeonagar H 23 H2 TRND
Tsunduru 49 F6 TSR
Tudiyalur 57 F5 TDE
Tuggali 53 G2 TGL
Tuglakabad 12 D3, 15 inset TKD
Tukaithad 31 F6 TTZ
Tuli 17 E6 TULI
Tulin 35 F3 THO
Tuljapur 41 H2 TGP
Tuljapur 47 F2 *
Tulsi Ashram 23 F4 TLAM
Tulsigam 30 A3 TUM
Tulsinagar Halt 23 E2 TLGR
Tulsipur 15 E5 TLR
Tulsitanr H 24 D6 TTN
Tulukapatti 60 D3 TY
Tulwara Jhil 11 H1 TLI
Tulyapani 32 D4 TPNI
Tumba 23 G5 TM
Tumboli Halt 60 B3 TMPY
Tumka 44 D2 TMKA
Tumkur 57 G1 TK
Tummalacheruvu 49 E5 TMLU
Tummanamgutta 54 A6 TAT
Tumsar Rd Jn 42 B1 TMR
Tumsar Town 42 B1 TMS
Tuna Port 28 C2 -
Tundaj 29 G5 TDJ
Tundla Jn 13 F6 TDL
Tundu H 45 inset TNO
Tung 25 F1 TUNG
Tungabhadra Dam 53 F2 TBDM
Tungi 24 B5 -
Tuni 50 B4 TUNI
Tunia 35 E4 TUX
Tupadih 35 E5 TPDH
Tupkadi 35 F2, inset TKB
Turbhe 38 inset TUH
Turekela Rd 43 G3 TRKR
Turinjapuram Halt 58 B3 TJM
Turkapalli 53 H3 TKPY
Turki 22 C6 TUR
Turki 24 B3 TUR
Turtipar 23 G3 TTI
Tuticorin 61 E5 TN
Tuti-Melur 61 E5 TME
Tuvvur Halt 57 E5 TUY
Tuwa 30 A3 TUWA
Twininganj 23 G3 TWG
Tyada 50 C2 TXD
Tyakal 57 H2 TCL

U

Ubarni 22 C3 UBN
Uchana 12 C1 UCA
Uchippuli 61 F4 UCP
Udagamandalam 57 F5 UAM
Udaipur City 19 F5 UDZ
Udaisagar 19 F5 UDSR
Udairampur 36 B5 URP
Udairampur 63 F6 -
Udaiyanpatti 58 B6 UDP
Udalguri 26 D1 ULG
Udalkachhar 33 G3 UKR
Udasar Halt 11 H3 UDS
Udayapur Halt 14 A3 -
Udgir 48 A1 UDGR
Udhampur 7 G5 UHP
Udhna Jn 39 F1 UDN
Udi 21 G1 *
Udramsar 11 F4 UMS
Udumalaipettai 60 C1 UDT
Udupi 52 C6 UD
Udvada 39 F2 UVD
Udwantnagar 23 H4 UNT
Udyankheri 31 F2 UDK
Ugamedi 29 F5 UGM
Ugaon 39 H3 UGN
Ugarkhurd 46 D5 UGR
Ugarpur 13 H6 UGP
Ugna Halt 24 C2 UGNA
Ugrasenpur 22 D4 URPR
Ugu Halt 22 A1 UGU
Ugwe 41 E2 UGWE
Ujalvav 29 F5 UJ
Ujhani 13 G4 UJH
Ujiarpur 24 B3 UJP
Ujjain Jn 31 E3 UJN
Ujjain C Cabin 31 E3 UJN'C'
Ukai Songadh 39 G1 USD
Ukhali Halt 40 D6 UKH
Ukhra 35 H2 UKA
Ukiler Hat 36 B6
Uklana 12 B1 UKN
Ukshi 46 B4 UKC
Ulavapadu 54 D3 UPD
Ulhasnagar 39 F5, 38 inset ULNR
Ulinda Konda 53 H2 UKD
Ullal 56 C2 ULL
Ulna Bhari 23 E2 ULN
Ultadanga Rd 37 inset ULR
Uluberia 36 B4, 37 inset ULB
Ulundurpet 58 C4 ULU
Umalla 29 H5 UML
Umar Tali 14 B6 UTA
Umardashi Rd 18 D6 UM
Umarha 23 F4 URH
Umaria 33 E2 UMR
Umaria Isra 32 B5 UIH
Umarpada 30 A6 UMPD
Umbargaon 39 F3 UBR
Umbermalli 39 G4 DMB
Umdanagar 48 C4, 51 inset UR
Umed 19 F1 UMED
Umesh Nagar 24 C4 UMNR
Umra 19 F5 UMRA
Umranala 32 B6 ULA
Umred 42 A2 URR
Umreth 29 H3 UMH
Umri 41 F6 UMRI
Umroli 39 F4 UOI
Una 38 C1 UNA
Una Himachal 9 E3 UHL
Unai & Vansada Rd 39 G2 UNI
Unaula 23 F1 UNLA
Unava Vasan 29 G2 UVSN
Unawa Aithor 29 G1 UAR
Unchadih 22 D5 UND
Unchahar Jn 22 C3 UCR
Unchaulia 14 A5 UCH
Unchehara 22 B6 UHR
Unchi Bassi 8 D2 UCB
Undasa Madhawpur 31 E3 UDM
Undi 49 H5 UNDI
Unguturu 49 H5 VGT
Unhel 30 D3 UNL
Unjalur 57 H5 URL
Unjha 29 G1 UJA
Unkal 52 C2 UNK
Unnao Jn 22 B2 ON
Untari Rd 23 G6 URD
Upariyala 29 F2 UAL
Uplai 47 F2 OPL
Upleta 28 C5 UA
Uppal 49 E2 UPL
Uppala 56 C2 UAA
Uppalavi 48 C2 UPW
Uppalluru 49 G5 UPL
Uppugundur 54 D2 UGD
Upramal 20 A4 URML
Uran 39 F6, 38 inset UNCT
Urapakkam 58 D2 UPM
Urdauli Halt 14 B5 UDX
Uren 24 C5 UREN
Urga 33 H5 URGA
Uri 7 F2 *
Urkura 43 E1 URK
Urlam Rd 50 D2 ULM
Urma 35 F3 URMA
Uruli 46 D1 URI
Usargaon 21 H3 URG
Usia Khas 23 G4 USK
Usilampatti 60 D2 USLP
Uska Bazar 15 F6 UB
Uslapur 33 G5 USL
Usmanpur 40 D5 UPR
Usra 30 B3 USRA
Utarlai 18 C2 UTL
Utarsanda 29 H3 UTD
Utraitia Jn 22 B1 UTR
Utran 39 F1 URN
Utripura 22 A UTP
Uttamarkovil Halt 58 B6 UKV
Uttangal Mangalam 58 C5 UMG
Uttar Bantra 63 F5 -
Uttar Kathani 16 D6 UKE
Uttar Radhanagar 36 B5 UTN
Uttarakosamangai 61 F4 UTK
Uttarpara 37 inset UPA
Uttukuli 57 G5 UKL

V

Vachaspatinagar 24 C2 VPH
Vachhanad 29 H5 VCH
Vadaj 30 A5 VRJ
Vadakannikapuram Halt 57 F6 VDK
Vadal 28 D5 VAL
Vadala Granthan 8 D2 VDGT
Vadali 29 H1 VAE
Vadali 29 H3
Vadalur 58 C5 VLU
Vadamadura 61 E1 VDM
Vadanam Kurushshi 57 E6 VDKS
Vadapalanji Halt 61 E2 VAJ
Vadarevu 55 E1 *
Vadavar 58 B6 VDU
Vadgaon 39 G6 VDN
Vadgaon Nila 40 D6 VDGN
Vadhvana 30 A4 VAN
Vadipatti 61 E2 VDP
Vadiya Devli 28 D5 VDV
Vadlamannadu 49 G6 VMD
Vadnagar 29 G1 VDG
Vadod 29 H4 VXD
Vadodara C Cabin 29 H4 BDA
Vadodara D Cabin 29 H4 BRGY
Vadodara E Cabin 29 H4 BRGZ
Vadodara Hump 29 H4 BRC HUMP
Vadodara Jn 29 H4 BRC
Vadtal Swaminarayan 29 H4 VTL
Vadviala 38 C1 VVL
Vagdiya 29 E3 VD
Vaghali 40 B2 VGL
Vaghania Juna 29 E5 WGN
Vaghodia 30 A4 WGR
Vaghpura 29 E1 VU
Vagra 29 H5 VGR
Vaibhavwadi Rd 46 B5 VBW
Vaikam 60 B3 *
Vaikam Rd 60 B3 VARD
Vailankanni 61 H1 *
Vaishali 24 A3 *
Vaitarna 39 F4, 38 inset VTN
Vaithilingapuram 60 D3 VPM
Vaithisvarankoil 58 C5 VDL
Vaiyampatti 61 E1 VPJ
Vajpadi Rd 29 E6 VJD
Vakav 47 F2 WKA
Valadar 38 C1 VLDR
Valadi 58 B6 VLDE
Valantaraval 61 F4 VTM
Valapattinam 56 D3 VAPM
Valappadi Gate Halt 58 A4 VGE
Valapuzha Halt 57 E6 VRZ
Valaramanikkam Halt 61 F2 VMM
Valathoor 58 B2 VLT
Valavanur 58 C4 VRA
Valha 46 C2 WLH
Valigonda 48 D4 VLG
Valivade 46 D5 VV
Vallabh Vidyanagar 29 H4 VLYN
Vallabhnagar 19 G5 VBN
Vallambram 57 E5
Vallampadugai Halt 58 C5 VMP
Vallanadi Rd 60 D2 VLNR
Vallarpadam 60 B2 *
Vallattol Nagar 57 E6 VTK
Vallikunnu 56 D5 VLI
Vallivedu 54 B6 VLV
Valliveru 49 F6 VRU
Valliyur 60 D5 VLY
Valmiki Nagar Rd 15 G6 VKNR
Valsad 39 F2 BL
Valtoha 8 C3 WLA
Vambori 40 A5 VBR
Vanchangiri 49 E3 SQZ
Vanchi Maniyachchi Jn 60 D5 MEJ
Vandalur 58 D2 VDR
Vandavasi 58 C3 *
Vangani 39 G5, 38 inset VGI
Vanganur 54 A3 VRN
Vangaon 39 F4 VGN
Vani Rd 29 F3 VNRD
Vani Vihar 44 D3 BNBH
Vaniambalam 57 E5 VNB
Vaniyambadi 58 B2 VN
Vaniyambadi IBH 58 B2 VKBH
Vanjipalayam 57 G5 VNJ
Vankal 29 H6 VKL
Vankia 29 E5 VNKA
Vanthali 28 C5
Vapi 39 F3 VAPI
Varadapur 58 A2 VRDP
Varahi 29 F1 VRX
Varakalpattu 58 D4 VKP
Varanasi City 23 F4 BCY
Varanasi Jn 23 E4 BSB
Varangaon 40 C2 VNA
Varediya 29 H5 VTDI
Varetha 29 G1 VTDI
Varkala 60 B5 VAK
Varkhedi 40 C2 VRKD
Varnama 29 H4 VRM
Vartej 29 F5 VTJ
Varud 41 H2 VARD
Varvala 28 A4 VVA
Vasad Jn 29 H4 VDA
Vasadva 29 F3 VSV
Vasai-Dabhla 29 G2 VAS
Vasai Rd Jn 39 F5, 38 inset BSR
Vasan Iyawa 29 G3 WSE
Vasco-da-Gama 52 A2 VSG
Vashi 38 inset VSH
Vasind 39 G5, 38 inset VSD
Vaso 29 G3 VASO
Vastrapur 29 G3, 28 inset VTP
Vasundhara 13 F5 VSR
Vatlur 49 G5 VAT
Vatva 29 G3, 28 inset VTA
Vatva Yard 28 inset VTA YARD
Vavadikhurd 30 A3 VKG
Vavaniya 28 D2 WWA
Vavdi 28 D5 VVD
Vavdi Rd 29 E5 VVF
Vavera 38 D1 VVV
Vayalar 60 B3 VAY
Vayalpad 54 B6 VLD
Vazeerpur Halt 13 H4 VZP
Vedaranyam 61 H1 VDY
Vedayapalem 54 D4 VDE
Vedchha 39 F2 VDH
Veer 46 B2 VEER
Veer Kunwar Singh Dharauli H 23 G4
Vejalka 29 F4 VJK
Vejalpar 29 E2 -
Vejalpore 29 H5 VJL
Vejendla 49 F6 VJA
Vejpur 30 A3 WJP
Velachery 59 inset
Velachha 29 H6 VLC
Velanandal 58 B3 VNL
Velavadar 29 F6 VAD
Veldurti 53 H2 VDI
Veli Halt 60 C5 VE
Velippalaiyam 58 D6 VXM
Vellalacheruvu 49 E6 VEP
Vellannur 61 F1 VEL
Vellarakkad Halt 56 D4 VEK
Vellayil Halt 56 D5 VLL
Velliyanai 57 H6 VEI
Vellodu 61 E2 VO
Vellore Cantt 58 B2 VLR
Vellore Town Halt 58 B2 VT
Vellur Halt 58 C5 VER
Velpuru 49 H5 VPU
Vemar 29 H5 VMR
Vembaditalam 57 H5 VBM
Vempalli 42 A5 VEM
Vemulapadu 53 H3 VML
Vemuru 49 G6 VMU
Vendodu 54 D5 VDD
Vendra 49 H5 VND
Venkatachalam 54 D4 VKT
Venkatagiri 54 C5 VKI
Venkatagirikote Halt 57 H1 VTE
Venkatampalle 53 G3 VPL
Venkatanarasimharajuvaripetta 58 C1 VKZ
Venkatesapuram 58 C4 VKM
Venkatnagar 33 G4 VKR
Venpura 29 F2 VNP
Ventrapragada 49 G6 VPG
Vepagunta 58 C1 VGA
Veppampattu 59 inset VEU
Veppilaipatti Chattiram 60 D3 VPC
Veraval 38 B1 VRL
Verka Jn 8 C2 VKA
Verna 52 A2 VEN
Verrampalli Halt 53 H4
Vetapalem 55 E1 VTM
Veysarpedi 59 inset VPY
Vidisha 31 H2 BHS
Viduraswatha 53 G5 VWA
Vidyanagar 51 inset VAN
Vidyapatinagar 24 B4 VPN
Vidyasagar 35 G1 VDS
Vidyavihar 38 inset VVH
Vijaipur 20 D6 V.IP
Vijapur 29 H2 VJF
Vijayamangalam 57 G5 VZ
Vijayanagara Colony 53 F4 VJC
Vijayawada Jn 49 F5 BZA
Vijayawada NE Cabin 49 F5
Vijayawada New West Blk Cab 49 F5 NWBC
Vijaynagar 46 D4 VJR

Vijaypur Jammu 7 G5 VJPJ
Vijaysota 33 F1 VST
Vikarabad Jn 48 B4 VKB
Vikasnagar 38 inset VKNA
Vikhran Rd 40 A1 VRD
Vikhroli 38 inset VK
Vikramgarh Alot 30 D2 VMA
Vikramnagar 31 E3 VRG
Vikravandi 58 C4 VVN
Vilad 40 A5 VL
Vilayatkalan Rd 33 E2 VYK
Vilegaon 41 F3 VLN
Vile Parle 38 inset VLP
Villianur 58 D4 VI
Villiambakkam 58 D2 VB
Villivakkam 58 D1, 59 inset VLK
Villupuram Jn 58 C4 VM
Vilvade 46 B4 VID
Vimanapura 57 H2 VMN
Vina 29 H3 VINA
Vina Ekma 24 D3 BNKM
Vinchhiya 29 E4 VCA
Vindyachal 23 E6 BDL
Vinnamangalam 58 B2 VGM
Vinnamangalam IBH 58 B2 VVBH
Vinukonda 54 D1 VKN
Viramdad 28 B4 VOD
Viramgam Jn 29 F2 VG
Virani Alur 60 C6 VRLR
Virapandiputhur 57 F5 VRPT
Virapandiyanpattanam H 61 E5 VYP
Virapandy Rd 57 H4 VRPD
Virapur 53 G3 VP
Virar 39 F4, 38 inset VR
Virarakkiam 57 H6 VRQ
Viravada 29 H2 VRV
Viravalli 49 G5 VRVL
Viravanallur 60 D5 VVR
Viravasaram 49 H5 VVM
Virbhadra 9 H5 VRH
Virinchipuram 58 B2 VJ
Virkudi 58 C6 VRK
Virol 29 G4 VOL
Virpar 28 D3 VRPM
Virpur 28 D5 VRR
Virsad 29 H4 VRS
Virudunagar Jn 61 E3 VPT
Virul 41 G2 VUL
Visakhapatnam Jn 50 C3 VSKP
Visakhapatnam Port 50 C3 VZP
Visakhapatnam Steel Plant 50 C3 VSP
Visakhapatnam Town 50 C3 VZT
Visalur 58 C6 VSL
Visapur 40 A6 VPR
Visapur 42 A4
Visavadar Jn 28 D6 VSW
Vishnupuram 49 E5 VNUP
Vishrambag 46 D4 VRB
Vishvamitri Jn 29 H4 VSI
Vishwanath Charali 16 C6 VNE
Vishwanath Puri 23 E5 VWP
Visnagar 29 G1 VNG
Vitawa 38 inset *
Vithalwadi 39 F5, 38 inset VLDI
Vivek Vihar 15 inset VVB
Vivekanand Puri H 15 inset VVKP
Vivekanandnagar 42 A4 VVKN
Vizianagaram Jn 50 C2 VZM
VOC Nagar 59 inset TNPM
Vondh 28 D2 VONB, VON
Vriddhachalam Jn 58 C5 VRI
Vriddhachalam Town 58 C5 VRT
Vrindavan 13 E5 BDB
Vrindavan Rd 13 E5 VRBD
Vyankatpura 30 A4 VNT
Vyara 39 G1 VYA
Vysanakeri 53 F2 VYS
Vysarpadi Jiva 59 inset VJM
Vyasnagar 23 F4 VYN

W

Wadakancheri 57 E6 WKI
Wadala Rd 38 inset VDLR
Wadali 38 D1 WAD
Wadawali Cabin 38 inset WDI
Wadegaon 42 B2 WDG
Wadharva 29 E2 WDHR
Wadhwan City 29 F3 WC
Wadi Jn 47 H4 WADI
Wadiaram 48 C2 WDR
Wadodara 40 D2 WDD
Wadrengdisa 27 F4 WDA
Wadsa 42 B3 WSA
Wadsinge 47 F2 WDS
Wadwal Nagnath 47 H1 WDLN
Wagdod 29 G1 WGD
Waghai 39 G2 WGI
Waghoda 40 D1 WGA
Wagholi 41 H3 WG
Wahiyal 29 G5 VHL
Wair 13 E3 WAIR
Walajah Rd Jn 58 C2 WJR
Walajabad 58 D2 WJ
Walayar 57 F6 WRA
Walgaon 41 F2 *
Wan Rd 41 E1 WND
Wanaparti Rd 48 B6 WPR
Wandal 47 F5 WDL
Wander Jatana 8 C4 WDJ
Wanegaon 41 E5 WNG
Wangapalli 48 D3 WP
Wani Jn 41 H4 WANI
Wankaner City 29 E3 WKRC
Wankaner Jn 29 E3 WKR
Wanlesswadi H 46 D4 WLS
Wansjaliya Jn 28 C5 WSJ
Warangal 49 E2 WL
Waraseoni 32 D6 WRI
Wardha Jn 41 H2 WR
Waria 35 H2 UYR
Warigaon Newada 23 E4 WRGN
Waris Aleganj 24 B5 WRS
Warsamedi 28 D2 WAR
Warora 42 A3 WRR
Warud 41 G1 *
Warud Khed 41 F3 WRD
Wasanapura 30 A4 VSP
Washermanpet 59 inset WST
Washim 41 E4 WHM
Washimbe 47 E1 WSB
Wa-Sojintra 29 G1 WSR
Wasud 47 E3 WSD
Water Pipe 38 inset WTP
Wathar 46 C2 WTR
Wav 29 G5 WAV
Wazirganj 24 A5 WZJ
Wellington 57 F5 WEL
Wena 24 B4 WENA
West Hill 56 D5 WH
West Outer BH B 23 F4 W/O BHB
Westpoint Halt 25 F1
Whitefield 57 H2 WFD
Wihirgaon 42 A4 VHGN
Wimco Nagar 59 E1, 59 inset WCN
Windmill 28 C3 WML
Wirur 42 A5 WIRR
Wishrampura 29 H4 WMP
WRS Colony 43 E1 WRS
Wyndhamganj 34 B1 WDM

Y

Yadalapur 48 A6 YDLP
Yadapalli 48 B1 YDP
Yadgir 47 H5 YG
Yadhavapuram 61 H1
Yadugram BH 24 B6 YGM
Yadvendranagar 23 E3 YDV
Yakutpura 51 inset YKA
Yalvigi 52 D3 YLG
Yamuna Bridge 13 E6 JAB
Yamuna South Bank 22 A3 JSB
Yaqutganj 13 H6 YAG
Yataluru 54 C5 YAL
Yavalkhed 41 E2 YAD
Yavatmal 41 G3 YTL
Yawarpura 29 G4 YVP
Yedamangala Halt 56 D2 YDM
Yedshi 47 G2 YSI
Yedukumeri 56 D1 YDK
Yelahanka Jn 57 H1 YNK
Yelgur 49 E3 YGL
Yeliyur 57 F2 Y
Yellakaru 54 C5 YLK
Yenor 41 H3 YNA
Yenugonda 48 B5 YNG
Yeola 40 A3 YL
Yeragoppa 52 D1 YGA
Yermaras 48 A6 YS
Yerpedu 54 C6 YPD
Yerragudipadu 54 B4 YGD
Yerraguntla 54 B4 YA
Yeshwantapuram 48 D3 YSPM
Yeshwantnagar 53 F3 YTG
Yeshwantpur Jn 57 G1 YPR
Yevat 46 D1 YT
Yogendradham Halt 14 D5 YEAM
Yusufpur 23 G4 YFP

Z

Zafarabad Jn 23 E4 ZBD
Zahirabad 48 B3 ZB
Zamania 23 F4 ZNA
Zampani 49 G6 ZPI
Zangalapalle 53 H4 ZPL
Zawar 19 F6 ZW
Zerpur Pali 12 C3 ZP
Zazpur 29 H5 ZR
Zindpura Halt 13 H4 ZNP
Zorawar Pura Halt 8 A6 ZPR

Metro Railway Stations

DMRC — Delhi Metro Railway Corpn.
Kol — Kolkata Metro

Adarshnagar [DMRC] 4 inset *
Ahimsa Sthal [DMRC] 4 inset *
AIMS [DMRC] 4 inset *
Andheria Bagh [DMRC] 4 inset *
Azadpur [DMRC] 4 inset *
Bansdroni [Kol] 4 inset *
Barakhamba Rd [DMRC] 4 inset *
Barwala [DMRC] 4 inset *
Belgachhia [Kol] 4 inset BEL
Bowbazar [Kol] 4 inset *
Central [Kol] 4 inset CEN
Central Park [Kol] 4 inset *
Chandni Chowk [Kol] 4 inset CWC
Chawri Bazar [DMRC] 4 inset *
Civil Lines [DMRC] 4 inset
Connaught Place [DMRC] 4 inset *
Dasnagar [Kol] 4 inset *
Daulatpur [DMRC] 4 inset *
Delhi Main [DMRC] 4 inset *
Derawal Nagar [DMRC] 4 inset *
Dilshad Garden [DMRC] 4 inset *
Dum Dum [Kol] 4 inset DMI
Dwarka Mor [DMRC] 4 inset *
Dwarka Sector 8 [DMRC] 4 inset *
Dwarka Sector 9 [DMRC] 4 inset *
Dwarka Sector 10 [DMRC] 4 inset *
Dwarka Sector 11 [DMRC] 4 inset *
Dwarka Sector 12 [DMRC] 4 inset *
Dwarka Sector 13 [DMRC] 4 inset *
Dwarka Sector 14 [DMRC] 4 inset *
Esplanade [Kol] 4 inset ESP
Ganesh Nagar [DMRC] 4 inset *
Garia Bazar [Kol] 4 inset *
Girish Park [Kol] 4 inset GPK
Green Park [DMRC] 4 inset *
Guru Tegh Bahadur Nagar [DMRC] 4 inset *
Hauz Khas Enclave [DMRC] 4 inset *
Howrah [Kol] 4 inset *
Howrah Maidan [Kol] 4 inset *
IGI Airport Terminal 1 [DMRC] 4 inset*
IGI Airport Terminal 2 [DMRC] 4 inset*
IIT [DMRC] 4 inset *
Inder Lok [DMRC] 4 inset
Indraprastha [DMRC] 4 inset *
Janakpuri [DMRC] 4 inset *
Jatin Das Park [Kol] 4 inset JPK
Jehangirpuri [DMRC] 4 inset *
Jhandewala [DMRC] 4 inset *
Kadamtala [Kol] 4 inset *
Kalighat [Kol] 4 inset KHG
Kanhaiya Nagar [DMRC] 4 inset *
Kankurgachi [Kol] 4 inset *
Karol Bagh [DMRC] 4 inset *
Kashmiri Gate [DMRC] 4 inset
Kendriya Sachivalaya [DMRC] 4 inset *
Keshavpuram [DMRC] 4 inset *
Kidwai Nagar [DMRC] 4 inset *
Kirti Nagar [DMRC] 4 inset *
Kohat Enclave [DMRC] 4 inset *
Kohli 7 G4 *
Kudghat [Kol] 4 inset *
Ladha Sarai [DMRC] 4 inset *
Lado Sarai [DMRC] 4 inset *
Laxmibai Nagar [DMRC] 4 inset *
Maidan [Kol] 4 inset MDI
Mandi House [DMRC] 4 inset *
Masudpur [DMRC] 4 inset *
Mayur Vihar [DMRC] 4 inset *
MG Road [Kol] 4 inset MHR
Model Town [DMRC] 4 inset *
Moti Nagar [DMRC] 4 inset *
Naktala [Kol] 4 inset *
National Highway 8 [DMRC] 4 inset *
Navjeevan Nagar[DMRC] 4 inset *
Netaji Bhawan [Kol] 4 inset NBN
Netaji Subhas Place[DMRC] 4 inset *
New Delhi [DMRC] 4 inset *
New Garia [Kol] 4 inset *
Nizamuddin [DMRC] 4 inset *
Noida City Centre [DMRC] 4 inset *
Noida Sector 21 [DMRC] 4 inset *
Noida Sector 63 [DMRC] 4 inset *
Om Vihar [DMRC] 4 inset *
Palika Place [DMRC] 4 inset *
Pehladpur [DMRC] 4 inset *
Park Street [Kol] 4 inset PKS
Patel Nagar [DMRC] 4 inset *
Patparganj [DMRC] 4 inset *
Patel Chowk [DMRC] 4 inset *
Pitampura [DMRC] 4 inset *
Pranabnagar [Kol] 4 inset *
Pratap Nagar [DMRC] 4 inset *
Prem Nagar [DMRC] 4 inset *
Pul Bangash [DMRC] 4 inset *
Rabindra Sadan [Kol] 4 inset RSN
Rabindra Sarobar [Kol] 4 inset RSB
Rajarhat [Kol] 4 inset *
Rajendra Place [DMRC] 4 inset *
Rajouri Garden [DMRC] 4 inset *
Ramesh Nagar [DMRC] 4 inset *
Ramrajtala [Kol] 4 inset *
Rangapuri[DMRC] 4 inset *
Rithala [DMRC] 4 inset *
Rohini East [DMRC] 4 inset *
Rohini West [DMRC] 4 inset *
Safdarjung Tomb [DMRC] 4 inset *
Sanjay Gandhi Transport Nagar [DMRC] 4 inset *
Sealdah [Kol] 4 inset *
Seelampur [DMRC] 4 inset
Shadipur [DMRC] 4 inset *
Shahdara [DMRC] 4 inset
Shastri Nagar [DMRC] 4 inset *
Shastri Park [DMRC] 4 inset
Shyambazar [Kol] 4 inset SHY
Sovabazar [Kol] 4 inset SHO
Subhashnagar [DMRC] 4 inset *
Tagore Garden [DMRC] 4 inset *
Tilak Nagar [DMRC] 4 inset *
Tollygunge [Kol] 4 inset TOL
Trilok Puri [DMRC] 4 inset *
Tri Nagar [DMRC] 4 inset *
Tughlak Rd [DMRC] 4 inset *
Uttam Nagar [DMRC] 4 inset *
Vasant Kunj Sector D[DMRC] 4 inset *
Vasant Kunj Sector A [DMRC] 4 inset *
Vasant Valley School [DMRC] 4 inset *
Vasundhara Enclave [DMRC] 4 inset *
Vidhan Sabha [DMRC] 4 inset
Vishwa Vidyalaya [DMRC] 4 inset
Welcome [DMRC] 4 inset
Yamuna Depot[DMRC] 4 inset *

Major Bridges & Tunnels

Ambed Tunnel 46 B4
Aravali Tunnel 46 B3
Ashti Tunnel 46 B3
Banewadi Tunnel 46 B4
Barcem Tunnel 52 B2
Barog Tunnel 9 F4
Berdewadi Tunnel 46 B4
Bhirkond Tunnel 46 B4
Bhor Gats 39 G6
Boggada Tunnel 54 B2
Braganza Ghat 52 B2
Byndoor Tunnel 52 C5
Cauvery Br., Erode 57 H5
Cauvery Br., Tiruchchirapalli 58 B6
Chambal Br., Dhaulpur 21 E1
Chambal Br., Kota 20 B4
Chelama Tunnel 54 B2
Chenab Br. (u/c) 7 G4
Chiplun Tunnel 46 B3
Curzon Br., Allahabad 22 D4
Doyang Viaduct 27 F4
Ehegaon Viaduct 39 G4
Farakka Barrage 25 F5
Garhmukteshwar Br., 13 F3
Godavari Br. 50 A4
Gopalwadi Tunnel 46 C5
Honnavar Tunnel 52 B4
Izat Br., Allahabad 22 D4
Jamuna Br., Allahabad 22 D4
Jubilee Br., Bandel 37 inset
Kachhla Br. 13 G4
Kalinadi Br., Karwar 52 B3
Kanpur Br. 22 A2
Karbude Tunnel 46 B4
Karwar Tunnel 52 B3
Khandala Tunnel 39 G6
Khershet Tunnel 46 B3
Koti Tunnel 9 F4
Krishna Br., Vijayawada 49 F5
Mahanadi Bridges, Cuttack area 44 D3
Malaviya Br., Varanasi 23 F4
Math Tunnel 46 B4
Nar Narayan Setu, Jogighopa 26 B2
Narmada Br., Bharuch 29 H5
Narmada Br., Hoshangabad 31 H4
Nathuwadi Tunnel 46 B2
Nilik Tunnel 46 B2
Padi Tunnel 52 B2
Pamban Br. 61 G4
Panval Nadi Viaduct 46 B4
Parchuri Tunnel 46 B4
Parsik Tunnel, Thane 38 inset
Pernem Tunnel 52 A1
Pir Panjal Tunnel (u/c) 7 G4
Rajendra Pul, Mokama 24 C4
Rajghat Br., Rajghat Narora 13 F4
Saraighat Br., Guwahati 26 D2
Savarde Tunnel 46 B3
Sharavati Br. 52 B4
Shinde Ambri Tunnel 46 C3
Shiravali Tunnel 46 B4
Son Br., Ara 23 H4
Tapti Br.,Surat 39 F1
Thal Ghats 39 G4
Tike Tunnel 46 B4
Tiware Tunnel 46 B4
Upper Son Br., Dehri-on-Sone 23 H5
Vasai Creek Br., Vasai 38 inset
Vivekananda Br., Dakshineshwar 37 inset
Wellingdon Br, Pandharpur 47 E3
Yamuna Br., Delhi 15 inset